ULTIMATE 3D GAME ENGINE
DESIGN & ARCHITECTURE

ULTIMATE 3D GAME ENGINE
DESIGN & ARCHITECTURE

ALLEN SHERROD

CHARLES RIVER MEDIA
Boston, Massachusetts

Cover Design: Tyler Creative
Cover Image: Allen Sherrod

CHARLES RIVER MEDIA
25 Thomson Place
Boston, Massachusetts 02210
617-757-7900
617-757-7969 (FAX)
crm.info@thomson.com
www.charlesriver.com

This book is printed on acid-free paper.

Allen Sherrod. *Ultimate 3D Game Engine Design & Architecture.*
ISBN: 1-58450-473-0

All brand names and product names mentioned in this book are trademarks or service marks of their respective companies. Any omission or misuse (of any kind) of service marks or trademarks should not be regarded as intent to infringe on the property of others. The publisher recognizes and respects all marks used by companies, manufacturers, and developers as a means to distinguish their products.

Library of Congress Cataloging-in-Publication Data
Sherrod, Allen.
  Ultimate 3D game engine design & architecture / Allen Sherrod. -- 1st ed.
    p. cm.
  Includes index.
  ISBN 1-58450-473-0 (hardcover with CD-ROM : alk. paper) 1. Computer games--Programming.
2. Computer graphics. 3. Computer games--Design. 4. Video games--Design. 5. Three-dimensional display systems. I. Title.

QA76.76.C672S538 2007
794.8'1526--dc22

                               2006033304

Printed in the United States of America
06 7 6 5 4 3 2 First Edition

CHARLES RIVER MEDIA titles are available for site license or bulk purchase by institutions, user groups, corporations, etc. For additional information, please contact the Special Sales Department at 800-347-7707.

Contents

Preface

My first book *Ultimate Game Programming with DirectX* was written to introduce the topic of Microsoft®'s DirectX® to hobby and student programmers wanting to learn how to make simple games with the popular Windows®-based suite of tools.

In this, my second book, *Ultimate Game Engine Design and Architecture* the goal is to teach aspiring game programmers, students, and those just beginning in the industry how to create their own game engine, or at least understand the fundamentals of the process. Although game engines are quite complex, I wanted to provide a simple introduction that was not too basic, but small enough to fit into one book, and the result is the Building Blocks Engine covered in the book.

Writing this book was particularly challenging for many different reasons, but mostly because I wanted it to be simple enough so that beginning and student programmers could read the code and understand it without much background in game engines. The challenge with this, however, is that any engine of considerable size and subsystems requires a lot of explanation and a great deal of background knowledge. Hopefully, the examination of the different parts of an engine and the exploration of how they work have met this challenge, and will provide you with the tools you need in your own game engine design and architecture journey.

About the Author

Allen Sherrod (Smyrna, GA) is the host of the game programming website *www.UltimateGameProgramming.com* for beginner and hobby game programmers. He regularly writes columns and develops code for this popular site. He has been programming in many different languages such as C, C++, Java, QBasic, Visual Basic, and Assembly for the past seven years. He graduated from DeVry University with a bachelor's degree in computer information systems. Allen Sherrod is also the author of the books *Ultimate Game Programming with DirectX* and *Data Structures for Game Developers*.

Acknowledgments

As a new author, a book of this magnitude was not an easy task. Many people gave me the support and help I needed to make this project possible. First, I thank my parents and my sister for always giving me support throughout my life. I also thank Jenifer Niles and Lance Morganelli of Charles River Media for keeping me motivated, Carl Granberg for the helpful review of this book, and the entire Charles River Media/Thomson Learning staff who helped make this book a reality. Among the many people who have given me great advice over the years, I must thank Professor Christopher Howard for being such a great help, teacher, and friend.

I also thank the loyal community at *UltimateGameProgramming.com*, and my readers. Without you, this book wouldn't be possible. I hope everything I do is of great use to people all over the world.

Acknowledgments

Introduction

OVERVIEW

In this book, we cover many topics that surface during the development of a cross-platform game engine. By the end of this book, you will have all you need to create your own 3D engine or build on top of the engine developed here. There are many books on the market about graphics programming, but not nearly as many on the design and architecture of a 3D game engine. It is my hope that you find great value in this text and can apply what you learn to your own projects. All the code and tools created in this book will be further expanded upon and improved at *UltimateGameProgramming.com*.

WHAT'S DIFFERENT ABOUT THIS BOOK

This book touches on the various aspects of engine development on an introductory level as a way to ease newcomers into the process. Professional game engine development is far more complex than what is presented here. This book presents information to help beginners get their first start in the fun yet challenging subject in game development.

The purpose of this book is to create a simple game engine. One thing that separates this book from others is that it does not focus on game programming or the creation of a game. At *UltimateGameProgramming.com* are step-by-step tutorials on creating different games using the engine developed here, but this book focuses on creating the technology using various examples to demonstrate that it works.

Although the engine will be simple, it is still far more complex than what is done in the majority of the books on the market. This is the main reason why the book focuses on engine programming and not game programming, and why it requires that you have at least some beginner-level knowledge about the different aspects of a game, especially beginner-level knowledge of graphics (i.e., being able to draw a triangle, texture mapping, and so forth).

WHOM THIS BOOK IS FOR

This book is for student and beginning C++ programmers, and beginning game develoers who want to create their own game engine. Each of the topics discussed can get pretty advanced in the real world, so everything here is done on an easy-to-read, introductory level. It is recommended that you have at least some beginner experience with the various topics discussed in this book, the most important of which are input, rendering, and application programming on the operating systems of your choice. It is also required that you have an understanding of your tool of choice. For example, if you are using Visual Studio 2003 to compile your code on Windows XP, it is required that you have an understanding about how to set up projects and compile code using that tool. The same can be said about the other operating systems if you plan to work with any outside of Windows.

WHAT YOU WILL NEED TO KNOW FOR THIS BOOK

In this book, it is assumed that you've never built a 3D game engine before, have some knowledge of a few technologies we will be using, and are familiar with Windows, Mac, or Linux and the creation of applications for one or all of these operating systems. The purpose of this engine is to run on the top three operating systems so no one will feel left out. Topics we assume you already know or have at least some beginner-level experience include:

- C++, since we'll be using it to implement all our code
- OpenGL
- Some understanding of Win32, Mac OS X, or Linux application programming
- Common game math
- Compiling and executing code
- Basic 3D knowledge such as primitives (triangles) and coordinate systems
- Some experience with input and sound
- Experience with common data structures such as arrays, etc.

- The ability to debug your own code
- A passion for programming

Since this is an engine book, it is assumed you have certain knowledge of the different technologies you'll be implementing. An example, again, is the graphics system. This book assumes you have knowledge with at least OpenGL. Appendix A, "Additional Resources," lists resources that can help you brush up on different technologies we will be using here. Newer technologies, such as using Xbox 360 controllers, will be discussed in detail, assuming you've never worked with these before.

HOW THIS BOOK IS ORGANIZED

This book is broken into five main parts. Each part goes a long way to the creation of the entire Building Blocks Engine. The first part is the introduction, where we discuss the engine core, input, sound, and networking systems.

The second part, "Graphics and Environments," deals with everything we can see on the screen. This section starts with the rendering system and the drawing of static models. It then moves on to more advanced rendering topics by looking at areas such as level of detail, scene graphs, graphical effects, resource management, and scene management for environments in general.

The third section, "Physics, AI, and Scripting," looks at the custom physics system that was built for the Building Blocks Engine, and at artificial intelligence and game scripting. In the physics section, we will be looking at point masses, rigid bodies, and soft bodies. In the artificial intelligence section, we'll look at a few different AI techniques, some of which we'll be implementing in some of the engine demos later in the book. For scripting, we'll look at command scripting, property scripting, and compiled scripting.

The fourth section is "Demos." By the time you get to the fourth section, the engine will be done, or at least the version of it for this book, and we will focus all our efforts on creating two demo applications. The first will create a black jack game, and the second will create a 3D walkthrough using a portal rendering system, which is first mentioned in Chapter 5 "Rendering Scenes and Scene Graphs."

The last section of this book, "Game Over," looks at what we've done, what we could do, and what resources we might need in the future to enhance our game engine. Even though the book will be finished at the end of the last section, this is just the beginning, as our engine will continue to grow over time.

While there is a plethora of information in this book, we cannot cover every subject in detail because each topic can easily span several books. That is why this engine is called the Building Blocks Engine, because it gets you started and allows you to add all the features you want by creating your own engine from scratch or building upon the existing framework. For example, the physics system will allow us to create some nice simulations, but will not be a complete physics system; meaning that there will be a ton of features you will be able to add if you need them. For our physics system, we'll add the information needed to create some cool simulations, while at the same time be lightweight enough to fit in a book that deals with engine programming as a whole and not just physics. The physics system will be built in a way that once you understand it, you can add whatever you can think of and need for future projects.

The Building Blocks Engine will continue its development at *UltimateGame Programming.com*. Feel welcome to come to the website and participate in the project. Creating a game engine is a complex process, and this book and game engine will help get you started in this very challenging field.

Part I

Introduction to Game Engines

1 Introduction to Game Engines

In This Chapter

- Overview of Game Engines
- Tools Used in Game Development
- Unified Modeling Language
- The Building Blocks Game Engine
- Tips and Practices

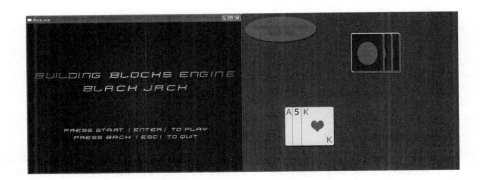

OVERVIEW OF GAME ENGINES

This book, *Ultimate Game Engine Design and Architecture,* is about the design and creation of a video game engine that can be used to create gaming applications on the PC. Today's video games are complex pieces of software that aim to push the envelope of modern technology. As technology increases in power and functionality, so does the engineering complexity involved in creating cutting-edge gaming software. The use of a game engine has gained tremendous importance and value that will continue to grow over the years to come in game development. One of the largest benefits of using a game engine is that it can save a developer time, money, and resources developing a game title. A development company can also earn additional revenue from the licensing and/or selling of a stable and proven game engine to other developers looking to save time and resources when developing a game engine themselves.

The purpose of this book is to discuss game engine design and architecture. Throughout this book, a game engine will be developed called the Building Blocks Engine and will be implemented on various Windows®, Mac, and Linux operating systems.

The term *game engine* is used to describe a set(s) of code used to build a gaming application. A game engine is more specifically a framework comprised of a collection of different tools, utilities, and interfaces that hide the low-level details of the various tasks that make up a video game. These tasks can include but are not limited to:

- Graphics
- Physics
- Input detection
- Audio playback and control
- Scripting
- Artificial intelligence (AI)
- Networking
- Core utilities

Each task in a game can have its own unique challenges and issues that can arise during the development of a game engine framework. This complexity is further increased because some tasks have to be compatible with other tasks but separate at the same time. For example, the physics system has to supply information the rendering system can use to orientate and position a 3D object once that information has been calculated. The following parts take a closer look at each of these areas of a game and some of the possible issues you will need to consider and address when designing a game engine framework from the ground up. In addition, each of these parts will be looked at in more detail throughout this book.

GAME GRAPHICS

Game graphics are at the forefront of game development mainly because they are a visual representation of the product itself. Graphics have come a long way from the days of 2D games to modern 3D games now on the marketplace. Computer graphics in games are mostly mathematics, numbers, and artwork. As programmable hardware becomes the main device used to create most modern games, it is important to understand the various mathematics that exist. From an engineering standpoint, it is important to understand the nature of graphics interfaces and devices to get the most out of a system and its hardware. Game graphics present a different kind of challenge when compared with other types of graphics (e.g., movies, print, TV, etc.), because they need to be processed and displayed many times a second dynamically in real time.

On the PC, the top-two application programming interfaces (APIs) used for 3D graphics are OpenGL and Direct3D. These rendering APIs hide many of the low-level details about how primitives are drawn and shaded on the screen using the underlying hardware, but are not high level enough that they can be used in a game engine without often times making them part of a larger, more complex rendering system. When designing a rendering system, many different obstacles and challenges will arise, including state management, resource management, scene management, and much more. More information on the graphics part of a game engine is discussed further in Chapter 4, "Rendering Systems," and Chapter 5, "Rendering Scenes and Scene Graphs."

PHYSICS AND COLLISIONS

Physics in video games has become a very important area of game development in recent years, allowing developers to apply forces upon objects in a virtual environment, oftentimes in a realistic manner. These physics-driven objects also interact with one another and their environment to further increase the level of realism in a simulation.

Currently, there are two main ways to do physics calculations in a game: use software processing with the CPU, or use a dedicated piece of hardware such as a PPU or a general-purpose GPU or multiple GPUs. Regardless of which path is taken, there is still the issue of whether to create a custom physics system or to integrate an existing system from companies such as Havok®, AGEIA, and so forth. This design choice must be made early on in the development of the game engine. Using a proven existing physics system can speed development time and reduce time spent debugging and fixing code.

Along with using physics to simulate natural forces acting on a virtual object, there are collisions between virtual objects in a computer-generated scene. Collision detection is the process of determining when two or more virtual bodies try to or are occupying the same virtual space. Once collision has been detected, the next step is to somehow respond to that collision. This collision response is often a realistic behavior that tries to mimic what real-world objects do. Although physics is used to simulate realistic behavior, it can also be used to do the opposite, depending on what the developers are after in the simulation.

When designing and implementing a physics system, you must consider how fast the physics can be processed for all objects in a virtual scene and how that information will be used to manipulate and orientate the renderable objects in the scene. Multithreading in physics can also play a large role in the implementation of a physics system and in other systems of the framework. Dynamic game objects and their animation systems can also affect the physics calculations in a game due to the geometry not being static in its topology. In physics, there are three main types of objects known as point masses, rigid bodies, and soft bodies. Point masses are used mostly for particle system effects, rigid bodies are used mostly for game objects that do not change their topology, and soft bodies are used for objects that can change their topology such as the dynamic cloth simulations seen in the original *Splinter Cell* games. Physics and collision detection and response are discussed in more detail in Chapter 6, "Physics."

INPUT DETECTION

Many different input devices can be used to control the interaction of a video game or other simulation. In a gaming application, it is important to be able to quickly detect and handle input from a device to keep the input response as smooth as possible. Input that is not smooth in its response can and often will frustrate gamers. Common input devices used in modern video games include but are not limited to:

- Keyboards
- Mice
- Joysticks
- Game pads
- Steering wheels
- Voice recognition
- Brain wave sensors
- Motion tracking sensors
- Touch screens

For PC games, the standard devices for video games include keyboards and mice. Other devices can be found on PC machines (e.g., joysticks, steering wheels, etc.), but are not as common as the standard keyboard and mouse combo. On home gaming consoles, the main input devices traditionally have been game pad controllers. With today's innovations, devices such as touch screens are starting to be used with great effect as seen with Nintendo®'s DS handheld portable gaming console. Sensors used to track motions are also being used in clever ways as seen with Nintendo's Wii™ and Sony's PlayStation® 3 gaming consoles. Although voice recognition is not a common form of input, it has been used by some companies to allow gamers to interact with a game using speech. Sensors to read brain waves, although currently mostly used in research with individuals with disabilities, have been used as a form of input device for applications.

The input system of a game engine has to be both fast and flexible. Input detection and response in video games is discussed further in Chapter 3, "Input, Sound, and Networking." For the Building Blocks Engine, the devices we will look at are keyboards, mice, and Xbox® 360™ game controllers.

AUDIO PLAYBACK AND CONTROL

Sound contributes to the overall interactivity of a video game. In today's games, the audio has become as important as it is in the movie and other entertainment industries. Game audio can be used to set mood, give clues and feedback, communicate with other gamers, and much more. A few types of different sounds are commonplace in today's games, including:

- Sound effects
- Ambient sounds
- Music tracks
- Speech

As time progresses, so does the technology available for handling sound in gaming applications. Along with mono and stereo, there is also surround sound types such as 5.1, which is used to give the impression of hearing 3D audio from multiple directions. The complexity of audio is now a specialized job in both programming and the recording arts. More information on game audio is discussed in Chapter 3.

SCRIPTING

Video games have benefited from game scripting systems for quite some time, with the feature being quite popular on PC games. Scripting allows the behavior of an application to be controlled outside the application itself. On the PC, scripting and the availability of game tools such as level editors have allowed gamers to create content and extend the life of their game titles. Various video game editors have been used on console games, as seen in games like the *Tony Hawk* series, but traditionally, game modifications have been done primarily on the PC. Game scripting can be used for AI, game logic, ways to define materials that are shaded on the surfaces of game objects, and so forth.

A more detailed discussion on game scripting can be found in Chapter 8, "Scripting," along with various scripting systems and the challenges and possibility of integrating existing scripting systems into a gaming application.

ARTIFICIAL INTELLIGENCE

All games need to display some kind of intelligence to make a scene believable and to pose a challenge to human players. Early games saw limited use of AI, but today with the complexity of 3D games and gameplay types, the AI in games has evolved to a much more complex level than previously seen. AI is part of the interactive experience, much like visual displays and audio. By using AI, game developers are able to present a challenge to gamers and submerse them in the virtual world. There are many different types of AI—path finding, flocking, and neural networks, to name a few.

AI in games is often game specific and is limited by the target hardware and the available resources a game has to work with on a system. AI systems are increasingly available over the Internet in the same way physics systems are starting to gain momentum. A detailed look at AI in games is discussed in Chapter 7, "Artificial Intelligence," and Chapter 9, "Demos," in which a number of small games and demos are developed. AI is a complex field and will be looked at briefly in this text.

NETWORKING

The networking system of a video game engine is used to transmit data across a network, be it a LAN setup or the Internet. In games, networking is often used to connect to a server across the Internet to use its services. Many households are connected to the Internet, and a large percent of those households have or will have a broadband connection. A few uses for networking in video games include, but are not limited to:

- Multiplayer gaming
- Downloading game fixes
- Downloading additional game content
- Downloading entire games
- Statistics tracking

The PC had the benefit of networking in applications and games much longer than the home gaming consoles. Home gaming consoles got their first taste of on-line networking connectivity on the Super Nintendo and Sega® Genesis™ through a device called XBAND™ that was created by a California-based company called Catapult. The XBAND service was ultimately a failure, but it did pave the way for the idea of bringing home gaming consoles online. The next system to go online was in 1999 with the Sega Dreamcast™ gaming console. The Xbox Live® gaming service that debuted on the original Xbox gaming system brought new life to taking a console online. Xbox Live was a milestone in the online gaming arena, as it demonstrated a very successful way to bring gamers to the Internet using home gaming consoles. Today, being able to go online in a game, be it multiplayer or not, is considered a very important feature. Networking is discussed in more detail in Chapter 3.

CORE UTILITIES

Core utilities can be classified as parts of the game engine framework that are not specific to any one system and are used to aid in the completion of a task. Such utilities focus on a single task and are there to make programming more efficient. Such utilities and tools that can be part of the core include but are not limited to:

- Various data structures
- Timers
- Memory management
- Resource management
- Journaling services
- File logging
- Application profilers
- Depreciation facilities
- Compression/decompression algorithms
- Encryption/decryption algorithms

A more detailed discussion on the engine core is in Chapter 2, "Engine Core." The core part is important because it can be a valuable resource to use during the development of a game engine and a gaming application. The core part of a game engine can be complex and very detailed.

NOTE

A developer can generate increased revenue by licensing their game engine technology to other developers, which is commonly done in the game industry.

TOOLS USED IN GAME DEVELOPMENT

Video games are content-driven applications. This content is created by various tools available on the market or developed in-house by a development team working on the project. Many resources and content make up any modern game, and the ability to work with such tools will allow a development team to create a number of gaming projects. These tools include but are not limited to:

- 3D modeling and animation packages
- Digital art creation tools
- Audio creation tools
- Profilers
- Environment editors
- Compilers (e.g., scripting)
- Motion capture tools
- Software design tools

Aside from various integrated development environments and compilers on Windows, Mac, and Linux, the content used in this book was created using the following tools:

- Photoshop for textures and images
- Microsoft's XACT cross-platform audio creation tool
- Garage Band for audio
- LightWave® for 3D geometry
- Visio® for UML diagrams
- DirectX® SDK for Microsoft DirectX–related applications
- NVIDIA®'s Cg for programmable high-level shaders
- Game Monkey Script for scripting support

The Game Monkey Scripting system will be used to demonstrate integrating an existing scripting system into an application built using the Building Blocks Engine, which will have its own various smaller text parsing classes as well. Scripting is discussed in more detail in Chapter 8. These tools are not necessary, but were used to prepare the assets used in each chapter.

UNIFIED MODELING LANGUAGE

The Unified Modeling Language (UML) is a standard that is used for data representation for object-oriented software design. When working in UML, static elements and dynamic elements can be modeled in the software. An example of a static element is a class, and an example of a dynamic element is a state machine. For the purposes of this book, UML is used to design the classes that make up the Building Blocks Engine, and Visio is used to model the UML class diagrams. In this book, the UML diagrams consist of classes with the planned members and some of their functions, and are kept simple.

There are tools available that allow developers to model in UML, one such tool being Visio. Some tools allow the user to model a system and have code generated based on the diagrams. For this book, Visio will only be used to model the classes used by the Building Blocks Engine.

A class in UML is represented by a box-shaped icon and is the fundamental base of a class diagram. Inside the icon is the class' name, functions, attributes, and so forth. The top part of the class icon is used for the name, the middle is used for the attributes, and the bottom part is used for the functions of the class. For the class functions and attributes, the scope of the item can be specified for each (e.g., public, protected, or private). Abstract classes or pure virtual functions are modeled by italicizing the name of the item. Figure 1.1 shows an example of a UML class icon.

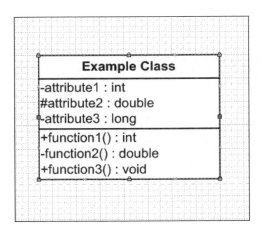

FIGURE 1.1   The class icon in UML.

To model inheritance in UML, an arrow icon is used. The arrow connects from the parent class to the child class, with the hollow arrow's tip connecting to the parent. Figure 1.2 shows an example of modeling a parent/child relationship using the arrow icon in UML.

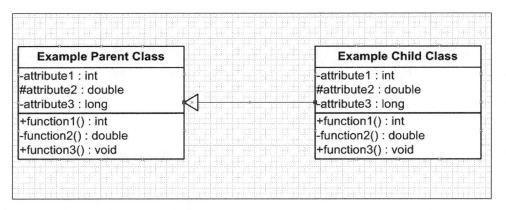

FIGURE 1.2   Modeling inheritance in UML.

To model a class relationship where one class knows about the other by some means—for example, if one class is used as a parameter to another's member function—a dotted-line solid arrow is used. This is called a weak dependency, and the arrow starts from the class that knows about the second class and ends at the second class by pointing the arrow tip toward it. Figure 1.3 illustrates a weak dependency in a UML class diagram.

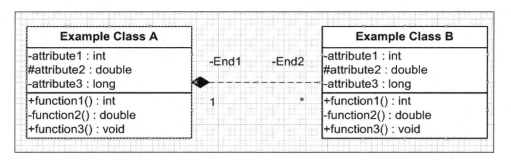

FIGURE 1.3   Weak dependency in UML.

ON THE CD
Additional information on UML can be found in Appendix A, "Additional Resources." Each of the Building Blocks Engine class diagrams can be found on the companion CD-ROM in the BUILDING BLOCKS ENGINE/DIAGRAMS folder. UML is used in this book to plan the various classes of the game engine and their relationships to one another in the system.

THE BUILDING BLOCKS ENGINE

The Building Blocks Engine that accompanies this book was designed to be small with the capability to be expanded upon. A game engine can be a complex system of programming engineering. By building on the Building Blocks Engine, users are provided with an entry point at which they can start video game engine development. Each part of the Building Blocks Engine has its own library that separates it from the rest of the framework. Figure 1.4 illustrates each of the libraries that make up the Building Blocks Engine. When creating applications using the Building Blocks Engine, the programmer can link to the necessary libraries of the framework for the features and areas needed in a gaming project.

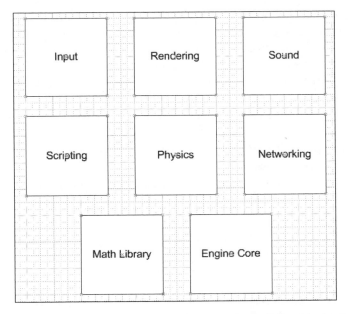

FIGURE 1.4   The libraries that make up the Building Blocks Engine.

The Building Blocks Engine will feature a rendering system, an input system, a math library, a sound system, a physics system, a networking system, scripting capabilities, and a core set of tools. The core of the engine is a set of code that operates on a lower level of the engine than the rest. For example, in the core of the engine you will find data structures, resource management routines, memory management, timers, file reading and writing code, and a number of other useful tools and utilities. The key to the core tools of the Building Blocks Engine requires them to be portable between all supported systems. Everything done in the framework must be portable in a transparent manner to allow for porting between different systems without needing to change any of the high-level code and interfaces. For the rendering system, the rendering API that will be used is the OpenGL graphics library. For hardware graphical effects, the use of NVIDIA's Cg shader will be used because it is supported by multiple APIs and systems such as OpenGL, Direct3D, PlayStation 2 and 3, Xbox and Xbox 360, Windows, Mac, and Linux, to name a few.

ENGINE FEATURES

The planned feature list for the Building Blocks Engine is kept to a minimum to allow the engine to stay small but useful in the educational context. Users can build their own creations from the existing code and interfaces, or can build their own engine framework from the ground up. This is a planned feature and allows room for improvement and expansion to the Building Blocks Engine.

It is important that the core of the Building Blocks Engine is useful and deep. The core system is the part of the engine that will be used by many different systems. The core will be made up of various data structures, resource management, timing, file handling, archive files, runtime type information, and classes used commonly for game math. Features that will make up the core system include:

- Support for common data structures such as arrays, link lists, queues, stacks, and hash tables
- Byte-ordering (endianness) handling for multibyte values
- File input and output
- Logging files
- Timing in milliseconds and seconds
- Resource management
- Archive files similar to .ZIP files used to pack multiple files into one larger archive file
- Common game math such as vectors, matrices, quaternions, bounding volumes, rays, and planes
- Runtime type information

Data structures are important because they are used to store an arrangement of data in memory in a useful manner. When working with that arrangement of data, various algorithms can be performed on the data structures to do something useful with them. For data structures, the C++ Standard Template Library (STL) will be used in the engine. STL will give the engine a standard set of C++ template classes that are very efficient.

The endian order specifies the order of multibyte values that are stored in the system, and can be little endian, big endian, or middle endian. To create a portable framework, the topic of endian order will need to be addressed. The endian order will have a large impact on reading and writing files across different systems, among other things. The Building Blocks Engine will have file reading and writing code, but the endian handling code will be separate.

Timing in video games is very important and is used heavily for real-time simulations. It is important that the Building Blocks Engine have some way to get the system's time in milliseconds and seconds.

The resource management system will be used to keep track of shared resources like textures and sounds and are explored in Chapter 4 in more detail. The runtime type information is a technique used to keep track of class types and what classes a certain class derives from, and can be useful when trying to cast from different types in a safe manner. The topics of creating a runtime type information class is further discussed in Chapter 2.

Archive files are created by packing multiple files into one; for example, WinZip's .ZIP archive file. Archive files have multiple benefits: improved performance by reducing the overhead of opening and closing multiple files, and a layer of data protection, to name a few. The Building Blocks Engine will implement its own archive filesystem and set of classes that are explored in Chapter 2.

The last part of our core system is the game math classes that represent rays, vectors, matrices, quaternions, and planes. The game math classes are code that will be used by both the rendering system and the physics system to great extent, and will be the key to implementing many of the physics that will be implemented by the custom physics system. The game math is first discussed in Chapter 4, the first rendering chapter, and in Chapter 6, the physics chapter.

The core system of the Building Blocks Engine is made up of various classes based on the previous information in this part. Many of these classes will be implemented in Chapter 2, while others will be spread throughout the book and implemented in the appropriate chapters. The details of the core system are discussed in detail in Chapter 2. Figure 1.5 illustrates the current plans for each of the classes that will appear in the core system.

The input system for the Building Blocks Engine will support standard keyboards and mice on the PC. In addition, the Windows XP and Windows Vista operating systems will also support Xbox 360 game controllers using XINPUT, which is part of the DirectX SDK. For sound, the Building Blocks Engine will use OpenAL (Open Audio Library) for cross-platform sound processing, and on Windows-based

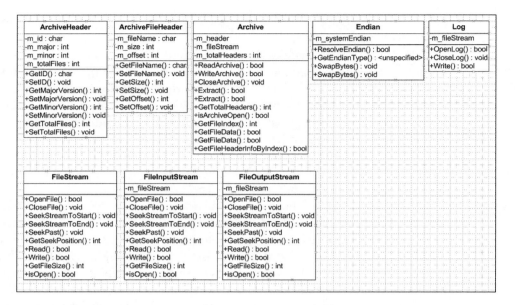

FIGURE 1.5   The class diagram for the core system.

operating systems, support for the use of XACT will be implemented in addition to OpenAL. Features dealing with the framework's input and sound systems include:

- Standard keyboard and mouse support
- Xbox 360 controller support through XINPUT
- OpenAL support for sound across all operating systems
- XACT support for sound on Windows

The input system can have classes for the Xbox 360 controllers, OpenAL, and XACT. For the standard keyboard and mouse functions, they can be used to test the device state of an object without necessarily needing an entire class. The input and sound systems of the Building Blocks Engine are discussed in further detail in Chapter 3. Figure 1.6 illustrates the planned class diagrams for the engine framework's input and sound systems.

Graphics are often among one of the most interesting topics in games for many, because they are a visual representation of the game itself. Graphics have gained tremendous importance in the last number of years as hardware capabilities have allowed for more to be done in higher resolutions. The rendering system for the Building Blocks Engine will have support for OpenGL on Windows, Mac, and

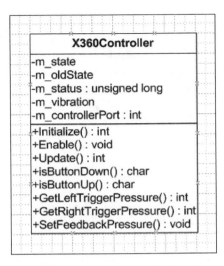

FIGURE 1.6   The class diagram for the input system.

Linux and the ability to be able to draw static meshes and allow the use of pro-grammable shaders. The rendering system will also have a simple scene graph for managing geometry objects, LOD, state management, octrees for space partition-ing, and a simple portal rendering system. The list of features the rendering system of the Building Blocks Engine will support includes:

- Ability to render static meshes
- Level of detail support for objects
- Simple scene graphs
- An octrees data structure
- A portal rendering system
- Texturing and multitexturing
- Support for programmable shaders
- Per-pixel lighting techniques such as traditional, bump mapping, normal map-ping, and extensions to bump mapping, which include parallax mapping
- Environment mapping
- Gloss mapping
- Alpha mapping
- Off-screen rendering
- OpenGL rendering

The rendering system of the Building Blocks Engine will have more classes than the rest of the framework. Each effect is planned to have its own class, and everything else mentioned for the rendering system. More detail and information about how the rendering system is designed and implemented are provided in Chapters 4 and 5. The class diagrams for the entire rendering system for the framework can be seen in Figure 1.7.

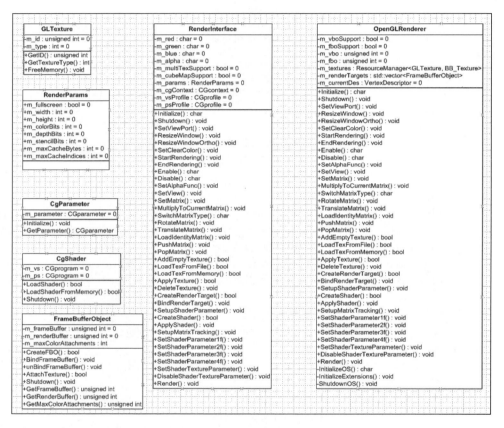

FIGURE 1.7   The class diagram for the graphics system.

Physics are becoming increasingly important in the gaming industry. Most modern games are built with realism in mind, and physics allow developers to take that level of realism to an even higher level than what has been seen in the past.

Currently, games are mostly all about graphics. In the future, games will still be about graphics, but also about physics and gameplay. It is possible that graphics will become less and less important, and gameplay and physics will take over as the key selling points of games. Physics and collision detection and handling are extremely important when creating a realistic simulation, because it doesn't matter how pretty a game is if the collisions are horrible, the feeling is unbalanced, and the overall gameplay experience is bad. For the Building Blocks Engine a physics system will be built from the ground up and will have support for point masses and soft bodies for cloth. The physics system of the Building Blocks Engine will include support for:

- Point mass representation
- Soft body representation
- Point mass collisions
- Soft body collisions
- Plane collisions
- Friction support for touching surfaces
- Drag support for objects traveling through a fluid
- Lift support for objects that can fly
- Buoyancy support for floating objects

In game physics, the use of point masses is mainly for objects such as particle systems, because in physics, point masses are infinitely small objects with no volume. Because point masses have no volume, there is a need for something else to represent the 3D objects such as characters, objects, weapons, and so forth. A rigid body is an object that can have its position and orientation, among other things, affected by physics, while a point mass has just its position. A third type of physics object is a soft body. Soft bodies are made up of point masses and springs and are used in games in the form of dynamic cloth simulations, for example. With the ability to update point masses and soft bodies, there will be support for collision detections and response. This will include plane collisions, friction against touching surfaces, drag for objects in fluids, lift for objects that can fly, and buoyancy for objects in water. The classes that make up the Building Blocks Engine's physics system are illustrated in Figure 1.8. The physics system is discussed in more detail in Chapter 6.

Game scripting is a very useful feature to have in a game. In the Building Blocks Engine, there will be support for a few different types of scripting systems, which

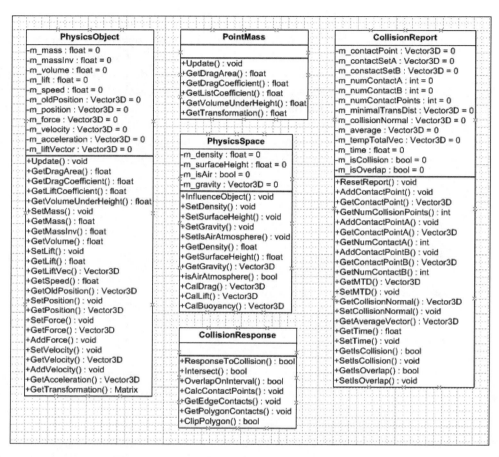

FIGURE 1.8 The class diagram for the physics system.

include property scripting, command scripting, and compiled scripts. Because the topic of scripting is complex, the compiled scripting system will be implemented using the third-party tool Game Monkey Script. Property scripts and command scripts will be implemented for the framework from the ground up. Features that make up the scripting system for the Building Blocks Engine include:

- Basic parser for tokens
- Property scripting

- Command scripting
- Compiled scripting with the help of Game Monkey Script

An additional tool that will be used by the property and command script will be a class used to parse tokens—a basic lexer. A lexer is a tool that breaks up a file into a list of tokens. This tool will be used for the property and command scripting systems, and for loading Wavefront .OBJ static geometry models in Chapter 4. Game scripting is discussed in more detail in Chapter 8. Figure 1.9 illustrates the class diagram that shows the planned classes for the entire scripting system for the Building Blocks Engine.

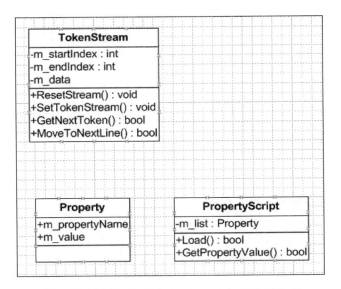

FIGURE 1.9   The class diagram for the scripting system.

The Building Blocks Engine will have one more system in addition to the previously mentioned ones in the framework—the networking system. This system will use sockets to connect an application to another computer. The networking system will simply take data from one application and send it to another using a class that wraps around sockets. On the receiving end, the information will be processed and some action will occur based on the interpretation of that information. The topic of networking is discussed in further detail in Chapter 3. Figure 1.10 is a visual look at the class diagram that makes up the entire networking system.

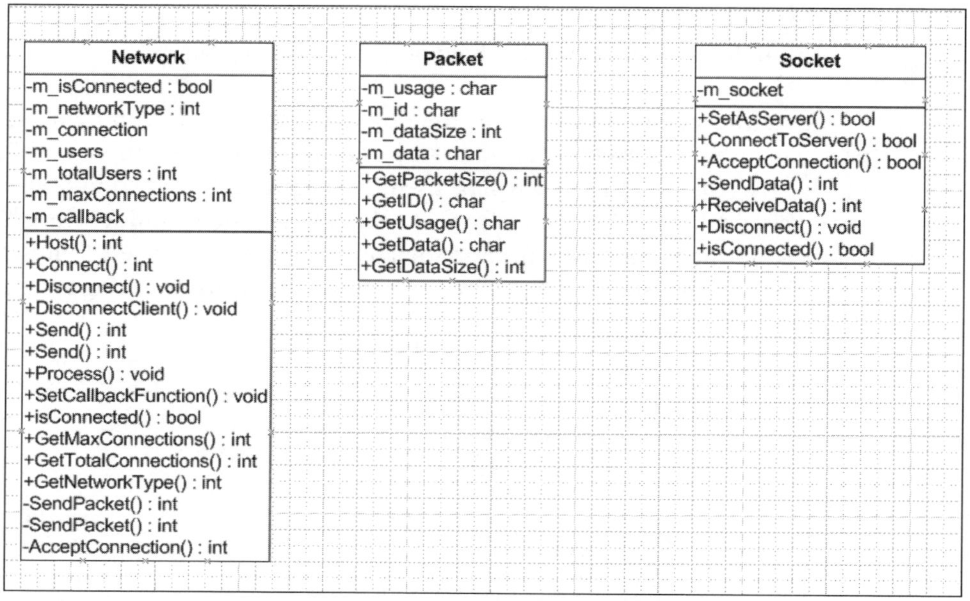

FIGURE 1.10 The networking system.

THE BUILDING BLOCKS ENGINE'S FUTURE

The game engine developed in this book is an early version of the Building Blocks Engine. An update for the first release of the Building Blocks Engine will appear on *UltimateGameProgramming.com* some time after the release of this book. The Building Blocks Engine is an early version of 0.5 because it needs heavy testing that is difficult to do at this time on a few different machines, needs many more features and tools to make creating games useful, and needs optimizations to speed up the game engine framework. The Building Blocks Engine will continue to grow at *UltimateGameProgramming.com* and will keep growing as long as it has some educational value for beginners. The purpose of the Building Blocks Engine is as a starting point for hobbyists and student game developers and will continue to target those audiences.

After this book is complete, there will be many tools created for the Building Blocks Engine that were not able to make it into this book. Examples of such tools are level editors, model format exporters (e.g., .3DS, .MAX, .LWO, etc.), memory management, and much more. Keeping with the spirit of *UltimateGameProgram-*

ming.com, all tools will have details on how they were designed and implemented. This information will be made available through online tutorials and Web articles that will take readers step by step through the addition of adding new features and tools. A list of possible additions to be added to the Building Blocks Engine in future releases includes but is not limited to:

- A complete and custom scripting system
- An enhanced physics system
- Additional rendering effects and techniques
- A general level editor
- Model exporters for the most popular file formats
- Model importers for the most popular file formats
- DirectX 10 support
- An enhanced archive filesystem and a GUI application to interface with the engine's archive files
- Optimizations to areas that have the heaviest bottlenecks
- XML files and XML-based material system for graphics
- Streaming audio files
- Support for additional input devices and device features
- An animation system for dynamic game objects
- Scripted animation paths for real-time cut scenes and artificial intelligence
- Memory management

Figures 1.11 and 1.12 are screenshots of two of the final demos created in this book with the Building Blocks Engine.

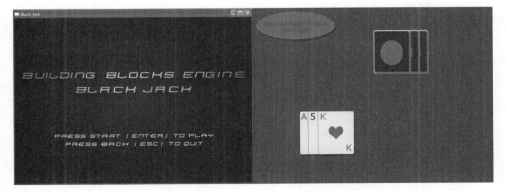

FIGURE 1.11   The blackjack game's menu (left), and the game being played (right).

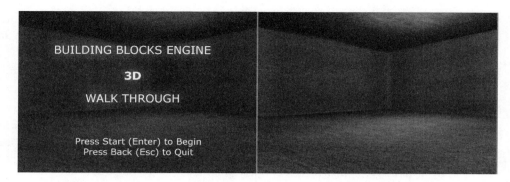

FIGURE 1.12   The 3D first-person walkthrough menu (left) and level (right).

TIPS AND PRACTICES

This part looks at the various coding styles and practices that are used in the code of the Building Blocks Engine. Everyone should be familiar with a few things in the C++ programming language, and a few of those concepts are looked at in the following parts. These topics include object construction, constructors and virtual destructors, C++ casting keywords, a brief look at the Standard Template Library, a brief look at design patterns, and how the Building Blocks Engine plans to encapsulate platform-specific code in the framework. There are many useful tips and practices for coding in C++. Appendix A lists a few resources on the C++ programming language, and on many of the topics discussed throughout this book.

THE BOOK'S CODING STYLE

Each programmer has his or her own programming style; everything from spaces, to tabs, to curly brace positions, to naming conventions, and so forth can change from one programmer to another. When working on a development team, it is important that each member adopt the programming style used by the team to make reading, editing, and working with code easier for each member. Without a generally accepted coding style, a development team can experience unnecessary slow downs when the code has many inconsistencies. The coding style in this book does not have to be used, but it is the style the engine is coded in. The purpose of this part is to give a quick overview of some of the aspects of how the framework was coded, so it is not a surprise later when code listings are shown. When coding in any language, the most important thing to remember is to stay consistent, especially with naming conventions for functions, variables, and classes.

Hungarian notation is a scheme created by Dr. Charles Simonyi as a way to standardize naming conventions. Although Hungarian notation is believed to be unnecessary in type-safe languages like C++, the Building Blocks Engine does use one or two ideas taken from the standard and deals with global variables and member variables of classes. Listing 1.1 lists an example where the g_ and m_ prefixes are used for the names of global variables and class member variables, respectively.

LISTING 1.1   An example of using the g_ and m_ prefixes for global and member variables.

```cpp
int g_globalVariable = (some value);


class SomeClass
{
    public:
        SomeClass()
        {

        }


        virtual ~SomeClass()
        {
            Shutdown();
        }


        bool Initialize()
        {
            ...

            return true;
        }


        void Shutdown()
        {
            ...

            return;
        }
```

```
private:
   int m_memberVar1;
   int m_memberVar2;
   int m_memberVar3;
};
```

The naming convention for variables in the Building Blocks Engine has the first letter of the variable's name lowercase, and every other word in the variable's name starts with an uppercase. This can be seen with the `g_globalVariable` where the word global starts with a lowercase and the word Variable starts with an uppercase. Since the global is in the global scope, it is also prefixed with the letter "g" and an underscore. For member variables, this is the same, except that member variables are prefixed with an `m_` to make them easier to identify in large functions of classes. Classes have capital letters for all words that make up a class name as seen in Listing 1.1 with the class `SomeClass`.

Another point to make in Listing 1.1 is that the class has an initialize and a shutdown function. Any class that must allocate memory that might or might not be needed when the object is first created will have an initialize function that returns the status of the creation. This is done because many times, some objects are created but are not used right away. This can happen in classes in which there are member objects of another class that might allocate memory if that information was specified in the constructor. If an object is not used or is not used for some time, the time spent allocating memory or performing other operations can prove an unnecessary overhead, especially if the object is not used for some reason (e.g., if the function returns early based on some condition). By using an initialize function, the operations a class needs to take to set up its internal variables, outside of setting default values, can be performed when needed. For any class that allocates data, that same data will need to be released. Releasing data is done in shutdown functions. To help to make sure classes release memory when the class object is no longer needed, the destructor of a class calls the shutdown function.

Each source file in the Building Blocks Engine uses three spaces instead of tabs. Curly braces appear on their own lines with semicolons following them with code that requires them (e.g., class declarations). In the body of a class, all public functions are declared first, followed by all protected members and then by all private members. An example of this can be seen in Listing 1.2.

LISTING 1.2 An example of ordering public from private from protected data.

```
int g_globalVariable = (some value);
```

```cpp
class SomeClass
{
   public:
      SomeClass()
      {

      }


      virtual ~SomeClass()
      {
         Shutdown();
      }


      bool Initialize()
      {
         ...

         return true;
      }


      void Shutdown()
      {
         ...

         return;
      }


   protected:
      void ProtectedFunction1();
      void ProtectedFunction2();
      virtual void ProtectedFunction3() = 0;


   protected:
      float m_protectedVar1;
      float m_protectedVar2;
      float m_protectedVar3;
```

```
      private:
          int m_memberVar1;
          int m_memberVar2;
          int m_memberVar3;
};
```

The only time the order of public from protected and private members changes is when grouping functions that are related but have different access privileges. For example, if the initialize function calls other functions to aid in doing its job but those function are not meant to be called by the programmer, they might be grouped together regardless of the privileges. An example of this can be seen in Listing 1.3.

LISTING 1.3   Grouping related functions regardless of access privileges.

```
class SomeClass
{
    public:
        SomeClass();
        virtual ~SomeClass();


        bool Initialize();


    protected:
        virtual bool InitializeInDerived() = 0;


    private:
        bool InitializeSomeThing();


    public:
        void Shutdown()
        {
            ...

            return;
        }


    protected:
        void ProtectedFunction1();
```

```
    void ProtectedFunction2();
    virtual void ProtectedFunction3() = 0;


protected:
    float m_protectedVar1;
    float m_protectedVar2;
    float m_protectedVar3;


private:
    int m_memberVar1;
    int m_memberVar2;
    int m_memberVar3;
};
```

C++ TIPS

This next part discusses various simple ideas to keep in mind when coding in an object-oriented language such as C++. Some of these topics can have an impact on performance depending on the situation, and are something to consider when creating a gaming or simulation application where performance is critical. In this part, class constructors and destructors are discussed, and things to remember when working with overloaded operators, casting, and the C++ Standard Template Library.

CLASS CONSTRUCTORS AND DESTRUCTORS

The first tip deals with not creating objects until they are needed. In the case of calling a function that uses an object of some class, if the function can quit early, the declaration of said class could have been unnecessary if the object was declared at the beginning of the function. When objects are created, their constructors are called, which is one form of overhead. If those objects must allocate memory, additional overhead is incurred. If the function quits early, this overhead could have been for nothing. Listing 1.4 lists an example of creating an object when it is not necessary. In the example, if the parameter passed into the function is invalid, the function returns. If the object was created before this test, there could be situations in which overhead is wasted. This overhead can add up with functions that are called many times per frame and quit early during the majority of those times.

LISTING 1.4   Don't create objects until they are needed.

```
void Function1(SomeObject *obj)
{
   AnotherObject obj2;


   if(obj == NULL)
      return;
}
```

The same idea presented in Listing 1.4 can be applied to loops. If in a loop an object is being declared, that object can be created, destroyed, and recreated many times. This is a waste of a lot of overhead if the process is unnecessary, especially if the object allocates memory. Instead of declaring objects inside the body of a loop, they should be defined before the loop as seen in Listing 1.5. This way, only the necessary operations that must be done for each iteration of a loop are performed instead of the additional overhead of creating, destroying, and so forth the same object.

LISTING 1.5   Declaring objects outside a loop.

```
// Instead of doing this...


void Function2()
{
   ...


   for(int i = 0; i < (some value); i++)
   {
      SomeObject obj;


      (body of loop that uses obj)
   }


   ...
}
```

```
// ... do this ...


void Function2()
{
    ...


    SomeObject obj;


    for(int i = 0; i < (some value); i++)
    {
        (body of loop that uses obj)
    }


    ...
}
```

The next tip deals with passing objects to another's constructor; for example, if an object must be passed into the constructor of a class and that object is assigned to a member object of the same type. The overhead involved in such a process includes the constructor of the parameter object being called so that the object being passed in can be copied, the overhead of the equal operator, the overhead of the new object being created, and any overhead associated with the allocation of any memory by the object being passed in. To improve on this overhead, instead of passing objects by value, they should be passed by reference; and instead of assigning one object to another in a constructor, the C++ : should be used to allow the member variables to be set before the body of the constructor is called. If the constructor is empty, some compilers can optimize it out. An example of this can be seen in Listing 1.6.

LISTING 1.6   Passing objects to constructors.

```
// Instead of doing this...


class SomeClass
{
    public:
        SomeClass(SomeObject obj)
        {
```

```
            m_obj = obj;
        }


    private:
        SomeObject m_obj;
};


// Do this...


class SomeClass
{
    public:
        SomeClass(const SomeObject &obj) : m_obj(obj)
        {

        }


    private:
        SomeObject m_obj;
};
```

The same idea from Listing 1.6 can be extended to member functions of a class. Taking a 3D vector class as an example, a lot of overhead can be wasted on overloaded operators, which can add up quickly over time, especially with objects that are used heavily in a game. As an example, take the operation of adding two 3D vectors and assigning the result to a third vector ($v1 = v2 + v3$). There exists overhead for the addition operator, the equals operator, and the constructor of a temp variable inside the function for the addition operation that is returned. For objects that are called in high frequency, like matrices and vectors in game development, this can have an impact depending on the game. An example of a 3D vector class with the addition and equal operators defined can be seen in Listing 1.7.

LISTING 1.7   An example 3D vector class with defined operators.

```
class Vector3D
{
    public:
        Vector3D()
        {
```

```
        x = 0;
        y = 0;
        z = 0;
    }


    void operator=(Vector3D v)
    {
        x = v.x;
        y = v.y;
        z = v.z;
    }


    Vector3D operator+(Vector3D v2)
    {
        return Vector3D(x + v2.x, y + v2.y, z + v2.z);
    }


    float x, y, z;
};
```

Creating operators for classes that deal with math is a natural and convenient way to work with objects, but that convenience comes at a price—and that price is performance. For nonperformance areas of an application, using these operators can have a negligible impact on the performance, but in other areas, functions and references should be used to minimize overhead as much as possible. An example of this can be seen in Listing 1.8, where an addition function is used to both add two vectors together and assign it to the object the function belongs to all in one call.

LISTING 1.8   A second 3D vector class example.

```
class Vector3D
{
    public:
        Vector3D() : x(0), y(0), z(0)
        {

        }
```

```
        void operator=(const Vector3D &v)
        {
           x = v.x;
           y = v.y;
           z = v.z;
        }


        Vector3D operator+(const Vector3D &v2)
        {
           return Vector3D(x + v2.x, y + v2.y, z + v2.z);
        }


        void Add(const Vector3D &v1, const Vector3D &v2)
        {
           x = v1.x + v2.x;
           y = v1.y + v2.y;
           z = v1.z + v2.z;
        }


        float x, y, z;
    };
```

When working with inheritance, it is important to declare destructors as virtual for the destructors to be called correctly. By not specifying a base class' destructor as virtual, the derived class' destructor will not be called. This problem does not concern constructors, but with destructors, it is something to keep in mind when using inheritance. An example of this can be seen in Listing 1.9.

LISTING 1.9   Declaring destructors as virtual.

```
  // When using inheritance make sure to have virtual destructor.


  class Base
  {
     public:
        Base()
        {

        }
```

```
        virtual ~Base()
        {

        }
};


class Derived1 : Base
{
    public:
        Derived1()
        {

        }


        virtual ~Derived1()
        {

        }
};
```

CASTING

Casting means taking something of one type and casting it to another. Two types of casting exist: implicit casting and explicit casting. Implicit castings are performed by the compiler, while explicit castings are performed by the programmer. In traditional C-styled casting, an explicit cast can look like the code seen in Listing 1.10. An implicit cast performed by the compiler can be seen listed in Listing 1.11.

LISTING 1.10   An example of a C-style cast.

```
SomeObject = (SomeObject)AnotherObject;
```

LISTING 1.11   An example of an implicit cast.

```
short a = 10;
int b = a;
```

The major problems with C-style casts is that they are hard to see when searching through a source file because of the (); it is hard for compilers and programmers alike to detect improper casts from proper casts, casts can't remove the "const-ness of an object," and it is really easy to use casts improperly, which can introduce bugs. In C++, there are four operators for casting:

- `static_cast`
- `const_cast`
- `dynamic_cast`
- `reinterpret_cast`

Using C++ style casts offer the following benefits:

- Clear casting
- Clear intensions with castings
- Type-safe castings

The first type of cast, `static_cast`, is used to cast one object to another similar to the cast that was performed in Listing 1.10. The second type of cast using the `const_cast` keyword is used to add or remove "const-ness" from an object. The third cast type through the `dynamic_cast` keyword is used to cast objects in an inheritance class hierarchy. The fourth and final cast type is used to reinterpret the data type pointers are pointing to, which is unsafe and is not supported by all compilers. The `reinterpret_cast` keyword is not recommended, and if you need to cast pointers from one type to another in a class hierarchy, the `dynamic_cast` keyword should be used instead. Listing 1.12 lists an example of how to use each of these keywords in C++.

LISTING 1.12   Examples of the various C++ casting.

```cpp
#include<iostream>


using namespace std;


void Display(char *str)
{
   cout << str << endl;
}


int main(int args, char argc[])
{
   int intVar = 10;
```

```
float floatVar = 5.85f;
const char *constStr = "Some message";


cout << "intVar = " << intVar << endl;
cout << "floatVar = " << floatVar << endl;


// static_cast example.
cout << "floatVar cast to int = "
     << static_cast<int>(floatVar) << endl;


// const_cast example.
Display(const_cast<char*>(constStr));


// reinterpret_cast example.
int *intPtr = &intVar;
float *floatPtr = reinterpret_cast<float*>(intPtr);


// dynamic_cast example.
class Base { };
class Derived: public Base { };

Base baseObj;
Base* basePtr = 0;

Derived derived;
Derived* derivedPtr = 0;

// Is valid.
basePtr = dynamic_cast<Base*>(&derived);

// Is not valid.
derivedPtr = dynamic_cast<Derived*>(&baseObj);


    return 1;
}
```

THE STANDARD TEMPLATE LIBRARY

Data structures are common in software development and are a way to organize data in memory by using structures or containers. By organizing data in containers, various algorithms can be performed on them to create useful output and other results. In video games, data structures are used in large numbers in many different sub-systems of a game and game engine and are almost impossible to avoid when creating a video game. Data structures in video games have to be performance friendly, efficient, and effective.

The C++ programming language has a set of code called the Standard Template Library (or STL for short) for various data structures. This book uses these various data structures as an efficient and effective means of organizing data in the Building Blocks Engine. Using STL can save a programmer a lot of time and energy from not having to create custom implementations of common data structures and algorithms used in programming. The topic of STL will be reviewed in Chapter 2 as well as the different data structures the Building Blocks Engine uses throughout its various interfaces. Various details about each STL data structure will need to be understood before implementing them in a performance-intensive application such as a video game.

DESIGN PATTERNS

Object-oriented programming in software development can become a complex subject. In programming, many different problems arise throughout the development of a piece of software. Often, these programming problems and issues are reoccurring and can be encountered by programmers and development teams everywhere. Design patterns in software development are general solutions to many of these repeatable issues.

A design pattern is a general solution to commonly re-occurring problems in software development where each design pattern has a different goal and is suited to a different problem. Design patterns in programming are code that is designed and implemented using various principles and methods and are not hard coded like template classes. A design pattern can be thought of as a template that developers can use when creating classes in their applications by following a set of guidelines. Common design patterns in software development include but are not limited to:

- Singleton
- Façade
- State
- Observer
- Decorator
- Factory

- Command
- Composite
- Proxy
- Adapter

ADAPTERS

One design pattern encountered later in this book is the adapter. An adapter design pattern allows developers to design code to wrap around classes to allow them to be used in a way they are not normally able to. An adapter pattern allows classes to "adapt" to a system so that a design expecting one interface can work with others. Like an electrical outlet adapter to allow U.S.-made devices to work in Europe and vice versa, adapters in programming are objects that sit between two incompatible interfaces and allow them to communicate to each other. In other words, an object-oriented adapter can be used to change the interface of a class into something another class or system is expecting.

Adapters try to solve two problems. The first problem, communication, deals with having a class that must be used with a new interface that is incompatible. The second problem of re-working code deals with having either to change the new interface or change the old interface so they are compatible. Changing one or more interfaces is not always possible, especially with third-party vendor classes. Forcing developers to change their own code can potentially cause the following problems:

- Bugs can be introduced.
- The difficult task of altering an already existing and working class so it can work with a new interface.
- The problem can arise again, causing the code to be reworked all over multiple times.
- Changing an already existing class can have a domino effect with the new class, derived classes, and all code that uses the class where changes must be made to reflect the new interface.

There are two different kinds of OOP adapters: object adapters and class adapters. An object adapter wraps an interface using composition, while a class adapter uses multiple inheritances to create an adapter class. In this part, we look at both types of adapters and how they can be made from classes. An example of using both object and class adapters can be seen in Listing 1.13. Note that the listing is just an example for demonstration purposes. In Listing 1.13, the object adapter class is called `DogObjectAdapter` and uses composition to wrap a `DogInterface` object, while `DogClassAdapter` uses multiple inheritances.

LISTING 1.13   An example of using object adapters.

```
#include<iostream>


class DogInterface
{
   public:
      DogInterface()
      {

      }

      virtual ~DogInterface()
      {

      }

      virtual void Bark()
      {
         std::cout << "Woof I'm a dog!" << std::endl;
      }
};


class CatInterface
{
   public:
      CatInterface()
      {

      }

      virtual ~CatInterface()
      {

      }

      virtual void Meow()
      {
         std::cout << "Meow I'm a cat!" << std::endl;
      }
};
```

```cpp
class DogObjectAdapter : public CatInterface
{
   public:
      DogObjectAdapter(DogInterface d)
      {
         m_dog = d;
      }

      virtual ~DogObjectAdapter()
      {

      }

      void Meow()
      {
         m_dog.Bark();
      }

   private:
      DogInterface m_dog;
};


class DogClassAdapter : public CatInterface, DogInterface
{
   public:
      DogClassAdapter()
      {

      }

      virtual ~DogClassAdapter()
      {

      }
};


void CatTalk(CatInterface &cat)
{
   cat.Meow();
}
```

```
int main(int args, char argc[])
{
   CatInterface cat;
   DogInterface dog;


   DogObjectAdapter dogObjectAdapter(dog);
   DogClassAdapter dogClassAdapter;


   CatTalk(cat);
   CatTalk(dogObjectAdapter);
   CatTalk(dogClassAdapter);


   return 1;
}
```

ENCAPSULATING PLATFORM-SPECIFIC CODE

The Building Blocks Engine is designed to work on multiple operating systems. Often, there are nonstandard ways to perform various tasks in C++ across different systems. Because the Building Blocks Engine must work on different systems, the issue can present a challenge when implementing the framework.

The solution in this book is to encapsulate the various platform-specific codes in a way to make an interface appear portable by using multiple source files. This method will allow the code to look portable and is an easy solution. For example, many different interfaces that are a part of the Building Blocks Engine are implemented with a header for a class declaration and a source file for the implementation. When it comes to platform-specific implementation, additional source files can be used. Taking a class used to get the time in milliseconds; for example, you can place the declaration in YourTimer.h and the Windows implementation in YourTimerWin32.cpp, Mac in YourTimerMac.cpp, and Linux in YourTimeLinux.cpp. An example of this can be seen in Listing 1.14.

LISTING 1.14 An example of encapsulating platform specifics in different source files.

```
// YourTimer.h


class YourTimer
{
```

```
    ...

    int GetTimeInMilliseconds();

    ...
};


// YourTimerWin32.cpp


int YourTimer::GetTimeInMilliseconds()
{
    // WIN 32 CODE HERE
}


// YourTimerMac.cpp


int YourTimer::GetTimeInMilliseconds()
{
    // MAC CODE HERE
}


// YourTimerLinux.cpp


int YourTimer::GetTimeInMilliseconds()
{
    // LINUX CODE HERE
}
```

SUMMARY

Video game engines play a large role in the game development scene. A game engine is a framework used to create games from and is a complex engineering project that requires skill and dedication. The development of a game engine is not trivial, and the design and architecture will take time, resources, and teamwork. As video games become more complex, so does the engineering challenges that come up during development of a game.

The Building Blocks Game Engine is a game engine created specifically for this book. All the information in this text has been implemented in the Building Blocks Engine as a demonstration of the various topics and techniques that will be discussed. It is recommended that readers read this text twice—first to understand the material in this book, and then to implement their own game engine framework from the ground up. Although many game development companies elect to license game engines from other companies, the need for game engineers is still important if not as common as the need for game programmers, game artist, level designers, and so forth.

In the next chapter, we discuss the core system in greater detail, and the implementation of the various core elements that make up the Building Blocks Engine. The core part makes up various classes and methods that will be used throughout the rest of the game engine's framework and any games created using the Building Blocks Engine.

CHAPTER EXERCISES

2 Engine Core

In This Chapter

- Data Structures
- Memory Allocation
- File I/O
- Timing Utilities
- Archive Files
- Additional Topics and Techniques

ArchiveHeader
-m_id : char
-m_major : int
-m_minor : int
-m_totalFiles : int
+GetID() : char
+SetID() : void
+GetMajorVersion() : int
+SetMajorVersion() : void
+GetMinorVersion() : int
+SetMinorVersion() : void
+GetTotalFiles() : int
+SetTotalFiles() : void

ArchiveFileHeader
-m_fileName : char
-m_size : int
-m_offset : int
+GetFileName() : char
+SetFileName() : void
+GetSize() : int
+SetSize() : void
+GetOffset() : int
+SetOffset() : void

Archive
-m_header
-m_fileStream
-m_totalHeaders : int
+ReadArchive() : bool
+WriteArchive() : bool
+CloseArchive() : void
+Extract() : bool
+Extract() : bool
+GetTotalHeaders() : int
+isArchiveOpen() : bool
+GetFileIndex() : int
+GetFileData() : bool
+GetFileData() : bool
+GetFileHeaderInfoByIndex() : bool

T
he core code that is part of a game engine is critical in aiding in the development of the engine technology and the games that will be developed because of that game engine. The low-level core system is made up of objects such as data structures, file I/O tools, timers, memory management, profilers, resource management, and much more that are used as tools that work at a low level within the framework. The code that makes up the core system will need to be fast, memory efficient, and easy to work with, especially in a real-time application such as a video game and other simulations. Being effective and efficient will help in the overall implementation and design of any games built from the game engine framework.

The purpose of this chapter is to examine a few classes, libraries, and methods that can be used in the game engine's core. A look at the various core objects that are a part of the Building Blocks Engine will also be examined in more detail as they are encountered. Reusability is the key idea throughout this chapter, as the code will need to be used by multiple systems that make up the game engine framework and the games themselves. Along with being reusable, speed is also a critical component of code that is developed to be used in a real-time application such as a video game and other dynamic simulations.

DATA STRUCTURES

All applications need some way to organize an arrangement of data in the computer's memory in a way that is useful to the application. Once such an arrangement has been created, various algorithms can be executed on them to produce some meaningful output and result. These arrangements of data are known as data structures in computer programming. Examples of data structures examined in this chapter, which only make up a small number of the data structures that exist, include arrays, link lists, queues, string objects, and hash tables. Additional data structures are binary trees, heaps, graphs, and stacks, to name a few.

To work with data structures, C++ developers generally face two main options. The first option is to create custom data structures that are written manually by the programmers on a development team, and the second option is to use existing code such as the C++ Standard Template Library (STL). The STL is a part of the C++ namespace called STD and is standard in the C++ programming language. STL is very popular and is well documented. The Building Blocks Game Engine and demo applications use the STL data structures in code for the following reasons:

- STL data structures are efficient.
- Using STL versus creating custom data structures or "re-inventing the wheel" saves time.
- STL is part of the C++ standard.

- STL was written by experienced professionals.
- The STL library is large with many different data structures for many different uses and situations that arise in computer programming.
- STL is optimized.

The benefits of using STL make it a viable option to use in C++ computer programming and for the Building Blocks Engine in this book. Some additional data structures that are used in various areas of game development (e.g., scene management) are discussed in Chapter 5, "Rendering Scenes and Scene Graphs." The following sections briefly discuss the main data structures commonly used throughout the Building Blocks Engine framework.

VECTOR ARRAYS

Arrays are the most basic data structures dealt with in computer programming. The STL library implements dynamically resizable arrays as a data structured called a vector. The data elements of a vector array can be accessed in the same way traditional arrays are by using the [] operator or by using iterators. Data items can be inserted and removed from a vector array by using the data structure's various methods such as push_back() and pop_back(). For developers, some of the things to keep in mind when using vectors are:

- Vectors can allocate more memory than is needed by an application, which can be a waste of resources.
- When a vector needs to be resized, there is overhead associated with the allocation of a new block of memory, copying of memory from one location to the other, and deletion of the old memory.
- When a vector reallocates memory, all iterators pointing to elements within the vector are invalid.

The vector template class has several different functions that can be called to manipulate an object, including:

`void push_back(const Type &val):` Used to add an item to the end of the array.

`void pop_back():` Used to remove an item at the end of the array.

`size_type size():` Returns the size (in total elements) of the array.

`size_type max_size():` Returns the max size of the array.

`void reserve(size_type count):` Allocates an array of a specified amount.

`void resize(size_type size):` Specifies a new size for the array.

`const_reference front():` Returns a reference to the first element in the array.

`const_reference back():` Returns a reference to the last element in the array.

`size_type capacity():` Returns the size the array can contain without needing to allocate more memory.

`void clear():` Clears the elements from the array.

`const_iterator begin():` Returns an iterator to the first element in the array.

`const_iterator end():` Returns an iterator to the last element in the array.

`bool empty():` Returns true if the array is empty; otherwise, false.

`operator[]:` Allows the vector array to have its elements accessed using the array subscripts.

An example of the `std::vector` array can be found on the companion CD-ROM in the BUILDING BLOCKS ENGINE/EXAMPLES/CHAPTER 2 folder and is called VECTOR. The demo application VECTOR demonstrates the basics to using the STL data structure in a console application. Listing 2.1 lists the main source file of this demo application for convenience.

LISTING 2.1   The VECTOR demo application.

```
#include<iostream>
#include<vector>

using namespace std;


int main(int args, char **argc)
{
   int i = 0;
   vector<int> array;

   array.push_back(10);
   array.push_back(20);
   array.push_back(30);
   array.push_back(40);
   array.push_back(50);

   cout << "Array contents(" << "Size: " << (int)array.size() <<
           " Capacity: " << (int)array.capacity() << ") - ";

   for(i = 0; i < (int)array.size(); i++)
   {
      cout << array[i] << " ";
   }
```

```
cout << endl;

array.pop_back();
array.pop_back();

cout << "Array contents(" << "Size: " << (int)array.size() <<
        " Capacity: " << (int)array.capacity() <<
        ") after 2 pop_back() - ";

for(i = 0; i < (int)array.size(); i++)
{
    cout << array[i] << " ";
}

cout << endl;

array.clear();

cout << "Array stats(" << "Size: " << (int)array.size() <<
        " Capacity: " << (int)array.capacity() <<
        ") after clear. ";

cout << endl << endl;

    return 1;
}
```

Listing 2.1 shows how to use a std::vector array by adding elements to the array, obtaining the size and capacity of the array, clearing the array, removing elements from the end of the array, and by using the operator [ ] to access elements of the array using random access. When items are added to the array, they are copied onto the list. When using pointers, the pointer address can be added to the list using the new operator, and elements of an array can be deleted from the list. Listing 2.2 lists an example of doing this using iterators with the vector array. This demo is called VECTOR 2 and can be found on the CD-ROM in the BUILDING BLOCKS ENGINE/EXAMPLES/CHAPTER 2 folder.

ON THE CD

LISTING 2.2   The second vector array example.

```
#include<iostream>
#include<vector>

using namespace std;
```

```
class DummyClass
{
   public:
      DummyClass(int val) : m_member(val)
      {

      }

      int GetMember()
      {
         return m_member;
      }

   private:
      int m_member;
};


int main(int args, char **argc)
{
   int i = 0;
   vector<DummyClass*> array;

   array.push_back(new DummyClass(10));
   array.push_back(new DummyClass(20));
   array.push_back(new DummyClass(30));
   array.push_back(new DummyClass(40));
   array.push_back(new DummyClass(50));


   cout << "Array contents(" << "Size: " << (int)array.size() <<
           " Capacity: " << (int)array.capacity() << ") - ";

   for(i = 0; i < (int)array.size(); i++)
   {
      cout << array[i]->GetMember() << " ";
   }

   cout << endl;


   for(vector<DummyClass*>::iterator it = array.begin();
       it != array.end(); ++it)
   {
```

```
    if(it != NULL)
    {
        cout << "Deleting DummyClass(" <<
                (*it)->GetMember() << ")" << endl;

        delete (*it);
        (*it) = NULL;
    }
}

cout << endl << endl;

return 1;
}
```

In Listing 2.2, the application adds dynamically allocated objects to the array. When accessing elements in any STL template class, an iterator can be used. In Listing 2.2, an iterator is used in the second for loop to transverse from the beginning of the array to the end. The element an iterator points to can also be accessed if necessary. In the second for loop in Listing 2.2, the dynamically allocated memory is deleted and nullified. This is important, because if dynamically allocated memory is added to a list as it is in Listing 2.2, that memory will need to be released manually because the template array class will not automatically do it when the array is destroyed.

STRINGS

Strings can be very useful in computer programs by allowing applications to have a character array used specifically for text messages. By using a structure specifically for storing and manipulating strings, the structure can make working with them natural and efficient. Strings in STL are exposed using the data structure string, which can be assessed by including the <string> header file. The STL string class has methods that allow coders to compare strings using comparison operators, concatenate strings, copy strings, finding substrings, reading data from an I/O stream, and a few other features. STL strings also have functions that are similar to the STL vectors such as push_back(), clear(), and size(). To read data from an input stream, the method getline() can be used to gather the data from a source. This can be used to read data from the std::cin stream, for example, which can be used to get data from the keyboard device attached to the computer. The string class is not a template class, unlike many of the other data structures that exist in the C++ STL. Some of the various functions that make up the string class include:

void swap(basic_string<CharType, Traits, Allocator>& _Left, basic_string<CharType, Traits, Allocator>& _Right): Used to swap the array data from one string to the other.

basic_istream<CharType, Traits>& getline(basic_istream<CharType, Traits>& _Istr, basic_string<CharType, Traits, Allocator>& _Str, CharType _Delim): Used to get a string from an input stream. This string can be specified by a delimiter.

void push_back(const Type &val): Used to add an item to the end of the string.

void pop_back(): Used to remove an item at the end of the string.

size_type size(): Returns the size of the string.

size_type max_size(): Returns the max size of the string.

void reserve(size_type count): Allocates a string of a specified amount.

void resize(size_type size): Specifies a new size for the string.

size_type capacity(): Returns the size the string can contain without needing to allocate more memory.

void clear(): Clears the elements from the string.

const_iterator begin(): Returns an iterator to the first element in the string.

const_iterator end(): Returns an iterator to the last element in the string.

bool empty(): Returns true if the string is empty; otherwise, false.

operator[], operator=, operator==, operator+, operator+=, operator<<, operator>>, operator!=, operator<, operator<=, operator>, and operator>=: Operators used for manipulating and comparing strings.

ON THE CD

On the companion CD-ROM in the BUILDING BLOCKS ENGINE/EXAMPLES/ CHAPTER 2 folder is a console application that demonstrates using STL strings called STRINGS. Listing 2.3 lists the main source file from the STRINGS console application for convenience. The STRINGS demonstration application shows the basics of using STL strings in a C++ console window. The use of the STL string class makes working with strings much easier and much more efficient than trying to create a manual string class or working with character arrays directly in code. In the example in Listing 2.3, the string is set, cleared, and displayed to the console window. When a new string is assigned to an STL string object and if the size of the new string is larger than the current capacity, the string is resized to be able to contain the entire data. This resizing operation does not occur when a string that is smaller than the capacity is set. STL strings, like vectors, can allocate more data than needed, which can or can't become an issue. For most applications, having objects that are the exact size needed to hold the data is not always necessary or is negligible when compared to the performance cost of having to resize data often in a program.

LISTING 2.3   The STRING demo application.

```cpp
#include<iostream>
#include<string>

using namespace std;


int main(int args, char **argc)
{
    string str("Hello World");

    cout << "String contents: " << str << endl;


    str.clear();
    cout << "New string contents: " << str << endl;


    str = "Goodbye World";
    cout << "New string contents: " << str << endl;


    cout << endl;


    cout << "Enter in a string and press enter: ";
    getline(cin, str);


    cout << endl;


    cout << "You've entered: " << str << endl;


    cout << endl;

    return 1;
}
```

LINK LISTS

Double-ended link lists in STL are implemented through the `list` data structure. With lists, the insertion and deletion are done in constant time. Also with lists, there is a loss of fast random access when compared to traditional arrays. Because the STL `list` is a double-ended link list, items can be inserted in the beginning or at the end of the list, which also means that inserting into the middle of the list is not as fast. One major advantage link lists have over arrays is that link lists can be resized very quickly and with less overhead. If random access is not a deal breaker, link lists can be a good choice to use for lists of objects in an application.

ON THE CD

On the companion CD-ROM in the BUILDING BLOCKS ENGINE/ EXAMPLES/CHAPTER 2 folder is a demo application called LISTS that demonstrates STL link lists in a console C++ application. The demo application also demonstrates the use of iterators to access the different elements in an STL data structure. Listing 2.4 lists the main source file from the LISTS demo application. An STL `list` has many of the same functions as vectors and strings with the addition of the following:

void merge(list &lst): Merge will combine two lists.

void remove(const TYPE &val): Removes all elements that are equal to `val`.

void remove_if(UnPred pr): Removes all elements from the list based on if the unary predicate `pr` is true.

void sort(): Sorts a list in ascending order.

void unique(): Removes all consecutive duplicates from a list.

LISTING 2.4   The LISTS demo application.

```cpp
#include<iostream>
#include<list>

using namespace std;


int main(int args, char **argc)
{
   int i = 0;
   list<int> linkList;
   list<int>::iterator it;

   linkList.push_back(10);
   linkList.push_back(20);
```

```
linkList.push_back(30);
linkList.push_back(40);
linkList.push_back(50);

cout << "Contents of the link list: ";

for(it = linkList.begin(); it != linkList.end(); it++)
{
    cout << *it << " ";
}

cout << endl;

linkList.pop_back();
linkList.pop_back();

cout << "Contents of the link list: ";

for(it = linkList.begin(); it != linkList.end(); it++)
{
    cout << *it << " ";
}

cout << endl << endl;

return 1;
}
```

QUEUES

A queue data structure has a first in/first out insertion and removal order and allows the access of one element at a time on the list. As a first in/first out data structure, the first item inserted into a queue list is the first object taken off the queue, also called being popped off the queue. To be able to access one item on the list, that item is popped off and worked with. The application can move to the next item on the queue list when necessary. If the item that is popped off the list needs to be back on the queue, it can be re-inserted into the list. An example of a use for a queue can be seen in a networking queue where the messages are placed in the queue and are processed when the application devotes resources to do so.

Another type of queue is known as a priority queue. A priority queue is used to order items in the queue based on their priority of importance. The priority allows items with a higher importance to be processed first before lower priority items on the queue list. That also means that the first object added to the queue is no longer guaranteed to be the first object off the queue when the item is removed. A priority queue can be a great data structure to use with objects that have a priority associated with them so that the critical elements can be taken care of first before the least important elements. The difference between a normal queue and a priority queue is that a priority queue orders the elements based on a condition. This condition can be to order all elements from less to greater, greater to less, and so on.

A third type of queue is called deque. A deque is a double-ended queue that allows for the insertion and removal of items on the queue from both ends of the list.

On the companion CD-ROM in the BUILDING BLOCKS ENGINE/EXAMPLES/ CHAPTER 2 folder is a C++ console application called QUEUE that demonstrates the use of both a traditional queue and a priority queue. Listing 2.5 lists the main source file of the QUEUE demo application. For the priority queue, it is possible to specify which underlying data structure it uses for the list, which in the case of Listing 2.5 is a vector array. For the priority comparison, a template class can be created and used to test two objects in the queue. The data structure is flexible so anything can be used with the priority queue as long as the comparison conditions are specified for the elements in the list. An example of a double-ended queue, or deque, can be seen listed in Listing 2.6, where items can be inserted (pushed) and removed (popped) from both ends of the queue. The double-ended queue example application can also be found on the companion CD-ROM in the same folder as the QUEUE demo application and is called DEQUE. A double-ended queue can work in constant time when it comes to insertions and deletions just like the STL vector array template class, and allows for random access of its elements.

LISTING 2.5   The QUEUE demo application.

```
#include<iostream>
#include<vector>
#include<queue>

using namespace std;


template<class T>
class BigToSmall
{
   public:
    inline bool operator()(T left, T right)
    {
```

```
        return (left < right);
      }
};


int main(int args, char **argc)
{
   queue<int> normalQueue;
   priority_queue<int, vector<int>,
                  BigToSmall<int> > priorityQueue;

   normalQueue.push(20);
   normalQueue.push(10);
   normalQueue.push(30);

   priorityQueue.push(99);
   priorityQueue.push(50);
   priorityQueue.push(2035);
   priorityQueue.push(35);
   priorityQueue.push(10);

   cout << "Queue contents (" << "Size: " <<
           (int)normalQueue.size() <<") - ";

   while(normalQueue.empty() == false)
   {
      cout << normalQueue.front() << " ";
      normalQueue.pop();
   }

   cout << endl;

   cout << "Priority Queue contents (" << "Size: " <<
           (int)priorityQueue.size() <<") - ";

   while(priorityQueue.empty() == false)
   {
      cout << priorityQueue.top() << " ";
      priorityQueue.pop();
   }

   cout << endl << endl;

   return 1;
 }
```

LISTING 2.6 An example of a deque.

```cpp
#include<iostream>
#include<deque>

using namespace std;


int main(int args, char **argc)
{
   deque<int> normalQueue;


   normalQueue.push_front(20);
   normalQueue.push_front(10);
   normalQueue.push_front(80);
   normalQueue.push_front(74);
   normalQueue.push_front(15);
   normalQueue.push_front(320);


   normalQueue.push_back(3);
   normalQueue.push_back(63);
   normalQueue.push_back(21);
   normalQueue.push_back(87);


   cout << "Deque contents (" << "Size: " <<
           (int)normalQueue.size() <<") - ";


   while(normalQueue.empty() == false)
   {
      cout << normalQueue.front() << " ";
      normalQueue.pop_front();
   }


   cout << endl << endl;


   return 1;
}
```

Stacks

A stack is a list of elements similar to the vector array that allows items to be pushed and popped off the list. The main different between stacks and arrays is that the stacks implement by default a deque, which can be changed to other underlying data structures if preferred, and only one item can be accessed at a time from the top of the stack. The STL stack template class has the following member functions:

bool empty(): Returns true if the stack is empty.

void push(const TYPE &val): Inserts an item on the top of the stack.

void pop(): Removes an item from the top of the stack.

size_type size(): Returns the size of the stack (total elements).

TYPE& top(): Returns the element from the top of the stack.

An example of creating and using a stack, both using the default deque and as a vector array, can be seen in Listing 2.7.

LISTING 2.7   A example of using a stack.

```
// Header file.
#include<stack>


// Creates a stack using a deque as the default.
std::stack<int> defaultIntStack;


// Creates a stack using a vector as the underlying data structure.
std::stack<int, std::vector<int> > vectorIntStack;


// Adds four elements to the stack.
defaultIntStack.push(10);
defaultIntStack.push(20);
defaultIntStack.push(30);
defaultIntStack.push(40);


// Removes the 40 which is on the top of the stack.
defaultIntStack.pop();
```

```
// Returns the 30 which is now on the top of the stack.
std::cout << defaultIntStack.top() << std::endl;


// Removes the 30 which is on the top of the stack.
defaultIntStack.pop();
```

HASH TABLES

A hash table is a data structure that offers very fast insertion and searching, especially beneficial with large data sets. Hash tables are faster than trees in some situations and can be used to great effect with a large amount of data in the table. Examples of some uses of hash tables include topics such as databases, spell checkers, search engines, and so forth. No matter how big a hash table is, the time it takes to do its job is close to a constant time in big O notation. That means that if a table has 100,000 items in it, it should be as fast, or close to being as fast depending on the collisions, with a list of 10,000,000 items.

Hash tables work by taking a key value and hashing it into an array index. Converting a key to a hash value is done using some math equation on the key, which will return an integer that can be used as an array index. This index is the location an object will be placed in the array within the hash table. For example, consider a list of employees, each with an employee ID. One can use the employee ID as the key for a hash table and the employee's data (i.e., name, address, phone, etc.) as the object that is inserted into the table.

Hash tables are based on arrays, which gives them the disadvantage of being inefficient to expand once they have been created. To further complicate things, there is a larger problem if the hash table is resized because the hashed values are based on the size of the array. If a hash table is resized, all hash values are invalid, all keys will need to be rehashed, and all items reinserted into the table. Such a process is slow and expensive to do, especially in a real-time application such as a video game or other simulation.

Another potentially huge problem is that different keys can actually hash to the same value, causing a collision in the hash table. When a collision occurs, a new item can't simply replace what is already there. Instead, there are techniques like double hashing, quadric probing, and separate chaining to solve the issue of hash table collisions. Double hashing will rehash the key in an attempt to find a new location for it. Quadric probing will go from the location the object would have been inserted into and move down the array by a value, like 4, until an empty space is found. Separate chaining will have an array at that location, so when a collision occurs the new value is just added to that index's array (i.e., in separate chaining there is a list of lists). Regardless of which method is used with the hash table, once the hash location has been determined, the next step would be to spend time comparing what is there with the key that is being searched on a collision. If the item at that location is not the correct one, the code will have to keep searching until all candidates have been checked at that location in the hash table.

The Building Blocks Engine uses separate chaining to handle hash table collisions. The C++ STL does not offer a standard hash table data structure. There are various nonstandard options available but no STL implementation at this time. To use hash tables in the Building Blocks Engine a custom implementation has been coded as a template class and was designed especially for this chapter. In the Building Blocks Engine, an item to be placed into the hash table uses a template class called HashItem. A hash item is made up of two values: a key that will be hashed by the hash table and used as an array index, and the data object itself. Listing 2.8 lists the class declaration for a hash item that can be used in the Building Blocks Engine's hash table.

LISTING 2.8   HashItem class.

```
template <class A>
class HashItem
{
   public:
      HashItem() : m_key(0) {}
      ~HashItem() {}


      int GetKey()
      {
         return m_key;
      }


      void SetKey(int k)
      {
         m_key = k;
      }


      A GetObject()
      {
         return m_obj;
      }
```

```
                void SetObj(A obj)
                {
                   m_obj = obj;
                }


                bool operator==(HashITem &item)
                {
                   if(m_key == item.GetKey())
                      return true;

                   return false;
                }


                void operator=(HashItem item)
                {
                   m_key = item.GetKey();
                   m_obj = item.GetObject();
                }


        private:
           int m_key;
           A m_obj;
    };
```

The hash table class used by the Building Blocks Engine has an array of STL vectors and the total number of hash elements as member variables. An array of STL vectors was chosen because it will allow for separate chaining to occur in the hash table by using an array for each hash element. The hash table has member functions to insert into the table, delete from the table, search the table, and two hash functions with one for hashing an integer key and another for hashing a string. The hash table itself calls the hash function to turn the key into an array index, and the object the class is trying to add to the hash table is inserted into the array at that index. Listing 2.9 lists the template class for the hash table used by the Building Blocks Engine.

LISTING 2.9 The template hash table.

```
            template <class A>
            class HashTable
            {
```

```cpp
public:
   HashTable(int size) : m_size(O)
   {
      if(size > O)
      {
         m_size = size;
         m_table = new vector<HashItem<A> >[m_size];
      }
   }


   virtual ~HashTable()
   {
      m_size = O;

      if(m_table != NULL)
      {
         delete[] m_table;
         m_table = NULL;
      }
   }


   void Insert(HashItem<A> &obj)
   {
      int hash = HashFunction(obj.GetKey());
      m_table[hash].push_back(obj);
   }


   void Delete(int key)
   {
      HashItem<A> item;
      item.SetKey(key);

      int hash = HashFunction(key);

      std::vector<HashItem<A> > *ptr = &m_table[hash];
      std::vector<HashItem<A> >::iterator it;

      for(it = ptr->begin(); it != ptr->end(); it++)
      {
         if(*it == item)
         {
```

```
            ptr->erase(it);
            break;
        }
    }
}


HashItem<A> Find(int key)
{
    HashItem<A> item, temp;
    item.SetKey(key);

    int hash = HashFunction(key);
    int i = 0;

    std::vector<HashItem<A> > *ptr = &m_table[hash];

    for(i = 0; i < (int)ptr->size(); i++)
    {
        temp = (*ptr)[i];

        if(temp == item)
            return temp;
    }

    item.SetKey(-1);
    return item;
}


int HashFunction(int key)
{
    return key % m_size;
}


int HashFunction(std::string &str)
{
    int hash = 0;
    int i = 0;

    for(i = 0; i < (int)str.size(); i++)
    {
        int val = (int)str[i];
```

```
                hash = (hash * 256 + val) % m_size;
            }

            return hash;
        }


        int GetSize()
        {
            return m_size;
        }


    private:
        std::vector<HashItem<A> > *m_table;
        int m_size;
};
```

ON THE CD

On the companion CD-ROM is a C++ demo application that demonstrates the use of the hash table discussed in this section called HASH TABLE, inside the folder BUILDING BLOCKS ENGINE/EXAMPLES/CHAPTER 2. The hash item and hash table classes are declared in the header file HASHTABLE.H located in the BUILD-ING BLOCKS ENGINE/SOURCE folder. The main source file from the HASH TABLE demo application is listed in Listing 2.10.

LISTING 2.10   The HASH TABLE demo application's main source file.

```
#include<iostream>
#include<string>
#include<HashTable.h>

using namespace std;


int main(int args, char **argc)
{
    bbe::HashTable<int> hashTable(21);
    bbe::HashItem<int> item;

    item.SetKey(112);
    item.SetObj(348);
    hashTable.Insert(item);
```

```
        item.SetKey(87);
        item.SetObj(841);
        hashTable.Insert(item);

        item.SetKey(24);
        item.SetObj(654);
        hashTable.Insert(item);

        item.SetKey(66);
        item.SetObj(11);
        hashTable.Insert(item);

        item.SetKey(222);
        item.SetObj(156);
        hashTable.Insert(item);

        item = hashTable.Find(87);
        cout << "Item: " << item.GetKey() << " has a value of " <<
                item.GetObject() << ".\n";

        item = hashTable.Find(112);
        cout << "Item: " << item.GetKey() << " has a value of " <<
                item.GetObject() << ".\n";

        hashTable.Delete(66);
        item = hashTable.Find(66);
        cout << "Item: " << item.GetKey() << " has a value of " <<
                item.GetObject() << ".\n";

        item = hashTable.Find(11);
        cout << "Item: " << item.GetKey() << " has a value of " <<
                item.GetObject() << ".\n";

        cout << "\n";

        string str("cats");
        int stringHash = hashTable.HashFunction(str);

        cout << "The string cats hash to " << stringHash << ".\n\n";

        return 1;
    }
```

ADDITIONAL DATA STRUCTURES

Additional data structures exist in computer programming. Examples include binary trees, red-black trees (balanced trees), 2-3-4 trees, K-D trees, heaps, graphs, circular link lists, and much more. There are many data structures used for games, some of which are explored and discussed in Chapters 5, "Rendering Scenes and Scene Graphs," and Chapter 10, "Conclusions". Data structures can save a ton of time and make coding easier on the developers using them in programming projects. Using the STL library allows developers to use a standard set of efficient code in their projects and is highly recommended.

MEMORY ALLOCATION

Memory management in computer science is a huge and complex field of study, and the topic of memory management is important for game engineers to tackle. Programmers on a development team are facing a large and complex challenge when trying to incorporate an efficient memory management system in any application project. Regardless of the challenges, the topic is extremely important and is covered as an introduction in this chapter. The early version of the Building Blocks Engine did not plan for the design and implementation for a memory management system for the following reasons:

- The games to be built with the Building Blocks Engine were never meant to be complex enough to where such a system would be vital to their development.
- The topic of memory management in applications can take up a book on its own and can not be adequately covered in a single chapter or in a single section in one chapter.
- Memory management requires a certain level of knowledge and skill, which requires a lot of research and experience.
- Due to the Building Blocks Engine being a starting point for hobby and student programmers, the memory management system of choice can be incorporated if one is desired and necessary by programmers who are implementing their own frameworks or are expanding on the Building Blocks Engine

The three main areas of memory management are application, hardware, and operating system. Memory management on the hardware level includes devices like RAM chips. On the operating system, memory management concerns the management of memory that is allocated to programs, virtual memory, and the release of memory that is no longer being used so it can be reused by other programs. The third area of memory management, the application, involves supplying memory the program needs to operate and recycling memory when it is no longer needed by the application.

The application area of memory management involves allocation and recycling of memory blocks received from the operating system. For allocation, an allocator is used to request a block of memory from the memory manager from a larger block of memory that was supplied by the operating system to the application. Recycling in application memory management involves taking blocks of memory that are no longer being used by an application and preparing them for reuse by other processes. Recycling is broken down into manual recycling, which is manually handled by the programmer, and automatic recycling, which is handled automatically by the memory management system.

With manual memory management, the programmer has direct and complete control over the memory use in an application. Bugs can be commonplace in manual memory management, as the programmer must do a ton of manual bookkeeping work and must explicitly tell the application when it needs or is done with a block of memory. Manual memory management involves memory that is requested from a stack, and memory variables that are locally defined. Suballocators can be created by a programmer to aid in the allocation and management of memory by trying to mimic the behavior of a memory manager when the original is inefficient. This type of suballocator is very challenging to create and can often hurt performance if not done efficiently.

Automatic memory management is memory managed by recycling blocks automatically when they are no longer in an application's reach by pointers. This type of memory management uses a *garbage collector* that handles unused blocks of memory so the programmer is freed from that responsibility. An example of an automatic memory management system can be seen in languages like Java and C#, where programmers do not have to manually free blocks of memory because the garbage collectors will take care of the recycling automatically as defined by the programming language.

When dealing with application memory management, developers must consider memory overhead, CPU overhead, and interactive delays. Memory management has other topics that must be addressed by the developer, including but not limited to:

- Memory fragmentation
- Memory leaks
- Dangling pointers
- Poor locality of reference
- Poor bookkeeping performance

Memory fragmentation is a severe issue that can bring down an application if the problem becomes too big. When memory blocks are requested, the block of memory is in one sequential area. If the memory is fragmented, there might not be enough sequential blocks of memory to allocate some specified amount even though there is space in the memory manager. If a poor allocator does not deal with fragmented memory when it is giving out blocks of memory, allocations can fail even though there is enough space to store the memory. The problem will be that the memory is just not in big enough sequential blocks to succeed.

Memory leaks are a common problem in computer programming. A memory leak occurs when memory that is allocated, used, and is no longer needed is not recycled for reuse. Memory is finite, and if enough memory is allocated but never recycled, a program can take up all of a computer's memory, causing performance issues and future allocations to fail. If memory becomes out of reach by an application from pointers, that memory can't be deleted by the application and a memory leak has occurred.

Dangling pointers are one of those potential problems that can crash a computer program instantly in some cases. When allocated memory is freed, all pointers pointing to that block of memory are no longer valid. If a program tries to access a pointer that pointed to a block of memory that is no longer valid, the program can either crash or behave unexpectedly. This problem deals with manual memory management and is a common problem that needs to be addressed. Although a block of memory has been freed, the pointer or pointers that pointed to it will need to be nullified to test if a pointer is dangling.

Poor locality of reference deals with the layout of memory blocks. Memory blocks that are not close by can cause a program to suffer from performance issues when memory is being accessed. Accessing memory blocks that are near one another allows for faster memory access in an application, which will increase the performance of the application.

Poor bookkeeping performance can come from memory managers that are designed to work around a certain set of conditions and assumptions but are used in a different manner in an application. This can include memory life spans, typical allocation block sizes, reference patterns, and so forth. A memory manager can spend more time than usual performing bookkeeping work if the memory manager is not being used as designed or set up.

We'll discuss memory management again in the final chapter of this book, along with some resources and references on the topic in Appendix A, "Additional Resources." For large game engine frameworks, memory management can be an unavoidable topic in the design process. The performance of a memory management system is too important to overlook, whether the application is being developed and executed on the PC, on a home video game console, or some other device. The information presented in this chapter serves as an introduction to a complex and large field of study in computer science. For game engine development, a memory management system can be used to great benefit in a gaming application.

FILE I/O

File reading and writing is standard in the C and C++ programming languages. In the C++ language are stream objects that can be used to manipulate data. When it comes to file input and file output, the stream objects used in C++ are `ifstream` and `ofstream`, respectively. Although file reading and writing is standard in the C++ programming language, a few issues can arise when files are shared between different platforms. In this section, the main topics discussed deal with endianness and archive files. Classes can be created to wrap around each of these topics in a convenient way—which the Building Blocks Engine has plans for. Classes might not totally be necessary for file I/O, but endianness and archive files will need a set of code to handle those topics.

According to the class diagrams of the core system of the Building Blocks Engine, there is a set of classes for reading and writing to a file within the framework (Figure 2.1). These classes are `FileInputStream` and `FileOutputStream` and derive from the base class `FileStream` and support both text and binary files. The operations of the file input and output classes include:

- Opening a file stream
- Closing a file stream
- Seeking to various positions within the file stream
- Reading data from a file stream
- Writing data to a file stream

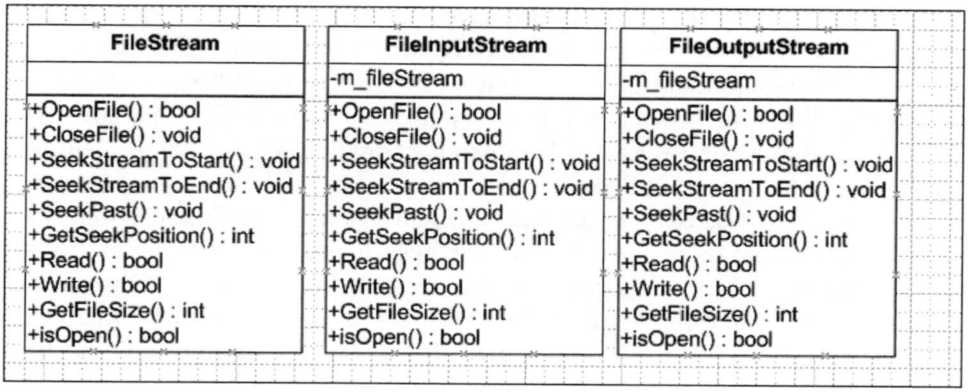

FileStream	FileInputStream	FileOutputStream
	-m_fileStream	-m_fileStream
+OpenFile() : bool	+OpenFile() : bool	+OpenFile() : bool
+CloseFile() : void	+CloseFile() : void	+CloseFile() : void
+SeekStreamToStart() : void	+SeekStreamToStart() : void	+SeekStreamToStart() : void
+SeekStreamToEnd() : void	+SeekStreamToEnd() : void	+SeekStreamToEnd() : void
+SeekPast() : void	+SeekPast() : void	+SeekPast() : void
+GetSeekPosition() : int	+GetSeekPosition() : int	+GetSeekPosition() : int
+Read() : bool	+Read() : bool	+Read() : bool
+Write() : bool	+Write() : bool	+Write() : bool
+GetFileSize() : int	+GetFileSize() : int	+GetFileSize() : int
+isOpen() : bool	+isOpen() : bool	+isOpen() : bool

FIGURE 2.1 The class diagrams for file I/O classes.

In the Building Blocks Engine, the file input and output related code are found on the companion CD-ROM in the BUILDING BLOCKS ENGINE/SOURCE folder inside the File.h and File.cpp files. Using the file I/O classes requires an application to bind to the core library and to include the File.h header file, or can include the File.cpp source file in the development project. Listing 2.11 partially lists the file I/O classes that make up the system.

LISTING 2.11   The file input and output classes.

```cpp
class FileInputStream : public FileStream
{
    public:
        FileInputStream();
        FileInputStream(const char *fileName,
                        BB_FILE_TYPE fileType);

        virtual ~FileInputStream();

        bool OpenFile(const char *fileName, BB_FILE_TYPE fileType);
        void CloseFile();

        void SeekStreamToStart();
        void SeekStreamToEnd();
        void SeekPast(int offset);
        int GetSeekPosition();

        bool Read(char *buffer, int bytesToRead);
        bool Write(char *buffer, int bytesToWrite);

        int GetFileSize();
        bool isOpen();

    private:
        std::ifstream m_fileStream;
};


class FileOutputStream
{
    public:
        FileOutputStream();
        FileOutputStream(const char *fileName,
                         BB_FILE_TYPE fileType);
```

```
        virtual ~FileOutputStream();

        bool OpenFile(const char *fileName, BB_FILE_TYPE fileType);
        void CloseFile();

        void SeekStreamToStart();
        void SeekStreamToEnd();
        void SeekPast(int offset);
        int GetSeekPosition();

        bool Read(char *buffer, int bytesToRead);
        bool Write(char *buffer, int bytesToWrite);

        int GetFileSize();
        bool isOpen();

    private:
        std::ofstream m_fileStream;
};
```

The file input and output classes were designed to be straightforward. The classes have functions to open a file in either text or binary mode, close a file stream, move around the file, read data from the file, and write data to the file. When designing the Building Blocks Engine, these features were the only ones considered necessary. In the future, if more functionality is desired, these classes can be extended upon to incorporate them. Listing 2.12 lists the FileInputStream class implementation. The FileOutputStream implementation is the same, but with write functions instead of read.

LISTING 2.12   The FileInputStream class implementation.

```
    bool FileInputStream::OpenFile(const char *fileName,
                                   BB_FILE_TYPE fileType)
    {
        if(isOpen() == true)
            CloseFile();

        if(fileType == BB_TEXT_FILE)
        {
            m_fileStream.open(fileName, std::ifstream::in);
        }
        else
        {
```

```
      m_fileStream.open(fileName, std::ifstream::in |
                         std::ifstream::binary);
   }

   return (isOpen() == true);
}


void FileInputStream::CloseFile()
{
   m_fileStream.close();
}


void FileInputStream::SeekStreamToStart()
{
   m_fileStream.seekg(0, std::ios::beg);
}


void FileInputStream::SeekStreamToEnd()
{
   m_fileStream.seekg(0, std::ios::end);
}


void FileInputStream::SeekPast(int offset)
{
   m_fileStream.seekg(offset, std::ios::cur);
}


int FileInputStream::GetSeekPosition()
{
   return m_fileStream.tellg();
}


bool FileInputStream::Read(char *buffer, int bytesToRead)
{
   if(isOpen() == false || buffer == NULL || bytesToRead <= 0)
      return false;
```

```
        m_fileStream.read(buffer, bytesToRead);

        return true;
}


bool FileInputStream::Write(char *buffer, int bytesToWrite)
{
        return false;
}


int FileInputStream::GetFileSize()
{
        int length = 0, streamPos = 0;

        streamPos = m_fileStream.tellg();
        m_fileStream.seekg(0, std::ios::beg);

        m_fileStream.seekg(0, std::ios::end);
        length = m_fileStream.tellg();

        m_fileStream.seekg(0, streamPos);

        return length;
}


bool FileInputStream::isOpen()
{
        if(m_fileStream.is_open() == false)
            return false;

        return true;
}
```

ENDIAN ORDER

Portability issues arise when working with files that store multibyte values in their data. Although file reading and writing is standard in C++, there can be times where one file that was written on one piece of hardware cannot be loaded by another. When working with files, there is something known as the endian order, which specifies the byte ordering of a multibyte value in memory. This topic is related to files and data storage. The endian orders that can be encountered are known as the little, big, or middle endian. For file I/O operations, if a system tries to read a value that is stored in little endian order but it works with data in big endian order, the value's bytes will be in reverse and will not be reported as the correct or intended value, which can lead to unexpected behavior in an application. PPC processors use big endian values, which are commonly used in Macs, and x86-based processors like Intel's Pentium processors use little endian order. Big endian values store the most significant bytes first, and little endian values store the least significant bytes first. Figure 2.2 shows an example of endian order.

value = 0xAABB

Little Endian
43707

Big Endian
48042

FIGURE 2.2 Example of endian order.

Converting the byte ordering of a value from little to big, or vice versa, requires applications to physically swap the bytes that make up the variable. All variables other than a character can be affected by the endian order of a value because characters are single byte, not multibyte. In the Building Blocks Engine's core class diagram, a class was planned to handle resolving endian orders called Endian, which can be seen in Figure 2.3. Listing 2.13 lists the class declaration for the Endian class, which can be found on the companion CD-ROM in the file Endian.h under the BUILDING BLOCKS ENGINE/SOURCE folder.

ON THE CD

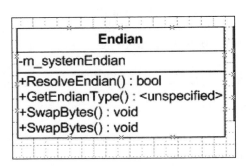

FIGURE 2.3 Example of Endian class diagram.

LISTING 2.13   Endian class declaration.

```
class Endian
{
   public:
      Endian();
      virtual ~Endian();


      void ResolveEndian(char *data, int size,
                         BB_ENDIAN_TYPE inputEndian);


      void SwapBytes(char *data, int size);
      void SwapBytes(char *data, int size, int number);


      BB_ENDIAN_TYPE GetEndianType()
      {
         return m_systemEndian;
      }


   private:
      BB_ENDIAN_TYPE m_systemEndian;
};
```

The implementation of the Endian class for the Building Blocks Engine works by determining the byte ordering used by the system that is running the code. This determination is handled in the class's constructor and its results are stored in the member variable m_systemEndian, which can be BB_ENDIAN_LITTLE, BB_ENDIAN_BIG, or BB_ENDIAN_MIDDLE. To determine a system's endian order a test is used in the constructor, which simply looks at a dummy variable and compares the individual bytes with what they would be if they were little, middle, or big endian. The constructor of the Endian class can be seen in Listing 2.14.

LISTING 2.14   The Endian class's constructor.

```
Endian::Endian()
{
   m_systemEndian = BB_ENDIAN_UNKNOWN;
```

```
unsigned long data = 0x12345678;
unsigned char *ptr = (unsigned char*)&data;

if(*ptr == 0x12 && *(ptr+1) == 0x34 &&
   *(ptr+2) == 0x56 && *(ptr+3) == 0x78)
{
   m_systemEndian = BB_ENDIAN_BIG;
}
else if(*ptr == 0x78 && *(ptr + 1) == 0x56 &&
        *(ptr + 2) == 0x34 && *(ptr + 3) == 0x12)
{
   m_systemEndian = BB_ENDIAN_LITTLE;
}
else if(*ptr == 0x34 && *(ptr + 1) == 0x12 &&
        *(ptr + 2) == 0x78 && *(ptr + 3) == 0x56)
{
   m_systemEndian = BB_ENDIAN_MIDDLE;
}
}
```

The ability to swap the byte order of a variable is straightforward by casting that variable to a character pointer, looping through the total number of bytes that make it up, and swapping accordingly. In the Endian class are two SwapBytes() functions. The first is used to swap the byte order of an individual variable, and the second is used to swap the byte order of an array of variables. Both overloaded SwapBytes() functions of the Endian class can be seen in Listing 2.15. When passing variables to the function, they can be cast to a character pointer in the first parameter.

LISTING 2.15   The two SwapBytes() functions of the Endian class.

```
void Endian::SwapBytes(char *data, int size)
{
   assert((size & 1) == 0);

   char *ptr = data;
   char temp = 0;

   for(int i = 0, j = size - 1; i < size / 2; i++, j-)
   {
      temp = ptr[i];
      ptr[i] = ptr[j];
      ptr[j] = temp;
   }
}
```

```
void Endian::SwapBytes(char *data, int size, int number)
{
    assert((size & 1) == 0);

    char *ptr = data;

    for(int n = 0; n < number; n++, ptr += size)
    {
        SwapBytes(ptr, size);
    }
}
```

The last function of the Endian class is ResolveEndian() and is the only function needed to handle endian portability in the Building Blocks Engine because it uses the SwapBytes() function. Whenever this function is called, it determines if there is an incompatibility between the system's endian order and the endian order of the variable being passed in. If there is, the variable is converted to the endian order of the system; otherwise, it is left as is. The Endian class would already know the endian order of the system, which is handled in the class' constructor. Therefore, the only parameters the ResolveEndian() function would need is the variable being tested and the endian order it is in. It is up to the programmer to know what endian order the variable being tested is in because there is no way to tell the endian order otherwise. For files, this means that whatever file is being loaded, the developers must be aware of the endian order to be able to work with it. This information is often commonly and publicly known about a file format. For example, LightWave's 7.5 .LWO object files are in big endian order. Listing 2.16 lists the ResolveEndian() function of the Endian class.

LISTING 2.16 The ResolveEndian() function.

```
void Endian::ResolveEndian(char *data, int size,
                           BB_ENDIAN_TYPE inputEndian)
{
    if(m_systemEndian == BB_ENDIAN_UNKNOWN ||
        inputEndian == BB_ENDIAN_UNKNOWN ||
        m_systemEndian == inputEndian)
    {
        return;
    }


    int half = size / 2;
```

```
// Test for middle vs big else middle vs little.
if((m_systemEndian == BB_ENDIAN_MIDDLE &&
    inputEndian == BB_ENDIAN_BIG) ||
   (m_systemEndian == BB_ENDIAN_BIG &&
    inputEndian == BB_ENDIAN_MIDDLE))
{
   SwapBytes(data, half);
   SwapBytes(data + half, half);

   return;
}
else if((m_systemEndian == BB_ENDIAN_MIDDLE &&
         inputEndian == BB_ENDIAN_LITTLE) ||
        (m_systemEndian == BB_ENDIAN_LITTLE &&
         inputEndian == BB_ENDIAN_MIDDLE))
{
   // Switch little to big then middle.
   SwapBytes(data, size);
   SwapBytes(data, half);
   SwapBytes(data + half, half);

   return;
}


// Little to Big or Big to Little Swap (NO MIDDLE).
SwapBytes(data, size);
}
```

ON THE CD

On the companion CD-ROM is a demo application called ENDIAN that is located in the BUILDING BLOCKS ENGINE/EXAMPLES/CHAPTER 2 folder. The purpose of this demo application is to test loading big endian values from a file into the system. Regardless of what endian order a system uses, the application will be able to load it from a file correctly in a portable manner. The same idea goes for sending multibyte variables across a network, and so forth.

TIMING UTILITIES

Timers are used often in computer simulations such as video games for things such as time-based animations, physics, and other calculations that can be affected by the changing of time. For the Building Blocks Engine, timing support was designed to work in the form of two functions. The first function, GetTimeMs(), is used to get the system time in milliseconds, and the second function, GetTimeSeconds(), is used to get the system time in seconds. Both functions are defined in the header file Timer.h on the companion CD-ROM under the BUILDING BLOCKS ENGINE/ SOURCE folder. The timing system for the Building Blocks Engine was designed this way as a quick and simple implementation for the early version of the framework. If more features and support are needed, a timer class can be created. High-resolution timers might be very useful for acquiring the system time in an application and might be a feature that can be considered for future versions of the framework.

The implementation of the function bodies is done by using different source files for each supported system. This will allow a single function to be used for getting the time on all systems in a manner that appears portable. The implementation is system specific, with the Windows code being defined in TimingWin32.cpp (Listing 2.17), the Mac-related code in TimingMacOSX.cpp (Listing 2.18) and the Linux-related code in TimingLinux.cpp (Listing 2.19). The implementation of timing functions was done to wrap around API-related calls as simply as possible. If higher resolution timers and more functionality are needed, additional timer functions or even a timer class can be designed and incorporated into the Building Blocks Engine. The entire timing code for all three supporting systems can be found on the companion CD-ROM for Windows, Mac, and Linux versions in the BUILD-ING BLOCKS ENGINE/SOURCE folder.

LISTING 2.17   Timing in Win32 defined in the TimerWin32.cpp file.

```
float GetTimeMs()
{
    return (float)timeGetTime();
}


float GetTimeSeconds()
{
    return (float)timeGetTime() * 0.001f;
}
```

LISTING 2.18   Timing for Mac defined in TimerMacOSX.cpp.

```
float GetTimeMs()
{
    float time = 0;
```

```
        AbsoluteTime current;
        Duration currentDur;
        current = UpTime();
        currentDur = AbsoluteToDuration(current);
        time = (float)currentDur;

        return time;
    }


    float GetTimeSeconds()
    {
        float time = 0;

        AbsoluteTime current;
        Duration currentDur;
        current = UpTime();
        currentDur = AbsoluteToDuration(current);
        time = (float)(0.001 * currentDur);

        return time;
    }
```

LISTING 2.19   Simple timing for Linux in TimerLinux.cpp.

```
#include<time.h>


float GetTimeMs()
{
    return (float)clock();
}


float GetTimeSeconds()
{
    return (float)clock() / CLOCKS_PER_SEC;
}
```

ARCHIVE FILES

Many files can make up an entire game, and can include texture images, static and dynamic game models, audio files, animations, scripts, shaders, and more. On top of being made up of many different files, the locations and folder hierarchy for each can be large.

This section is on archive files and creating the ability to store multiple files inside one larger file. In this section, the archive filesystem of the Building Blocks Engine is discussed as it was planned in Chapter 1, "Introduction to Game Engines," and archive files will be looked at in general. An example of an archive file is WinZip's .ZIP and Stuffit's .SIT. Archive files have been used in game development by some of the most popular games (e.g., *Doom 3™*). Some benefits of using archive files in an application include but are not limited to:

- Increased performance when loading multiple files out of an archive.
- Can be used to help protect game files and resources.
- One file can be used to access multiple files that are possibly related.
- Creating a custom archive file format is not a difficult task; especially minus compression and encryption.
- Data in archive files can be compressed and stored using less storage space on the disk containing the file.
- Data in archive files can be encrypted to add another layer of protection.

The Building Blocks Engine has its own archive file with the extension .AC1. The main purpose for adding archive files to the Building Blocks Engine was to increase performance for loading multiple files from an archive and to have a small layer of protection for the resources a game uses. The archive filesystem for the engine works by creating a file that has multiple files inside it. Reading a file that was packed into an archive for the Building Blocks Engine is accomplished by reading a file header, which contains information about the block of data in the archive that specifies a specific file, and reading the file itself. The file header for the archive filesystem of the Building Blocks Engine specifies the name of the file, the size of the file, and the offset from the beginning of the archive to the position that marks the start of the file's data. A header for the archive itself is read first from the file when the archive is initially opened. This header has general information about the archive file, such as the number of total files in the archive and the archive ID and version for compatibility testing. With this system, creating an archive file would require writing an archive header and then writing all the file headers/file data for each file that is to be packed in the archive.

Building Blocks Engine's Archive File Structure

An archive file for the Building Blocks Engine is a binary file. The first block of information in the archive file is the archive header, which specifies the archives ID, major and minor version, and the total number of files that are packed into the archive. Beyond the archive header is the information for each file that is packed within the archive. This information is specified by a file header and the character data that makes up the entire file. The file header is made up of the file name, the size in bytes that make up the file, and the offset from the beginning of the archive to the position that marks the start of the file's data. Figure 2.4 illustrates an archive file that is used for the Building Blocks Engine. Figure 2.5 illustrates the classes that were designed in Chapter 1 that pertain to the archive filesystem of the Building Blocks Engine's archive filesystem.

FIGURE 2.4   The archive file.

ArchiveHeader	ArchiveFileHeader	Archive
-m_id : char	-m_fileName : char	-m_header
-m_major : int	-m_size : int	-m_fileStream
-m_minor : int	-m_offset : int	-m_totalHeaders : int
-m_totalFiles : int	+GetFileName() : char	+ReadArchive() : bool
+GetID() : char	+SetFileName() : void	+WriteArchive() : bool
+SetID() : void	+GetSize() : int	+CloseArchive() : void
+GetMajorVersion() : int	+SetSize() : void	+Extract() : bool
+SetMajorVersion() : void	+GetOffset() : int	+Extract() : bool
+GetMinorVersion() : int	+SetOffset() : void	+GetTotalHeaders() : int
+SetMinorVersion() : void		+isArchiveOpen() : bool
+GetTotalFiles() : int		+GetFileIndex() : int
+SetTotalFiles() : void		+GetFileData() : bool
		+GetFileData() : bool
		+GetFileHeaderInfoByIndex() : bool

FIGURE 2.5   Class diagrams dealing with the archive filesystem.

The archive header is represented by the ArchiveHeader class defined in Chapter 1. This class stores as member variables the ID of the archive file in a character array, the major and minor version numbers in integers, and the total number of files as an integer. For functions, the class has get and set methods for accessing and manipulating each of the member variables in the class. Initially, the ID is "BBEI" and version numbers are 1.0. Listing 2.20 lists the archive header class implementation based on the class diagram that was designed as shown in Figure 2.6.

ArchiveHeader	ArchiveFileHeader	Archive
-m_id : char	-m_fileName : char	-m_header
-m_major : int	-m_size : int	-m_fileStream
-m_minor : int	-m_offset : int	-m_totalHeaders : int
-m_totalFiles : int	+GetFileName() : char	+ReadArchive() : bool
+GetID() : char	+SetFileName() : void	+WriteArchive() : bool
+SetID() : void	+GetSize() : int	+CloseArchive() : void
+GetMajorVersion() : int	+SetSize() : void	+Extract() : bool
+SetMajorVersion() : void	+GetOffset() : int	+Extract() : bool
+GetMinorVersion() : int	+SetOffset() : void	+GetTotalHeaders() : int
+SetMinorVersion() : void		+isArchiveOpen() : bool
+GetTotalFiles() : int		+GetFileIndex() : int
+SetTotalFiles() : void		+GetFileData() : bool
		+GetFileData() : bool
		+GetFileHeaderInfoByIndex() : bool

FIGURE 2.6   Class diagrams for the archive system.

LISTING 2.20 The archive and file headers.

```cpp
#define ARCHIVE_ID        "BBE1"
#define ARCHIVE_MAJOR     1
#define ARCHIVE_MINOR     0


class ArchiveHeader
{
    public:
        ArchiveHeader()
        {
            m_id[0] = '\0';
            m_majorVersion = 0;
            m_minorVersion = 0;
            m_totalFiles = 0;
        }


        char *GetID() { return m_id; }
        int GetMajorVersion() { return m_majorVersion; }
        int GetMinorVersion() { return m_minorVersion; }
        int GetTotalFiles() { return m_totalFiles; }


        void SetID(char *id)
        {
            if(id == NULL)
                return;

            memcpy(m_id, id, 4);
            m_id[4] = '\0';
        }


        void SetMajorVersion(int major) { m_majorVersion = major; }
        void SetMinorVersion(int minor) { m_minorVersion = minor; }
        void SetTotalFiles(int total) { m_totalFiles = total; }


    private:
        char m_id[5];
        int m_majorVersion;
```

```
            int m_minorVersion;
            int m_totalFiles;
    };
```

The individual file headers for the packed files are stored in the ArchiveFile-Header class, which was designed in Chapter 1 and is shown in Figure 2.6. The file header has planned as member variables the filename, size of the file (which tells the application how big the file is), and the offset of the file from the start of the archive in bytes so the file stream can quickly seek to the start of the file's data. Similar to the archive header class, the file header class is made up of various get and set methods used to access and manipulate the member variables of the class. Listing 2.21 lists the ArchiveFileHeader class that was created based on the class diagram in Figure 2.6.

LISTING 2.21   The Archive Header class.

```
class ArchiveFileHeader
{
    public:
        ArchiveFileHeader()
        {
            m_fileName[0] = '\0';
            m_size = 0;
            m_offset = 0;
        }


        char *GetFileName() { return m_fileName; }
        int GetSize() { return m_size; }
        int GetOffset() { return m_offset; }


        void SetFileName(char *fileName)
        {
            int len;
            m_fileName[0] = '\0';

            if(fileName == NULL)
                return;

            len = strlen(fileName);
```

```
        if(len > 255)
            return;

        memcpy(m_fileName, fileName, len);
        m_fileName[len] = '\0';
    }


    void SetSize(int size) { m_size = size; }
    void SetOffset(int offset) { m_offset = offset; }


    void operator=(ArchiveFileHeader &header)
    {
        m_size = header.GetSize();
        SetFileName(header.GetFileName());
        m_offset = header.GetOffset();
    }


private:
    char m_fileName[256];
    int m_size;
    int m_offset;
};
```

The archive file is loaded and created with a class called `Archive`. In Chapter 1, it was planned that a single class be used to load or write an archive file. The class diagram for the `Archive` class can be seen in Figure 2.6. The `Archive` class has functions to open an archive file, write an archive file, extract a file from the archive based on its index and filename, and to get a file's data from the archive based on its index filename. As member variables, it was designed to have a file input stream object, a list of file headers, and the total number of files in the archive. The input stream object is used to open an archive file and to keep it open so multiple files can be loaded without the overhead of opening and closing many times. Loading all the file headers and keeping the file stream open will allow the class to look up file data quickly so it can be accessed. Listing 2.22 lists the `Archive` class declaration, which can be found in the header file Archive.h on the companion CD-ROM under the BUILDING BLOCKS ENGINE/SOURCE folder. The implementation to the classes that make up the archive system can be found in the source file Archive.cpp.

ON THE CD

LISTING 2.22   The Archive class.

```
class Archive
{
   public:
      Archive();
      virtual ~Archive();

      bool ReadArchiveFile(char *fileName);
      bool WriteArchiveFile(char *fileName,
                            ArchiveFileHeader *headers,
                            int totalHeaders);
      void CloseArchive();


      bool Extract(int index, char *location);
      bool Extract(char *fileName, char *location);


      int GetFileIndex(char *fileName);
      bool GetFileData(int index, char *buffer, int bytesToRead);
      bool GetFileData(char *fileName, char *buffer,
                       int bytesToRead);
      bool GetFileHeaderInfoByIndex(int index,
                                    ArchiveFileHeader *fh);

      int GetTotalHeaders() { return m_totalHeaders; }


      bool isArchiveOpen()
      {
         return (m_fileStream.isOpen() == true);
      }


   private:
      ArchiveFileHeader *m_headers;
      int m_totalHeaders;

      FileInputStream m_fileStream;
};
```

An archive file is opened and read by calling the class' `ReadArchiveFile()` function. The design was for this function to open a file stream to the archive file and keep it open until closed by the application. When an archive file is first read, according to the design for the archive file, the first five bytes are the file's ID, and the next eight bytes are used for the major and minor versions of the file. This information can be tested to ensure that what is being read is a compatible archive file. The `ReadArchiveFile()` reads in all file headers, which by design allows the class to be able to locate file data either by index or by filename. Listing 2.23 lists the entire `ReadArchiveFile()` function from the `Archive` class.

LISTING 2.23 The `ReadArchiveFile()` function.

```
bool Archive::ReadArchiveFile(char *fileName)
{
    Endian endianSwap;
    ArchiveHeader archiveHeader;
    int temp = 0, temp2 = 0, offset = 0;

    if(fileName == NULL)
        return false;

    if(m_fileStream.OpenFile(fileName, BB_BINARY_FILE) == false)
        return false;

    m_fileStream.Read((char*)&archiveHeader,
                    sizeof(ArchiveHeader));

    if(strcmp(archiveHeader.GetID(), ARCHIVE_ID) != 0)
        return false;

    temp = archiveHeader.GetMajorVersion();
    endianSwap.ResolveEndian((char*)&temp, 4, BB_ENDIAN_LITTLE);

    temp2 = archiveHeader.GetMinorVersion();
    endianSwap.ResolveEndian((char*)&temp, 4, BB_ENDIAN_LITTLE);

    if(temp != ARCHIVE_MAJOR && temp2 != ARCHIVE_MINOR)
        return false;

    m_totalHeaders = archiveHeader.GetTotalFiles();
    endianSwap.ResolveEndian((char*)&m_totalHeaders, 4,
                    BB_ENDIAN_LITTLE);
```

```
   if(m_totalHeaders <= 0)
      return false;

   m_headers = new ArchiveFileHeader[m_totalHeaders];

   if(m_headers == NULL)
      return false;

   for(int i = 0; i < m_totalHeaders; i++)
      {
         m_fileStream.Read((char*)&m_headers[i],
                             sizeof(ArchiveFileHeader));

         offset = m_headers[i].GetSize();
         endianSwap.ResolveEndian((char*)&offset, 4,
                             BB_ENDIAN_LITTLE);

         m_fileStream.SeekPast(offset);
      }

   return true;
}
```

Archive files have to be able to retrieve file data so it can be loaded by an application. The Archive class has as part of its design two functions for extracting files and two functions used to get the file data into a buffer. The extracting functions will get the file data and save it to a specified location, which is listed in Listing 2.24. The functions used to get the file's data into a buffer will read the file's entire data into a pre-allocated buffer. By design the function used to read in a file's data, GetFileData(), copies the data into a buffer. This forces the programmer to supply one that is the correct size. The functions used to get a file's data are listed in Listing 2.25.

LISTING 2.24   The Extract() functions.

```
bool Archive::Extract(int index, char *location)
{
   FileOutputStream fileOutput;
   std::string str;
   char *buffer = NULL;
   int size = 0;
```

```
    if(isArchiveOpen() == false || index < 0 ||
      index >= m_totalHeaders || location == NULL)
      {
        return false;
      }

    size = m_headers[index].GetSize();

    if(size > 0)
      {
        buffer = new char[size];

        if(buffer == NULL)
          return false;
      }
    else
      {
        return false;
      }

    GetFileData(index, buffer, size);

    str = location;
    str += "/";
    str += m_headers[index].GetFileName();

    fileOutput.OpenFile(str.c_str(), BB_TEXT_FILE);
    fileOutput.Write(buffer, size);
    fileOutput.CloseFile();

    delete[] buffer;

    return true;
}


bool Archive::Extract(char *fileName, char *location)
{
    int index = GetFileIndex(fileName);

    return (Extract(index, location));
}
```

LISTING 2.25 The Remaining Archive functions.

```
int Archive::GetFileIndex(char *fileName)
{
   int i = 0;

   for(i = 0; i < m_totalHeaders; i++)
      {
         if(strcmp(fileName, m_headers[i].GetFileName()) == 0)
            return i;
      }

   return -1;
}


bool Archive::GetFileData(int index, char *buffer, int bytesToRead)
{
   if(index < 0 || index >= m_totalHeaders)
      return false;

   m_fileStream.SeekPast(m_headers[index].GetOffset() -
                         m_fileStream.GetSeekPosition());

   return m_fileStream.Read(buffer, bytesToRead);
}


bool Archive::GetFileData(char *fileName, char *buffer, int
bytesToRead)
{
   int index = GetFileIndex(fileName);

   return (GetFileData(index, buffer, bytesToRead));
}


bool Archive::GetFileHeaderInfoByIndex(int index, ArchiveFileHeader
*header)
{
   if(index < 0 || index >= m_totalHeaders || header == NULL)
      return false;
```

```
        *header = m_headers[index];

        return true;
    }
```

ADDITIONAL TOPICS AND TECHNIQUES

This chapter marks the beginning of many different tools and utilities that can be part of a game engine's core system. We can add many things to the core system. Among those tools are many other data structures, math objects, and tools that can aid developers greatly in the development of an engine and games. Many optimizations can be performed, such as SSE for our math library, for example. In the following sections, we'll look at a few topics that will most likely arise when programmers start to create their own engine or extend upon the Building Blocks Engine framework.

COMPRESSION

Compression is a technique used to take a piece of data and make it smaller, using one algorithm or another. JPEG images use lossy compression to remove data from an image file so it can be saved to a file smaller than its original version. There are two main types of compression: lossy compression and lossless compression. Lossy compression sacrifices quality for size, while lossless compression gets the smallest size without affecting the quality of the source material.

In this book, the topic of compression will be looked at later for images like textures maps, normal maps, and so forth. For the purposes of this book, there will not be a need to compress anything else, but for those readers thinking about making a game with a engine they've created or with the Building Blocks Engine, compression might be something worth looking into further. Compression can also be useful for archive files as mentioned previously.

ENCRYPTION

Encryption is the science of taking some data and changing it with an algorithm into a form not recognizable from the original. Encryption is a powerful tool in the age of the Internet where a great deal of sensitive information is being passed around from one location to another. Outside of the Internet, many other types of applications can use encryption to protect sensitive files, such as game files that when altered can lead to cheating and other unfair advantages in gameplay.

Encryption (i.e., cryptography) is outside the scope of this book. If readers are dealing with information that must stay private but needs to be passed around (e.g., credit card information over the Internet, sensitive game files, etc.), it might be worth picking up a textbook on cryptography and applying what is learned to a custom-built engine or to the Building Blocks Engine framework.

APPLICATION PROFILING

Performance is important in game development. In a real-time application like a video game, many factors can affect the performance of the overall application. The challenge developers face is trying to figure out what parts of their system are running the slowest so they can know where they need to start optimizing first. If developers assume certain areas are moving slowly and they are not, developers can waste a lot of time optimizing code that does not necessarily need it or is not the cause for the most serious bottlenecks. Using an application profiler can give developers valuable information about how their code is running on a machine. An example of a profiler is NVIDIA's NVPerfHud, which works with an application to give information on everything from individual API rendering calls, to CPU performance information, and much more.

STREAMING DATA

Modern video games are pieces of software that must handle a lot of data at one time. In open-world-style games, there is often a large environment the player can explore and navigate. Sometimes, more data needs to be loaded and used than there is on the system in total. In games, the total amount of storage space on a source disk is often much larger than the total amount of memory the system has at its disposal. To display an environment in a gaming application, the main options are to either be able to load the environment off a disk in whole, or to load only some of the data initially and then dynamically load additional data as the need arises. This process allows resources that are not used to be swapped for resources that are needed to display the scene at that moment.

Streaming game data information can be very useful in a video game that must run on target hardware where the total amount of memory is not enough to fully load and process an environment in its entirety. Even in situations where there is enough memory, developers can still stream large environments to save memory for other parts of the game and framework. This feature opens up many new opportunities for game developers by allowing them to go outside the limitations of the target hardware's finite memory size and allow for much more content to be displayed dynamically in a virtual scene in real time.

Streaming game data is not done in the Building Blocks Engine, but might be a feature that will be added later in future releases. In the past, streaming was done quite often in games like *Legacy of Kain Soul Reaver™*, *Grand Theft Auto 3*, *Need for Speed Most Wanted™*, and many more.

SUMMARY

This chapter dealt with the details of the design and implementation of the core system of the Building Blocks Engine. The core system is a set of code that was developed to help make creating the various sections of the Building Blocks Engine and games much easier and efficient. These tools include an archive filesystem, a file I/O system, an endianness handling system, and timing methods. Also discussed in this chapter are C++ Standard Template Library data structures and an additional data structure created from scratch to deal with hash tables. Much more can go into the core section of a video game engine. Many of these possible additions and improvements are discussed in Chapter 10, "Conclusions."

The next chapter looks at the input, sound, and networking sections of the Building Blocks Engine. Each of these sections was briefly touched on in Chapter 1 and will be discussed in more detail in the next chapter. After Chapter 3, the rendering and physics chapters start.

CHAPTER EXERCISES

1. Create high-resolution timer classes for Windows, Mac, and Linux to replace the timer code that currently exists for the Building Blocks Engine.
2. Alter the archive system so it allows individual items to be inserted one at a time. Also, alter the system so that the total number of files in an archive is not stored and instead is gathered through loading the file and counting how many file headers there are until it reaches the end of the file. The code already loads each file header from the file, so the change here will be to have it read until it reaches the end of the file (instead of by a set amount read from the archive header). This will allow individual files to be added to the file (appended) without interfering with the other files in the archive or the archive header.
3. On the companion CD-ROM is a tool called ARCHIVE CREATOR that creates archive files for the Building Blocks Engine in the BUILDING BLOCKS ENGINE/TOOLS folder. Edit the code for this tool to allow individual items to be inserted into an archive. The tool uses the code from the archive filesystem, so minor changes to the tool and a re-compilation of the code will need to be performed.

ON THE CD

3

Input, Sound, and Networking

In This Chapter

- Game Input
- Xbox 360 Controllers and XInput
- OpenAL for Game Audio
- XACT for Game Audio
- The Building Blocks Sound Systems
- Networking with Sockets
- The Building Blocks Networking System

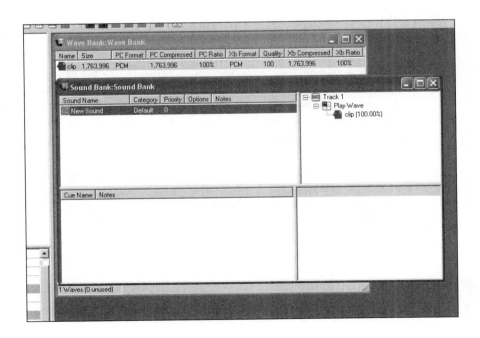

The purpose of this chapter is to focus on input detection and response, audio playback, and networking in gaming applications. Each of these areas of game development is pretty commonplace in modern video games and will be implemented in some form or another into the Building Blocks Engine. Simply put, the input in gaming is the primary way gamers interact with a video game, sound is a way for gamers to receive audio feedback, and networking is a way to connect a machine to another across a network such as the Internet. The quality of each of these areas in a game can have a huge effect on the overall gaming experience. A game with poor input detection and response can frustrate players and turn many gamers off a game title. Poor sound in a video game can decrease the gaming experience or distract the player in a negative way, while poor networking connectivity can have adverse affects on online games or the downloading of information to a client machine.

This chapter is broken into three sections: input detection, sound, and networking. Input detection covers gathering input from keyboards, mice, and Xbox 360 game controllers. Sound playback uses both the OpenAL audio library on all supported system and XACT (Audio Creation Tool) on Windows. For networking, the task will be implemented using sockets. Xbox 360 game controllers through XINPUT and XACT are technologies that pertain to the Windows operating systems and both the Xbox and Xbox 360 home video gaming consoles.

GAME INPUT

There is a large range of input devices that users can or cannot have attached to their personal computer. The two most common devices found on PCs are the keyboard and mouse combination. Other devices such as steering wheels, joysticks, game pads, and others are also used, but are not as common as the standard keyboard and mouse setup. Because of such wide use of a keyboard and mouse, the Building Blocks Engine has support for those two devices. To go one step beyond this, the Building Blocks Engine also has support for Xbox 360 game controllers on Windows XP, Windows Vista, and beyond. Xbox 360 game controller support can be added to a Win32 application using the library XINPUT, which is part of the DirectX SDK and XNA framework. The DirectX SDK can be downloaded directly from Microsoft's DirectX Web site. The XNA framework is not covered in this book, as it deals with the C# programming language and, at the time of writing, is still in beta form on the PC.

GETTING DEVICE KEY STATES

The easiest way to detect input from a keyboard and a mouse is to obtain the device's state and test for the action of interest. On Windows, input from the keyboard and mouse can be obtained by using the message pump or by manually requesting and testing the device's state using API calls. For the Mac, the same options exist to either use a message pump to allow the operating system to notify the application of an event, or to obtain the device's state manually. With Linux, the input detection of the mouse and keyboard can take place by using events to notify the application of when an action has occurred. Another way to detect input with the keyboard and mouse in an application would be to use a library such as Direct Input, which is used to obtain the key states of a device directly.

The Building Blocks Engine design from Chapter 1, "Introduction to Game Engines," required the input system to use functions for detecting keyboard and mice input. The design also called for creating a class for Xbox 360 controllers for the Windows side of input detection. Mac and Linux will use the straightforward input functions as a means to gather input through the keyboard and mouse but will not support Xbox 360 controllers. The design of the input system was done in this manner to keep the input system simple and straightforward. Xbox 360 controller support on Windows PCs was added to the engine design as a bonus feature, since playing games created out of the game engine framework would be more impressive with a very popular console input device.

The plan for the input system of the Building Blocks Engine specified that button input for keyboards and mice would be handled by the `isButtonDown()` function, and the mouse position would be handled by the `GetMousePosition()` function. The `GetMousePosition()` function takes addresses to variables that hold the mouse's x and y position, while the `isButtonDown()` function takes a flag that defines what button is being tested. This design was chosen to keep the input and gathering of the mouse movements as straightforward and simple as possible. Listings 3.2 and 3.3 list the function bodies for the `isButtonDown()` and `GetMousePosition()` functions for Win32 as an example. The button flags are converted internally to the system's key-code by the `GetButtonKeyCode()` function, which allows the initial `isButtonDown()` function to appear portable. A partial look at the `GetButtonKeyCode()` can be seen listed in Listing 3.4 for the Win32 version as an example. Listing 3.1 lists a partial listing of the enumeration for the button flags, which can be found in the header file Defines.h on the companion CD-ROM under the BUILD-ING BLOCKS ENGINE/SOURCE folder. An example of using the input detection function `isButtonDown()` is listed in Listing 3.5. The Mac and Linux versions implement the bodies of `isButtonDown()` and `GetMousePosition()` based on their specifics, which can be viewed in the source files InputMac.cpp and InputLinux.cpp on the CD-ROM.

ON THE CD

LISTING 3.1 The enumeration `BB_INPUT_BUTTON`.

```
enum BB_INPUT_BUTTON {BB_BUTTON_ARROW_UP,
                      BB_BUTTON_ARROW_DOWN,
                      BB_BUTTON_ARROW_LEFT,
                      BB_BUTTON_ARROW_RIGHT,
                      BB_BUTTON_A,
                      ...
                      BB_BUTTON_Z,
                      ... ETC ...};
```

LISTING 3.2 The `isButtonDown()` function.

```
bool isButtonDown(BB_INPUT_BUTTON btn)
{
   int key = 0;
   key = GetButtonKeyCode(btn);


   if(key == -1)
      return false;


   if(GetKeyState(key) & 0x80)
      return true;


   return false;
}
```

LISTING 3.3 The `GetMousePosition()` function.

```
void GetMousePosition(int *mx, int *my)
{
   POINT mousePos;
   GetCursorPos(&mousePos);


   if(mx) *mx = mousePos.x;
   if(my) *my = mousePos.y;
}
```

LISTING 3.4 A partial listing of the `GetButtonKeyCode()` function.

```
int GetButtonKeyCode(BB_INPUT_BUTTON btn)
{
    switch(btn)
    {
        case BB_BUTTON_ESCAPE: return VK_ESCAPE; break;
        case BB_BUTTON_SPACE: return VK_SPACE; break;
        case BB_BUTTON_MOUSE_LEFT: return VK_LBUTTON; break;
        case BB_BUTTON_MOUSE_RIGHT: return VK_RBUTTON; break;

        ... ETC ...

        default: return -1; break;
    }


    return -1;
}
```

LISTING 3.5 An example of using the input functions for keyboard key presses.

```
if(bbe::System.isButtonDown(BB_BUTTON_ESCAPE))
{
    g_quitDemo = true;
}

if(bbe::System.isButtonDown(BB_BUTTON_SPACE))
{
    g_spaceBtnDown = true;
}
else
{
    g_spaceBtnDown = false;
}
```

ADDITIONAL INPUT

The one additional input device for the Building Blocks Engine that will also be supported is the Xbox 360 controllers. The purpose of this section is to look at how XINPUT can be used for detecting input from the Xbox 360 game pad. XINPUT is a relatively new library that was recently added to the DirectX SDK some time before writing this chapter. In Chapter 1, Xbox 360 support was designed to take place in a class called `Xbox360Controller`. In the future, other console input devices might be added to the Building Blocks Engine such as the PlayStation 3 game controllers. The PlayStation 3 allows homebrewed applications to be developed on the system, much as it was for the original PlayStation with the Net Yarooza and on the PlayStation 2 with the PS2 Linux Kit. When new devices are added to the framework that can have drastically different features from the other devices, new classes can be designed and implemented. For example, the PlayStation 3 and the Wii controllers have motion sensors built in to the main controllers.

Xbox 360 Controllers and XInput

The ability to play a game developed with the Building Blocks Engine on a console controller is appealing. Traditionally, using console controllers has been strictly a feature for console games and professional developers. Today, a few new game consoles allow the ability to develop games for them outside the professional field. Moreover, the fact that some devices use the USB standard, like the Xbox 360 controller, allows for new options for nonprofessionals in game development. Creating game controllers that are USB devices allows those same devices to be used on the PC by plugging the devices into a USB slot and, if necessary, installing the latest drivers for the device. This very idea lead to the purpose of this section and it is here that the discussion will explore the possibility of using Xbox 360 console controllers on the PC.

To use Xbox 360 controllers on the PC will require users to first obtain an Xbox 360 wired controller. The next step is to download the drivers from Microsoft's Web site and install them on the client machine. There exists the option of buying an Xbox 360 controller with a special CD-ROM with the drivers on it called the *Xbox 360 Controller for Windows*. Purchasing a controller with this CD is optional since the drivers can be downloaded over the Internet. When working with Xbox 360 controllers on the PC, this applies to wired controllers and not wireless controllers because if a user tries to turn on a wireless controller it will automatically be picked up by an Xbox 360 console that is within range, or nothing will happen. The Xbox 360 *Plug-and-Play Recharge Kit* is not meant to be used to turn a wireless controller into a wired one because its purpose is to recharge the batteries in a wireless game pad.

Xbox 360 controllers can also be used on normal game pads in the same way any other PC game pad can be used that can be purchased on the market. However, to use the special features of the Xbox 360 controller and to be able to easily obtain input from the devices, the Building Blocks Engine will use XINPUT. XINPUT is an application programming interface (API) for using Xbox 360 controllers on the PC and on the Xbox consoles. As mentioned previously, XINPUT can be downloaded with the DirectX SDK from Microsoft's DirectX Web site for Windows XP and higher.

When using Xbox 360 controllers on the PC, make sure they are indeed wired controllers. Don't try to use the plug-and-play recharge kit with wireless controllers because the kit is not designed for that.

Enabling Xbox 360 Controllers

Enabling Xbox 360 controllers using XINPUT can be done by plugging the controller into the client machine and starting an application that uses XINPUT. When an application starts execution, any Xbox 360 controller attached to the machine will light up around the media button on the device and bind to a controller port from 1 through 4. This is the same action that occurs when a controller is plugged into the Xbox 360 or when a wireless controller is turned on. Applications that use XINPUT have to include the header file xinput.h and bind the library xinput.lib.

It is not necessary to enable XINPUT in code within an application to ON because that is the default, but there is still a way to enable and disable XINPUT if the need ever arises. This is done with the API function XInputEnable(), which takes as a parameter a Boolean value indicating what state to set XINPUT to. This can be useful if, for example, the application was minimized and focus has been lost from the program. This function can be used to stop the input from being detected from the controllers, and when the user re-focuses on the window, the application can reactivate it. Listing 3.6 lists the function prototype for XInputEnable() and illustrates an example of its use.

LISTING 3.6   The XInputEnable() function prototype and example use.

```
// Function prototype...
void XInputEnable(BOOL enable);


// Example of use...
XInputEnable(true);
```

Detecting Button Presses

The main benefit to using XINPUT to gather input from Xbox 360 controllers is that everything is done in a straightforward and simple manner. XACT, another new addition to the DirectX SDK, makes sound programming easier in a similar fashion as XINPUT than when compared to Direct Sound. Button presses on the

Xbox 360 controllers comes down to the arrow pad (directional pad's up, down, left, right), the face buttons (A, B, X, Y), the thumb buttons (left thumb = pressing in the left stick, right = pressing in the right stick), the start button, the back button, and the shoulder buttons. The shoulder buttons are on top of the controller in front of the triggers. On a PlayStation controller, these would be the L1 and R1 buttons, while on the Xbox 360 they are known as the left and right shoulder buttons (also known as bumpers). Table 3.1 lists all the flags that will be tested for when trying to detect input. Notice that triggers or the joystick movements are not in this table. Those are handled different from button presses and will be looked at later in this section.

TABLE 3.1   Button Flags for Xbox 360 Controller Buttons

XINPUT_GAMEPAD_LEFT_SHOULDER XINPUT_GAMEPAD_RIGHT_SHOULDER	Top front two buttons of the controller.
XINPUT_GAMEPAD_LEFT_THUMB XINPUT_GAMEPAD_RIGHT_THUMB	The joysticks are buttons just as they are in PS2 and PS3 controllers. They can be clicked by pressing the controller sticks in.
XINPUT_GAMEPAD_START XINPUT_GAMEPAD_BACK	The start and back buttons on the sides of the media button (green X logo button).
XINPUT_GAMEPAD_DPAD_UP XINPUT_GAMEPAD_DPAD_DOWN XINPUT_GAMEPAD_DPAD_LEFT XINPUT_GAMEPAD_DPAD_RIGHT	The array (directional) pad buttons flags.
XINPUT_GAMEPAD_A XINPUT_GAMEPAD_B XINPUT_GAMEPAD_X XINPUT_GAMEPAD_Y	The face buttons flags.

The buttons for a game pad are located in the Gamepad.wButtons variable of the XINPUT_STATE *object. A device is first updated before this object is tested for a particular button press.*

To gather the input from a controller device, the first thing is to obtain the current state of that device. The current state information is all the information dealing with the controller, from button presses to joystick positions to the trigger's pressures.

To obtain the controller state XINPUT supplies the function `XInputGetState()`, and it takes as parameters the controller index (0 for controller 1, 1 for controller 2, etc.) and an `XINPUT_STATE` object used to store the state information. The function `XInput-GetState()` returns `ERROR_SUCCESS` if the function was successful, `ERROR_DEVICE_NOT_CONNECTED` if there are no controllers connected to the index the function is looking for, and any other value if the function failed. Listing 3.7 lists the `XInputGet-State()` function prototype and an example of how to use it in an application.

LISTING 3.7   `XInputGetState()` function prototype and example.

```
// Function prototype...
DWORD XInputGetState(DWORD dwUserIndex, XINPUT_STATE *pState);


// Example of its use.
XINPUT_STATE state;
XInputGetState(0, &state);


if(state.Gamepad.wButtons & XINPUT_GAMEPAD_A) { /* Action */ }
if(state.Gamepad.wButtons & XINPUT_GAMEPAD_B) { /* Action */ }
```

Detecting Joystick Movements

As mentioned previously, calling `XInputGetState()` gives the application everything it needs to know about an Xbox 360 controller, including the joystick positions. For the left and right joysticks, their values can be in the range of −32,768 to +32,767 on each axis. When dealing with the joystick's X-axis, a negative values means that the joystick is going to the left while a positive value means right. With the joystick's Y-axis, a negative value is down while a position value is up. Both sticks and axes use a value of 0 for being in the center position. The more the joystick is moved, the higher the number of its axis. If there is a left stick X-axis value of −32,768, the joystick is all the way to the left, which allows an application to easily determine how far a player is moving a joystick in a given direction. This can be used to control a character's animation. For example, if the joystick that is used to control movement is being pressed slightly, the character can walk; if the joystick is being pressed far the character can run.

An application can get the current state of a device by calling `XInputGetState()`. All that is needed to determine the joystick's positions is to read the values in the state object's `Gamepad` variable. The left stick's X- and Y-axes are stored in the `Gamepad.sThumbLX` and `Gamepad.sThumbLY` variables, and the right stick's information can be found in the `Gamepad.sThumbRX` and `Gamepad.sThumbRY` variables. Listing 3.8 lists an example of getting the joystick's X and Y positions.

LISTING 3.8 Getting the joystick positions on a 360 controller.

```
XINPUT_STATE state
XInputGetState(0, &state);


short leftX = state.Gamepad.sThumbLX;
short leftY = state.Gamepad.sThumbLY;

short rightX = state.Gamepad.sThumbRX;
short rightY = state.Gamepad.sThumbRY;
```

Working with Triggers

The last two buttons on the Xbox 360 controller that have not been discussed are the triggers. Triggers are the top back buttons on the controller and are pressure sensitive. Like joysticks, the triggers have a range of values associated with them that depends on how much they are being pressed down. For the triggers, which would correspond to L2 and R2 on PlayStation 1/2/3 controllers, the values range from 0 to 255. This range of values means that the variables used to hold the trigger values are of the char data type. The more a player presses a trigger button the higher this value. Once that value gets to 255 the trigger is pressed all the way down. As with buttons and joystick information, the trigger states are gathered during the call to XInputGetState(). The left trigger is stored in the Gamepad.bLeftTrigger variable, and the right trigger is stored in the Gamepad.bRightTrigger variable. Listing 3.9 lists an example of getting the values of the triggers.

LISTING 3.9 Working with triggers.

```
XINPUT_STATE state
XInputGetState(0, &state);

/* Values range from 0 to 255 */
/* A value of 255 = pressed all the way down */

char leftTrigger = state.Gamepad.bLeftTrigger;
char rightTrigger = state.Gamepad.bRightTrigger;
```

Rumble Feedback (Force Feedback) Vibrations

XINPUT makes working with the Xbox 360 controllers easy with the use of a few API functions. With one function call an application is able to do just about everything with the Xbox 360 controller when it comes to input detection, but there is one thing that was not yet talked about: force feedback. Nintendo was the first home console maker to use force feedback on the Nintendo 64 with their rumble pack controller add-on device that was bundled with *Star Fox 64*, and sold separately. Since that time, many consoles added the force feedback feature. Although the PlayStation 3 gaming consoles no longer use force feedback in their game controller, the Xbox 360 does and it can be programmed using XINPUT.

There are two motors in an Xbox 360 controller, with one on the left and one on the right. The motors' speed can be in the range of 0, for no vibrations, to 65,535, for max power. Both the left and right motors can have their own separate speeds with which to work. To set the vibrations of a controller it is necessary to call XInputSetState() and pass to it the controller index of the device to set, and an XINPUT_VIBRATION object. Before calling XInputSetState() it is necessary to set the vibration object's wLeftMotorSpeed and wRightMotorSpeed variables. Once this is done, a call to this XINPUT function will immediately cause the controller to start shaking. Listing 3.10 list an example of how to make a controller rumble.

LISTING 3.10   Making the controller shake.

```
XINPUT_VIBRATION vibration


// SETTING THE VIBRATION OF EACH MOTOR.
vibration.wLeftMotorSpeed = (some value);
vibration.wRightMotorSpeed = (some value);


XInputSetState(0, &vibration);
```

Working with the Xbox 360 Headset

The only remaining parts of the Xbox 360 controller are the media button and the Xbox 360 headset for voice communication. The media button, the Xbox logo button in the middle of the controller, is used only by the game system and is not actually programmed. The media button is used to access the system panel of the Xbox 360 console. The Xbox 360 headset is an additional device that can be plugged into the bottom of the controller. Its primary use is voice communication with other gamers in online games and chat rooms. The Xbox 360 headset is not covered mainly because it uses Direct Sound and can be quite complex when compared to the rest of XINPUT and working with Xbox 360 controllers. For convenience and for the interested there is an application at *UltimateGameProgramming.com* that demonstrates how to use Xbox 360 headsets in applications using both Direct Sound and XINPUT. A demo application that comes with the DirectX SDK demonstrates this as well.

ON THE CD

On the companion CD-ROM is a simple demo application that demonstrates how to use XINPUT in a Win32 program. The demo can be found in the BUILD-ING BLOCKS ENGINE/EXAMPLE/CHAPTER 3 folder and is called XINPUT. Xbox 360 controllers will be used at the end of this book for the game demo applications.

THE BUILDING BLOCKS ENGINE XINPUT SYSTEM

ON THE CD

The Xbox 360 input system for the Building Blocks Engine can be found on the companion CD-ROM in the BUILDING BLOCKS ENGINE/SOURCE folder in the X360Input.h header file. The Building Blocks Engine's Xbox 360 controller class, called X360Controller, was first designed in Chapter 1 to be a single class. The class diagram for the X360Controller class can be seen in Figure 3.1.

X360Controller
-m_state
-m_oldState
-m_status : unsigned long
-m_vibration
-m_controllerPort : int
+Initialize() : int
+Enable() : void
+Update() : int
+isButtonDown() : char
+isButtonUp() : char
+GetLeftTriggerPressure() : int
+GetRightTriggerPressure() : int
+SetFeedbackPressure() : void

FIGURE 3.1 The class diagram for the X360Controller class.

The Xbox 360 controller class has a constructor, destructor, an enabling function to wrap around XInputEnable(), an update function to update the device's state, a function to get the button pressure amount of the triggers, functions to test button presses, a function to set the controller's force feedback, and a function to get the joystick's positions. The Xbox 360 device class has member variables for the controller port it is attached to (0 through 3 for controllers 1, 2, 3, and 4), the current and last state of a device stored in XINPUT_STATE structures, the status of a device that tells the application if the controller is connected, and the vibration's state stored in the XINPUT_VIBRATION structure. The only purpose of the initialize function is to set the member variable for which controller port the object is using. The class marks a value of −1 for the status as being a controller that has not been set to any controller port. Listing 3.11 lists the Xbox 360 controller class declaration based on the design for the controller's class. The Xbox 360 controller class was designed this way to wrap all the capabilities of the Xbox 360 controller into one class that can be expanded to support more features. If Xbox 360 headset functionality is desired, it can be added to this class.

LISTING 3.11   The Xbox 360 controller input device class X360Controller.

```
class X360Controller
{
    public:
        X360Controller() : m_controllerPort(-1) { }
        virtual ~X360Controller() { }


        BRESULT Initialize(int controllerPort);
        void Enable(bool flag);
        BRESULT Update();


        BSTATE isButtonDown(BB_INPUT_BUTTON button);
        BSTATE isButtonUp(BB_INPUT_BUTTON button);


        int GetLeftTriggerPressure();
        int GetRightTriggerPressure();


        void GetStickPos(int deadzone, int *lx, int *ly,
                         int *rx, int *ry);


        void SetFeedBackPressure(int left, int right);


    private:
        XINPUT_STATE m_state;
        XINPUT_STATE m_oldState;
```

```
        unsigned long m_status;
        XINPUT_VIBRATION m_vibration;
        short m_controllerPort;
};
```

The first functions in the Xbox 360 class are Initialize(), Enable(), and Update(). The Initialize() function takes as a parameter the controller port for the device. The Initialize() function also calls Update() once to test that the state of the device was successfully gathered. If not, then it can be assumed that there is some problem with the device or a device is not attached. For the controller port, it can be any value between 0 and 3, which maps to controllers 1, 2, 3, and 4 on the Xbox 360.

Also with Update(), the function's job is to get the current state of the object. The function XInputGetState() returns a status value that is used to set the status member variable, m_status, so the class can know if a device is connected or was successfully detected. The last function is Enable(), which calls XInputEnable() by passing the flag to the function.

The class can keep track of the status of a controller. It would then be possible to unplug the device from the system and plug it back it while the game is running. As with the Xbox 360 console, players can plug and unplug a controller while in a game. If this happens and the Xbox 360 controller is the only device being used for input, the game can pause and display a message like "please attach an Xbox 360 controller to the system."

The next to last functions in the class are button up/down, left and right trigger pressure, and GetStickPos(). An application can test if a button is down by testing the current state object. To determine if a button has been released, an application can test the current state to see if the button is up, and if so, it can test if the last state is the opposite. The pressure functions GetLeftTriggerPressure() and GetRight-TriggerPression() return to the caller the pressure amount, from 0 to 255, a trigger is being pressed. The joystick position function, GetStickPos(), is used to get the joystick positions of the controller device. The first two parameters, lx and ly, are used to get the left stick's X- and Y-axis, while the last two parameters, rx and ry, are used to get the right stick's position.

The last function is SetFeedBackPressure(), which takes a value for the left motor speed and right motor speed. These values are in the range of 0 to 65,353, which fits into an integer data type. In an application, it can keep track of the current motor speeds and manipulate them based on what is going on inside a game. Each of the functions of the XBOX360Controller can be seen in Listing 3.12.

LISTING 3.12   The implementation for the XBOX360Controller class.

```
BRESULT X360Controller::Initialize(int controllerPort)
{
   if(controllerPort < 0 || controllerPort > 3)
      return BB_FAIL;

   m_controllerPort = controllerPort;

   return Update();
}


void X360Controller::Enable(bool flag)
{
   XInputEnable(flag);
}


BRESULT X360Controller::Update()
{
   if(m_controllerPort < 0 || m_controllerPort > 3)
      return BB_FAIL;

   m_oldState = m_state;

   m_status = XInputGetState(m_controllerPort, &m_state);

   if(m_status != ERROR_SUCCESS)
      return BB_FAIL;

   return BB_SUCCESS;
}


int X360Controller::GetLeftTriggerPressure()
{
   return (int)m_state.Gamepad.bLeftTrigger;
}


int X360Controller::GetRightTriggerPressure()
{
   return (int)m_state.Gamepad.bRightTrigger;
}
```

```
BSTATE X360Controller::isButtonDown(BB_INPUT_BUTTON button)
{
   unsigned long buttonCode = GetButtonCode(button);

   if(button == BB_BUTTON_LEFT_TRIGGER)
      if(m_state.Gamepad.bLeftTrigger > 0)
         return BB_SUCCESS;

   if(button == BB_BUTTON_RIGHT_TRIGGER)
      if(m_state.Gamepad.bRightTrigger > 0)
         return BB_SUCCESS;

   if(buttonCode == -1)
      return BB_FAIL;

   if(m_state.Gamepad.wButtons & buttonCode)
      return BB_SUCCESS;

   return BB_FAIL;
}


BSTATE X360Controller::isButtonUp(BB_INPUT_BUTTON button)
{
   unsigned long buttonCode = GetButtonCode(button);

   if(button == BB_BUTTON_LEFT_TRIGGER)
      if(m_state.Gamepad.bLeftTrigger == 0)
         if(m_oldState.Gamepad.bLeftTrigger > 0)
            return BB_SUCCESS;

   if(button == BB_BUTTON_RIGHT_TRIGGER)
      if(m_state.Gamepad.bRightTrigger == 0)
         if(m_oldState.Gamepad.bRightTrigger > 0)
            return BB_SUCCESS;

   if(buttonCode == -1)
      return BB_FAIL;

   if(!(m_state.Gamepad.wButtons & buttonCode))
      if(m_oldState.Gamepad.wButtons & buttonCode)
         return BB_SUCCESS;
```

```
      return BB_FAIL;
}


void X360Controller::GetStickPos(int deadzone, int *lx, int *ly,
                                 int *rx, int *ry)
{
   if(deadzone)
   {
      BB_X360_DEADZONE_CHECK(m_state.Gamepad.sThumbLX,
                             m_state.Gamepad.sThumbLY,
                             deadzone);

      BB_X360_DEADZONE_CHECK(m_state.Gamepad.sThumbRX,
                             m_state.Gamepad.sThumbRY,
                             deadzone);
   }

   if(lx) *lx = (int)m_state.Gamepad.sThumbLX;
   if(ly) *ly = (int)m_state.Gamepad.sThumbLY;
   if(rx) *rx = (int)m_state.Gamepad.sThumbRX;
   if(ry) *ry = (int)m_state.Gamepad.sThumbRY;
}


void X360Controller::SetFeedBackPressure(int left, int right)
{
   if(left < 0) left = 0;
   if(right < 0) right = 0;

   if(m_controllerPort >= 0 && m_controllerPort < 4)
   {
      m_vibration.wLeftMotorSpeed = left;
      m_vibration.wLeftMotorSpeed = right;

      XInputSetState(m_controllerPort, &m_vibration);
   }
}
```

ON THE CD

The implementation for the Xbox 360 controller device can be found on the companion CD-ROM in the BUILDING BLOCKS ENGINE/SOURCE folder. A demo application that demonstrates using XINPUT in an OpenGL Win32 application can also be found on the CD-ROM in the BUILDING BLOCKS ENGINE/EXAMPLES/CHAPTER 3 folder. The X360Controller class and the input functions isButtonDown() and GetMousePosition() are part of the input library of the Building Blocks Engine framework.

OpenAL for Game Audio

This section looks at playing sounds in an application using popular sound APIs. As mentioned previously, game audio is very important in game development and can be used as a great tool. Sound is a type of feedback, and is common in all modern games and has been for many decades. With sound, gamers can be immersed deeply into a virtual environment and atmosphere. The purpose of this section is to create a straightforward sound system that is capable of loading and playing audio files in a game.

The Building Blocks Engine will implement an OpenAL (Open Audio Library) sound system and an XACT sound system. XACT can be used on Windows and on the Xbox 360, while OpenAL can be used by Xbox, Xbox 360, Windows, Mac OS 8 through 10, and Linux, to name a few. Before going over the engine-specific sound systems, the following sections briefly discuss each of the sound-processing APIs that will be used in the framework. The OpenAL SDK can be downloaded from the Creative Labs developer Web site, which is listed in Appendix A, "Additional Resources." The OpenAL utility library (ALUT), which makes working with OpenAL easier, can be downloaded from the OpenAL Web site, which is also listed in Appendix A. Microsoft's XACT tools and SDK can be downloaded with the current DirectX SDK. Like XInput, XACT comes with the DirectX SDK and has a few beginner level demos that can be found in the DirectX Sample Browser that covers a lot of material in the API.

OpenAL in General

In the Building Blocks Engine when working with OpenAL the sound library will use the OpenAL utility kit called ALUT. ALUT for OpenAL is similar to GLUT for OpenGL by simplifying the process of playing sounds in an application. To play a sound in OpenAL, a sound buffer and a source object will need to be initialized. A sound buffer in OpenAL is the sound data that is to be played. Source objects are used to play sound buffers much like texture IDs in OpenGL are used to access texture data. In OpenAL, a source is a literal source that is emitting a sound. In an application there can be more than one source referencing the same sound buffer. When the application loads the sound data in memory, the sound buffer is just an ID for that memory. Source objects are IDs used to specify information about the source of the sound, which includes the sound buffer it uses and its position, velocity, and so forth, which is used for 3D sound effects. Listing 3.13 lists an example of how to declare a sound buffer and source object in OpenAL.

LISTING 3.13 Defining a sound buffer and source object.

```
ALuint SoundBuffer;
ALuint Source;
```

To initialize the OpenAL API with ALUT, the `alutInit()` function can be called. `alutInit()` will initialize OpenAL for a single call and takes as parameters an argument list and a number of arguments. `alutInit()`can take as a parameter the command-line arguments from the `main()` function, or NULL can be passed. Once initialized, the major and minor version numbers can be checked to make sure the values in the alut.h header file are compatible with the libraries on the system. Listing 3.14 lists the function prototype for the `alutInit()` function. Listing 3.15 lists an example of version checking.

LISTING 3.14 Calling the `alutInit()` function.

```
// Function prototype...
ALboolean alutInit (int *argcp, char **argv);



// Example...
if(alutInit(NULL, 0) != AL_TRUE)
{
    /* SOME ERROR */
}
```

LISTING 3.15 Checking the ALUT version numbers.

```
if(alutGetMajorVersion() != ALUT_API_MAJOR_VERSION &&
    alutGetMinorVersion() != ALUT_API_MINOR_VERSION)
{

    /* ERROR - HEADERS DON'T MATCH LIBRARIES */

}
```

To code with OpenAL it is required to include the header files al.h and alc.h. To use the OpenAL utility, which will be used by the Building Blocks Engine, it is required to include alut.h. In addition, all libraries will need to be linked to the projects.

LOADING SOUNDS

In OpenAL, the application can load and play wave files (.WAV) in an application. The application can also use streaming OggVorbis (.OGG) sound files, which are not used and not covered in the Building Blocks Engine. To load a sound file in OpenAL, the first step would be to create a sound buffer to reference the sound data that is loaded into memory. ALUT has a function that makes this process easy—`alutCreateBufferFromFile()`. `alutCreateBufferFromFile()` takes a sound file, loads it, creates a sound buffer object, binds the data to it, and returns the sound buffer on the function's exit. `alutCreateBufferFromFile()` takes a filename in the form of a character string as a parameter. The return value for `alutCreateBufferFromFile()` is the ID for the created sound buffer object.

The second object needed is a source object so the application can manipulate the sound (play, stop, pause, position, etc.) in code. This is done by creating a source object with the OpenAL API function call `alGenSources()`. The OpenAL API was designed to be similar to the style of OpenGL, so there are similarities in how both APIs create and destroy objects. The function `alGenSources()` takes as parameters the number of sources to generate and the address to a list of variables to save them to. This can be used for arrays of sources of just single source objects as with the OpenGL functions `glGenTextures()`, `glDeleteTextures()`, and so forth. Listing 3.16 lists the function prototypes for `alutCreateBufferFromFile()` and `alGenSources()` along with examples of how to use each.

LISTING 3.16 Prototypes and examples of `alutCreateBufferFromFile()` and `alGenSources()`.

```
// Function prototypes...
ALuint alutCreateBufferFromFile (const char *filename);

void alGenSources (ALsizei n, ALuint *sources);


// Examples...
ALuint SoundBuffer, Source;

SoundBuffer = alutCreateBufferFromFile("clip.wav");

alGenSources(1, &Source);
```

As mentioned previously, OpenAL is very similar in syntax to OpenGL. In OpenAL once the application generates (creates) a source object it can bind properties to it. The first property that can be bound is the sound buffer object to the source. The other sound properties can vary from the sound position (position of the object making the sound in 3D space), the sound velocity, and the listener properties (player position). The OpenAL documentation that comes with the OpenAL SDK has a list of all properties that can be set. As an example, we will set the sound's position, velocity, and listener's position, orientation (look direction), and up vector for 3D sound effects. Listing 3.17 lists an example of setting properties of a source object. Various functions can be used: alSourcei() to set an integer property, alSourcef() to set a floating-point property, alSourcefv() to set a floating-point array of values, and so forth.

More than one source can bind to the same sound buffer. This is because sound data can take up resources, and loading the same sound data more times than necessary is a waste. If it uses the same sound, have the sources bind to the same buffer. Sources are used to set individual properties of a sound source such as position, velocity, and so forth; to have each source with its own unique sound buffer is not necessary.

LISTING 3.17 Setting some source object properties.

```
ALfloat SourcePosition[] = {0.0f, 0.0f, 0.0f};
ALfloat SourceVelocity[] = {0.0f, 0.0f, 0.0f};

ALfloat ListenerPosition[] = {0.0f, 0.0f, 0.0f};
ALfloat ListenerVelocity[] = {0.0f, 0.0f, 0.0f};
ALfloat ListenerOrientation[] = {0.0f, 0.0f, -1.0f,
                                 0.0f, 1.0f, 0.0f};


alSourcei(Source, AL_BUFFER, SoundBuffer);
alSourcefv(Source, AL_POSITION, SourcePosition);
alSourcefv(Source, AL_VELOCITY, SourceVelocity);
alSourcei(Source, AL_LOOPING, true);

alListenerfv(AL_POSITION, ListenerPosition);
alListenerfv(AL_VELOCITY, ListenerVelocity);
alListenerfv(AL_ORIENTATION, ListenerOrientation);
```

PLAYING/PAUSING/STOPPING SOUNDS AND CLEANING UP

Once an application has a source object and a sound buffer it is ready to start playing sounds. To play a sound the application can call alSourcePlay(), to pause a sound it can call alSourcePause(), and to stop a sound it can call alSourceStop().

Each of these functions takes a single parameter, which is the source object ID of the object emitting the sound. When playing a sound, the application can call `alSourcePlay()` more than once on the same source object to play the sound multiple times, even overlapping at the same time. Listing 3.18 lists examples of using each of these functions on a source object.

LISTING 3.18 Playing, pausing, and stopping a sound.

```
alSourcePlay(Source);

alSourcePause(Source);

alSourceStop(Source);
```

When the application is done with the sounds, it must clean up all the OpenAL objects that were used. This can be done by deleting the sound buffer with `alDelete-Buffers()`, deleting the source object with `alDeleteSources()`, and exiting ALUT with `alutExit()`. The function `alutExit()` takes no parameters, returns no value, and shuts down ALUT, which was initialized with `alutInit()`. The `alDeleteBuffers()` and `alDeleteSources()` functions have the same parameters as their creation counterparts `alGenBuffers()` and `alGenSources()`. These functions match the syntax and style of the OpenGL delete function `glDeleteTextures()`. Examples of using the `alDelete-Buffers()`, `alDeleteSources()`, and `alutExit()` functions can be seen in Listing 3.19.

LISTING 3.19 Deleting the OpenAL buffers and exiting ALUT.

```
if(SoundBuffer)
    alDeleteBuffers(1, &SoundBuffer);

if(Source)
    alDeleteSources(1, &Source);

alutExit();
```

ON THE CD

There is a demo on the companion CD-ROM in the BUILDING BLOCKS ENGINE/EXAMPLES/CHAPTER 3 folder called OPENAL. This demo is a C++ console application that will load a .WAV sound file and play it using all the information discussed in this chapter for OpenAL. This demo does not use the engine's sound system, which will be looked at later, and is just a simple application that shows off the information recently covered.

XACT FOR GAME AUDIO

XACT is Microsoft's Cross-Platform Audio Creation Tool. With it, developers can create sound files in the form of wave and sound banks and use them in their applications. XACT is used to give power to the sound designers and relieves the programmers from a lot of the work. With XACT, the sound designers can use the XACT tool to specify properties and effects that can be used in a game without even touching game code. The XACT API comes with the DirectX SDK. Although Direct Sound is still part of DirectX, XACT is another option developers have to use and might become a solution to the aging API. XACT allows applications to load wave files (.WAV), .AIFF files, and .XMA. The .XMA files are based on Windows .WMA file format.

CREATING PROJECTS

The XACT tool can be launched by going to the Start menu of Windows XP, Vista, and so forth and going to Programs/Microsoft's DirectX SDK/DirectX Utilities. Another option is to use the DirectX SDK Sample Browser to launch the tool by going to the XACT section and clicking the executable link. When the XACT is first opened, users are greeted with a graphical user interface (GUI). This screen is initially blank. A user can create a new project and save it from the menu before beginning to work. Figure 3.2 illustrates what the XACT tool looks like when it is first launched.

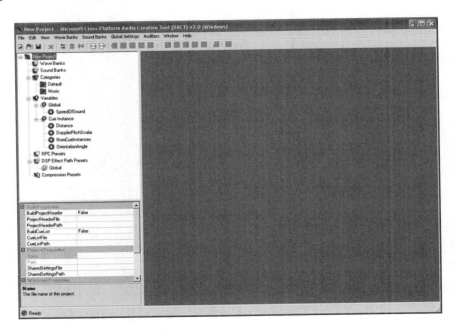

FIGURE 3.2   The XACT tool.

WAVE BANKS

Once a new project has been created and saved, it is ready to be worked on. A panel on the left side, which can be seen in Figure 3.3, has in it a tree list. In this tree list are seven major sections: Wave Banks, Sound Banks, Categories, Variables, RPC Presets, DSP Effect Path Presets, and Compress Presets. Wave Banks is used to store all the wave (.WAV) files in an audio resource. When users build the project, XACT will create a file with the extension .XWB, which represents a wave bank file. In the wave bank are all waves that are going to be played in an application. A new wave bank can be created by going to the application's menu and selecting Wave Bank/New Wave Bank. A blank window will appear in the middle of the screen similar to the one in Figure 3.4. Adding .WAV files to the wave bank can be done from the menu and selecting Wave Banks/Insert Wave Files. Every time a new wave file is added to the wave bank, it appears in the Wave Bank window as seen in Figure 3.5.

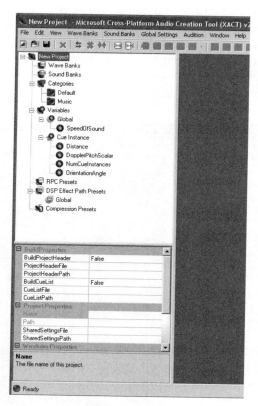

FIGURE 3.3 The left panel in the XACT tool.

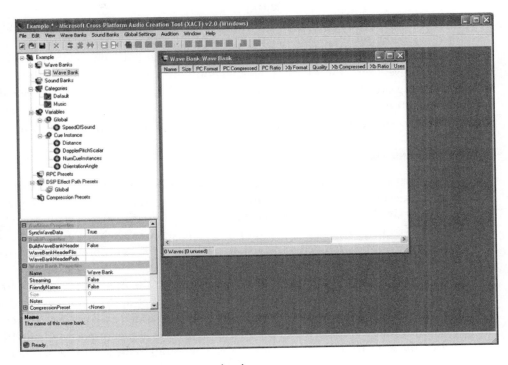

FIGURE 3.4   A new but empty wave bank.

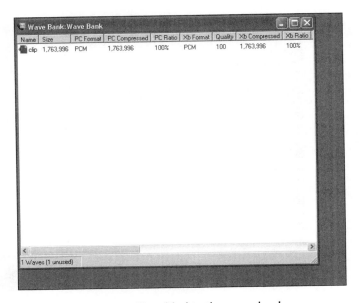

FIGURE 3.5   A Wave file added to the wave bank.

A wave in the wave bank can be selected to see/edit its properties in the Properties panel on the lower left side of the XACT tool. Some properties users will come across are used for the Xbox 360, and will be labeled as such. If working on Windows, users don't have to worry about any Xbox 360 settings unless they are working on both the PC and the console. For some audio files, a user can also set the compression preset by clicking on the wave file and editing the Compression Preset property listed in the Properties window on the lower left panel.

Sound Banks and Sound Cues

The next section in the tree list in the left panel is for the sound bank, which is a list of sounds in the audio resource and those sounds' properties. A sound in the sound bank is similar to the source object in OpenAL. When a new sound is added to the sound bank, a user can edit the sound's properties like pitch, volume, and so forth. Different sounds can be bound to the same wave file as different OpenAL sources can be bound to the same sound buffer.

A new sound bank can be created by going to the menu and selecting from it Sound Banks/New Sound Bank. An empty window will appear much as it did for the wave bank. A new sound to the sound bank can be added by going to the menu and selecting Sound Banks/New Sound. To attach a wave to the sound, users can drag and drop the wave from the wave bank to the new sound in the sound bank (Figure 3.6). Once the new wave has been attached to the sound, users can click on the track next to it in the sound bank for more information and view/edit additional properties.

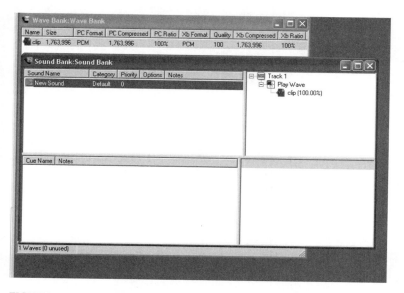

FIGURE 3.6   Creating a new sound in the sound bank.

The last thing needed to play a sound, technically, is a sound cue, which is called inside a game when a sound needs to be played. A sound cue is bound to a sound in the sound bank much like a sound in the sound bank is bound to a wave file. A new sound cue can be created by going to Sound Banks/New Cue from the menu. Then, a sound can be dragged from the top of the sound bank next to the cue it is to be bound to. By clicking on the new sound cue, a user can view/edit additional properties dealing with the cue. As mentioned previously, XACT allows sound designers a lot of power and control to the point where programmers have little work ahead of them. Figure 3.7 shows how to add a sound cue in the XACT tool window.

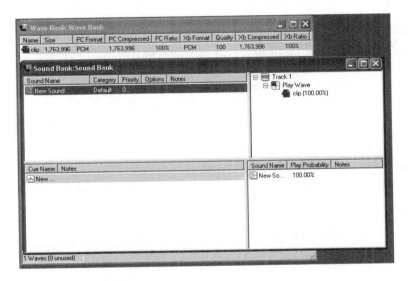

FIGURE 3.7 Creating sound cues.

In a game or any other application using XACT, sound cues are used to play a sound. In the application, the index of a sound cue can be obtained from the sound bank. If that sound cue does not exist, nothing happens if the application tries to play it. If it does exist, the sound is played with the various properties associated with the cue, the sound it is bound to, and the wave file. This can allow a programmer to specify all the sound cues in a game (e.g., weapon shots, footsteps, etc.), and a sound designer can add those sounds later or edit them as needed. Sounds can be added, deleted, modified, and so forth without bothering a programmer.

An XACT project can be built by pressing F7 on the keyboard. When a project is built, two new files will be created in the location the project is saved. If wave and sound banks were created in the project, files for these will appear when the project is built. If any categories were specified in the category section, a file for those will also appear with the other build files. Additional information on XACT can be found in the DirectX documentation. Demos of the various aspects of XACT can also be found in the DirectX SDK.

LOADING SOUNDS

Loading audio resources in XACT is a little more work than with OpenAL. To work with XACT there has to at least be a wave and a sound bank. The sound banks have the sound cues and the wave bank has the actual audio data. In code, a wave bank is stored in the structure IXACTWaveBank and the sound bank is stored in the structure IXACTSoundBank. Listing 3.20 shows a structure that was created to hold a sound and wave bank in the XACT demo application on the companion CD-ROM. The additional two variables, of type void pointer, will hold the file data for when the application creates the actual banks.

ON THE CD

To use XACT the application will need to create an XACT audio engine. This object is of the type IXACTEngine. When the application actually plays sounds, it will need to use sound cues. Sound cues are defined in the sound banks and the application must get indexes to them to call them to be played. A sound cue has the type XACTINDEX.

NOTE

When creating applications with XACT, the header file xact.h must be included.

LISTING 3.20 A structure to hold all we need to play sounds.

```
struct stXACTAudio
{
    IXACTWaveBank *waveBank;
    IXACTSoundBank *soundBank;

    void *waveBankData;
    void *soundBankData;
};
```

XACT, like DirectX, uses COM; therefore, the application must initialize COM using CoInitializeEx() before it can create the XACT engine. The XACT engine can be created by calling the XACTCreateEngine() function, which takes as parameters the creation flag, which can be XACT_FLAG_API_AUDITION_MODE or XACT_FLAG_API_DEBUG_MODE, and the address of the IXACTEngine sound engine object.

With a sound engine object, the application can set the parameters for the run-time engine. These parameters are similar to Direct3D's present parameters and have a type XACT_RUNTIME_PARAMETERS. A number of parameters can be set, and coders can refer to the DirectX SDK for a complete list. The look-ahead time for the sound engine can be set to 250, which is the same value used by the DirectX SDK demo applications. To apply the parameters, a call to the sound engine's Initial-ize() function can be made that takes a single parameter: the runtime parameters. Listing 3.21 displays an example of setting up the XACT runtime and applying its parameters to the engine.

LISTING 3.21   A code example that can load sound and wave banks.

```
bool SetupXACT(char *waveBank, char *soundBank)
{
   ZeroMemory(&g_xactSound, sizeof(stXACTAudio));

   // Init com. COINIT_APARTMENTTHREADED can be used.
   if(FAILED(CoInitializeEx(NULL, COINIT_MULTITHREADED)))
      return false;


   // Create XACT engine.
   if(FAILED(XACTCreateEngine(XACT_FLAG_API_AUDITION_MODE,
      &g_soundEngine)))
   {
      return false;
   }

   if(g_soundEngine == NULL)
      return false;


   // Set XACT parameters.
   XACT_RUNTIME_PARAMETERS xparams = {0};
   xparams.lookAheadTime = 250;

   if(FAILED(g_soundEngine->Initialize(&xparams)))
      return false;


   // Load wave bank.
   if(!LoadBank(waveBank, WAVE_BANK_TYPE))
      return false;
```

```
   // Load sound bank.
   if(!LoadBank(soundBank, SOUND_BANK_TYPE))
      return false;

   return true;
}
```

There are two main ways to create sound and wave banks: creating memory mapped file I/O handles, or allocating the buffers manually. In the DirectX SDK, those demos create the wave banks using memory mapped handles, and the sound banks using allocated pointers to the data. According to the SDK, using memory mapped I/O is faster in most situations, so that method will be used for both the sound and wave banks. To create the in-memory data, an application can first get a handle to the file it is loading by calling CreateFile() and getting the size of the file by calling GetFileSize(). With that information, the application can call CreateFileMapping() to get a handle to the file mapping and MapViewOfFile() to get a pointer to the file data. The last step would be to call CreateInMemoryWaveBank() when creating a wave bank, or CreateSoundBank() when creating a sound bank. Detailed information about each of these functions can be obtained from the documentation, but their names and the parameters they take are clear to their purpose. Listing 3.22 lists an example of creating a function that can be used to load a wave or a sound bank.

LISTING 3.22   Example of loading a wave and sound bank.

```
bool LoadBank(char *fileName, int bankType)
{
   HANDLE file;
   DWORD fileSize;
   HANDLE mapFile;
   void *ptr;
   bool result = true;


   // Create file in memory.
   file = CreateFile(fileName, GENERIC_READ, FILE_SHARE_READ,
                     NULL, OPEN_EXISTING, 0, NULL);

   if(file == INVALID_HANDLE_VALUE)
      return false;
```

```
// Get the file's size and make sure its ok.
fileSize = GetFileSize(file, NULL);

if(fileSize == -1)
{
   CloseHandle(file);
   return false;
}


// Create memory mapped data since its it's faster.
mapFile = CreateFileMapping(file, NULL, PAGE_READONLY, 0,
                            fileSize, NULL);

if(!mapFile)
{
   CloseHandle(file);
   return false;
}

ptr = MapViewOfFile(mapFile, FILE_MAP_READ, 0, 0, 0);

if(!ptr)
{
   CloseHandle(mapFile);
   CloseHandle(file);
   return false;
}


// Load depending on the type bank we are creating.
if(bankType == WAVE_BANK_TYPE)
{
   g_xactSound.m_waveBankData = ptr;

   if(FAILED(g_soundEngine->CreateInMemoryWaveBank(
      g_xactSound.m_waveBankData, fileSize, 0, 0,
      &g_xactSound.m_waveBank)))
   {
      result = false;
   }
}
else
```

```
      {
         g_xactSound.m_soundBankData = ptr;

         if(FAILED(g_soundEngine->CreateSoundBank(
            g_xactSound.m_soundBankData, fileSize, 0, 0,
            &g_xactSound.m_soundBank)))
         {
            result = false;
         }
      }


      // Close handles now that we are done.
      CloseHandle(mapFile);
      CloseHandle(file);

      return result;
   }
```

Once the sound and wave banks are loaded, the next step is to get the sound cues, which is as easy as calling the sound bank's GetCueIndex() function. GetCueIndex()takes as a parameter the name of the sound cue and returns the index. If the sound cue is not found, and the application tries to play the sound, nothing will happen. This allows programmers to specify cues in their games without them actually being ready yet. Listing 3.23 shows an example of calling the previously talked about SetupXACT() function that was created to load both a wave and sound bank and how to get a cue. In Listing 3.23, the code uses the same function created in Listing 3.22.

LISTING 3.23   Getting a sound cue once the sound and wave banks are loaded.

```
      // Example of setting up XACT and load the banks.
      if(!SetupXACT("Sound/Win/TapWaveBank.xwb",
         "Sound/Win/TapSoundBank.xsb"))
      {
         return false;
      }


      // Get sound cue indexes.
      g_tapCue = g_xactSound.m_soundBank->GetCueIndex("tap");
```

PLAYING SOUNDS

When working with XACT, applications must occasionally update the XACT run-time engine by calling the sound engine's function DoWork(). DoWork() in a game can be called every iteration of the game loop. Calling this function too often can affect performance, but calling it not often enough might cause glitches in the streaming content.

To play a sound cue an application can call the sound bank's Play() function. Play() takes as parameters a sound cue, playback flags, the offset time in millisec-onds from which to start, and an optional out pointer to the cue index. The state of a cue can be obtained by calling GetState() of the sound bank and sending to it the address of an unsigned long variable that will hold the state of the cue. An applica-tion can test this cue for different states. To test if the sound is playing, the appli-cation can look for the XACT_CUESTATE_PLAYING flag, and respond to the result. Listing 3.24 shows how to update the runtime and to play a cue. Listing 3.25 lists an example of getting the cue's state and testing if it is already playing.

LISTING 3.24   Updating the XACT runtime and playing a cue.

```
// Update XCT engine.
if(g_soundEngine)
   g_soundEngine->DoWork();


g_xactSound.m_soundBank->Play(g_tapCue, 0, 0, NULL);
```

LISTING 3.25   Getting the state of a cue.

```
unsigned long state = 0;

// Update XCT engine.
if(g_soundEngine)
   g_soundEngine->DoWork();



g_xactSound.m_soundBank->GetState(&state);

// If statement allows cue to be played 1 at a time.
if(!(state && XACT_CUESTATE_PLAYING))
   g_xactSound.m_soundBank->Play(g_tapCue, 0, 0, NULL);
```

CLEANING UP

As with most things in programming, when an application is done with any resources it must free them before the application closes. To shut down the XACT engine, a call to the engine's ShutDown() function is used to clean up XACT. Then, a call to the Release() function is used to release the object from memory. The ShutDown() function must be called before Release(), because once Release() is called, the pointer is no longer valid.

When releasing the sound and wave banks a slightly different approach must be taken than what was done with other objects. The memory was mapped in the application, so a call to UnmapViewOfFile() is needed and COM is released by calling CoUninitialize(). An example of releasing all of the objects mentioned can be seen in Listing 3.26.

LISTING 3.26 Releasing everything we've used with XACT.

```
// Release XACT engine.
if(g_soundEngine)
{
   g_soundEngine->ShutDown();
   g_soundEngine->Release();
}


// MUST use UnmapViewoFile() for memory mapped banks.
if(g_xactSound.m_soundBankData)
{
   UnmapViewOfFile(g_xactSound.m_soundBankData);
   g_xactSound.m_soundBankData = NULL;
}


// MUST use UnmapViewoFile() for memory mapped banks.
if(g_xactSound.m_waveBankData)
{
   UnmapViewOfFile(g_xactSound.m_waveBankData);
   g_xactSound.m_waveBankData = NULL;
}


// Shutdown COM.
CoUninitialize();
```

THE BUILDING BLOCKS ENGINE SOUND SYSTEMS

When it comes to sound, the design for the Building Blocks Engine was straightforward. For all three operating systems, it was desired to have them use the same sound system for all game audio operations by using OpenAL. It was also desired to create a simple XACT sound system that can be built upon over time to be used on the Windows OS and possibly on the Xbox 360. When thinking about how the sound system should be coded, it was decided that the easier route to take was to create wrappers around each of the main APIs. This would mean, using OpenAL as an example, that there would be a class for the source objects, sound buffers, and the OpenAL system itself. Each of the classes used for XACT and OpenAL was first mentioned in Chapter 1 and can be seen in Figure 3.8.

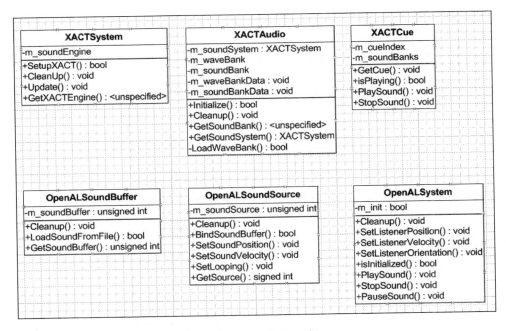

FIGURE 3.8   The Building Blocks Engine sound class diagrams.

The sound buffer will have a class that can load a sound from a file using ALUT, and the source object can have a class that has wrapper functions used to set the various properties of a source sound. For the sound buffer the only planned member variable that is an unsigned integer and the planned functions are called `Cleanup()`, `LoadSoundFromFile()`, and `GetSoundBuffer()`. The source sound class is planned to have an unsigned integer member variable for the source object, and the functions Cleanup(), BindSoundBuffer(), SetSoundPosition(), SetSoundVelocity(), SetLooping(), and GetSource(). Each of these functions is self-explanatory. The class declaration for the sound buffer class can be seen in Listing 3.27, and the source sound class can be seen in Listing 3.28.

LISTING 3.27 The OpenALSoundBuffer.

```
class OpenALSoundBuffer
{
   public:
      OpenALSoundBuffer() : m_soundBuffer(0)
      {

      }


      virtual ~OpenALSoundBuffer()
      {
         Cleanup();
      }


      void Cleanup()
      {
         if(m_soundBuffer)
            alDeleteBuffers(1, &m_soundBuffer);

         m_soundBuffer = 0;
      }


      bool LoadSoundFromFile(char *fileName)
      {
         m_soundBuffer = alutCreateBufferFromFile(fileName);

         if(alGetError() == AL_NO_ERROR)
         return true;

         return false;
      }
```

```
unsigned int GetSoundBuffer()
{
    return m_soundBuffer;
}

private:
    unsigned int m_soundBuffer;
};
```

LISTING 3.28   The OpenALSoundSource class.

```
class OpenALSoundSource
{
    public:
        OpenALSoundSource() : m_soundSource(0)
        {

        }


        virtual ~OpenALSoundSource()
        {
            Cleanup();
        }


        void Cleanup()
        {
            if(m_soundSource)
                alDeleteSources(1, &m_soundSource);

            m_soundSource = 0;
        }


        bool BindSoundBuffer(OpenALSoundBuffer &buff)
        {
            if(m_soundSource == 0)
                alGenSources(1, &m_soundSource);

            alSourcei(m_soundSource, AL_BUFFER,
buff.GetSoundBuffer());
```

```
           if(alGetError() == AL_NO_ERROR)
           return true;

           return false;
      }


      void SetSoundPosition(float x, float y, float z)
      {
         alSource3f(m_soundSource, AL_POSITION, x, y, z);
      }


      void SetSoundVelocity(float x, float y, float z)
      {
         alSource3f(m_soundSource, AL_VELOCITY, x, y, z);
      }


      void SetLooping(bool enable)
      {
         alSourcei(m_soundSource, AL_LOOPING, enable);
      }


      unsigned int GetSource()
      {
         return m_soundSource;
      }

   private:
      unsigned int m_soundSource;
};
```

The only thing left for an OpenAL sound system is the sound system itself. An OpenAL sound system would have to take a source object so it can be played, paused, and stopped. Since the framework will be working with 3D sounds in OpenAL, it also needs to be able to set the listener information within the sound system. The class's constructor and destructor functions are used to initialize and un-initialize the ALUT library. Listing 3.29 lists the OpenAL sound system's class.

LISTING 3.29   The `OpenALSystem`.

```
class OpenALSystem
{
   public:
      OpenALSystem()
      {
         alutInit(NULL, 0);
         m_init = true;

         if(alGetError() != AL_NO_ERROR)
         m_init = false;

         if(alutGetMajorVersion() != ALUT_API_MAJOR_VERSION &&
            alutGetMinorVersion() != ALUT_API_MINOR_VERSION)
         {
            m_init = false;
         }
      }


      virtual ~OpenALSystem()
      {
         Cleanup();
      }


      void Cleanup()
      {
         if(m_init == true)
            alutExit();

         m_init = false;
      }


      void SetListenerPosition(float x, float y, float z)
      {
         if(m_init == true)
            alListener3f(AL_POSITION, x, y, z);
      }
```

```
void SetListenerVelocity(float x, float y, float z)
{
   if(m_init == true)
      alListener3f(AL_VELOCITY, x, y, z);
}


void SetListenerOrientation(float dx, float dy, float dz,
                            float ux, float uy, float uz)
{
   float orientation[] = { dx, dy, dz, ux, uy, uz };

   if(m_init == true)
      alListenerfv(AL_ORIENTATION, orientation);
}


void PlaySound(OpenALSoundSource &source)
{
   if(m_init == true)
      alSourcePlay(source.GetSource());
}


void PauseSound(OpenALSoundSource &source)
{
   if(m_init == true)
      alSourcePause(source.GetSource());
}


void StopSound(OpenALSoundSource &source)
{
   if(m_init == true)
      alSourceStop(source.GetSource());
}


bool isInitialized()
{
   return m_init;
}
```

```
    private:
        bool m_init;
};
```

Each class in this section that is a part of the OpenAL sound system uses all the information we talked about earlier in this chapter. Since OpenAL and ALUT will perform much of the work, these classes are straightforward and small when compared to the classes seen for systems later in this book. The OpenAL sound system can be found on the companion CD-ROM in the BUILDING BLOCKS ENGINE/ SOURCE folder in the header file OpenALSystem.h.

ON THE CD

THE BUILDING BLOCKS ENGINE **XACT** SYSTEM

As seen earlier in this chapter, XACT is much different from OpenAL. In XACT, there is the XACT runtime engine, XACT sound cues, and audio resources for the sound and wave banks. When designing an XACT sound system, the same approach can be taken as was done with the OpenAL system by creating classes for the XACT system, sound cues, and audio resources. For the sound system, it is necessary to initialize the XACT API, release the API, and update the runtime (`DoWork()`). Each of the sound system's functions will wrap what has already been seen with the setup and cleanup of XACT, and the system's class can be seen in Listing 3.30. In the XACT sound system class, the only member variable is the XACT runtime object. The functions for the class include `SetupXACT()`, `Cleanup()`, `Update()`, and `GetXACTEngine()`. The implementation for the `XACTSystem` class can be seen in Listing 3.31, which can also be found in the file XACTSystem.cpp on the companion CD-ROM.

ON THE CD

LISTING 3.30 The `XACTSystem`.

```
class XACTSystem
{
    public:
        XACTSystem();
        virtual ~XACTSystem();


        bool SetupXACT();
        void Cleanup();
        void Update();


        IXACTEngine *GetXACTEngine()
        {
```

```
            return m_soundEngine;
        }


    private:
        IXACTEngine *m_soundEngine;
};
```

LISTING 3.31 The implementation for the XACTSystem class.

```
bool XACTSystem::SetupXACT()
{
    if(FAILED(XACTCreateEngine(XACT_FLAG_API_AUDITION_MODE,
        &m_soundEngine)))
        return false;

    if(m_soundEngine == NULL)
        return false;

    XACT_RUNTIME_PARAMETERS xparams = {0};
    xparams.lookAheadTime = 250;

    if(FAILED(m_soundEngine->Initialize(&xparams)))
        return false;

    return true;
}


void XACTSystem::Cleanup()
{
    if(m_soundEngine)
    {
        m_soundEngine->ShutDown();
        m_soundEngine->Release();
    }

    m_soundEngine = NULL;
}


void XACTSystem::Update()
{
```

```
    if(m_soundEngine)
        m_soundEngine->DoWork();
}
```

Audio resources can be made up of sound banks, wave banks, streaming wave banks, global categories, and more. This chapter discussed only sound and wave banks and how to play audio with them. The XACT audio resource class has as member variables the IXACTWaveBank and IXACTSoundBank objects, and handles (void*) to the files. The member functions include Cleanup(), Initialize(), and LoadBank(). Listing 3.32 lists the XACTAudio class from the Building Blocks Engine. The implementation for the XACTAudio class can be seen in Listing 3.33.

LISTING 3.32   The XACTAudio.

```
class XACTAudio
{
    public:
        XACTAudio();
        virtual ~XACTAudio();


        void Cleanup();


        bool Initialize(char *waveBank, char *soundBank,
                        XACTSystem *soundSystem);


    private:
        enum BB_BANK_TYPE { BB_WAVE_BANK_TYPE = 1,
                            BB_SOUND_BANK_TYPE };


        bool LoadBank(char *fileName, BB_BANK_TYPE bankType);


    public:
        IXACTSoundBank *GetSoundBank();
        XACTSystem *GetSoundSystem();


    private:
        XACTSystem *m_soundSystem;
```

```
        IXACTWaveBank *m_waveBank;
        IXACTSoundBank *m_soundBank;


        void *m_waveBankData;
        void *m_soundBankData;
};
```

LISTING 3.33 The implementation to the XACTAudio class.

```
void XACTAudio::Cleanup()
{
   if(m_soundBankData)
   {
      UnmapViewOfFile(m_soundBankData);
      m_soundBankData = NULL;
   }

   if(m_waveBankData)
   {
      UnmapViewOfFile(m_waveBankData);
      m_waveBankData = NULL;
   }

   m_soundSystem = NULL;
}


bool XACTAudio::Initialize(char *waveBank, char *soundBank,
                           XACTSystem *soundSystem)
{
   if(soundSystem == NULL)
      return false;

   m_soundSystem = soundSystem;

   if(m_soundSystem == NULL)
      return false;

   if(!LoadBank(waveBank, BB_WAVE_BANK_TYPE))
      return false;
```

```
    if(!LoadBank(soundBank, BB_SOUND_BANK_TYPE))
        return false;

    return true;
}


bool XACTAudio::LoadBank(char *fileName, BB_BANK_TYPE bankType)
{
    HANDLE file;
    DWORD fileSize;
    HANDLE mapFile;
    void *ptr;
    bool result = true;
    IXACTEngine *xactEngine = NULL;

    if(m_soundSystem == NULL)
        return false;

    file = CreateFile(fileName, GENERIC_READ, FILE_SHARE_READ,
                      NULL, OPEN_EXISTING, 0, NULL);

    if(file == INVALID_HANDLE_VALUE)
        return false;

    fileSize = GetFileSize(file, NULL);

    if(fileSize == -1)
    {
        CloseHandle(file);
        return false;
    }

    // Create memory mapped data since its faster.
    mapFile = CreateFileMapping(file, NULL, PAGE_READONLY,
                                0, fileSize, NULL);

    if(!mapFile)
    {
        CloseHandle(file);
        return false;
    }
```

```
ptr = MapViewOfFile(mapFile, FILE_MAP_READ, 0, 0, 0);

if(!ptr)
{
   CloseHandle(mapFile);
   CloseHandle(file);
   return false;
}

xactEngine = m_soundSystem->GetXACTEngine();

if(xactEngine != NULL)
{
   if(bankType == BB_WAVE_BANK_TYPE)
   {
      m_waveBankData = ptr;

      if(FAILED(xactEngine->CreateInMemoryWaveBank(m_waveBankData,
         fileSize, 0, 0, &m_waveBank)))
      {
         result = false;
      }
   }
   else
   {
      m_soundBankData = ptr;

      if(FAILED(xactEngine->CreateSoundBank(m_soundBankData,
         fileSize, 0, 0, &m_soundBank)))
      {
         result = false;
      }
   }
}
else
{
   result = false;
}

CloseHandle(mapFile);
CloseHandle(file);

return result;
}
```

The last object that is a part of the XACT sound system is the sound cue. The sound cue class will have the cue index as a member variable and the functions GetCue(), isPlaying(), PlaySound(), and StopSound(). The sound cue class is used directly to play, stop, or pause a sound in an application. Listing 3.34 lists the class declaration for the XACTCue class. Listing 3.35 lists the implementation for the XACTCue class.

LISTING 3.34   The XACTCue class.

```
class XACTCue
{
   public:
       XACTCue();
       virtual ~XACTCue();


       void GetCue(char *name, XACTAudio *audioBanks);


       bool isPlaying();
       void PlaySound();
       void StopSound();


    private:
       XACTINDEX m_cueIndex;
       XACTAudio *m_soundBanks;


   };
```

LISTING 3.35   The implementation for the XACTCue class.

```
void XACTCue::GetCue(char *name, XACTAudio *audioBanks)
{
   IXACTSoundBank *sBank = NULL;

   if(audioBanks == NULL)
       return;

   m_soundBanks = audioBanks;

   if(m_soundBanks != NULL)
       sBank = m_soundBanks->GetSoundBank();
```

```
      if(sBank != NULL)
         m_cueIndex = sBank->GetCueIndex("tap");
}


bool XACTCue::isPlaying()
{
   unsigned long state = 0;
   IXACTSoundBank *sBank = NULL;

   if(m_soundBanks == NULL)
      return false;

   if(m_soundBanks != NULL)
      sBank = m_soundBanks->GetSoundBank();

   if(sBank == NULL)
      return false;

   sBank->GetState(&state);

   if(state && XACT_CUESTATE_PLAYING)
      return true;

   return false;
}


void XACTCue::PlaySound()
{
   IXACTSoundBank *sBank = NULL;

   if(m_soundBanks != NULL)
      sBank = m_soundBanks->GetSoundBank();

   if(sBank != NULL)
      sBank->Play(m_cueIndex, 0, 0, NULL);
}


void XACTCue::StopSound()
{
   IXACTSoundBank *sBank = NULL;
```

```
    if(m_soundBanks != NULL)
        sBank = m_soundBanks->GetSoundBank();

    if(sBank != NULL)
        sBank->Stop(m_cueIndex, 0);
}
```

The XACT sound system can be found on the companion CD-ROM in the BUILDING BLOCKS ENGINE/SOURCE folder in the header file called XACTSystem.h and in the source file XACTSystem.cpp.

NETWORKING WITH SOCKETS

Playing a game over a network is an experience unto itself. The number of players available, the level of competition, and so forth are all heightened with the ability to connect a computer or game console to the Internet. The Internet is giving new life to games that are completed offline and can offer game developers the ability to expand a game beyond its release with additional content. On the Xbox 360, the industry is seeing how popular the Xbox Live Marketplace is becoming and how companies can generate additional revenue by offering premium content that was not available at the launch of a game title. Eventually, most media will be electronically distributed. Many media are already electronically distributed, and that will most likely continue to grow. This chapter is about networking in an application using sockets. At the end of the chapter, the networking system used by the Building Blocks Engine framework is discussed in detail.

WORKING WITH SOCKETS

Berkley sockets are objects that are used to connect to a network using TCP/IP and a client/server model. Sockets will work for Windows, Mac, and Linux with the same code with minor exceptions. For example, on Windows a socket has a data type of SOCKET, while on Mac and Linux it is just an integer (int). This chapter assumes some prior experience with sockets, and a refresher will be given in the next section. For additional detailed information, the various functions that make up the API can be looked up in documentation, with the MSDN being one possible source.

It was mentioned previously that there tends to be minor differences between the operating systems that are being supported by the Building Blocks Engine. This can first be seen with the need to call WSAStartup() before using sockets, and WSACleanup()when the application is done with sockets on Windows. These two functions are API functions on Windows that load and unload the Winsock dynamic link library. The WSAStartup() takes the version of Winsock it is to load and an address to a structure that will hold the details of the implementation, and WSACleanup() takes no parameters. Both function prototypes and examples of how they are used can be seen in Listing 3.36. On Windows, it is necessary to link the ws2_32.lib library to any projects that use sockets.

If a socket is opened by an application, it must be closed at some point. To close a socket, a call to closesocket() is used and takes as a parameter the socket to close. Once the socket is closed, it can be set to INVAILD_SOCKET, which is −1 on Windows. Listing 3.37 lists the function prototype and example use for the closesocket() function.

LISTING 3.36   WSAStartup() and WSACleanup() prototypes.

```
// Prototypes...
int WSAStartup(WORD wVersionRequested, LPWSADATA lpWSAData);
int WSACleanup(void);


// Usage Examples...
WSADATA WinSockData;
WSAStartup(MAKEWORD(2, 0), &WinSockData);

WSACleanup();
```

Sockets in Windows have the data type SOCKET. *On Mac and Linux, a socket is an integer. For non-Windows systems, a macro can be defined and used to match the Windows counterpart.*

LISTING 3.37   The closesocket() function prototype.

```
// Prototype...
int closesocket(SOCKET s);


// Usage Example...
SOCKET mainSocket = (open);

closesocket(mainSocket);
mainSocket = INVALID_SOCKET;
```

Hosting as a Server

Connections can be created to connect as a client or as a server. When working with sockets, there are blocking calls and nonblocking calls. A blocking call means that the function will wait for some action to occur indefinitely. When a blocking call is executed, the program continues to loop until whatever action the blocking call was waiting for occurs. With sockets, two main blocking call functions will be encountered in this chapter: `accept()` and `recv()`. To solve the problem of blocking calls with `accept()`, an application can call `ioctlsocket()` on Windows and `ioctl()` on non-Windows prior to calling it. The functions `ioctlsocket()` and `ioctl()` control the input/output mode of a socket and take as parameters the socket object, a command, and the argument. The command parameter when making the socket nonblocking prior to calling `accept()` is `FIONBIO` and the argument is 1. This will successfully make the socket nonblocking for accepting connections when it is acting as a server. When a nonblocking call is called, it executes once and then returns regardless if the action it was looking for occurs. Listing 3.38 lists the function prototypes for `ioctl()` and `ioctlsocket()`. These functions are pretty much the same with the exception that `ioctlsocket()` takes a socket of type `SOCKET` and an argument of type `unsigned long*`, while `ioctl()` takes a socket of type `int` and an argument of type `char*`. To combat these differences a macro can be created (e.g., `IOCTL_TYPE`), which will be defined on Windows as `unsigned long`, and `char` on non-Windows systems. In addition, on non-Windows systems a macro define can be created for `ioctlsocket` to be replaced by `ioctl`.

LISTING 3.38   Function prototype for `ioctl()` and `ioctlsocket()`.

```
int ioctl(int s, long cmd, char * argp);
int ioctlsocket(SOCKET s, long cmd, u_long* argp);
```

Four functions are called when setting up as a server: `socket()`, `bind()`, `accept()`, and `listen()`. `socket()` is used to create a new socket object and takes as parameters the address family, the socket type, a protocol flag, and returns a new socket. `bind()` is used to bind a socket to a port on the computer and takes as parameters the socket that is binding, a `sockaddr` structure address with all the information in it about the connection, and a size in bytes for the second parameter. `listen()` is used to listen for clients attempting to connect to the server, is called after a socket is bound to a port, and takes as parameters the socket that is listening and a size for the queue that will be used to hold the total number of pending connections. `accept()` is used to accept a client connection and takes as a parameter the socket for the server, a `sockaddr` structure address with the information describing the socket, and a size for the second parameter. `accept()` returns a client socket, and if that client is equal to `INVALID_SOCKET` (−1), there were no clients trying to connect.

Listing 3.39 lists the function prototypes for each of these functions. An example of setting up the server can be seen in Listing 3.40, which uses the socket(), bind(), and listen() functions, and an example of accepting a client's connection can be seen in Listing 3.41, which uses accept().

LISTING 3.39   Function prototypes for socket(), bind(), accept(), and listen().

```
SOCKET socket(int af, int type, int protocol);

int bind(SOCKET s, const struct sockaddr* name,
         int namelen);

SOCKET accept(SOCKET s, struct sockaddr *addr, int *addrlen);

int listen(SOCKET s, int backlog);
```

LISTING 3.40   Setting up a server socket.

```
sockaddr_in address;
unsigned long arg = 1;
SOCKET mainSocket;

mainSocket = socket(AF_INET, SOCK_STREAM, 0);

if(mainSocket == INVALID_SOCKET)
   return false;

memset(&address, 0, sizeof(sockaddr_in));
address.sin_family = AF_INET;
address.sin_addr.s_addr = htonl(INADDR_ANY);
address.sin_port = htons(port);

ioctlsocket(mainSocket, FIONBIO, &arg);

if(bind(mainSocket, (sockaddr*)&address, sizeof(sockaddr)) ==
   SOCKET_ERROR)
{
   return false;
}

if(listen(mainSocket, 32) == SOCKET_ERROR)
   return false;
```

LISTING 3.41   Accepting a client connection.

```
SOCKET client;
sockaddr_in addr;
int size = sizeof(sockaddr_in);
memset(&addr, 0, size);

client = accept(mainSocket, (struct sockaddr*)&addr, &size);

if(client == INVALID_SOCKET)
    return false;
```

Connecting to a Server

Connecting to a server requires a call to the connect() function. When connecting to another connection, an application is making that socket a client. The connect() function takes as parameters the socket the application is using to connect to some host, a sockaddr structure address with the information filled in it that describes who and how it will connect to the host, and the size of the second parameter.

When connecting to a server or setting up as a server, an application uses a sockaddr structure. This structure is a list of parameters that are set before calling the socket functions that are needed to either connect or set up as a server. This structure has all the information in it; for example, it has the host IP and port the application is connecting to if it is a client along with other necessary information. The function prototype for the connect() function and an example of how it is used can be seen in Listing 3.42.

LISTING 3.42   The connect() function prototype and example.

```
// Function prototype...
int connect(SOCKET s, const struct sockaddr *name, int namelen);


// Example of use...
sockaddr_in addr;
LPHOSTENT lphost;
char *serverIP = "192.168.1.1";
int port = 6000;
SOCKET mainSocket;

memset(&addr, 0, sizeof(sockaddr_in));
addr.sin_family = AF_INET;
addr.sin_addr.s_addr = inet_addr(serverIP);
```

```
// Set the host based on IP address.
if(addr.sin_addr.s_addr == INADDR_NONE)
{
    lphost = gethostbyname(serverIP);
}
else
{
    lphost = gethostbyaddr((const char*)&addr.sin_addr.s_addr, 4,
                           AF_INET);
}

if(lphost == NULL)
    return false;

addr.sin_addr.s_addr = ((LPIN_ADDR)lphost->h_addr)->s_addr;
addr.sin_port = htons(port);

mainSocket = socket(AF_INET, SOCK_STREAM, 0);

if(mainSocket == INVALID_SOCKET)
    return false;

if(connect(mainSocket, (struct sockaddr*)&addr,
    sizeof(sockaddr)) == SOCKET_ERROR)
{
    return false;
}
```

Sending and Receiving Information

Once a machine is set up as a server or is connected to a server, it is ready to start sending and receiving information. To send information from the application's socket to one that is connected to it requires a call to the function send(). send() takes as parameters the socket that is sending the information, the data it is sending as a character pointer, the size of the data being sent in bytes, and a list of flags that can be set to 0. Listing 3.43 lists the function prototype for send() and an example of how it is used.

LISTING 3.43 Sending data.

```
// Function prototype...
int send(SOCKET s, const char *buf, int len, int flags);
```

```
// Example of use...
char *ptr= (some data);
int size = (the size of the data in ptr);

send(mainSocket, ptr, size, 0);
```

To receive information from a connection, the application uses the function `recv()`. `recv()` is a blocking call, so a call to `ioctl()` (`ioctlsocket()` on Windows) can be made to test if there is any data waiting to be read. By using the `ioctl()` function the application can send to it as the command (second parameter) `FIONREAD`. By using `FIONREAD`, the third parameter will store the amount of bytes waiting to be read in by the socket. If the third parameter is 0, there is no data and the application can skip calling `recv()`. See Listing 3.44 for the `recv()` function prototype and an example of how it is used.

LISTING 3.44   Receiving data.

```
// Function prototype...
int recv(SOCKET s, char *buf, int len, int flags);



// Example of use...
ioctlsocket(mainSocket, FIONREAD, &readAmt);

if(readAmt > 0)
    recv(mainSocket, ptr, readAmt, 0);
```

THE BUILDING BLOCKS ENGINE NETWORKING SYSTEM

The design of the Building Blocks Engine networking system at first took quite a bit of planning. It was determined early on that the system should use sockets because the API is not difficult to work with, and sockets can be used on all the systems the Building Blocks Engine was to support. In Chapter 1, the class design documents for the networking system were shown, and can be seen again in Figure 3.9.

A class used to wrap around sockets was first conceived and designed. This class, `Socket`, had a single member variable that represented a socket and had functions to connect to a server, act as a server, send data, receive data, listen to a port, bind to a port, accept connections, and disconnect. The `Socket` class represents a single socket connection. If an application is set up as a server, it can accept connections. To accept a connection, another `Socket` class object will need to be created. This object can be passed to the member function `AcceptConnection()`, which

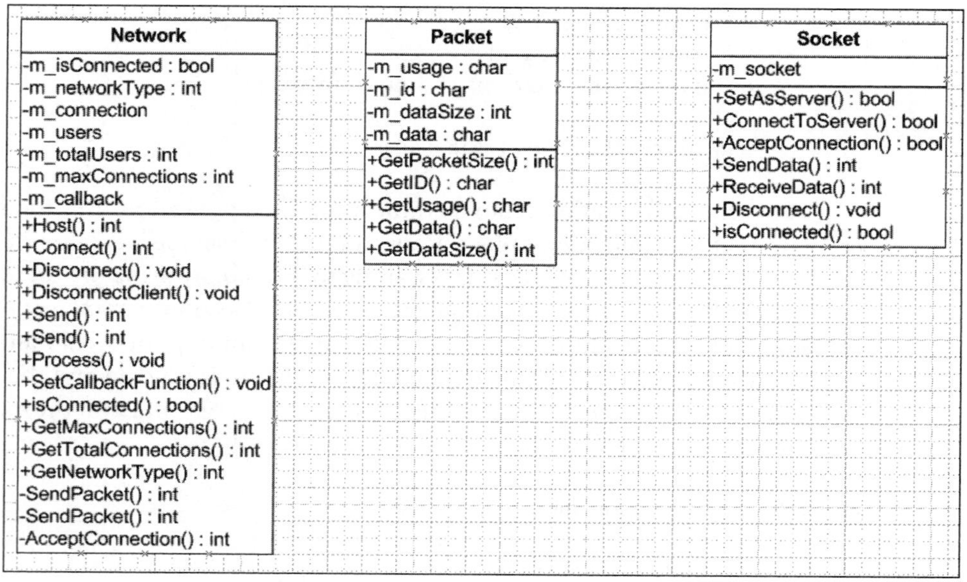

Network	Packet	Socket
-m_isConnected : bool	-m_usage : char	-m_socket
-m_networkType : int	-m_id : char	+SetAsServer() : bool
-m_connection	-m_dataSize : int	+ConnectToServer() : bool
-m_users	-m_data : char	+AcceptConnection() : bool
-m_totalUsers : int	+GetPacketSize() : int	+SendData() : int
-m_maxConnections : int	+GetID() : char	+ReceiveData() : int
-m_callback	+GetUsage() : char	+Disconnect() : void
+Host() : int	+GetData() : char	+isConnected() : bool
+Connect() : int	+GetDataSize() : int	
+Disconnect() : void		
+DisconnectClient() : void		
+Send() : int		
+Send() : int		
+Process() : void		
+SetCallbackFunction() : void		
+isConnected() : bool		
+GetMaxConnections() : int		
+GetTotalConnections() : int		
+GetNetworkType() : int		
-SendPacket() : int		
-SendPacket() : int		
-AcceptConnection() : int		

FIGURE 3.9 The class diagrams for the networking system.

will initialize the client socket that is trying to connect. This means that any application that is going to use this class must have one socket for the main application and one for each potential client. If a game allows 16 players at one time, this can translate to having one socket for the user's application and 15 for others that try to connect to the application. The Socket class can be seen in Listing 3.45.

LISTING 3.45 The socket class Socket.

```
class Socket
{
    public:
        Socket() { m_socket = INVALID_SOCKET; }
        virtual ~Socket() { Disconnect(); }

        bool SetAsServer(int port, int numPending);
        bool ConnectToServer(char *IP, int port);
        bool AcceptConnection(Socket &client);

        BNETWORKRESULT SendData(Packet &packet);
        BNETWORKRESULT ReceiveData(Packet &packet, int *bytesRead);
```

```
        void Disconnect();

        bool isConnected() { return (m_socket != INVALID_SOCKET); }

        bool operator==(Socket &s) { return(m_socket==s.m_socket); }
        void operator=(Socket &s) { m_socket = s.m_socket; }

        BB_SOCKET GetSocket() { return m_socket; }

    private:
        BB_SOCKET m_socket;
};
```

BNETWORKRESULT *and* BRESULT *are defined in the file Defines.h, and are actually* typedefs *for chars. The results returned by functions that use them are macro defines. For example,* BB_FAIL *is a define with the value 0.*

The parameters the SetAsServer() function takes is the port to bind to and the number of pending connections to allow. The ConnectToServer() function takes the IP address and the port to connect to. AcceptConnection() takes a client socket that will be initialized if a connection is pending. The SendData() and ReceiveData() functions take a packet of information to send, discussed later in this section. The ReceiveData() also takes as a second parameter the number of bytes that were read in successfully. Listing 3.46 lists the SetAsServer(), ConnectToServer(), and Accept-Connection() functions. Listing 3.47 lists the SendData(), ReceiveData(), and Disconnect() functions.

LISTING 3.46 The SetAsServer(), ConnectToServer(), and AcceptConnection() functions.

```
bool Socket::SetAsServer(int port, int numPending)
{
    sockaddr_in address;
    IOCTL_TYPE arg = 1;

    m_socket = socket(AF_INET, SOCK_STREAM, 0);

    if(m_socket == INVALID_SOCKET)
        return false;

    memset(&address, 0, sizeof(sockaddr_in));
    address.sin_family = AF_INET;
```

```cpp
   address.sin_addr.s_addr = htonl(INADDR_ANY);
   address.sin_port = htons(port);

   ioctlsocket(m_socket, FIONBIO, &arg);

   if(bind(m_socket, (sockaddr*)&address,
      sizeof(sockaddr)) == SOCKET_ERROR)
   {
      Disconnect();
      return false;
   }

   if(listen(m_socket, numPending) == SOCKET_ERROR)
      return false;

   return true;
}


bool Socket::ConnectToServer(char *serverIP, int port)
{
   sockaddr_in addr;
   LPHOSTENT lphost;

   memset(&addr, 0, sizeof(sockaddr_in));
   addr.sin_family = AF_INET;
   addr.sin_addr.s_addr = inet_addr(serverIP);

   if(addr.sin_addr.s_addr == INADDR_NONE)
      lphost = gethostbyname(serverIP);
   else
      lphost = gethostbyaddr((const char*)&addr.sin_addr.s_addr,
                             4, AF_INET);

   if(lphost == NULL)
   {
      WSASetLastError(WSAEINVAL);
      return false;
   }

   addr.sin_addr.s_addr = ((LPIN_ADDR)lphost->h_addr)->s_addr;
   addr.sin_port = htons(port);

   m_socket = socket(AF_INET, SOCK_STREAM, 0);
```

```
   if(m_socket == INVALID_SOCKET)
      return false;

   if(connect(m_socket, (struct sockaddr*)&addr,
      sizeof(sockaddr)) == SOCKET_ERROR)
   {
      Disconnect();
      return false;
   }

   return true;
}


bool Socket::AcceptConnection(Socket &client)
{
   sockaddr_in addr;
   int size = sizeof(sockaddr_in);
   memset(&addr, 0, size);

   client.m_socket = accept(m_socket, (struct sockaddr*)&addr,
                            &size);

   if(client.m_socket == INVALID_SOCKET)
      return false;

   return true;
}
```

LISTING 3.47 The SendData(), ReceiveData(), and Disconnect() functions.

```
   BNETWORKRESULT Socket::SendData(Packet &packet)
   {
      int sent = -1, size = 0;
      void *ptr = (char*)&packet;
      BNETWORKRESULT result = BB_DATA_SUCCESS;

      if(packet.GetPacketSize() <= 0)
         return BB_DATA_FAIL;

      size = packet.GetPacketSize();

      sent = send(m_socket, (char*)ptr, size, 0);
```

```
   if(sent == SOCKET_ERROR)
      result = BB_DATA_FAIL;


   if(sent != packet.GetPacketSize())
      result = BB_PARTIAL_DATA;


   return result;
}



BNETWORKRESULT Socket::ReceiveData(Packet &packet, int *bytesRead)
{
   int read = 0;
   unsigned long readAmt = 0, maxSize;
   void *ptr = (char*)&packet;
   BNETWORKRESULT result = BB_DATA_SUCCESS;

   maxSize = packet.GetPacketSize();

   if(maxSize <= 0)
      return BB_DATA_FAIL;

   if(ioctlsocket(m_socket, FIONREAD, &readAmt) != 0)
      result = BB_NO_DATA;

   if(readAmt == 0)
      result = BB_NO_DATA;

   if(readAmt > maxSize)
   {
      result = BB_PARTIAL_DATA;
      readAmt = maxSize;
   }

   read = recv(m_socket, (char*)ptr, readAmt, 0);

   if(read <= 0)
      result = BB_DATA_FAIL;

   if(bytesRead)
      *bytesRead = read;
```

```
    return result;
}


void Socket::Disconnect()
{
    if(m_socket != INVALID_SOCKET)
        closesocket(m_socket);

    m_socket = INVALID_SOCKET;
}
```

NETWORKING AND PACKET CLASSES

The next class is the Packet class, which is small, straightforward, and simple. A packet is a piece of information that is sent across a network (message). A packet in the Building Blocks Engine is one that is first made up of two IDs that are of a data type BPACKETVALUE (which is a typedef for char). These IDs are used by the application to determine what kind of packet it is so it knows what to do with it. The reason for this is that chars only go up to 256 (0 to 255). Therefore, instead of having a max ID of 255, having the additional value only adds one byte to the packet and gives a higher range if needed. The class could use a short since the short data type is two bytes, like using two char objects, but this method was thought to be clearer because each message can have a type identifier and a message identifier clearly specified. The two IDs are called usage (m_usage) and id (m_id) in the Packet class. Engine system messages have a usage of 0, so when creating packets in the Building Blocks Engine, applications must use 1 and up. System packets are packets that only the network system internally can send. These include disconnection messages, connection requests, and so forth and are not specific to any game. More on system messages later in this section.

The packet will also have a size for the data that is being sent along with the packet and the actual data. The data will be of type BPACKETVALUE (char), so casting will be used with creating packet objects. Figure 3.10 shows what a packet looks like. To keep things simple, the class will be using a max packet size, which is defined by a macro in the header file Defines.h, for the packet data. The class could have dynamic packet sizes, but that will further complicate the system. It might be worth looking into dynamic packet sizes later when improvements are being made to the framework. Listing 3.48 lists the Packet class declaration. In the packet class, all multibyte values are stored as little endian values. Whenever one of these values is requested, it is copied to a temporary variable, converted to the correct system endian if needed, and that temp variable is returned. This can be seen with the member variable m_dataSize in Listing 3.48.

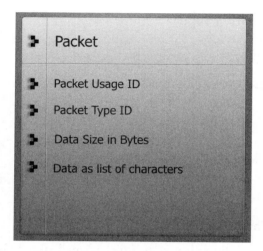

FIGURE 3.10 A visual look at packets.

LISTING 3.48 The Packet class.

```
class Packet
{
   public:
      Packet(BPACKETVALUE usage, BPACKETVALUE id,
            const char *data, int size)
      {
         m_usage = usage;
         m_id = id;
         m_dataSize = 0;
         m_data[0] = '\0';

         m_dataSize = size;

         if(data != NULL)
            memcpy(m_data, data, m_dataSize);

         Endian endian;
         endian.ResolveEndian((char*)&m_dataSize,
                              sizeof(m_dataSize),
                              BB_ENDIAN_LITTLE);
      }
```

```
virtual ~Packet()
{

}


int GetPacketSize() { return sizeof(*this); }
BPACKETVALUE GetUsage() { return m_usage; }
BPACKETVALUE GetID() { return m_id; }
BPACKETVALUE *GetData() { return m_data; }


int GetDataSize()
{
    Endian endian;
    int temp = m_dataSize;

    endian.ResolveEndian((char*)&temp, sizeof(temp),
                    BB_ENDIAN_LITTLE);

    return temp;
}


private:
    BPACKETVALUE m_usage;
    BPACKETVALUE m_id;
    int m_dataSize;
    BPACKETVALUE m_data[BB_MAX_PACKET_SIZE];
};
```

The last class in the networking system of the Building Blocks Engine is Network. The Network class has member variables that include a main socket, a list of client sockets that is used only if the application is hosting, a total connected user count, a max connections count, a function pointer to a callback function, and a flag for the network type. If the application is set up as a server, the network type will be marked as a server; otherwise, a client. The networking system class has member functions to host as a server, connect to a server, disconnect, disconnect a specific client (boot), send packets, accept connections, and a process (update) function.

The networking class was designed to be able to specify a max number of connections, which is game dependent. To send information, the class has two overloaded functions: one to send to all connected users, and the other to send to a specific user. The disconnect functions in the class are used to disconnect the server from all clients or from the server if the application is acting as a client. The over-loaded disconnect function takes a specific client to disconnect, which can be use-ful for booting users, and is only used if the class is acting as a server. The accept connection function `AcceptConnection()` will test if there is a pending connection trying to connect. If so, the next available client object is created and connected. If there is no more room or there is an error accepting the connection, the class can ignore the request since nothing can be done if there is no one trying to connect or couldn't for some reason.

The function of interest in this entire class is `Process()`, since the rest wrap around the `Socket` class and are straightforward. The purpose of this function is to receive data from connected users and process them and to look for new connec-tions if the application is acting as a host. The incoming data is processed by call-ing the callback function that is set to the class. The callback function, `m_callback`, is an application supplied function pointer that points to a function used to handle all messages. This is similar to Win32's message proc function. Whenever incom-ing data is received, it is passed to the callback function if a callback function was bound to the class. Inside the callback function, it can have a set of if statements to determine how the data was intended to be used (usage) and the type of data (type) that is being passed in. The `Process()` function is called once per frame to look for any new changes in the network. When something happens, be it a new connection, a new packet, and so forth, the class processes it. When a new user connects, a special system message is passed to the callback function. This message tells the application that a new connection was accepted. In a game, this can translate to displaying a message on the screen that someone has joined the game. Listing 3.49 lists the networking system class for the framework.

 `BB_NETWORK_CALLBACK()` *is a macro defined in defines.h and is just a function pointer. Using the macro takes less space than writing out* `void(*callback)(int,` `int, char*, int)`. *The define is for convenience.*

LISTING 3.49   The networking system class `Network`.

```
class Network
{
    public:
        Network(int maxConnections)
        {
            m_isConnected = 0,
            m_callback = NULL;
```

```
   m_networkType = BB_NETWORK_NULL;
   m_totalUsers = 0;
   m_users = NULL;

   if(maxConnections > 0)
   {
      m_users = new Socket[maxConnections];
      m_maxConnections = maxConnections;
   }
}

virtual ~Network()
{
   if(m_users != NULL)
   {
      delete[] m_users;
      m_users = NULL;
   }
}


BRESULT Host(int port, int numPending);
BNETWORKRESULT Connect(char *ip, int port);


void Disconnect();
void DisconnectClient(int index);


BNETWORKRESULT Send(Packet &packet)
{
   // ONLY SYSTEM MESSAGES CAN HAVE USAGE OF 0.
   if(packet.GetUsage() == 0)
      return BB_DATA_FAIL;

   return SendPacket(packet);
}

BNETWORKRESULT Send(Packet &packet, int sendTo)
{
   // ONLY SYSTEM MESSAGES CAN HAVE USAGE OF 0.
   if(packet.GetUsage() == 0)
      return BB_DATA_FAIL;
```

```
            return SendPacket(packet, sendTo);
        }


    private:
        BNETWORKRESULT SendPacket(Packet &packet);
        BNETWORKRESULT SendPacket(Packet &packet, int sendTo);


    public:
        void Process();

        void SetCallBackFunction(BB_NETWORK_CALLBACK(funcPtr))
        {
            m_callback = funcPtr;
        }


        bool isConnected() { return m_isConnected; }
        int GetMaxConnections() { return m_maxConnections; }
        int GetTotalConnections() { return m_totalUsers; }
        BB_NETWORK_TYPE GetNetworkType() { return m_networkType; }


    private:
        BRESULT AcceptConnection();


    private:
        bool m_isConnected;
        BB_NETWORK_TYPE m_networkType;

        Socket m_connection;
        Socket *m_users;
        int m_totalUsers;
        int m_maxConnections;

        BB_NETWORK_CALLBACK(m_callback);
};
```

The first functions in the class are Host(), AcceptConnection(), and Connect(). These functions more or less wrap around the Socket class' functions. Host() passes the parameters to the Socket class' SetAsServer() function and sets the network

class' member variables m_isConnected to true and m_networkType to BB_NETWORK_
SERVER, which flags it as a server.

AcceptConnection()calls the Socket class' AcceptConnection() function of the
next available client object. If all goes well, it will return true. Connect() is used only
by client setup connections. It passes the workload to the Socket class and returns
the result. All three functions can be seen in detail in Listing 3.50.

LISTING 3.50   The Host(), AcceptConnection(), and Connect() functions.

```
BRESULT Network::Host(int port, int numPending)
{
   if(m_connection.SetAsServer(port, numPending) == false)
      return BB_FAIL;

   m_isConnected = true;
   m_networkType = BB_NETWORK_SERVER;

   return BB_SUCCESS;
}


BNETWORKRESULT Network::Connect(char *ip, int port)
{
   if(m_connection.ConnectToServer(ip, port) == false)
      return BB_DATA_FAIL;

   m_isConnected = true;
   m_networkType = BB_NETWORK_CLIENT;

   return BB_DATA_SUCCESS;
}


BRESULT Network::AcceptConnection()
{
   if(m_networkType != BB_NETWORK_SERVER)
      return BB_FAIL;

   if(m_totalUsers >= m_maxConnections)
      return BB_FAIL;

   if(m_connection.AcceptConnection(m_users[m_totalUsers]) ==
      false)
      return BB_FAIL;
```

```
        m_totalUsers++;

        return BB_SUCCESS;
    }
```

The next functions in the networking class are `Disconnect()`, `Disconnect-Client()`, and `SendPacket()`. `Disconnect()` will disconnect the main socket and any clients that are connected to the application. However, before that is done, a message is sent to all clients that the server is disconnecting. That way, on the client's side they are not just dropped with no explanation. `DisconnectClient()` is the same way, but is only used if the connection is a server and it is used to kick (boot) a single user from the server. Listing 3.51 lists the two disconnect functions from the networking class of the framework.

LISTING 3.51   The disconnect functions.

```
void Network::Disconnect()
{
    int i = 0;
    BB_NETWORK_MESSAGE_TYPE type;

    if(m_networkType == BB_NETWORK_NULL)
        return;

    if(m_networkType == BB_NETWORK_SERVER)
        type = BB_MESSAGE_SERVER_DISCONNECT;
    else
        type = BB_MESSAGE_CLIENT_DISCONNECT;

    Packet packet(BB_NETWORK_SYSTEM_USAGE, type, NULL, 0);
    SendPacket(packet);

    for(; i < m_totalUsers; i++)
    {
        if(m_users[i].isConnected())
            m_users[i].Disconnect();
    }

    m_connection.Disconnect();
}
```

```
void Network::DisconnectClient(int index)
{
   BB_NETWORK_MESSAGE_TYPE type;

   if(m_networkType != BB_NETWORK_SERVER)
      return;

   type = BB_MESSAGE_FORCE_DISCONNECT;

   Packet packet(BB_NETWORK_SYSTEM_USAGE, type, NULL, 0);
   SendPacket(packet, index);

   if(index < m_totalUsers)
   {
      if(m_users[index].isConnected())
         m_users[index].Disconnect();
   }
}
```

The second to last two functions are the SendPacket() functions. The first of these functions is used to send a single packet to all connected clients if the connection is a server, or will send a packet to the server if the connection is a client. The second SendPacket() function is used only by servers to send information to a particular user. This can be useful if the client has requested some kind of information and is the only one that needs to receive it. Both SendPacket() functions can be seen in Listing 3.52.

LISTING 3.52 The SendPacket() functions.

```
BNETWORKRESULT Network::SendPacket(Packet &packet)
{
   int i = 0;

   if(m_networkType == BB_NETWORK_NULL)
      return BB_DATA_FAIL;

   if(m_networkType == BB_NETWORK_SERVER)
   {
      for(; i < m_totalUsers; i++)
      {
         if(SendPacket(packet, i) != BB_DATA_SUCCESS)
         {
```

```
                     if(m_callback)
                     {
                        m_callback(BB_NETWORK_SYSTEM_USAGE,
                                   BB_MESSAGE_SEND_ERROR,
                                   (char*)&i, sizeof(int));
                     }
                  }
               }
            }
            else
            {
               if(m_connection.SendData(packet) != BB_DATA_SUCCESS)
                  return BB_DATA_FAIL;
            }

            return BB_DATA_SUCCESS;
         }


         BNETWORKRESULT Network::SendPacket(Packet &packet, int sendTo)
         {
            if(sendTo < 0 || sendTo >= m_totalUsers)
               return BB_DATA_FAIL;

            if(m_networkType != BB_NETWORK_SERVER)
               return BB_DATA_FAIL;

            if(m_users[sendTo].isConnected() == false)
               return BB_NO_DATA;

            if(m_users[sendTo].SendData(packet) != BB_DATA_SUCCESS)
               return BB_DATA_FAIL;

            return BB_DATA_SUCCESS;
         }
```

The last function is Process(). The purpose of this function is to process the networking messages. It starts by checking for client connections, if this is a server calling this function. Next, it checks for any data that is to be received either from the server if this is a client, or from all clients if this is a server. Once it has that information, it passes it to the callback function so the application can process it as necessary. Since network messages are often game specific, the only thing the system can do is pass them to the callback function whenever messages come in. Listing 3.53 lists the `Process()` function from the `Network` class. If a callback function is not specified, packets can't be received and clients can't be accepted into the server.

LISTING 3.53   The `Process()` function.

```
void Network::Process()
{
   int i = 0, read = 0;
   Packet packet(0, 0, NULL, 0);

   if(m_networkType == BB_NETWORK_NULL)
      return;

   if(AcceptConnection())
   {
      if(m_callback)
      {
         m_callback(BB_NETWORK_SYSTEM_USAGE,
                    BB_MESSAGE_CONNECT_ACCEPTED,
                    NULL, 0);
      }
   }

   if(m_networkType == BB_NETWORK_SERVER)
   {
      for(; i < m_totalUsers; i++)
      {
         if(m_users[i].isConnected() == FALSE)
            continue;

         m_users[i].ReceiveData(packet, &read);

         if(read > 0)
         {
            if(m_callback)
            {
               m_callback((int)packet.GetUsage(),
                          (int)packet.GetID(),
```

```
                              packet.GetData(),
                              packet.GetDataSize());
                    }
                }
            }
        }
        else
        {
            m_connection.ReceiveData(packet, &read);

            if(read > 0)
            {
                if(m_callback)
                {
                    m_callback((int)packet.GetUsage(),
                            (int)packet.GetID(),
                            packet.GetData(),
                            packet.GetDataSize());
                }
            }
        }
    }
}
```

On the companion CD-ROM is an = application that demonstrates a simple client/server setup in a C++ console application. It is a small demo, but uses everything discussed in this chapter so far. The demo can be found in the BUILDING BLOCKS ENGINE/EXAMPLES/CHAPTER 3 folder and will run on Windows, Mac, and Linux.

SUMMARY

In this chapter, we created an input system that was able to detect input from keyboards, mice, and Xbox 360 controllers; a sound system for OpenAL and XACT to play audio files; and a networking system using sockets. The systems created in this chapter were simple and straightforward, which is one of the goals of the Building Blocks Engine. Because of the nature of these systems, many improvements can be made. Many of these ideas and topics are discussed in Chapter 10, "Conclusions." The next chapter deals with the first of the two chapters on the rendering system of the Building Blocks Engine.

CHAPTER EXERCISES

1. Using the DirectX SDK, add support for Xbox 360 headsets to the `XBOX360Controller` class. The DirectX SDK has an intermediate level demo application with all the information on how this can be done inside it.

2. Use OggVorbis for streaming audio files in OpenAL. For OggVorbis, an article on DevMaster.net in the articles section explains this in detail. Also, use streaming wave banks in XACT to add streaming audio to Microsoft's latest sound API. The DirectX SDK has a beginner-level demo application that shows how to do this.

3. In the network system, add varying packet sizes to the `Packet` class to replace the static sized array for sending data across a network.

Part II

Graphics and Environments

4 | Rendering Systems

In This Chapter

- Overview to Rendering
- Math Library
- Rendering Interface and Systems
- Render States and Geometry Types
- Resource Management
- Rendering

I n game development, a lot of time and effort are invested in graphics. Although graphics is not the only important area of game development, it is one of the top areas where many resources are dedicated to the task of making scenes pleasant to look at. In games, graphics is the area that is first noticed by gamers and is often a selling point for a game. As with many other areas of entertainment, the visual look of a product is very important. As graphics become more realistic, they also become more complex. This increase in complexity also increases the engineering efforts needed by a development team.

In this chapter is a discussion on the design and creation of the rendering system used by the Building Blocks Engine. We will cover rendering with the OpenGL API, programmable shaders using the OpenGL Shading Language, and rendering on Windows, Mac, and Linux operating systems. Chapter 5, "Rendering Scenes and Scene Graphs," will build on the information in this chapter to create the complete rendering system for the Building Blocks Engine. This chapter also discusses the various challenges that arose when developing the rendering system. The information presented in this chapter assumes that you have some prior experience and knowledge of OpenGL and high-level programmable shaders. If not, several resources can be found in Appendix A, "Additional Resources," that can help in learning about rendering and advanced graphical effects.

OVERVIEW TO RENDERING

Game graphics is a combination of mathematics, hardware power, and artwork. Today's games are primarily developed in three dimensions, and push the hardware that is available to its limits. When it comes to rendering, you must consider static geometry, animated geometry, special effects, GUIs, limitations in the target hardware, environment rendering, and much more. The goal of any rendering system for a real-time application is the performance speed at which scenes can be rendered. Bottlenecks in the rendering system can easily affect the overall application and hurt the performance observed by the end users. This performance hit often comes in the form of a reduced frame rate, which can also make a game hard to play or even unplayable.

On the PC, fast hardware rendering is done using rendering APIs such as OpenGL, Direct3D, and so forth. OpenGL is a very common and very popular cross-platform rendering API solution, and the Building Blocks Engine's design included support for OpenGL. For advanced graphics using programmable shaders, NVIDIA's Cg was chosen for the following reasons:

- Cg can be used on the Building Blocks Engine's supported operating systems Windows, Mac, and Linux.
- Cg can be used on the PlayStation 3, Xbox/Xbox 360, and other home gaming consoles.
- Adding new rendering systems outside of OpenGL to the Building Blocks Engine won't require the re-writing of shader files as long as it is supported by Cg.
- Cg can compile to high-level shading languages if needed (e.g., OpenGL's GLSL, Direct3D's HLSL, etc.).

The Building Blocks Engine focuses on 3D rendered scenes. Two-dimensional rendered scenes can be done with the same code, and since it is hardware accelerated, any 2D application built with the Building Blocks Engine should be fast. Additional tools and classes needed for 2D-specific topics can be added to the framework if necessary. In games, the most-used type of geometrical shape is the triangle. Triangles, also called polygons (which are defined as any shape made up of three or more connected points), are used a great deal in all modern 3D games. Graphics hardware is highly optimized and efficient at processing triangle polygons, so that is what the design of the Building Blocks Engine's rendering system focuses on.

When generating scenes, the amount of detail used in describing the geometry can help increase the realism of the rendered scenes; however, scenes are more than just polygons and are just one step toward creating realistic imagery. The problem with polygons is that there is a threshold that, when passed, can have a negative effect on performance. Another obstacle that can affect performance involves other issues like fill-rate, bottlenecks in the pipeline, and so forth. When it comes to adding detail to a scene, lighting and shadows play an important role in creating 3D images, and when combined in a game can be the something that takes scenes to another level. Programmable shaders are used to create realistic effects for the Building Blocks Engine. Many graphical techniques require post-processing capabilities, so off-screen rendering is also needed.

Normal mapping is a technique that can be used to somewhat sidestep the polygon count limitations of the hardware much like texture mapping was in the beginning of 3D games by simulating detail. Normal mapping is discussed in the next chapter and is a type of per-pixel lighting.

CONSIDERATIONS AND OBSTACLES

When rendering graphics on the PC, many things must be considered. One issue is the window creation process because it is operating system dependent. Creating a system with a higher level set of code that can allow the framework to give the perception of using the same code on multiple operating systems is not an easy task. For cross-platform APIs, like OpenGL, which depend on operating system–specific objects to initialize, the problem is even more complex. Even though OpenGL is cross platform, there are still objects OpenGL can use that are operating system specific in their creation and release. One example is the objects OpenGL needs when it has to swap rendering buffers from the primary buffer to the secondary, and vice versa. Another example is using objects such as p-buffers for off-screen rendering.

Another challenge that arises comes from the fact that the engine might need to be ported to other systems where OpenGL is not an option. What if a development team wanted to port the engine to the Xbox 360 or to the Nintendo Wii? Not considering or planning for another rendering API can cause many problems in porting the framework. The challenges in porting the rendering system can introduce bugs, take up many resources, and eat up a deal of development time. With OpenGL, challenges exist when working with OpenGL on multiple platforms. On Windows, the use of OpenGL extensions has different requirements than on Mac and Linux because on Windows, programmers have to manually obtain function pointers to the features they want to use from the OpenGL dynamic link libraries.

In the following sections, the OpenGL rendering system for the Building Blocks Engine will be carefully discussed in general and the system's implementation.

DESIGN OF THE RENDERING SYSTEM

When designing the rendering system for the Building Blocks Engine, it was important to come up with a few features necessary to achieve the rendering results implemented in the book demos later. In the future, if new features are desired they can be added to the rendering system at that time. Some general features planned for the Building Blocks Engine's rendering system include:

- OpenGL support for Windows, Mac, and Linux
- A common interface class that can be built upon when creating rendering systems for the framework
- Support for programmable shaders
- Resource management
- Implementation for common game math objects
- Culling tools
- The ability to render static meshes
- Simple scene graph

- Octree data structure for scene partitioning
- Simple portal rendering system
- 3D camera

Creating an interface class from which all rendering systems will derive can help to insure that all rendering systems are built from the same base and implement the same methods—which can make it easier to port the rendering system, if needed, to different rendering APIs. For individual graphical effects, the Building Blocks Engine has classes for each type. For example, there exists a texture mapping class that operates on a high enough level where it only needs to store handles to the resources it needs (shader and texture handles, for example), and calls the rendering system's functions, passed in as a base class, to perform the task. This also allows programmers using the framework to create their own effects by simply creating their own effect classes. More on this and resource handles later in this chapter.

Programmable shaders allow the ability to write code that runs on the graphics hardware. This allows developers to surpass the limitations of the fixed-function pipeline with their own routines and operations. Using shaders can also allow developers to create virtually any effect imaginable, which is not possible using the fixed-function pipeline alone. Developers can write their own code for effects, and can optimize them for the games based on the hardware. Programmable shaders can be either low level or high level. Since high-level languages are easier to develop and read, those shaders will be used in the Building Blocks Engine. The benefits to using high-level shading languages are similar to the benefits of programming applications in high-level languages like C and C++.

The Building Blocks Engine's rendering system will create a tool that can be used to manage resources. This is important because games re-use a lot of redundant information—textures, geometry models, animations, and so forth. The resource manager is responsible for keeping redundant data from being loaded more than once. This means that objects that use the same textures, shaders, models, and so forth will share those resources and limit the amount of memory consumed by the game application. Resources in the Building Blocks Engine will be stored in the manager. Access to these resources is done using handles. A handle in the Building Blocks Engine will boil down to an array index. The resource manager is discussed in more detail later in this chapter.

Games are math-intensive applications. Creating classes that represent the operations used in game development can allow the framework to have a common code set to work with. The Building Blocks Engine implements rays, planes, vectors, quaternions, matrices, and bounding geometry. The bounding geometry classes include axis-aligned bounding boxes, bounding spheres, and oriented bounding boxes for bounding volumes.

In games, many objects and polygons cannot be seen by the viewer at one time. These polygons can be behind the viewer, behind another object, and so forth. Rendering these objects even though they are not visible will take more resources and have a negative impact on the game's performance. For the Building Blocks Engine, the two culling methods that will be added to the framework are frustum culling and occlusion culling. Each is discussed further in this chapter in more detail.

The last feature the Building Blocks Engine implements in this version is the ability to draw static meshes, a simple scene graph used for object relationships, the ability to draw out a large polygon mesh using an octree, the ability to render an indoor scene using a portal rendering system, and a 3D camera. The need to draw static meshes is necessary. Using a scene graph allows the games to define relationships between the objects, and can be used for state management. Along with the scene graph, the ability to render data structures called an octree and a portal rendering system will also be implemented. Octrees can allow for fast culling of things like terrains and other types of environments and portals are an old but effective way to render environments that are made up of different sectors. The last item, the 3D camera, is used to allow the viewer to move around in the 3D environment. The ability to draw static meshes and 3D cameras are discussed later in this chapter, and the remaining items are discussed in the next chapter.

Math Library

The math is a huge part of game development. Math and numbers are used for representing geometry, graphics algorithms, physics, and collision detection and response, to name a few. Three-dimensional game engines need to have a strong math library to aid in the creation of the games that will be built from them. This section looks at the math classes used in the Building Blocks Engine, and includes vectors, matrices, quaternions, rays, bounding volumes, frustums, and planes. Game math encompasses many different types of math, such as physics, calculus, algebra, and much more. Therefore, it is important to have a solid understanding of different mathematics that go into games.

Vectors

Vectors are used heavily in 3D games. A vector represents a direction in a virtual space. In 3D games are 3D vectors that are made up of an X-, Y-, and Z-axis. For the

Building Blocks Engine, there is a class for 3D vectors called Vector3D. The 3D vector's axes are three floating-point variables. The member functions of the vector class are overloaded operators used to make working with the class easier. These operators include =, +, -, *, /, +=, -=, *=, and /=. The class also has functions to negate a vector, find the dot product between two vectors, find the magnitude of a vector, calculate the cross product between two vectors, and normalize a vector. These are very common operations to perform on vectors and are definitely something useful to add to a vector class. Listing 4.1 lists the 3D vector class declaration used in the Building Blocks Engine. The class Vector3D can be found on the companion CD-ROM in the BUILDING BLOCKS ENGINE/SOURCE folder in the header and source files Vector3D.h and Vector3D.cpp.

ON THE CD

LISTING 4.1   The Vector3D class.

```
class Vector3D
{
    public:
        Vector3D();
        Vector3D(scalar X, scalar Y, scalar Z);

        void Add(Vector3D &v1, Vector3D &v2);
        void Subtract(Vector3D &v1, Vector3D &v2);
        void Multiply(Vector3D &v1, Vector3D &v2);
        void Divide(Vector3D &v1, Vector3D &v2);

        void Add(Vector3D &v1, float f);
        void Subtract(Vector3D &v1, float f);
        void Multiply(Vector3D &v1, float f);
        void Divide(Vector3D &v1, float f);

        void operator=(Vector3D &v);
        void operator+=(Vector3D &v);
        void operator-=(Vector3D &v);
        void operator/=(Vector3D &v);
        void operator*=(Vector3D &v);

        Vector3D operator+(Vector3D &v2);
        Vector3D operator-(Vector3D &v2);
        Vector3D operator/(Vector3D &v2);
        Vector3D operator*(Vector3D &v2);
```

```
Vector3D operator+(float f);
Vector3D operator-(float f);
Vector3D operator/(float f);
Vector3D operator*(float f);

void Negate();
scalar Dot3(Vector3D &v);
scalar Magnitude();

void Normalize();
void Normalize(Vector3D &p1, Vector3D &p2,
               Vector3D &p3);

Vector3D CrossProduct(Vector3D &v);

float x, y, z;
};
```

For the Building Blocks Engine, the main operators are for addition, subtraction, multiplication, and division between both vectors and floating-point values. The addition of a vector can be seen in Equation 4.1. The multiplication, division, and subtraction are the same, but with different operators as seen in Equation 4.2. Each component is operated on when performing arithmetic similar to normal variables. By using overloaded operators, the entire structure can have an operation applied to it instead of working with one component at a time.

```
v3.x = v1.x + v2.x
v3.y = v1.y + v2.y
v3.z = v1.z + v2.z

v3.x = v1.x + f
v3.y = v1.y + f
v3.z = v1.z + f
```
(4.1)

```
Multiplication

v3.x = v1.x * v2.x
v3.y = v1.y * v2.y
v3.z = v1.z * v2.z

v3.x = v1.x * f
v3.y = v1.y * f
v3.z = v1.z * f
```

```
Subtraction
v3.x = v1.x - v2.x
v3.y = v1.y - v2.y
v3.z = v1.z - v2.z


v3.x = v1.x - f
v3.y = v1.y - f
v3.z = v1.z — f

Division
v3.x = v1.x / v2.x
v3.y = v1.y / v2.y
v3.z = v1.z / v2.z


v3.x = v1.x / f
v3.y = v1.y / f
v3.z = v1.z / f
```

(4.2)

Obtaining a vector's magnitude is also known as getting its length. When a vector has a length of 1, it is known as a unit-vector or a normal. Many calculations are done using unit-length vectors with many of those calculations dealing with lighting. To create a unit-length vector—in other words, to normalize a vector—the length of the vector is divided by each component that makes up the vector. Equation 4.3 shows how to get a vector's magnitude and how to normalize a vector. Figure 4.1 shows a visual of the equation in Equation 4.3.

$$\|V\| = \sqrt{V_x^2 + V_y^2 + V_z^2}$$

FIGURE 4.1   Normalizing a vector.

Length = sqrt(X * X + Y * Y + Z * Z)

X = X / Length
Y = Y / Length
Z = Z / Length

(4.3)

The dot product of a vector is similar to the length, but without the square root operation. In mathematics, the dot product is also known as the scalar product (and inner product) and is obtained by multiplying each component of two vectors together and then adding each. The purpose of a dot product is to find the measurement of difference between two vectors. Equation 4.4 shows how to get the dot product of two vectors *v1*, *v2*.

```
Dot product = (v1.x * v2.x + v1.y * v2.y + v1.z * v2.z)
```
(4.4)

The cross product, also known as the vector product or outer product, is used to find the vector that is orthogonal to two other vectors. One use of a cross product is when normalizing a triangle, which is done by finding two edge vectors, normalizing them, and getting the cross product between them. Equation 4.5 shows how to get the cross product of a vector, and Equation 4.6 shows how to normalize a triangle.

```
Result.x = y * v.z - z * v.y
Result.y = z * v.x - x * v.z
Result.z = x * v.y - y * v.x
```
(4.5)

```
edge1 = p1 - p2;
edge2 = p2 - p3;

edge1.Normalize();
edge2.Normalize();

this = CrossProduct(edge1, edge2);
Normalize(this);
```
(4.6)

The implementation to the Vector3D class can be seen in Listing 4.2. Each of the operations discussed up to this point is implemented into the class. For the arithmetic operations, overloaded operators are available for nonperformance critical code, and functions for performance-critical areas are also available.

LISTING 4.2 The implementation for the Vector3D class.

```
void Vector3D::Add(Vector3D &v1, Vector3D &v2)
{
    x = v1.x + v2.x;
```

```
   y = v1.y + v2.y;
   z = v1.z + v2.z;
}


void Vector3D::Subtract(Vector3D &v1, Vector3D &v2)
{
   x = v1.x - v2.x;
   y = v1.y - v2.y;
   z = v1.z - v2.z;
}


void Vector3D::Multiply(Vector3D &v1, Vector3D &v2)
{
   x = v1.x * v2.x;
   y = v1.y * v2.y;
   z = v1.z * v2.z;
}


void Vector3D::Divide(Vector3D &v1, Vector3D &v2)
{
   x = v1.x / v2.x;
   y = v1.y / v2.y;
   z = v1.z / v2.z;
}


void Vector3D::Add(Vector3D &v1, float f)
{
   x = v1.x + f;
   y = v1.y + f;
   z = v1.z + f;
}


void Vector3D::Subtract(Vector3D &v1, float f)
{
   x = v1.x - f;
   y = v1.y - f;
```

```
        z = v1.z - f;
    }


    void Vector3D::Multiply(Vector3D &v1, float f)
    {
        x = v1.x * f;
        y = v1.y * f;
        z = v1.z * f;
    }


    void Vector3D::Divide(Vector3D &v1, float f)
    {
        if(f != 0)
            f = 1 / f;

        x = v1.x * f;
        y = v1.y * f;
        z = v1.z * f;
    }


    void Vector3D::operator=(Vector3D &v)
    {
        x = v.x;
        y = v.y;
        z = v.z;
    }


    void Vector3D::operator+=(Vector3D &v)
    {
        x += v.x;
        y += v.y;
        z += v.z;
    }


    void Vector3D::operator-=(Vector3D &v)
    {
```

```
    x -= v.x;
    y -= v.y;
    z -= v.z;
}


void Vector3D::operator/=(Vector3D &v)
{
    x /= v.x;
    y /= v.y;
    z /= v.z;
}


void Vector3D::operator*=(Vector3D &v)
{
    x *= v.x;
    y *= v.y;
    z *= v.z;
}


Vector3D Vector3D::operator+(Vector3D &v2)
{
    return Vector3D(x + v2.x, y + v2.y, z + v2.z);
}


Vector3D Vector3D::operator-(Vector3D &v2)
{
    return Vector3D(x - v2.x, y - v2.y, z - v2.z);
}


Vector3D Vector3D::operator/(Vector3D &v2)
{
    return Vector3D(x / v2.x, y / v2.y, z / v2.z);
}
```

```
Vector3D Vector3D::operator*(Vector3D &v2)
{
   return Vector3D(x * v2.x, y * v2.y, z * v2.z);
}


Vector3D Vector3D::operator+(float f)
{
   return Vector3D(x + f, y + f, z + f);
}


Vector3D Vector3D::operator-(float f)
{
   return Vector3D(x - f, y - f, z - f);
}


Vector3D Vector3D::operator/(float f)
{
   return Vector3D(x / f, y / f, z / f);
}


Vector3D Vector3D::operator*(float f)
{
   return Vector3D(x * f, y * f, z * f);
}


void Vector3D::Negate()
{
   x = -x;
   y = -y;
   z = -z;
}


scalar Vector3D::Dot3(Vector3D &v)
{
   return x * x + y * y + z * z;
}
```

```
scalar Vector3D::Magnitude()
{
    return (scalar)sqrt(x * x + y * y + z * z);
}


void Vector3D::Normalize()
{
    scalar len = Magnitude();

    if(len <= 0.00001)
        len = 1;

    len = 1 / len;

    x *= len;
    y *= len;
    z *= len;
}


void Vector3D::Normalize(Vector3D &p1, Vector3D &p2, Vector3D &p3)
{
    Vector3D e1 = p1 - p2;
    Vector3D e2 = p2 - p3;

    e1.Normalize();
    e2.Normalize();

    *this = e1.CrossProduct(e2);
    Normalize();
}


Vector3D Vector3D::CrossProduct(Vector3D &v)
{
    return Vector3D(y * v.z - z * v.y,
                    z * v.x - x * v.z,
                    x * v.y - y * v.x);
}
```

MATRICES

Matrices are used greatly in 3D game development. In OpenGL and Direct3D, they mostly deal with 4×4 matrices, which are made up of 16 elements for a total of four rows and four columns, for both rotations and translations (3×3 for just rotations). Because 4×4 matrices are a large part of the rendering OpenGL API that will be implemented, matrices will be supported. A visual look at a 4×4 matrix can be seen in Figure 4.2. Matrices are implemented using an array of floating-point values. For 4×4 matrices, this is equal to an array of 16 with four rows and four columns.

$$M = \begin{vmatrix} m1 & m2 & m3 & m4 \\ m5 & m6 & m7 & m8 \\ m9 & m10 & m11 & m12 \\ m13 & m14 & m15 & m16 \end{vmatrix}$$

FIGURE 4.2 4×4 matrix visual.

Like the vector class, the `Matrix4x4` class in the Building Blocks Engine has support for overloading operators like =, -, +, *, and /. The matrix class also has functions for common matrix operations, such as set the matrix to an identity matrix, zero matrix, translations, inverse translations, inverse of a matrix, invert of a matrix, matrix rotations, scaling, and multiplying a vector by a matrix. Matrices are very important, but whenever possible, rotations will be done using quaternions since they are more efficient to work with. Listing 4.3 lists the matrix class, which can also be found on the companion CD-ROM in the BUILDING BLOCKS ENGINE/SOURCE folder in the header and source files Matrix4×4.h and Matrix4×4.cpp. A zero matrix is a matrix where all elements are 0, and an identity matrix is a matrix where the first, sixth, eleventh, and fifteenth elements are equal to 1, whereas all others are 0.

ON THE CD

LISTING 4.3   The `Matrix4x4` class.

```
class Matrix4x4
{
```

```cpp
public:
    Matrix4x4();
    Matrix4x4(float r11, float r12, float r13, float r14,
              float r21, float r22, float r23, float r24,
              float r31, float r32, float r33, float r34,
              float r41, float r42, float r43, float r44);

    void Add(Matrix4x4 &m1, Matrix4x4 &m2);
    void Subtract(Matrix4x4 &m1, Matrix4x4 &m2);
    void Multiple(Matrix4x4 &m1, Matrix4x4 &m2);

    void operator=(Matrix4x4 &m);
    Matrix4x4 operator-(Matrix4x4 &m);
    Matrix4x4 operator+(Matrix4x4 &m);
    Matrix4x4 operator*(Matrix4x4 &m);

    void Identity();
    void Zero();

    void Translate(Vector3D &v);
    void Translate(float x, float y, float z);

    Vector3D inverseTranslateVector(Vector3D &v);

    bool inverseMatrix(Matrix4x4 &m);
    void invertMatrix(Matrix4x4 &m);

    Vector3D VectorMatrixMultiply(Vector3D &v);
    Vector3D VectorMatrixMultiply3x3(Vector3D &v);
    Vector3D VectorMatrixMultiply3x3Inv(Vector3D &v);

    void Transpose(Matrix4x4 &m);

    void Scale(Vector3D &scale);

    void SetRotationRadians(double x, double y, double z);
    void Rotate(float angle, int x, int y, int z);
    void RotateAxis(double angle, Vector3D axis);
    void RotateX(double angle);
    void RotateY(double angle);
    void RotateZ(double angle);
```

```
        void CreateViewMatrix(Vector3D &pos, Vector3D &dir,
                              Vector3D &up, Vector3D &right);

        float matrix[16];
};
```

Each element of a matrix is added and subtracted linearly. For the overloaded minus and plus sign operators, this can be seen in Listing 4.4. Multiplication, on the other hand, is done by multiplying the row of the first matrix with the column of the second. This can be seen in Listing 4.5. The matrix class has support for both overloaded operators and straightforward functions similar to the vector class.

LISTING 4.4 The subtraction and addition of matrices.

```
Matrix4x4 Matrix4x4::operator-(Matrix4x4 &m)
{
    return Matrix4x4(matrix[0] - m.matrix[0],
                     matrix[1] - m.matrix[1],
                     matrix[2] - m.matrix[2],
                     matrix[3] - m.matrix[3],
                     // Row 2 start.
                     matrix[4] - m.matrix[4],
                     matrix[5] - m.matrix[5],
                     matrix[6] - m.matrix[6],
                     matrix[7] - m.matrix[7],
                     // Row 3 start.
                     matrix[8] - m.matrix[8],
                     matrix[9] - m.matrix[9],
                     matrix[10] - m.matrix[10],
                     matrix[11] - m.matrix[11],
                     // Row 4 start.
                     matrix[12] - m.matrix[12],
                     matrix[13] - m.matrix[13],
                     matrix[14] - m.matrix[14],
                     matrix[15] - m.matrix[15]);
}


Matrix4x4 Matrix4x4::operator+(Matrix4x4 &m)
{
    return Matrix4x4(matrix[0] + m.matrix[0],
                     matrix[1] + m.matrix[1],
```

```
            matrix[2] + m.matrix[2],
            matrix[3] + m.matrix[3],
            // Row 2 start.
            matrix[4] + m.matrix[4],
            matrix[5] + m.matrix[5],
            matrix[6] + m.matrix[6],
            matrix[7] + m.matrix[7],
            // Row 3 start.
            matrix[8] + m.matrix[8],
            matrix[9] + m.matrix[9],
            matrix[10] + m.matrix[10],
            matrix[11] + m.matrix[11],
            // Row 4 start.
            matrix[12] + m.matrix[12],
            matrix[13] + m.matrix[13],
            matrix[14] + m.matrix[14],
            matrix[15] + m.matrix[15]);
}
```

LISTING 4.5   The multiple of two matrices in the matrix class.

```
Matrix4x4 Matrix4x4::operator*(Matrix4x4 &m)
{
    return Matrix4x4(
        matrix[0] * m.matrix[0] + matrix[4] * m.matrix[1] +
        matrix[8] * m.matrix[2] + matrix[12] * m.matrix[3],
        matrix[1] * m.matrix[0] + matrix[5] * m.matrix[1] +
        matrix[9] * m.matrix[2] + matrix[13] * m.matrix[3],
        matrix[2] * m.matrix[0] + matrix[6] * m.matrix[1] +
        matrix[10] * m.matrix[2] + matrix[14] * m.matrix[3],
        matrix[3] * m.matrix[0] + matrix[7] * m.matrix[1] +
        matrix[11] * m.matrix[2] + matrix[15] * m.matrix[3],
        // Row 2 start.
        matrix[0] * m.matrix[4] + matrix[4] * m.matrix[5] +
        matrix[8] * m.matrix[6] + matrix[12] * m.matrix[7],
        matrix[1] * m.matrix[4] + matrix[5] * m.matrix[5] +
        matrix[9] * m.matrix[6] + matrix[13] * m.matrix[7],
        matrix[2] * m.matrix[4] + matrix[6] * m.matrix[5] +
        matrix[10] * m.matrix[6] + matrix[14] * m.matrix[7],
        matrix[3] * m.matrix[4] + matrix[7] * m.matrix[5] +
        matrix[11] * m.matrix[6] + matrix[15] * m.matrix[7],
```

```
                         // Row 3 start.
                         matrix[0] * m.matrix[8] + matrix[4] * m.matrix[9] +
                         matrix[8] * m.matrix[10] + matrix[12] * m.matrix[11],
                         matrix[1] * m.matrix[8] + matrix[5] * m.matrix[9] +
                         matrix[9] * m.matrix[10] + matrix[13] * m.matrix[11],
                         matrix[2] * m.matrix[8] + matrix[6] * m.matrix[9] +
                         matrix[10] * m.matrix[10] + matrix[14] * m.matrix[11],
                         matrix[3] * m.matrix[8] + matrix[7] * m.matrix[9] +
                         matrix[11] * m.matrix[10] + matrix[15] * m.matrix[11],
                         // Row 4 start.
                         matrix[0] * m.matrix[12] + matrix[4] * m.matrix[13] +
                         matrix[8] * m.matrix[14] + matrix[12] * m.matrix[15],
                         matrix[1] * m.matrix[12] + matrix[5] * m.matrix[13] +
                         matrix[9] * m.matrix[14] + matrix[13] * m.matrix[15],
                         matrix[2] * m.matrix[12] + matrix[6] * m.matrix[13] +
                         matrix[10] * m.matrix[14] + matrix[14] * m.matrix[15],
                         matrix[3] * m.matrix[12] + matrix[7] * m.matrix[13] +
                         matrix[11] * m.matrix[14] + matrix[15] * m.matrix[15]);
        }
```

The translation of a 4×4 matrix is done by setting the next to last three elements of the matrix to the position in question. The first three rows and columns deal with the rotational part of the matrix, while the translation deals with the last row. When working with 3×3 matrices, those are rotation matrices. The inverse translation of a matrix is the subtraction of its translation part from a 3D vector. These operations can be seen in Listing 4.6.

LISTING 4.6   Translating a matrix.

```
        void Matrix4x4::Translate(Vector3D &v)
        {
           matrix[12] = v.x;
           matrix[13] = v.y;
           matrix[14] = v.z;
           matrix[15] = 1.0f;
        }


        void Matrix4x4::Translate(float x, float y, float z)
        {
```

```
    matrix[12] = x;
    matrix[13] = y;
    matrix[14] = z;
    matrix[15] = 1.0f;
}


Vector3D Matrix4x4::inverseTranslateVector(Vector3D &v)
{
    return Vector3D(v.x - matrix[12],
                    v.y - matrix[13],
                    v.z - matrix[14]);
}
```

Transforming a vector by a matrix is a very useful and common operation to perform in games. By multiplying a vector against a matrix, a matrix can apply its information to the vector. This can be seen when transforming a vector from one space to another space. Equation 4.7 is used for transforming a vector by a matrix. Listing 4.7 lists the matrix code for transforming a vector by a 4×4 matrix, 3×3 matrix, and the inverse of a 3×3 matrix. The remaining functions of the `Matrix4x4` class can be found in the Matrix.h and Matrix.cpp files on the companion CD-ROM in the BUILDING BLOCKS ENGINE/SOURCE folder.

ON THE CD

$$v' = m * v \tag{4.7}$$

LISTING 4.7   Transforming a vector by a matrix.

```
Vector3D Matrix4x4::VectorMatrixMultiply(Vector3D &v)
{
    Vector3D out;

    out.x = (v.x * matrix[0]) + (v.y * matrix[4]) +
            (v.z * matrix[8]) + matrix[12];
    out.y = (v.x * matrix[1]) + (v.y * matrix[5]) +
            (v.z * matrix[9]) + matrix[13];
    out.z = (v.x * matrix[2]) + (v.y * matrix[6]) +
            (v.z * matrix[10]) + matrix[14];

    return out;
}
```

```
Vector3D Matrix4x4::VectorMatrixMultiply3x3(Vector3D &v)
{
   Vector3D out;

   out.x = (v.x * matrix[0]) + (v.y * matrix[4]) +
           (v.z * matrix[8]);
   out.y = (v.x * matrix[1]) + (v.y * matrix[5]) +
           (v.z * matrix[9]);
   out.z = (v.x * matrix[2]) + (v.y * matrix[6]) +
           (v.z * matrix[10]);

   return out;
}


Vector3D Matrix4x4::VectorMatrixMultiply3x3Inv(Vector3D &v)
{
   Vector3D out;

   out.x = (v.x * matrix[0]) + (v.y * matrix[1]) +
           (v.z * matrix[2]);
   out.y = (v.x * matrix[4]) + (v.y * matrix[5]) +
           (v.z * matrix[6]);
   out.z = (v.x * matrix[8]) + (v.y * matrix[9]) +
           (v.z * matrix[10]);

   return out;
}
```

RAYS

Rays have an origin and a direction, and are used in 3D graphics mostly for performing ray-traced operations, collision detection, and other things. Rays are simple in nature but powerful in their use. In the Building Blocks Engine, there is a class to represent rays. The ray class has two member variables for the origin and direction, which are both 3D vectors. The ray class also has functions to test for intersection (i.e., if a ray goes through something) with spheres, triangles, planes, and bounding volumes. With the code in the math library, it would be easy to create a simple ray tracer. Listing 4.8 is a look at the ray class Ray. A visual look at a ray can be seen in Figure 4.3.

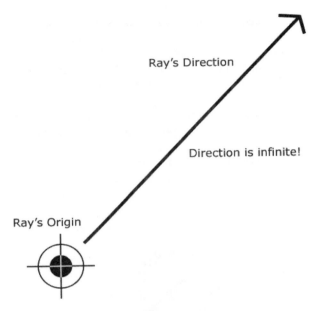

FIGURE 4.3   A visual look at rays.

The main operators done on rays are finding if a ray intersects an object so they are not visually drawn. The direction of a ray is a unit-length vector that infinitely points in a direction from the ray's origin. A ray can have a specified length if an infinite direction is not desired, which can be useful for many things such as limiting the range of a ray when testing for collision between it and another object. Using a sphere as an example, Figure 4.4 shows a visual of what a ray/sphere intersection looks like in 2D, while Listing 4.9 lists the ray/sphere intersection code from the Ray class.

LISTING 4.8   The Ray class.

```
class Ray
{
   public:
      Ray();
      Ray(Vector3D &origin, Vector3D &dir);

      bool Intersect(Vector3D &pos, float radius, float *dist);
```

```
bool Intersect(Vector3D &p1, Vector3D &p2,
               Vector3D &p3, bool cull, float *dist);

bool Intersect(Plane &pl, bool cull,
               Vector3D *intersectPoint, float *dist);

bool Intersect(Vector3D &bbMin, Vector3D &bbMax,
               Vector3D *intersectPoint);

Vector3D m_origin;
Vector3D m_direction;
};
```

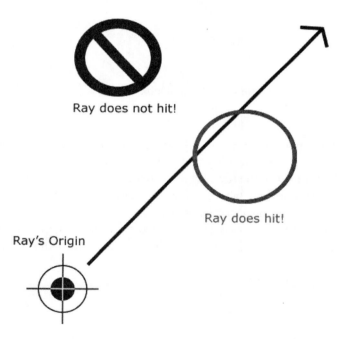

FIGURE 4.4 Testing rays to see if they intersect objects.

LISTING 4.9 Testing a sphere for intersection.

```
bool Ray::Intersect(Vector3D &pos, float radius, float *dist)
{
```

```
Vector3D RayToSphereDir;
float RayToSphereLength = 0.0f;
float IntersectPoint = 0.0f;
float SquaredPoint = 0.0f;

RayToSphereDir = pos - m_origin;
RayToSphereLength = RayToSphereDir.Dot3(RayToSphereDir);

IntersectPoint = RayToSphereDir.Dot3(m_direction);

if(IntersectPoint < 0 )
   return false;

SquaredPoint = (radius * radius) - RayToSphereLength +
               (IntersectPoint * IntersectPoint);

if(SquaredPoint < 0)
   return false;

if(dist)
   *dist = IntersectPoint - (float)sqrt(SquaredPoint);

return true;
}
```

BOUNDING VOLUMES

Bounding volumes are used to represent a geometrical object using a simplified shape. These shapes can be boxes, spheres, ellipsoids, cylinders, and so forth. The main purpose of bounding volumes is for fast culling and fast collision detection. By using a simplified piece of geometry like a bounding volume, there is a decrease in accuracy when they are used for things like collision detection. Often, this decrease in accuracy is acceptable for the speed gains that are realized.

In the Building Blocks Engine are three bounding volume classes. The first is for an axis-aligned bounding box, which is used to create a box that surrounds an object's extreme points on each axis. The second is a bounding sphere, used to create a sphere around an entire model using a center position and a radius. The third is for an oriented bounding box. Oriented bounding boxes differ from axis-aligned bounding boxes in that they specify three lengths along three axes instead of two points for the min and max extremes. An example of an axis-aligned bounding box can be seen in Figure 4.5, and the axis-aligned bounding box class, BoundingBox, can

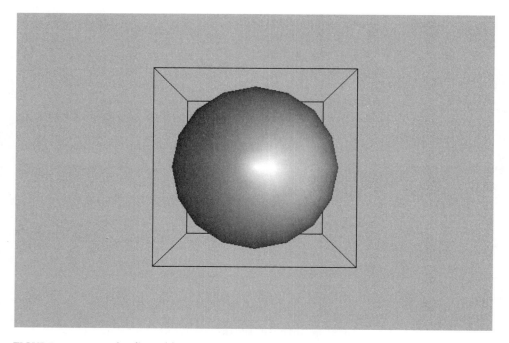

FIGURE 4.5 An axis-aligned bounding box.

be seen in Listing 4.10 and its implementation can be seen listed in 4.11. An example of a bounding sphere can be seen in Figure 4.6, and the class, `BoundingSphere`, can be seen in Listing 4.12 and its implementation can be seen in Listing 4.13. The last volume type, oriented bounding box (OBB), can be seen in Figure 4.7 and the class can be seen listed in Listing 4.14. Some of the functions in each of the bounding volume classes are used for physics and collisions. Those functions are discussed later in Chapter 6, "Physics," along with more detailed information on oriented bounding boxes. The remaining functions are self-explanatory, with functions like `Calculate()` that is used to calculate the bounding volume, `Translate()` that is used to move a bounding volume, and so forth.

LISTING 4.10 The `BoundingBox` class.

```
class BoundingBox
{
    public:
        BoundingBox();
```

```
BoundingBox(BoundingBox &aabb);

void Calculate(Vector3D *v, int numPoints);
void Expand(float amt);

void Translate(Vector3D v);

bool CollisionCheck(BoundingBox &aabb);
bool CollisionCheck(Vector3D &v);

Vector3D m_min, m_max, m_center;
};
```

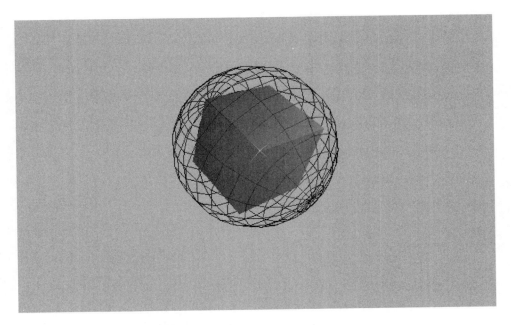

FIGURE 4.6   A bounding sphere (sphere drawn as a tri-mesh).

LISTING 4.11   The implementation for the BoundingBox class.

```
void BoundingBox::Calculate(Vector3D *v, int numPoints)
{
    int i = 0;
```

```
   for(i = 0; i < numPoints; i++)
   {
      if(v[i].x < m_min.x) m_min.x = v[i].x;
    if(v[i].x > m_max.x) m_max.x = v[i].x;

    if(v[i].y < m_min.y) m_min.y = v[i].y;
    if(v[i].y > m_max.y) m_max.y = v[i].y;

    if(v[i].z < m_min.z) m_min.z = v[i].z;
    if(v[i].z > m_max.z) m_max.z = v[i].z;
   }

   m_center = (m_min + m_max) * 0.5f;
}


void BoundingBox::Expand(float amt)
{
   m_max = m_max + amt;
   m_min = m_min - amt;
}


void BoundingBox::Translate(Vector3D v)
{
   m_min += v;
   m_max += v;
   m_center += v;
}


bool BoundingBox::CollisionCheck(BoundingBox &aabb)
{
   Vector3D b(aabb.m_min.x, aabb.m_max.y, aabb.m_min.z);
   Vector3D c(aabb.m_max.x, aabb.m_max.y, aabb.m_min.z);
   Vector3D d(aabb.m_max.x, aabb.m_min.y, aabb.m_min.z);
   Vector3D e(aabb.m_min.x, aabb.m_min.y, aabb.m_max.z);
   Vector3D f(aabb.m_min.x, aabb.m_max.y, aabb.m_max.z);
   Vector3D h(aabb.m_max.x, aabb.m_min.y, aabb.m_max.z);

   if(CollisionCheck(aabb.m_min) == true)
      return true;
```

```
    if(CollisionCheck(b) == true)
        return true;

    if(CollisionCheck(c) == true)
        return true;

    if(CollisionCheck(d) == true)
        return true;

    if(CollisionCheck(e) == true)
        return true;

    if(CollisionCheck(f) == true)
        return true;

    if(CollisionCheck(aabb.m_max) == true)
        return true;

    if(CollisionCheck(h) == true)
        return true;

    return false;
}


bool BoundingBox::CollisionCheck(Vector3D &v)
{
 if(m_max.x <= v.x)
        return false;

    if(m_min.x >= v.x)
        return false;

    if(m_max.y <= v.y)
        return false;

    if(m_min.y >= v.y)
        return false;

    if(m_max.z <= v.z)
        return false;
```

```
    if(m_min.z >= v.z)
        return false;

    return true;
}
```

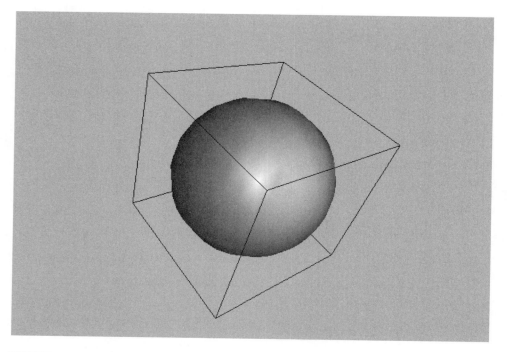

FIGURE 4.7 An oriented bounding box.

LISTING 4.12 The BoundingSphere class.

```
class BoundingSphere
{
    public:
        BoundingSphere();
        BoundingSphere(BoundingSphere &bs);
```

```
        void Calculate(Vector3D *v, int numPoints);

        bool CollisionCheck(BoundingSphere &bs);
        bool CollisionCheck(Vector3D &v);
        bool CollisionCheck(Vector3D &p1, Vector3D &p2,
                            Vector3D &p3);
        bool CollisionCheck(BoundingBox &aabb);

        Vector3D m_center;
        double m_radius;
    };
```

LISTING 4.13   The implementation for the `BoundingSphere` class.

```
    void BoundingSphere::Calculate(Vector3D *v, int numPoints)
    {
       float distance = 0.0f;
       float tempDist = 0.0f;
       int i = 0;

       for(i = 0; i < numPoints; i++)
       {

          tempDist = ((v[i].x - m_center.x) * (v[i].x - m_center.x)) +
                     ((v[i].y - m_center.y) * (v[i].y - m_center.y)) +
                     ((v[i].z - m_center.z) * (v[i].z - m_center.z));

          if(tempDist > distance)
             distance = tempDist;
       }

       m_radius = sqrt(distance);
    }


    void BoundingSphere::Translate(Vector3D v)
    {
       m_center += v;
    }
```

```
bool BoundingSphere::CollisionCheck(BoundingSphere &bs)
{
    Vector3D vec = m_center - bs.m_center;

    if(sqrt(vec.Dot3(vec)) < m_radius + bs.m_radius)
        return true;

    return false;
}


bool BoundingSphere::CollisionCheck(Vector3D &p1)
{
    Vector3D vec = m_center - p1;

    if(sqrt(vec.Dot3(vec)) < m_radius + 0.01f)
        return true;

    return false;
}


bool BoundingSphere::CollisionCheck(Vector3D &p1, Vector3D &p2,
                                    Vector3D &p3)
{
    if(CollisionCheck(p1) == true)
        return true;

    if(CollisionCheck(p2) == true)
        return true;

    if(CollisionCheck(p3) == true)
        return true;

    return false;
}


bool BoundingSphere::CollisionCheck(BoundingBox &aabb)
{
    Vector3D b(aabb.m_min.x, aabb.m_max.y, aabb.m_min.z);
    Vector3D c(aabb.m_max.x, aabb.m_max.y, aabb.m_min.z);
```

```
    Vector3D d(aabb.m_max.x, aabb.m_min.y, aabb.m_min.z);
    Vector3D e(aabb.m_min.x, aabb.m_min.y, aabb.m_max.z);
    Vector3D f(aabb.m_min.x, aabb.m_max.y, aabb.m_max.z);
    Vector3D h(aabb.m_max.x, aabb.m_min.y, aabb.m_max.z);

    if(CollisionCheck(aabb.m_min) == true)
       return true;

    if(CollisionCheck(b) == true)
       return true;

    if(CollisionCheck(c) == true)
       return true;

    if(CollisionCheck(d) == true)
       return true;

    if(CollisionCheck(e) == true)
       return true;

    if(CollisionCheck(f) == true)
       return true;

    if(CollisionCheck(aabb.m_max) == true)
       return true;

    if(CollisionCheck(h) == true)
       return true;

    return false;
}
```

LISTING 4.14   The OBB class.

```
class OBB : public Polytope
{
   public:
      OBB();
      OBB(OBB &obb);
      OBB(BoundingBox &aabb);
```

```
void Calculate(Vector3D *vertices, int numVerts);
void Calculate(BoundingBox &aabb);

void Transform(OBB &obb, Matrix4x4 &mat);
void ObjectTransform(OBB &obb, Matrix4x4 &mat);

void ProjectionInterval(Vector3D &axis, float &center,
                        float &ext, float &min,
                        float &max);

unsigned int GetSupport(Vector3D &axis,
                        Vector3D *contacts);


Vector3D GetFaceNormal(int index);
Vector3D GetEdgeDirection(int index);

// Accessor functions.
Vector3D GetCenterPos() { return m_center; };
void SetCenter(Vector3D &center) { m_center = center; }

float GetHalfAxis1() { return m_halfAxis1; }
float GetHalfAxis2() { return m_halfAxis2; }
float GetHalfAxis3() { return m_halfAxis3; }
float GetHalfAxis(int index);

void SetHalfAxis1(float val) { m_halfAxis1 = val; }
void SetHalfAxis2(float val) { m_halfAxis2 = val; }
void SetHalfAxis3(float val) { m_halfAxis3 = val; }

Vector3D GetAxis1() { return m_axis1; }
Vector3D GetAxis2() { return m_axis2; }
Vector3D GetAxis3() { return m_axis3; }

Vector3D GetAxis(int index);

void SetAxis1(Vector3D &axis) { m_axis1 = axis; }
void SetAxis2(Vector3D &axis) { m_axis2 = axis; }
void SetAxis3(Vector3D &axis) { m_axis3 = axis; }

// Members.
Vector3D m_center;
float m_halfAxis1, m_halfAxis2, m_halfAxis3;
Vector3D m_axis1, m_axis2, m_axis3;
};
```

CAMERAS AND FRUSTUMS

Three-dimensional games require the ability to move around environments in three dimensions. This is accomplished using a camera. There are various types of cameras: first-person cameras, third-person cameras, top-down camera, side-scrolling camera, and so forth. In OpenGL and Direct3D, cameras, or views, can be set by supplying the position, look direction, and up direction vectors to API functions. In OpenGL, for example, this function is `gluLookAt()`. Working with cameras requires us to create view matrices. These view matrices are in turn applied to the model matrix to create the model-view matrix. Combine this with the projection matrix and we have the model-view project matrix, or MVP. Combining two matrices together is done by multiplying them. Using a function like OpenGL's `gluLookAt()` will create and apply the view matrix for us. The only information this function needs is the view's position, the position it is looking at, and which direction points up. The `Matrix4x4` class discussed earlier in this chapter can construct a view matrix out of a camera's information.

The Building Blocks Engine has a camera class called `Camera`. The class has member functions to allow the camera to be moved, strafed (moved side to side), and rotated using quaternions. Rotation can happen around an axis using an angle. The remaining functions of the class are accessor get and set functions. The `Camera` class can be seen in Listing 4.15 and its implementation can be seen in Listing 4.16. The `MoveCamera()` function moves the position and the look-at position in a direction based on a set number of units (speed) using vector addition. The function used to strafe the camera moves the camera strictly to the left or to the right depending on if the speed is negative or positive. The rotation function creates a quaternion out of the axis and the angle, and then applies that quaternion to the right and view vectors. The member variables of this class can be used by OpenGL to set the view matrix.

LISTING 4.15   The `Camera` class.

```
class Camera
{
   public:
      Camera();

      Camera(Vector3D &pos, Vector3D &lookAt,
             Vector3D &up, Vector3D &right);


      void MoveCamera(Vector3D &direction, float speed);
      void StrafeCam(float speed);
```

```
            void RotateCamera(float angle, Vector3D &axis);

            void SetPosition(Vector3D &pos) { m_pos = pos; }
            void SetLookDirection(Vector3D &at) { m_lookAt = at; }
            void SetUpDirection(Vector3D &up) { m_up = up; }
            void SetRightDirection(Vector3D &right) { m_right = right; }

            Vector3D GetPosition() { return m_pos; }
            Vector3D GetLookDirection() { return m_lookAt; }
            Vector3D GetUpDirection() { return m_up; }
            Vector3D GetRightDirection() { return m_right; }


        private:
            Vector3D m_pos, m_lookAt, m_up, m_right;
    };
```

LISTING 4.16   The implementation for the Camera class.

```
        void Camera::MoveCamera(Vector3D &direction, float speed)
        {
           m_pos += direction * speed;
           m_lookAt += direction * speed;
        }


        void Camera::StrafeCam(float speed)
        {
           MoveCamera(m_right, speed);
        }


        void Camera::RotateCamera(float angle, Vector3D &axis)
        {
           Quaternion qRotation, qView, qNewView;

           qRotation.RotationAxisToQuaternion(angle, axis);

           qView.x = m_lookAt.x - m_pos.x;
           qView.y = m_lookAt.y - m_pos.y;
           qView.z = m_lookAt.z - m_pos.z;
           qView.w = 0;
```

```
        qNewView = ((qRotation * qView) * qRotation.Conjugate());

        m_right.x = m_pos.x + qNewView.x;
        m_right.y = m_pos.y + qNewView.y;
        m_right.z = m_pos.z + qNewView.z;

        m_lookAt.x = m_pos.x + qNewView.x;
        m_lookAt.y = m_pos.y + qNewView.y;
        m_lookAt.z = m_pos.z + qNewView.z;
    }
```

A frustum is a volume that encloses an area. In games, frustums are usually created out of the camera's view to create a volume that represents what can be seen. Objects can be tested against this volume to determine if the objects lie within the view frustum. If they do, the objects can be drawn; otherwise, they are culled out (not drawn). This process can speed rendering times because it is often much less work to test an object's bounding volume against a frustum to see if it is visible rather than rendering the entire model. This increase in performance can add up for many different objects. A visual example of a frustum can be seen in Figure 4.8.

Another use of a frustum is to cull entire sections of an environment. In 3D games, the fewer polygons processed the better. This translates to only rendering what can be seen. For environments, data structures are used to split the world into hierarchies of bounding volumes. These bounding volumes can be tested against the frustum. If a section of the world is not visible, it and its leaf nodes are skipped and not drawn. One example of such a data structure is an octree. An octree splits a world recursively into bounding boxes. By being able to discard a parent node in the tree, the algorithm can also discard the child nodes because the children can't be visible if the parent is not. This allows for fast processing of a 3D scene and allows only what is visible to be drawn, which speeds renderings. Another example of a data structure used to split up an environment is a binary space partitioning (BSP) tree. The Frustum class can be seen in Listing 4.17. The frustum is calculated by creating planes from the view-projection matrix as seen in Listing 4.18. The coordinate type that is passed to the function used to create a frustum can be either left- or right-handed. The coordinate system (e.g., OpenGL uses right-handed system while Direct3D uses left) will determine if the planes are flipped so that they point inward and objects can be correctly tested. Otherwise, with left-handed systems, the planes will face the wrong way and all objects inside the frustum will be read as being outside and all outside objects will be read as being inside.

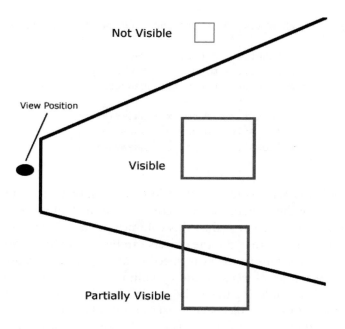

FIGURE 4.8   An example of a frustum.

LISTING 4.17   The Frustum class.

```
class Frustum
{
   public:
      Frustum();

      void CalculateFrustum(float angle, float ratio, float near,
                            float far, Vector3D &camPos,
                            Vector3D &lookAt, Vector3D &up);

      void AddPlane(Plane &pl);
      bool GetPlane(int index, Plane *out);
      int GetTotalPlanes() { return (int)m_frustum.size(); }

      bool isPointVisible(float x, float y, float z);
      bool isSphereVisible(float x, float y, float z,
                           float radius);
```

```
    bool isCubeVisible(float x, float y, float z, float size);
    bool isBoxVisible(Vector3D min, Vector3D max);
    bool isOBBVisible(OBB &obb);

private:
    std::vector<Plane> m_frustum;
};
```

LISTING 4.18   Creating a frustum.

```
void Frustum::CalculateFrustum(float angle, float ratio,
                               float near, float far,
                               Vector3D &camPos, Vector3D &lookAt,
                               Vector3D &up)
{
    Vector3D xVec, yVec, zVec;
    Vector3D vecN, vecF;
    Vector3D nearTopLeft, nearTopRight,
             nearBottomLeft, nearBottomRight;
    Vector3D farTopLeft, farTopRight,
             farBottomLeft, farBottomRight;

    float radians = (float)tan((DEG_TO_RAD(angle)) * 0.5);
    float nearH = near  * radians;
    float nearW = nearH * ratio;
    float farH = far    * radians;
    float farW = farH   * ratio;

    zVec = camPos - lookAt;
    zVec.Normalize();

    xVec = up.CrossProduct(zVec);
    xVec.Normalize();

    yVec = zVec.CrossProduct(xVec);

    vecN = camPos - zVec * near;
    vecF = camPos - zVec * far;

    nearTopLeft     = vecN + yVec * nearH - xVec * nearW;
    nearTopRight    = vecN + yVec * nearH + xVec * nearW;
    nearBottomLeft  = vecN - yVec * nearH - xVec * nearW;
    nearBottomRight = vecN - yVec * nearH + xVec * nearW;
```

```
        farTopLeft      = vecF + yVec * farH - xVec * farW;
        farTopRight     = vecF + yVec * farH + xVec * farW;
        farBottomLeft   = vecF - yVec * farH - xVec * farW;
        farBottomRight  = vecF - yVec * farH + xVec * farW;

        m_frustum.clear();

        Plane plane;

        plane.CreatePlaneFromTri(nearTopRight, nearTopLeft,
                                 farTopLeft);
        AddPlane(plane);

        plane.CreatePlaneFromTri(nearBottomLeft, nearBottomRight,
                                 farBottomRight);
        AddPlane(plane);

        plane.CreatePlaneFromTri(nearTopLeft, nearBottomLeft,
                                 farBottomLeft);
        AddPlane(plane);

        plane.CreatePlaneFromTri(nearBottomRight, nearTopRight,
                                 farBottomRight);
        AddPlane(plane);

        plane.CreatePlaneFromTri(nearTopLeft, nearTopRight,
                                 nearBottomRight);
        AddPlane(plane);

        plane.CreatePlaneFromTri(farTopRight, farTopLeft,
                                 farBottomLeft);
        AddPlane(plane);
    }
```

PLANES AND QUATERNION OBJECTS

The last two types of math classes that are a part of the Building Blocks Engine are planes and quaternions. A plane is an infinitely small surface that extends along two axes, and is defined by a direction (direction it is facing) and a distance (D) from the origin. Planes are used mostly for collisions and culling, which is seen in later chapters. The Plane class for the Building Blocks Engine can be seen in Listing 4.19.

The Plane class has member functions that allow users to create a plane from a triangle, intersect two planes, intersection with bounding volumes, classification functions to determine where an object lines in relation to the plane, and a member function to get the distance a vector is from the plane. Planes are usually made up of four floating-point values, with the first three being a normal vector and the last being the distance. The equation for a plane is commonly written as:

$$Ax + By + Cz + D = 0$$

A quaternion is used to represent a rotation. Quaternions are better than matrices because they can be represented using 4 floating-point variables instead of 9 or 16, are more efficient, and do not suffer from gimbal lock like matrices when Euler angles are used. The Quaternion class used by the Building Blocks Engine will have member functions to allow users to get the magnitude of a quaternion, normalization of a quaternion, conjugate, cross product between two quaternions, to interpolate between two quaternions spherically, and two functions used to convert a quaternion to a matrix and a matrix to a quaternion. Listing 4.20 lists the Quaternion class.

LISTING 4.19   The Plane class.

```
class Plane
{
    public:
        Plane();
        Plane(scalar A, scalar B, scalar C, scalar D);

        void CreatePlaneFromTri(Vector3D &t1,
                                Vector3D &t2,
                                Vector3D &t3);

        bool Intersect(Plane &pl, Vector3D *intersectPoint);
        bool Intersect(Vector3D &bbMin, Vector3D &bbMax);
        bool Intersect(Vector3D &position, float radius);
        bool Intersect(OBB &obb);

        BB_PLANE_STATUS ClassifyPoint(Vector3D &v);
        BB_PLANE_STATUS ClassifyPoint(Vector3D &v, float *dist);
        BB_PLANE_STATUS ClassifyPoint(float x, float y, float z);
        BB_PLANE_STATUS ClassifyPoint(float x, float y, float z,
                                      float *dist);
```

```
        scalar GetDistance(Vector3D &v);
        scalar GetDistance(float x, float y, float z);

        Vector3D Reflect(Vector3D &vec, float e);

        bool ClipTriangle(Vector3D *inVerts, int totalInVerts,
                          Vector3D *outFrontVerts,
                          int *totalOutFrontVerts,
                          Vector3D *outBackVerts,
                          int *totalOutBackVerts);

        Vector3D GetNormal();
        void SetNormal(Vector3D n);

        void SetPointOnPlane(Vector3D p);

        bool operator==(Plane p);
        void operator=(Plane p);


        float a, b, c, d;
        Vector3D m_pointOnPlane;
};
```

LISTING 4.20 The Quaternion class.

```
class Quaternion
{
   public:
      Quaternion();
      Quaternion(const Quaternion &q);
      Quaternion(float X, float Y, float Z, float W);

      Quaternion operator*(const Quaternion &q);
      void operator=(const Quaternion &q);

      float Magnitude();
      void Normalize();
      Quaternion Conjugate();
```

```
void RotationAxisToQuaternion(float angle, Vector3D &axis);
void EulerToQuaternion(Vector3D &euler);

Quaternion CrossProduct(const Quaternion &q);

void CreateMatrix(float *matrix);
void MatrixToQuaternion(float *matrix);

void Slerp(const Quaternion &q1, const Quaternion &q2,
           float t);

float w, y, z, x;
};
```

RENDERING INTERFACE AND SYSTEMS

All rendering systems will derive from a base render interface class in the Building
Blocks Engine. The render interface will contain all the functions that will be exposed to the application. One of these functions will have to be an initialize
method. The problem with an initialize method is that it requires users to pass in
objects and variables that are dependent on the operating system. For example, to
initialize a WGL OpenGL window will require an HDC device context, HRGC rendering context, and so forth. On the Mac, the system will be using AGL and requires
objects used only on the Mac. Another issue to consider is the number of parameters an initialize function can take. The system will need to define things like resolution width and height, color bits, depth bits, and many other things. Instead of
having a few dozen parameters, some of which can be OS specific, or trying to create a complex method, the system will use a different approach—a special parameter class. The motivation for the parameter class came from Direct3D's present
parameters structure. The parameters class, RenderParams, can store information
such as full-screen mode, resolution, buffer bits, OS window information, and
information about the vertex cache, which is the vertex buffer object used for
rendering. The window-specific objects are handled by a class called WindowHandle.
A WindowHandle object is a member variable in the parameter class. The purpose
of the WindowHandle class is to sneak OS-specific variables into the rendering system without the high-level system being aware. The member variables of the
WindowHandle are set using #define macros depending what OS the code is being

compiled on. An example of using such a class can be seen in Listing 4.21 using the Windows OS (the OS-specific object is in bold). The parameters in a game application can be set with values from a file that is specific to a game as well. This can be done using a property script, which is discussed later in this book.

LISTING 4.21   Setting up the parameters.

```
int WINAPI WinMain(HINSTANCE h, HINSTANCE p, LPSTR cmd, int show)
{
    bbe::CRenderParams params;
    params.m_colorBits = 24;
    params.m_depthBits = 16;
    params.m_stencilBits = 8;
    params.m_fullscreen = true;
    params.m_width = 800;
    params.m_height = 600;
    params.m_maxCacheBytes = 2000;
    params.m_maxCacheIndices = 2000;
    params.m_handle.m_hInstance = hInstance;


    if(!DemoInitialize(&params))
    {
        MessageBox(NULL, "Error in initialize!", "Error", MB_OK);
    }
    else
    {
        ... GAME LOOP ...
    }

    ... SHUTDOWN ...
}
```

As mentioned previously in this book, games today use many resources. Many of these resources are shared among the different objects in the game world, and can include:

■ Textures
■ Shaders
■ Geometry
■ Scripts

- Audio files
- Materials
- Animations

All games need someway to manage this data in a high level and efficient way. If resources can be shared among objects, they should, to save the amount of memory an application is consuming. Such a resource manager can be a class that has a list of objects that outside code references either by a pointer, an ID, and so forth.

The Building Blocks Engine will have a simple class used to handle resources in a game. This class is used as a resource manager and is a template class. The primary use for the resource manager is to hold textures, shaders, and character models, to name a few. Resources are accessed from the resource manager using handles. For each resource, a handle will be created. A handle in the framework is a template class that wraps around an integer index. This index is used as an array into the resource list in the resource manager. Creating different handles for each type of resource allows the handles meant for one manager (e.g., textures) to only work with that one manager. The texture handle is defined in the same file as the rendering base interface class, since all rendering systems will use it along with the rendering parameters class. Both the texture handle and render parameters can be seen in Listing 4.22. Both of these are defined in the file RenderInterface.h on the companion CD-ROM in the BUILDING BLOCKS ENGINE/SOURCE folder. More variables can be added to the parameters class during the development of the engine if the need arises to have more functionality. More information on the resource manager appears later in this chapter.

LISTING 4.22   Texture handle and render parameters.

```
struct stTexture { };
typedef bbe::Handle<bbe::stTexture> BB_TEXTURE;


class RenderParams
{
  public:
    RenderParams()
    {
        m_fullscreen = 0;
        m_width = m_height = 0;
        m_colorBits = m_depthBits = m_stencilBits = 0;
        m_maxCacheBytes = m_maxCacheIndices = 0;
    }
```

```
public:
    bool m_fullscreen;
    int m_width, m_height;
    int m_colorBits, m_depthBits, m_stencilBits;
    int m_maxCacheBytes, m_maxCacheIndices;

    WindowHandle m_handle;
};
```

When creating a rendering system, there are a few different options. One would be to use a singleton design pattern to create a class where only one instance of it can exist in an application. A second option would be to use inheritance by creating classes that derive from a general base. The second option allows for new rendering systems to be created by deriving from a base. The downside is that it is harder to implement new functionality into those classes or to modify existing interfaces. A third option would be to use other design patterns such as the decorator pattern. The decorator pattern allows for new features and functionality to be added to classes, but it is harder to create new systems using this pattern, which is the opposite of the second option of using inheritance. For the Building Blocks Engine, inheritance is used mostly because it is easier to grasp and is more common than various design patterns, although both have their pros and cons.

The render interface class of the rendering system for the engine is `RenderInterface`. The first few functions of this class are virtual initialization, shutdown, view port, and resizing functions. The initialize function can take as a parameter an object of the `RenderParams` class. The function used to shut down the system cleans up everything that was used by the rendering class. The function to set the view port does just that by specifying the window dimensions. The functions used to resize the window reset the projection matrix using perspective projection and orthogonal projection. Each of these functions can be seen in Listing 4.23, which is a partial look at the `RenderInterface` class.

LISTING 4.23   Partial look at the `RenderInterface` class.

```
class RenderInterface
{
    BB_RTTI_EXPOSE_TYPE;

public:
    RenderInterface();
    virtual ~RenderInterface();
```

```
virtual BRESULT Initialize(const RenderParams *params);
virtual void Shutdown() = 0;


virtual void SetViewPort(int x, int y, int width,
                         int height) = 0;

virtual void ResizeWindow(float fov, float nearDist,
                          float farDist, int width,
                          int height) = 0;

virtual void ResizeWindowOrtho(int left, int right,
                               int bottom, int top,
                               float nearDist,
                               float farDist) = 0;
};
```

The rendering system will have a way to clear the screen to a specified color and to start and stop rendering. For clearing, the buffers the code will allow for clearing the color buffer, depth buffer, and stencil buffers are also the buffers that are most used by the OpenGL rendering API. For the function used to start rendering, it can receive Boolean values to determine which buffers to clear. Another option would be to use flags and bit operators so we can have a single parameter that can be used to set several different values—this isn't necessary but could be preferred. The function used to end a rendering will swap the buffers.

The next three functions that will be added to the RenderInterface class are used to enable and disable various rendering states and to set the alpha state. Enabling/disabling states can include depth buffering, texture mapping, alpha blending, and so forth and is similar to how OpenGL can toggle states by using the API functions glEnable() and glDisable(). The function that deals with the alpha specifically is used for alpha blending by setting the alpha function. Listing 4.24 lists the second partial look at the RenderInterface class.

LISTING 4.24   The second partial look at the RenderInterface class.

```
class RenderInterface
{
      virtual void SetClearColor(int r, int g, int b, int a) = 0;
      virtual void StartRendering(bool color, bool depth,
                                  bool stencil) = 0;
      virtual void EndRendering() = 0;
```

```
virtual BRESULT Enable(BB_RENDER_STATE state) = 0;
virtual BRESULT Disable(BB_RENDER_STATE state) = 0;
virtual void SetAlphaFunc(BB_ALPHA_STATE state,
                          float val) = 0;
};
```

When working in 3D there is a need to get around the virtual space. There exists the option of setting the view matrix and the model view matrix (also projection, texture, etc.), and that will be used in the rendering system for the framework. For the view matrix, the rendering API can use a virtual camera that is used to specify a viewer's location, look direction, and which way is up. In the RenderInterface class is a function called SetView() that can set the view matrix of the 3D scene. In OpenGL and Direct3D, it is not necessary to have to manually calculate the matrix because the option to use API functions will do the work. For example, in OpenGL this can be done by calling gluLookAt() to set a view. Since more than one matrix can be manipulated, other functions in the rendering class are used to switch the current matrix, load an identity matrix, apply a matrix, and to push and pop matrices off a stack. Each of these functions would be simple in nature and easy to use. The ease of these functions comes from the fact that the rendering API class will wrap around the underlying graphics API and have it do the work with matrices. When it comes to the view matrix, the Matrix4x4 class can calculate it and the results can be multiplied to the current model-view matrix by using the Multiply-ToCurrentMatrix() function of the rendering system, which will be discussed in the upcoming paragraphs.

The functions used to manipulate the matrices talked about in the last paragraph are SetView(), SetMatrix(), SwitchMatrixType(), GetMatrix(), MultiplyTo CurrentMatrix(), LoadIdentityMatrix(), PushMatrix(), and PopMatrix(). The functions dealing with the matrices of the render interface class can be seen in Listing 4.25. Additional functions used to manipulate the current matrix are RotateMatrix() and TranslateMatrix() and are used to perform rotations and translations. Listing 4.26 lists the enumerations for the type of matrix the functions are working with, the format of the matrix (identity, inverse, transpose, etc.), and matrices used for the type of projections being supported. These enumerations are defined in Defines.h, which is located in the BUILDING BLOCKS ENGINE/SOURCE folder on the companion CD-ROM.

ON THE CD

LISTING 4.25   The matrix manipulation functions of the RenderInterface.

```
class RenderInterface
{
```

```
    virtual void SetView(float posX, float posY, float posZ,
                         float lookX, float lookY, float lookZ,
                         float upX, float upY, float upZ) = 0;


    virtual void SetMatrix(const float *matrix) = 0;
    virtual void MultiplyToCurrentMatrix(const float *m) = 0;
    virtual BRESULT SwitchMatrixType(BB_MATRIX_TYPE type) = 0;
    virtual void GetMatrix(BB_MATRIX_TYPE type,
                           float *matrix) = 0;


    virtual void RotateMatrix(float angle, float x,
                              float y, float z) = 0;
    virtual void TranslateMatrix(float x, float y, float z) = 0;


    virtual void LoadIdentityMatrix() = 0;
    virtual void PushMatrix() = 0;
    virtual void PopMatrix() = 0;
};
```

LISTING 4.26   Matrix-related enumerations in defines.h.

```
    enum BB_MATRIX_TYPE { BB_PROJECTION_MATRIX = 1,
                          BB_MODELVIEW_MATRIX,
                          BB_TEXTURE_MATRIX, BB_MVP_MATRIX };


    enum BB_MATRIX_FORMAT { BB_IDENTITY_MATRIX = 1,
                            BB_TRANSPOSE_MATRIX,
                            BB_INVERSE_MATRIX,
                            BB_INVERSE_TRANSPOSE_MATRIX };


    enum BB_PROJECTION_TYPE { BB_PROJECTION_NULL = 0,
                              BB_PERSPECTIVE_TYPE,
                              BB_ORTHO_TYPE };
```

Texture mapping in the Building Blocks Engine will use 2D textures or cube maps. For texture mapping, there will be functions to load textures from a file or from memory. The load from memory functions will be used to load textures that have been loaded from an archive file. The engine framework will support .TGA texture images. Other types can be added if desired later. TGA textures are the only supported type. When it comes to cube maps, a custom cube map file format is created for the Building Blocks Engine (more on cube maps in the next chapter).

To load a texture, the application must specify the name of the texture (file-name if loading from a file), the type of texture (2D or cube), and a handle that will be used to represent the texture resource. It was mentioned previously that textures will be managed by a resource manager. The handles are used for accessing loaded texture data from the management system, which will be looked at later in the chapter. Additionally, there will be a function used to create empty textures. This will be useful for off-screen rendering where the contents of the texture aren't filled until sometime after the texture has been created. All functions that deal with the creation of a texture—whether from a file, empty, etc.—will need to specify some name for the resource. This is used by the resource manager to check for duplicates of texture resources.

The remaining functions that deal with textures are used to create an off-screen surface, apply a texture, delete a texture handle, apply filters to a texture, and add a texture to a render target's color unit. Deleting a texture handle just means making its index to an invalid value such as –1. A function in the rendering system to do this isn't necessary, but some users using the framework might find it natural to use the same system that created a handle to release it. The function used to apply filters will apply a list of filters to an image. For example, the filter list might tell the rendering system to enable bi-linear filtering on the image.

Each of these topics can be seen by their functions in Listing 4.27. These functions are `ApplyFilters()`, `AddEmptyTexture()`, `LoadTexFromFile()`, `LoadTexFromMemory()`, `ApplyTexture()`, `DeleteTextures()`.

LISTING 4.27   Texture functions of the `RenderInterface`.

```
class RenderInterface
{
   public:
      virtual void ApplyFilters(BB_TEXTURE &handle,
                                BB_FILTER_LIST_PTR filters) = 0;

      virtual bool AddEmptyTexture(char *name, int width,
                                   int height,
                                   int components,
                                   BB_TEXTURE_TYPE type,
                                   BB_TEXTURE_FORMAT format,
                                   BB_TEXTURE *handle) = 0;
```

```
virtual bool LoadTexFromFile(char *fileName,
                             BB_TEXTURE_TYPE type,
                             BB_TEXTURE *handle) = 0;

virtual bool LoadTexFromMemory(char *name, char *fileData,
                               int length,
                               BB_TEXTURE_TYPE type,
                               BB_TEXTURE *handle) = 0;

virtual bool ApplyTexture(int texUnit,
                          BB_TEXTURE &handle) = 0;

virtual void DeleteTexture(BB_TEXTURE &handle) = 0;
};
```

Programmable shaders are important in the Building Blocks Engine. In this engine, the framework will be using GLSL shader. For the rendering interface class, there needs to be a way to create shaders, apply shaders, and set various uniform parameters. The creation of a shader will create a GLSL shader object upon success, which can be used to apply an effect later. When setting parameters, various functions can be used such as setting a single float-point value, three values, four, and so on. In addition, a function used to bind textures to shader uniform variables is added to the interface. Along with a class for the GLSL shader, another class exists in the framework used for individual parameters. When binding parameters in the rendering system, the only items needed are the parameter object and a value.

The create and apply shader functions are CreateShaderFromFile(), Create ShaderFromMemory(), and ApplyShader() and are straightforward. CreateShader FromFile() will take a shader filename and an out pointer handle to the created shader, while ApplyShader() will take the shader to enable. The CreateShaderFrom Memory() function takes the same parameters as its counterpart with the exception that the first parameter is the file data instead of a filename. Parameters for GLSL are wrapped in a class, GLSLParameter, which is looked at later in this chapter. When binding to parameters in a shader file, a function is used, SetupShaderParameter(), which will take the parameter's name in the shader file, the shader in which it is located (vertex or pixel), the shader object, and an out pointer to the filled-in GLSL parameter object.

LISTING 4.28 Shader functions of the `RenderInterface`.

```
class RenderInterface
{
   public:
      virtual bool CreateShaderFromFile(char *vs, char *ps,
                                  ShaderHandle *handle) = 0;

      virtual bool CreateShaderFromMemory(char *vsFile,
                                  char *psFile,
                                  ShaderHandle *handle) = 0;

      virtual void ApplyShader(ShaderHandle shader) = 0;

      virtual void SetupShaderParameter(char *pname,
                                  ShaderHandle shader,
                                  ParameterHandle *param) = 0;

      virtual void SetShaderParameter1i(ParameterHandle param,
                                  float val) = 0;

      virtual void SetShaderParameter1f(ParameterHandle param,
                                  float val) = 0;

      virtual void SetShaderParameter2f(ParameterHandle param,
                                  float x, float y) = 0;

      virtual void SetShaderParameter3f(ParameterHandle param,
                                  float x, float y,
                                  float z) = 0;

      virtual void SetShaderParameter4f(ParameterHandle param,
                                  float x, float y,
                                  float z, float w) = 0;
};
```

The final piece of the framework's render interface is the need to render some geometry and the rendering interface's class member variables. The first member variable is used to set the clear color (RGBA) of the color buffers. The next member variables are used to store whether certain features are supported. This is used because some pieces of hardware might or might not support some features the rendering system can attempt. The last member variables deal with GLSL contexts and profile versions.

When rendering a model, the system will need some information. The first piece of information is the vertices that are a part of the geometry. The problem is that this information can vary. For example, a user of the system might have a 3D position and a set of texture coordinates for one model, and might have a position, texture coordinate, a normal, and a tangent for another. One option is to always restrict the programmers of the engine to use a vertex structure that is pre-specified, but not all cases need to use the same information. For example, if a user were just drawing out a texture object, he wouldn't have to specify normal data or S and T tangets. If the rendering system tried to create individual functions for every possible case, the setup will limit the use of the framework and make the system large and messy. Another option would be to take the Direct3D approach and allow users to create their own vertex structures and tell the rendering system how it is laid out. This will give the system much more flexibility and will not limit it in any way. This is the approach taken by the Building Blocks Engine's rendering system.

The rendering system has a single function used to draw out information—`Render()`. This function takes the vertices as a list of custom per-vertex information (e.g., positions, texture coordinates, etc.), a number of total vertices, list of indices, and total number of indices, vertex stride, a vertex descriptor, and the primitive type. The vertices are the list of vertices that make up the model that are cast to a character pointer. The stride of the vertices specifies the total number of bytes that make up each vertex. For example, an x, y, and z position along with a set of texture coordinates would be 3 * 4 for the position and 2 * 4 for the texture cords (which equals 20 bytes). The primitive type can be a triangle list, point list, triangle fan, and so forth. The vertex descriptor tells the rendering system how the data is laid out. The vertex descriptor is a class called `VertexDescriptor` that simply has a list of flags. The order of these flags tells the system the order of the data. For example, if the custom vertex structure that is being passed in has a 3D position and a pair of texture coordinates, the flags in the vertex descriptor will start with a flag that represents a 3D vertex followed by a flag that represents a 2D texture coordinate pair. The vertex descriptor class will be looked at later in this chapter. Listing 4.29 lists the final section of the `RenderInterface` class `RenderInterface`.

LISTING 4.29   The last part of the `RenderInterface` class.

```
class RenderInterface
{
    public:
```

```
    virtual void Render(BB_PRIMITIVE_TYPE type,
                        VertexDescriptor *desc,
                        char *vertexData,
                        unsigned int *indices,
                        int totalVertices,
                        int totalIndices) = 0;

protected:
    int m_red, m_green, m_blue, m_alpha;
    bool m_multiTexSupport, m_cubeMapSupport;

    RenderParams m_params;

    CGcontext m_cgContext;
    CGprofile m_vsProfile, m_psProfile;
};
```

RENDER STATES AND GEOMETRY TYPES

The Enable() and Disable() functions take as a parameter a BB_RENDER_STATE variable. This parameter variable is an enumeration and can be used to set depth testing, texture mapping, and so forth to the on or off state. For the texture mapping filtering functions, the parameters are an array of BB_FILTER_TYPE variables. These variables are used to set different filter properties like linear filtering on the min and mag, anisotropic filtering, and so forth. There is also an enumeration called BB_TEXTURE_TYPE and BB_TEXTURE_FORMAT that was seen earlier. The BB_TEXTURE_TYPE can be either BB_TEX2D_TYPE or BB_CUBE_TYPE for 2D and cube map textures. The BB_TEXTURE_FORMAT can be, at this time, BB_TEX_UNSIGNED_BYTE and BB_TEX_FLOAT for unsigned character and floating-point textures.

ON THE CD

The render state, filter type, texture type, and texture formation enumerations can be seen in Listing 4.30. On the companion CD-ROM, these enumerations and defines are in the Defines.h header file in the BUILDING BLOCKS ENGINE/ SOURCE folder.

LISTING 4.30 Rendering enumerations.

```
enum BB_RENDER_STATE { BB_DEPTH_TESTING = 1, BB_SMOOTH_SHADING,
                       BB_TEXTURE_2D, BB_TEXTURE_CUBE,
                       BB_TOTAL_RENDER_STATES };
```

```
enum BB_FILTER_TYPE { BB_NO_FILTER = 0, BB_MIN_POINT_FILTER,
                      BB_MAG_POINT_FILTER, BB_MIP_POINT_FILTER,
                      BB_MIN_LINEAR_FILTER, BB_MAG_LINEAR_FILTER,
                      BB_MIP_LINEAR_FILTER, BB_USE_ANSIO_FILTER,
                      BB_S_REPEAT_FILTER, BB_T_REPEAT_FILTER,
                      BB_S_CLAMP_FILTER, BB_T_CLAMP_FILTER,
                      BB_S_EDGE_CLAMP_FILTER,
                      BB_T_EDGE_CLAMP_FILTER };


enum BB_TEXTURE_TYPE { BB_TEX2D_TYPE = 1, BB_CUBE_TYPE };


enum BB_TEXTURE_FORMAT { BB_TEX_UNSIGNED_BYTE = 1, BB_TEX_FLOAT };
```

GEOMETRY PRIMITIVES

Rendering geometric objects is done using custom defined vertex structures. To help make this possible, there is a vertex descriptor class whose sole purpose is to accurately describe the layout of the custom vertex structure that is being passed to the Render() function. When planning and designing the vertex descriptor, it was thought that it would be easier to have an array of vertex elements. That way, the vertex descriptor can be a class that has an array of vertex elements as its member object. A vertex element is an object that stores information on the type of element, how many bytes in size it is, and its offset from the previous element. When it comes to the type of element, this value can represent something like vertex 3D, vertex 4D, normal 3D, texture coordinate set 1, texture coordinate set 2, and so forth. The vertex type is kept in an enumeration, BB_ELEMENT_TYPE, and depending on the type will depend on the size the element is in bytes. For example, the flag BB_ELEMENT_VERTEX_3F will tell the rendering system that an element is an X, Y, Z position and is to be sent as the position of the vertex point. Since it has three floats, its size will be 12 bytes. When dealing with OpenGL, the system will be using vertex arrays and vertex buffer objects if supported by the hardware. When using vertex arrays, certain functions are used for certain purposes. For example, in OpenGL, glVertexPointer() is used to set a vertex stream. Knowing what an element is used for and how big it is will allow the system to send in any data the user specifies into the correct vertex array streams. Listing 4.31 lists the enumerations dealing with the vertex element type and the primitive type. The primitive types supported by the Building Blocks Engine are point lists, triangle lists and strips, and line lists and strips.

LISTING 4.31 The vertex element type enumeration and primitive type enumeration.

```
enum BB_ELEMENT_TYPE { BB_ELEMENT_TYPE_NULL = 0,
                       BB_ELEMENT_TYPE_IGNORE_2F,
                       BB_ELEMENT_TYPE_IGNORE_3F,
                       BB_ELEMENT_TYPE_VERTEX_3F,
                       BB_ELEMENT_TYPE_NORMAL_3F,
                       BB_ELEMENT_TYPE_COLOR_3F,
                       BB_ELEMENT_TYPE_TEX1_2F,
                       BB_ELEMENT_TYPE_TEX2_2F,
                       BB_ELEMENT_TYPE_TEX3_2F,
                       BB_ELEMENT_TYPE_TEX4_2F,
                       BB_ELEMENT_TYPE_TEX5_2F,
                       BB_ELEMENT_TYPE_TEX6_2F,
                       BB_ELEMENT_TYPE_TEX7_2F,
                       BB_ELEMENT_TYPE_TEX8_2F };

enum BB_PRIMITIVE_TYPE { BB_PRIMITIVE_NULL = 0,
                         BB_PRIMITIVE_POINT_LIST,
                         BB_PRIMITIVE_TRI_LIST,
                         BB_PRIMITIVE_TRI_STRIP,
                         BB_PRIMITIVE_LINE_LIST,
                         BB_PRIMITIVE_LINE_STRIP };
```

Vertex elements are a class of type VertexElement that stores the element type, its size in bytes, and its offset. Each of these is filled in by the vertex descriptor class and is never set directly. The vertex descriptor class, VertexDescriptor, has an array of vertex elements and a total stride. The stride is needed so the rendering function can know how big a particular vertex is in a list of vertices so it can get from one to the next. The only functions needed by the vertex descriptor class are a function to clear the list, get the stride, get the total number of elements, and add and get elements. To add an element, a user can send in the flag for the element type. Inside the vertex descriptor class, it calculates the size in bytes the element is based on its flag, and the current stride. To get an element from the list, an array index is used.

When building vertex descriptor objects, users can specify the elements based on the order and data format they are in the custom structure. As long as this is done, users can create any vertex structure they want with the data in any order. Listing 4.32 lists the VertexElement class. Note that the members are public so the VertexDescriptor class can directly set them. This is done because individual elements are not used outside the descriptor and therefore have no effect. Listing 4.33 lists the VertexDescriptor class.

LISTING 4.32   The `VertexElement` class.

```cpp
class VertexElement
{
   public:
      VertexElement()
      {
         m_type = BB_ELEMENT_TYPE_NULL;
         m_bytes = 0;
         m_offset = 0;
      }

      bool operator==(VertexElement &e)
      {
         return (m_type == e.m_type &&
                 m_bytes == e.m_bytes &&
                 m_offset == e.m_offset);
      }

      BB_ELEMENT_TYPE m_type;
      int m_bytes;
      int m_offset;
};
```

LISTING 4.33   The `VertexDescriptor` class.

```cpp
class VertexDescriptor
{
   public:
      VertexDescriptor()
      {
         m_currentStride = 0;
      }

      void Clear()
      {
         m_elements.clear();
         m_currentStride = 0;
      }
```

```
BRESULT AddElement(BB_ELEMENT_TYPE type)
{
   VertexElement element;

   element.m_type = type;

   switch(type)
   {
      case BB_ELEMENT_TYPE_IGNORE_3F:
      case BB_ELEMENT_TYPE_VERTEX_3F:
      case BB_ELEMENT_TYPE_NORMAL_3F:
      case BB_ELEMENT_TYPE_COLOR_3F:
         element.m_bytes = sizeof(float) * 3;
      break;

      case BB_ELEMENT_TYPE_IGNORE_2F:
      case BB_ELEMENT_TYPE_TEX1_2F:
      case BB_ELEMENT_TYPE_TEX2_2F:
      case BB_ELEMENT_TYPE_TEX3_2F:
      case BB_ELEMENT_TYPE_TEX4_2F:
      case BB_ELEMENT_TYPE_TEX5_2F:
      case BB_ELEMENT_TYPE_TEX6_2F:
      case BB_ELEMENT_TYPE_TEX7_2F:
      case BB_ELEMENT_TYPE_TEX8_2F:
         element.m_bytes = sizeof(float) * 2;
      break;

      default:
         break;
   };

   if(type == BB_ELEMENT_TYPE_NULL || element.m_bytes <= 0)
   {
      return BB_FAIL;
   }

   element.m_offset = m_currentStride;
   m_currentStride += element.m_bytes;

   m_elements.push_back(element);
```

```
        return BB_SUCCESS;
    }

    VertexElement GetElement(int index)
    {
        VertexElement element;

        if(index >= 0 && index < (int)m_elements.size())
        {
            element = m_elements.GetElement(index);
        }

        return element;
    }

    int GetTotalElements();
    int GetStride();

private:
    std::vector<VertexElement> m_elements;
    int m_currentStride;
};
```

PROGRAMMABLE SHADERS

Shaders come in two types (three after Shader Model 4.0): vertex and pixel (fragment). When working with GLSL, users can specify both shaders in a single file, which is what will be done in the shader files used by the framework. Uniform variables in a shader are called parameters. In the Building Blocks Engine is a parameter class that is used to store an individual parameter. The enumeration for the shader type is BB_SHADER_TYPE and can be seen in Listing 4.34. The ParameterHandle class can be seen in Listing 4.35.

LISTING 4.34 An enumeration for the type of shader.

```
enum BB_SHADER_TYPE { BB_VERTEX_SHADER = 1, BB_PIXEL_SHADER };
```

LISTING 4.35 The ParameterHandle.

```
typedef int ParameterHandle;
```

A GLSL shader is made up of vertex and fragment programs. When a user loads a GLSL shader, an already existing GLSL context object and a vertex and fragment profile will need to be ready. The profiles are used to compile shaders to the highest supported profile version of the hardware. The creation of the GLSL context and the profile types is done in the rendering API's constructor and is used by all shaders that are created. These objects were first seen during the discussion of the rendering interface class' member variables.

To load a shader, users can call the function LoadShaderFromFile(), which takes the shader, GLSL context, and profiles. To clean up after a shader, the class calls in the destructor, cgDestroyProgram(), which is wrapped up into a Shutdown() function. To load a shader from memory, the LoadShaderFromMemory() function can be used and takes the same parameters as LoadShaderFromFile(), except the first parameter is the file data instead of a filename. Listing 4.36 lists the ShaderHandle declaration.

LISTING 4.36   The ShaderHandle class.

```
typedef int ShaderHandle;
```

TEXTURE RESOURCES

Textures are resource managed in the engine's framework. These managed objects in the OpenGL rendering system use the class GLTexture. The GLTexture has as member variables the OpenGL texture ID and a flag that indicates what kind of texture it is (i.e., 2D or Cube).

ON THE CD

For the Building Blocks Engine, the framework will support uncompressed RGB and RGBA .TGA image files. The code used to load a .TGA image can be found in the header file TGA.h on the companion CD-ROM in the BUILDING BLOCKS ENGINE/SOURCE folder. The code to load a cube map can also be found in that same folder in the file CubeMap.h. Listing 4.37 lists the OpenGL texture resource.

LISTING 4.37   The OpenGL texture source.

```
class GLTexture
{
   public:
      GLTexture(int id, BB_TEXTURE_TYPE type)
      {
         m_id = id;
         m_type = type;
      }
```

```
    virtual ~GLTexture()
    {
       FreeMemory();
    }

    unsigned int GetID() { return m_id; }
    BB_TEXTURE_TYPE GetTextureType() { return m_type; }

private:
    void FreeMemory()
    {
       if(m_id > 0)
          glDeleteTextures(1, &m_id);

       m_id = 0;
    }

private:
    unsigned int m_id;
    BB_TEXTURE_TYPE m_type;
};
```

RESOURCES FROM ARCHIVE FILES

Resources can be loaded from an archive file and passed to the rendering system. For example, when dealing with textures, by using functions like LoadTexFromMemory() users can send that loaded file data from the archive to the function to be processed. Shaders are also handled in this manner as was seen during the discussion of the rendering interface class.

RESOURCE MANAGEMENT

The resource management system is a template class. The resource manager is handle based, meaning that handles are used to access resources in the manager. A handle in the Building Blocks Engine is a template class that has a member variable of an integer. This integer is used as an array index into the resource manager for accessing a resource. The Handle class is a template class as a way to create different handles for different types of resources. This makes handles of one type incompatible with resource managers that expect handles of another type. The Handle class' declaration can be seen in Listing 4.38.

LISTING 4.38 The template `Handle` class.

```
template<typename TAG>
class Handle
{
   public:
      Handle() { m_index = BB_NULL_HANDLE; }

      void Initialize(int index) { m_index = index; }
      void Nullify() { m_index = BB_NULL_HANDLE; }
      int GetIndex() { return m_index; }
      bool isNull() { return (m_index <= BB_NULL_HANDLE); }

      bool operator==(Handle<TAG> handle)
      {
         return m_index == handle.GetIndex();
      }

   private:
      int m_index;
};
```

The resource manager uses the hash table from Chapter 2, "Engine Core" inside it. This hash table allows duplicates to be kept out of the resource manager. This works by creating a hash table that stores the names of resources and the index to where they appear in the manager's resource list. Every time a new resource is about to be added, the name of the resource is searched in the hash table. If it is not found, the item is added to the resource list. The name of a resource is hashed as used as the key for the hash table that was created and discussed in Chapter 2. Whenever a resource is to be added to the resource manager, a name must be specified if the hash table is being used. Using a hash table is optional. The resource name and index are wrapped in a class called `ResourceName`, and can be seen in Listing 4.39.

LISTING 4.39 The `ResourceName` class for the hash table.

```
class ResourceName
{
   public:
      ResourceName()
      {
```

```
        m_index = -1;
    }

    std::string GetName() { return m_name; }
    int GetIndex() { return m_index; }

    void SetName(std::string name) { m_name = name; }
    void SetIndex(int index) { m_index = index; }

    bool operator==(ResourceName resName)
    {
        return (m_name == resName.GetName() &&
                m_index == resName.GetIndex());
    }

private:
    std::string m_name;
    int m_index;
};
```

The resource manager itself is a template class. The constructor of the class allows the size of the hash table to be specified. If a size of 0 or lower is used, the hash table is not used and all resources are added regardless of whether they are duplicates. The resource manager has functions to add a resource to the list, release a handle, and get the index of a resource in the manager's list. There are also functions used to add a name to the hash table, delete the memory used by the manager, get a resource, get the size of the resource list, and get a pointer to the list of resources.

The function used to add a resource to the list, Create(), takes as parameters the resource to add, its name, and the address to a handle that will be initialized upon success. The function used to release handles, Release(), takes the address of the handle to release and invalidates its member.

The functions used to get the index of a resource is GetRegisteredIndex() and takes as a parameter the name of the resource. If the hash table has not been created, this function returns an invalid value. The function SetRegisteredName() takes as parameters the name of the resource and its array index. This function is private and is only used by the manager. The remaining functions of the class are access functions. The two member variables of the class are the hash table and an array of resources, which is an STD vector. The resource manager's declaration is listed in Listing 4.40. The resource manager's `Create()` function can be seen in Listing 4.41, the `Release()` function can be seen in Listing 4.42, and `GetRegisteredIndex()` and `SetRegisteredName()` can be seen in Listing 4.43.

LISTING 4.40   The resource manager.

```
template<typename A, typename HANDLE>
class ResourceManager
{
   public:
      ResourceManager(int hashSize = 0)
      {
         m_resourceHash = NULL;

         if(hashSize > 0)
            m_resourceHash = new HashTable<ResourceName>(hashSize);
      }

      virtual ~ResourceManager()
      {
         DeleteAllMemory();
      }

      bool Create(A *res, char *name, HANDLE *handle);
      void Release(HANDLE &handle);

      int GetRegisteredIndex(char *name);

   private:
      void SetRegisteredName(char *name, int index);

      void DeleteAllMemory()
      {
         for(int i = 0; i < GetSize(); i++)
         {
            if(m_objects[i])
               delete m_objects[i];

            m_objects[i] = NULL;
         }
```

```
        if(m_resourceHash != NULL)
           delete m_resourceHash;

        m_resourceHash = NULL;
     }

   public:
      A *GetResource(HANDLE handle)
      {
         int index = handle.GetIndex();

         if(index >= GetSize() || index <= BB_NULL_HANDLE)
            return NULL;

         return m_objects[handle.GetIndex()];
      }

      int GetSize();
      std::vector<A*> *GetObjects();

   private:
      std::vector<A*> m_objects;
      HashTable<ResourceName> *m_resourceHash;
};
```

LISTING 4.41   The resource manager's `Create()` function.

```
template<typename A, typename HANDLE>
bool ResourceManager<A, HANDLE>::Create(A *res, char *name,
                                        HANDLE *handle)
{
   int index = -1;

   if(res == NULL)
      return false;

   if(handle)
      handle->Nullify();

   index = GetRegisteredIndex(name);
```

```
   if(index == -1)
   {
      m_objects.push_back(res);

      index = (int)m_objects.size() - 1;

      if(index < 0)
         return false;

      SetRegisteredName(name, index);
   }

   if(handle)
      handle->Initialize(index);

   return true;
}
```

LISTING 4.42   The resource manager's `Release()` function.

```
template<typename A, typename HANDLE>
void ResourceManager<A, HANDLE>::Release(HANDLE &handle)
{
   int index = handle.GetIndex();

   if(handle.isNull())
      return;

   handle.Nullify();
}
```

LISTING 4.43   The resource manager's `GetRegisteredIndex()` and `SetRegisteredName()` functions.

```
template<typename A, typename HANDLE>
int ResourceManager<A, HANDLE>::GetRegisteredIndex(char *name)
{
   HashItem<ResourceName> tempHashItem;
   ResourceName tempRes;
```

```
   int key = -1;
   std::string str(name);

  if(name == NULL)
     return -1;

  if(m_resourceHash != NULL)
  {
     key = m_resourceHash->HashFunction(str);
     tempHashItem = m_resourceHash->Find(key);

     if(tempHashItem.GetKey() != -1)
     {
        return tempHashItem.GetObject().GetIndex();
     }
  }

  return -1;
}


template<typename A, typename HANDLE>
void ResourceManager<A, HANDLE>::SetRegisteredName(char *name,
                                                   int index)
{
  if(name == NULL || m_resourceHash == NULL || index < 0)
     return;

  HashItem<ResourceName> hashItem;
  std::string str(name);

  ResourceName resName;
  resName.SetName(name);
  resName.SetIndex(index);

  hashItem.SetKey(m_resourceHash->HashFunction(str));
  hashItem.SetObj(resName);

  m_resourceHash->Insert(hashItem);
}
```

RENDERING

On the companion CD-ROM is a demo application called OPENGL in the BUILD-
ING BLOCKS ENGINE/EXAMPLES/CHAPTER 4 folder. This application demonstrates texture mapping, off-screen rendering, using shaders, and displaying a 3D
model of a 3D cube. The demo application is made up of three files: main.h,
main.cpp, and WindowsMain.cpp (for the Win32 version, MacMain.cpp for Mac,
LinuxMain.cpp for Linux). The main.h header file has includes and application-
specific defines such as the window's name, resolution, function prototypes, and so
forth. The main.cpp source file is the main source file with all the demo functions
implemented, such as an initialize function, rendering function, and so forth. The
last file has operating-specific main functions inside it. For example, on Windows
this is where the WinMain() function is implemented. There will be more on this file
later in the chapter.

The OpenGL rendering system is currently the only system the Building Blocks
Engine uses. The class derives from the RenderInterface class and implements all of
the virtual functions discussed in this chapter with OpenGL-specific code. The
member variables of the OpenGL rendering class include a pointer to the current
vertex descriptor, flags if cube mapping and vertex buffer objects are supported,
OpenGL IDs for a vertex and index buffer, a resource manager for textures, and a
list of rendering targets. The current descriptor is used to allow the class to keep
track of which vertex descriptor was used the last time the rendering function was
called. This can allow the function to skip setting up the same vertex descriptor for
objects that share it or if the same object is being drawn multiple times. Some hardware might or might not support cube mapping or vertex buffer objects, so flags for
those are also included in the OpenGL rendering class.

Vertex buffer objects are a fast way to use vertex arrays to send data to the hardware. If support is found, the feature is used; otherwise, normal vertex arrays are
used. Since it is possible to specify geometry that is indexed, an index buffer must
also be created along with vertex buffers to help maximize rendering speed. The last
objects are the resource manger for the OpenGL textures and a list of OpenGL
frame buffer objects. The OpenGL member variables for the OpenGL rendering
class can be seen in Listing 4.44. The rest of the class is identical to the RenderInterface class, with the exception that the functions are not marked virtual.

LISTING 4.44   The member variables of the OpenGL class.

```
class OpenGLRenderer : public RenderInterface
{
```

```
    private:
        VertexDescriptor *m_currentDesc;
        bool m_vboSupport, m_fboSupport;
        unsigned int m_vbo, m_ibo;

        ResourceManager<GLTexture, BB_TEXTURE> *m_texManager;
        std::vector<FrameBufferObject> m_renderTargets;
};
```

The OPENGL demo application is meant to be a simple application to check to make sure the rendering system works as expected. Because of this, in the main.cpp source file is a simple and straightforward test and is not an actual game. The first section of the main.cpp file has a group of globals, which include the OpenGL rendering system, a model used for display, two texture handles for multitexturing the model, a texture handle for the rendering target, the rendering target itself, a shader, a group of parameters the shader requires, and values used to rotate the scene using the mouse. The global section of the OPENGL demo can be seen in Listing 4.45. The class ModelData wraps up everything required by the Render() function to draw a piece of geometry to the screen and is an optional class that was created for convenience. The ModelData class defined in ModelData.h can be seen in Listing 4.46.

LISTING 4.45   The global section of the OPENGL demo.

```
// Rendering System.
bbe::OpenGLRenderer g_Render;

// Main model object.
bbe::ModelData g_model;

// Decals and render target texture.
bbe::BB_TEXTURE g_tex, g_tex2;
bbe::BB_TEXTURE g_rt;

// Render target ID.
bbe::BB_RENDER_TARGET g_offscreen = -1;

// Shader.
bbe::CgShader g_shader;

// Shader parameters.
bbe::CgParameter g_mvpParam;
```

```
bbe::CgParameter g_decalParam,
                 g_decal2Param;

// Flag used to quit.
bool g_quitDemo = false;

// Scene rotations.
int g_xRot = 0, g_oldXRot = 0;
int g_yRot = 0, g_oldYRot = 0;
```

LISTING 4.46 The ModelData class defined in ModelData.h.

```
class ModelData
{
   public:
      ModelData();
      virtual ~ModelData();

      void Clear();
      void ClearDescriptor();

      BRESULT AddDescriptorElement(BB_ELEMENT_TYPE type);
      VertexDescriptor *GetDescriptor();

      bool SetIndices(int totalIndices, unsigned int *indices);
      int GetTotalIndices();
      unsigned int *GetIndices();

      bool SetVertices(BB_PRIMITIVE_TYPE type, int totalVertices,
                       int stride, char *vertices);
      int GetTotalVertices();
      char *GetVertices();

      int GetVertexSizeInBytes();
      int GetVertexStride();
      BB_PRIMITIVE_TYPE GetPrimitiveType();

   private:
      unsigned int *m_indices;
      int m_totalIndices;
```

```
      char *m_vertices;
      int m_totalVertices;

      VertexDescriptor m_descriptor;

      BB_PRIMITIVE_TYPE m_primitiveType;
};
```

The first two functions in the main.cpp source file are DemoResize() and DemoInitialize(). The DemoResize() function is used to resize the window whenever necessary. This function is called after the rendering system is initialized in the DemoInitialze() function and can be seen in Listing 4.47.

The DemoInitialize() function is used to initialize the rendering system, load all textures, load all shaders, and prepare all other data the application is going to use. In the first section of this function the RenderParams object that will be sent to the rendering system's Initialize() function is filled in. The last two variables in the parameter object are used to set the max size for the vertex buffer and the index buffer of the rendering class. Once the rendering system has successfully initialized, the window is re-sized, which means that the projections view-ports, and initial rendering states are set. The first section of the DemoInitialize() function can be seen in Listing 4.48.

LISTING 4.47   The DemoResize() function in the main.cpp source file.

```
void DemoResize(int width, int height)
{
    g_Render.SetViewPort(0, 0, width, height);
    g_Render.ResizeWindow(45.0f, 0.1f, 1000, width, height);
}
```

LISTING 4.48   The DemoInitialize() function in the main.cpp source file.

```
bool DemoInitialize(bbe::RenderParams &params)
{
    bool result = false;

    params.m_colorBits = 24;
    params.m_depthBits = 16;
    params.m_stencilBits = 8;
    params.m_fullscreen = WINDOW_FULLSCREEN;
```

```
params.m_height = WINDOW_HEIGHT;
params.m_width = WINDOW_WIDTH;
params.m_maxCacheBytes = 2000;
params.m_maxCacheIndices = 2000;

if(g_Render.Initialize(&params) != BB_SUCCESS)
   return false;

DemoResize(WINDOW_WIDTH, WINDOW_HEIGHT);

g_Render.SetClearColor(0, 0, 0, 255);
g_Render.Enable(BB_DEPTH_TESTING);
g_Render.Enable(BB_SMOOTH_SHADING);
g_Render.Enable(BB_TEXTURE_2D);
```

The next section of the `DemoInitialize()` function loads a .OBJ model that will be displayed to the screen and loads the textures used in the demo. Model loading is discussed in more detail in the next chapter. The code for the OBJ model loading feature can be found in OBJLoader.h and OBJLoader.cpp on the companion CD-ROM in the BUILDING BLOCKS ENGINE/SOURCE folder and is discussed in more detail in the next chapter. When the textures are loaded, they are loaded from a file into the resource manager. Filters are added to the textures once they are loaded to get the desired look for each surface. The second section of the `DemoInitialize()` function can be seen in Listing 4.49.

LISTING 4.49 The second section of the `DemoInitialize()` function.

```
result = CreateOBJMesh("resources/model/TexturedBox.obj",
                       &g_model);

if(result == false)
   return false;

std::vector<BB_FILTER_TYPE> filters;
filters.push_back(BB_MIN_LINEAR_FILTER);
filters.push_back(BB_MAG_LINEAR_FILTER);
filters.push_back(BB_MIP_LINEAR_FILTER);
filters.push_back(BB_USE_ANSIO_FILTER);

result = g_Render.LoadTexFromFile("resources/textures/decal.tga",
                                  BB_TEX2D_TYPE, &g_tex);
```

```
g_Render.ApplyFilters(g_tex, &filters);

if(result == false)
    return false;

result = g_Render.LoadTexFromFile("resources/textures/decal2.tga",
                                  BB_TEX2D_TYPE, &g_tex2);

g_Render.ApplyFilters(g_tex2, &filters);

if(result == false)
    return false;
```

The final section of the DemoInitialize() function creates the render target, adds a color destination to the render target, filters the destination texture, and loads the shader used by the demo. The render target is created to be 800 × 600, which is also the size of the window. The destination texture is also set to the size of the rendering target. When the texture is created, it is given a name. This name can be referenced by the resource manager and is used just like a filename is used in the LoadTexFromFile() function. The last part of the function loads the shader from a file and sets up its three shader uniform parameters. The final section of the DemoInitialize() function can be seen in Listing 4.50.

LISTING 4.50   The final section of the DemoInitialize() function.

```
filters.clear();
filters.push_back(BB_MIN_LINEAR_FILTER);
filters.push_back(BB_MAG_LINEAR_FILTER);

result = g_Render.CreateRenderTarget(800, 600, &g_offscreen);

if(result == false)
    return false;

result = g_Render.AddRenderTargetTexture("fullscreen", 800, 600,
                                         3, 0, BB_TEX2D_TYPE,
                                         BB_TEX_UNSIGNED_BYTE,
                                         g_offscreen, &g_rt);
```

```
        g_Render.ApplyFilters(g_rt, &filters);

        if(result == false)
            return false;

        result = g_Render.CreateShaderFromFile("resources/shaders/
                                               passThrough.cg",
                                               &g_shader);

        if(result == false)
            return false;

        g_Render.SetupShaderParameter("mvp", BB_VERTEX_SHADER,
                                      &g_shader, &g_mvpParam);
        g_Render.SetupShaderParameter("decal", BB_PIXEL_SHADER,
                                      &g_shader, &g_decalParam);
        g_Render.SetupShaderParameter("decal2", BB_PIXEL_SHADER,
                                      &g_shader, &g_decal2Param);

        return true;
    }
```

The OPENGL demo uses the input code discussed in Chapter 3, "Input, Sound, and Networking." It uses the GetMousePosition() function to allow the model displayed to the screen to be rotated by the mouse. It also uses isButtonDown() to detect when the left mouse button is being pressed, or the rotations, and for when the escape button is pressed. When the escape button is pressed, a flag called g_quitDemo is set to true. In the WinMain() function, using Win32 as an example, the application loop checks this value to see if it is true. If so, the application cleans up and closes. The variable is a global variable that is specified external with the keyword extern variable that is defined in main.h. The DemoUpdate() function can be seen in Listing 4.51. The DemoUpdate() function is called once per frame during the application loop and is where all updates occur. The application loop is discussed later in this section.

LISTING 4.51 The DemoUpdate() function.

```
void DemoUpdate()
{
    int mouseX = 0, mouseY = 0;
```

```
bbe::GetMousePosition(&mouseX, &mouseY);

if(bbe::isButtonDown(BB_BUTTON_ESCAPE))
{
    g_quitDemo = true;
}

if(bbe::isButtonDown(BB_BUTTON_MOUSE_LEFT))
{
    g_xRot -= (mouseX - g_oldXRot);
    g_yRot -= (mouseY - g_oldYRot);
}

g_oldXRot = mouseX;
g_oldYRot = mouseY;
}
```

The OPENGL demo tests the render targets and shader capability of the rendering system along with texture mapping. In the demo are two rendering passes. The first pass renders the multitextured box to the render target. The multitexturing is done in the shader that is enabled before the shape is drawn. During the second pass, the render target is detached and the box is drawn to the regular buffers, but this time the box is drawn without the shader and with the results of the rendering target as a texture. Also in the second pass, the box is allowed to be rotated by the mouse. Both functions, DemoRenderPass1() and DemoRenderPass2(), can be seen in Listing 4.52. Note that the macro BB_RENDER_MODEL_DATA_PARAMS is defined in ModelData.h and is just a macro that fills in the Render() function's parameters. The macro allows the function call code to appear smaller and is optional. Without the macro, users would have to send the parameters that Render() requires by calling the accessor functions of the g_model object (e.g., g_model.GetPrimitiveType() for the first parameters, etc.).

The last two functions in the OPENGL demo application are DemoRender() and DemoShutdown(). DemoRender()is called by the application loop every frame after DemoUpdate(). DemoShutdown()is called when the application starts shutting down to clean up all demo-specific objects used by the system. In the OPENGL demo, the rendering system can be shut down, which in turns deletes all textures, shaders, rendering targets, and so forth. The final two functions of the main.cpp source file can be seen in Listing 4.53.

LISTING 4.52   The rendering pass functions.

```
void DemoRenderPass1()
{
    g_Render.BindRenderTarget(g_offscreen);
    g_Render.SetClearColor(255, 255, 255, 255);

    g_Render.StartRendering(1, 1, 0);
    g_Render.LoadIdentityMatrix();

    g_Render.SetView(0, 0, 6, 0, 0, 0, 0, 1, 0);

    g_Render.ApplyShader(&g_shader);

    g_Render.SetupMatrixTracking(g_mvpParam, BB_MVP_MATRIX,
                                 BB_IDENTITY_MATRIX);
    g_Render.SetShaderTextureParameter(g_decalParam, g_tex);
    g_Render.SetShaderTextureParameter(g_decal2Param, g_tex2);

    g_Render.Render(BB_RENDER_MODEL_DATA_PARAMS(g_model));
}


void DemoRenderPass2()
{
    g_Render.BindRenderTarget(-1);
    g_Render.SetClearColor(0, 0, 0, 255);

    g_Render.StartRendering(1, 1, 0);
    g_Render.LoadIdentityMatrix();

    g_Render.SetView(0, 0, 6, 0, 0, 0, 0, 1, 0);
    g_Render.RotateMatrix((float)g_xRot, 0, 1, 0);
    g_Render.RotateMatrix((float)g_yRot, 1, 0, 0);

    g_Render.ApplyShader(NULL);
    g_Render.ApplyTexture(0, g_rt);

    g_Render.Render(BB_RENDER_MODEL_DATA_PARAMS(g_model));
}
```

LISTING 4.53   The final functions in the OPENGL demo application.

```
void DemoRender()
{
    DemoRenderPass1();
    DemoRenderPass2();

    g_Render.EndRendering();
}


void DemoShutdown()
{
    g_Render.Shutdown();
}
```

Each operating system has its own special source file that declares its main function along with any other OS specific code required to display a window. Using Win32 as an example, the function WindowsMain.cpp contains all the Win32 specific code needed to display a Win32 window. Among this code is the WinMain() function and is the entry point into the application. The only portion of this function that concerns the demo application is the application loop. Before the loop, the DemoInitialize() function is called. This function is sent the RenderParams object, which has the OS specific objects OpenGL needs to launch and swap buffers. It was mentioned early in the chapter that the RenderParams object will be used to sneak OS specific objects into the rendering system while appearing to look portable on the outside. In the main.cpp function, there is no difference and no discrimination between the operating systems running the code. The only operating system specific code is handled in the OS specific source file such as WindowsMain.cpp.

If the initialize fails, the application displays an error and quits; otherwise, it starts the application loop. During this loop, a check for if g_quitDemo is performed to see if the application is done executing. If it is, the DemoShutdown() function is called and the WinMain() function returns. Otherwise, the loop calls Win32 specific code to check for OS messages and calls DemoUpdate() and DemoRender() once during each iteration of the loop. A partial look at the WinMain() function that deals with the application loop can be seen in Listing 4.54. A screenshot of the running application can be seen in Figure 4.9.

FIGURE 4.9 A screenshot of the OPENGL demo application.

LISTING 4.54 The application loop (partial look at the `WinMain()` function).

```
int WINAPI WinMain(HINSTANCE hInst, HINSTANCE p, LPSTR c, int s)
{
   HWND hwnd;

   ...

   bbe::RenderParams params;
   params.m_handle.m_hwnd = hwnd;
   params.m_handle.m_hInstance = hInst;

   if(!DemoInitialize(params))
   {
      MessageBox(NULL, "Error in initialize!", "Error", MB_OK);
   }
```

```
        else
        {
           while(!g_quitDemo)
           {
               if(PeekMessage(&msg, 0, 0, 0, PM_REMOVE))
               {
                   if(msg.message == WM_QUIT) break;
                   TranslateMessage(&msg);
                   DispatchMessage(&msg);
               }
               else
               {
                   DemoUpdate();
                   DemoRender();
               }
           }

           DemoShutdown();
        }

        ...
    }
```

RENDERING BILLBOARDS

In games, it is often useful to be able to render a polygon that is always facing the camera. This can be seen with particle systems where the particles are flat 2D squares that are rendered facing the camera. When the camera moves the billboard, polygons are adjusted to remain facing the camera. In OpenGL and Direct3D, developers have the option of using point sprites, which are squares that are rendered facing the camera that is done by the hardware.

In the past, some games used billboards for objects and enemies in the game world. This can be seen with the original *Doom* by ID Software. Later in the book, we look at how to render particle systems using point sprites. Although point sprites can be used, the technique to do it manually is simple and can be done on hardware that does not support point sprites.

To render a billboard, a few pieces of information are needed. First, the model-view matrix will need to be obtained. This can be gathered by using the `GetMatrix()` function of the rendering system. The second piece of information is the width and height size of the desired billboard. From the model-view matrix, the right and up vectors are extracted. These vectors correspond to the first two columns of the model-view matrix as seen in Listing 4.55.

LISTING 4.55   Obtaining the right and up vectors from the model-view matrix.

```
Vector3D right(matrix[0], matrix[4], matrix[8]),
             top(matrix[1], matrix[5], matrix[9]);
```

With the right and up vectors, a square can be created by using these vectors to make two triangles. This billboard can be rendered to the screen using the rendering system's Render() function like any other piece of geometry. Constructing the billboard out of the right and up vectors can be seen in Listing 4.56.

LISTING 4.56   Creating a billboard square.

```
Vector3D billBoardVerts[6] =
    {
        { (right - top) *  size },
        { (right + top) * -size },
        { (top   - right) *  size },
        { (top   - right) *  size },
        { (right + top) *  size },
        { (right - top) *  size }
    };
```

ON THE CD

On the companion CD-ROM is a demo application called BILLBOARDS in the BUILDING BLOCKS ENGINE/EXAMPLES/CHAPTER 4 folder that demonstrates how to render a billboard using the information in the previous section. Regardless of where the camera is placed or rotated, the billboard will always face it. The billboard in the demo is a square rendered around the origin (0, 0, 0). The render function from the BILLBOARDS demo application can be seen in Listing 4.57. A screenshot of the demo application can be seen in Figure 4.10. The code in Listing 4.57 creates a billboard where the position and texture coordinates for each vertex are calculated.

LISTING 4.57   The rendering function from the BILLBOARDS demo application.

```
void DemoRender()
{
    g_Render.SetClearColor(0, 0, 0, 255);

    g_Render.StartRendering(1, 1, 0);
    g_Render.LoadIdentityMatrix();

    g_Render.SetView(10, 0, 4, 0, 0, 0, 0, 1, 0);
    g_Render.ApplyTexture(0, g_tex);
```

```
float matrix[16], size = 1;

g_Render.GetMatrix(BB_MODELVIEW_MATRIX, matrix);

bbe::Vector3D right(matrix[0], matrix[4], matrix[8]),
              top(matrix[1], matrix[5], matrix[9]);

stVertex billBoardVerts[6] =
{
    { (right - top) * size, 1, 0 },
    { (right + top) * -size, 0, 0 },
    { (top - right) * size, 0, 1 },
    { (top - right) * size, 0, 1 },
    { (right + top) * size, 1, 1 },
    { (right - top) * size, 1, 0 }
};


g_Render.Render(BB_PRIMITIVE_TRI_LIST, &g_descriptor,
                (char*)&billBoardVerts, NULL,
                g_descriptor.GetStride() * 6, 0,
                g_descriptor.GetStride());

    g_Render.EndRendering();
}
```

FIGURE 4.10 A screenshot from the BILLBOARDS demo.

Summary

Rendering is a huge area of game development, and this chapter looked at the graphics system used by the Building Blocks Engine. This system has the capability to render geometrical models, texture map surfaces, use programmable shaders. Although there was a great deal of information in this chapter and lots of code, there is still much more to a rendering system, most of which is covered in the next chapter. The information in this chapter that was only briefly touched upon is also covered in more detail in the next chapter.

The next chapter focuses on looking at more advanced rendering topics such as scene management, state management, scene graphs, specific graphical effects, model loading, and level of detail. The graphical techniques discussed include topics such as cube mapping, specular mapping, alpha mapping, per-pixel lighting, normal mapping, reflections, and more.

ON THE CD

The entire OpenGL rendering system can be found on the companion CD-ROM in the BUILDING BLOCKS ENGINE/SOURCE folder. The purpose of this chapter was to understand the high-level design of the framework's rendering system and why it was designed and coded the way it was. There is a demo application in the EXAMPLES/CHAPTER4 folder called OPENGL that demonstrates drawing a textured object to the screen. The next chapter completes the look at the design and implementation of the Building Blocks Engine's rendering system.

Chapter Exercises

1. Create a multitextured square where one texture is a decal.
2. Draw an animated billboard by displaying a different texture after every 1/10 of a second on a square that is always facing the camera.
3. Add the ability to render text. Do so by adding textured squares to the screen. The texture itself should be an image with all the letters and numbers on it. When rendering out text, the texture coordinates for each square will have to be calculated so the texture of the correct letter/number is used. The number of squares depends on the number of characters in the text being displayed. A text message that is being displayed needs to specify the texture with the font, a starting location on the screen, and a size for each character.

5 Rendering Scenes and Scene Graphs

In This Chapter

- Overview
- Scene Graphs
- Level of Detail
- Geometry Sorting and Culling
- Effects
- Models and Meshes

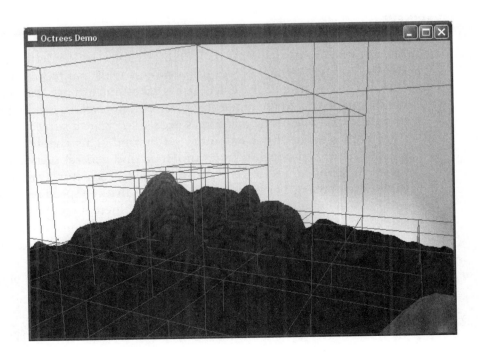

A rendering system is only as good as the objects that are feeding it the information it needs to perform its job. Modern games have complex scenes and environments that require real-time rendering. These scenes are far too complex to simply pass to the rendering system all at once. This is because scenes of any complexity will most likely be made up of far more polygons than can be rendered in a decent number of frames per second at the same time. Therefore, a rendering system must create objects and various data structures that are used to manage the scene data and to feed information to the rendering system when it comes time to draw a scene. The aim of this is to feed the rendering system in an optimized way to speed up the processing time of each frame. The key to creating complex scenes is to draw as little as possible, only drawing what can be seen and in a level of detail that is acceptable. Other topics can also affect performance, which are discussed later in this chapter.

A rendering system must be able to render complex scenes, or the engine framework will have a very limited use when trying to make 3D-driven gaming applications and simulations. Techniques and algorithms have been used to speed up a game's performance ever since the beginning of 3D games and will continue to be used as the complexity of gaming environments exceed what can be done on the hardware without them.

OVERVIEW

The purpose of this chapter is to build off Chapter 4, "Rendering Systems," and add the ability to render scenes using various tools and techniques. Rendering complex scenes in modern video games takes much more than just sending a number of objects to the rendering system. High-level data management is very important and one of the many keys needed to create a successful game engine from both a rendering standpoint and beyond. This chapter looks at scene graphs, state management, levels of detail, and general scene partitioning in games. When it comes to scene partitioning, data structures are used heavily in game development. There exist data structures that can speed rendering, physics, and so forth by splitting an environment into different sections. These manageable sections can be used for many different optimizations, which are discussed later in this chapter. The main idea behind using various data structures to speed calculations is that the algorithms used on those data structures are often much faster to process than the brute force alternative. This increase in performance is often drastic in comparison.

The main challenges with rendering scenes with a rendering system lie with the behind-the-scenes data management and organization. In games, the management of resources and data is so important that they can make or break a project. Bottlenecks can exist in many different areas of the rendering system, which will also affect performance. The overall performance of any rendering system is trying to balance as many different areas as possible, because it is not always possible to achieve 100-percent optimization in a dynamic simulation like a video game.

SCENE GRAPHS

A scene graph is a data structure used to specify relationships between objects in the virtual environment. Scene graphs are used to arrange a graphical scene into its logical and, possibly, spatial relationships. This arrangement is a hierarchy that resembles a tree with n-dimensions. For example, a binary tree has two subnodes for every node. In a scene graph, the number of children a single node can have is not limited; hence, it has n-dimensions. In the game industry, scene graphs are more general data structures than others. This means that the definition of a data structure is not as concrete or made up of a hard set of rules as it is with other data structures. It can be said that a scene graph is more or less defined by the application for which it is being used. An application that does not use textures or materials would not need a way to define special relationships based on this, but one that does use textures and materials might. Game developers take the basic ideas and principles of scene graphs and adapt them to the needs of the game being developed.

A scene graph is a collection of nodes that form a tree of n-dimensions. The parent/child relationship means that all nodes that have a parent are also affected by its parents and their parents' parents. For example, take a group of individual boxes where each box has its own location that is specified in its own local coordinate space. If the group of boxes as a whole has a parent transformation, the hierarchy can look like the illustration in Figure 5.1, in which the parent node specifies the transformation for the entire group. Each child node transformation represents the individual box positions. When rendering a transformation hierarchy, the child nodes are multiplied to the parent node's transformation. If the boxes are geometrical shapes, a child of the local transformation node for each box can be a node that represents the renderable geometry (Figure 5.2). Concatenating transformations in this manner is very easy to understand and natural to represent in a scene graph.

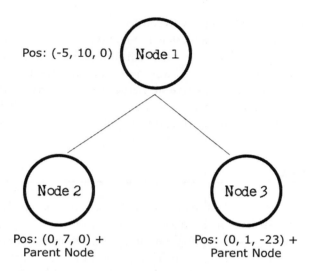

FIGURE 5.1 A parent/child relationship using transformation nodes.

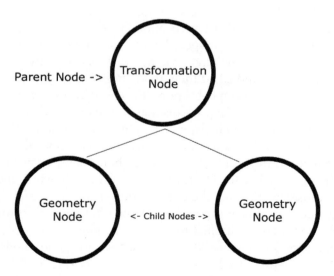

FIGURE 5.2 Transformation nodes used to position geometry node data.

In games, scene graphs can be used in a powerful way. For example, take a character that is controlled in some manner, whether by human or is an NPC, in a virtual scene that has the ability to attach itself to other objects. In the game *Halo 2* for the Xbox video game console, characters are able to ride in vehicles. By attaching a character node to a vehicle node, for example, the vehicle can be moved throughout the 3D environment while automatically moving the character model as well. By specifying a relationship between the two objects, the vehicle's transformation is being applied to the character model as well. The character model at that point can take a pose, such as sitting, and give the appearance of driving the vehicle through various model animations such as turning the steering wheel or shifting gears.

Scene graphs can be used to reduce the memory footprint of a game by using instances of resources. The Building Blocks Engine has a resource manager that is capable of creating handles for resources that are in its list. Resources can be shared by simply sharing the handle, which is an array index. In a scene graph, nodes that represent geometrical data, or any other kind of resource, can reference the same physical memory in the same way. For example, take a model of a tree in nature. In a 3D game, that same tree can be referenced by many different geometry nodes, each with its own location. By using a single reference to a resource such as a texture, model, shader, and so forth, the game can instance many different copies without loading the resource multiple times. Another benefit to instancing is that the data for the textures, shaders, and so forth does not need to be sent to the rendering system again, because it is already there and ready, thus reducing bandwidth. This assumes that the relationships between the objects are grouped by materials in the hierarchy.

Scene graphs can be implemented in many different ways. A programmer can use arrays, link lists, or another underlying data structure when creating a scene graph system. Most scene graphs use a tree as the underlying data structure. This tree can be easy to implement, because the nature of scene graphs fits trees very well. A scene graph starts with a root node. In any tree structure, the root node is a node in the list that has no parent and is the node that all other nodes are children of. When processing a scene graph, the root node is the first to be executed. From there, all other nodes are processed using recursion or by accessing the member pointers of each node that points to its children. The root node applies itself to every other node by moving down the tree during transversal. This continues until the final node has been processed. This type of transversal takes a top-down approach where the transversal starts at the top (root) and continues down through the hierarchy. Another approach is a down-top transversal, which works in the opposite direction.

When creating a scene graph, it is effective to separate it from the rendering system of the game. A scene graph node can have API function calls in it to perform a task (e.g., OpenGL or Direct3D rendering calls to render geometry). This process will make the scene graph too dependent on the API, which also makes it harder to port if the scene graph needs to be used by different rendering APIs. There are better ways to handle this by not coupling the API and the scene graph in a tight and ineffective relationship where there is no benefit to doing so in a game.

Typical scene graphs do not deal with bounding volume hierarchies. A bounding volume hierarchy, as mentioned previously, is a way to speed renderings, collisions, and so forth by using a hierarchy. Based on the nature of scene graphs, they can be turned into a bounding volume hierarchy, which extends the general definition of a scene graph; or nodes that represent references to the root node of a bounding volume can be used in the scene graph, which is more effective than the former. Because scene graphs are not bounding volume hierarchies, they should be de-coupled from them, but there is no hard set of rules when creating a scene graph, as they are application specific. Keeping the bounding volume hierarchy separate from the scene graph has no benefit either way and can keep the two systems from becoming hybrids that might end up making the system not as efficient or harder to maintain.

DESIGNING THE SCENE GRAPH

The design for the Building Blocks Engine was kept simple to leave room for the addition of more functionality. For the Building Blocks Engine, the scene graph uses a tree hierarchy as the underlying data structure of n-dimensions. The nodes have pointers to their first child and their first sibling. The sibling relationship is similar to a link list where the sibling node (next pointer) chains together all children of a parent node.

The scene graph for the Building Blocks Engine is used to logically group object relationships based on transformation. The nodes of the scene graph will be implemented using inheritance by deriving nodes from a base class. The benefit to using inheritance is that it is easy to implement additional types of nodes. The downside is that it is more difficult to add additional features to the nodes. For this version of the Building Blocks Engine, there are three types of general nodes, which include transformations and geometry. For the transformation node, a transformation matrix is used to apply to the current model-view matrix. The geometrical node is used to render an actual model in the environment. Each of these types of nodes are classes that derive from the same base. The base class is made up of a few pure virtual functions.

WORKING WITH NODES

In the Building Blocks Engine, the scene graph is a class with a node pointer member variable that acts as the root node of the hierarchy. When nodes are added to the scene graph, they are added to the root node. The node class allows child and sibling nodes to be attached to it. Because of this, groups of nodes can be specified in the application, and entire groups can be added to the scene graph with one call. This will be seen in the examples later in this book where entire sub-trees can be added to the scene graph instead of one item at a time.

In the Building Blocks Engine, the base node class, Node, has functions to attach child and sibling nodes and to process a node. The node process is a function that calls the Process() function of every child of the node and then every sibling. In the Node class, the next pointer, m_next, refers to the next sibling, while the previous pointer, m_prev, refers to the previous sibling. The Node class can be seen listed in Listing 5.1.

LISTING 5.1   The Node class.

```
class Node
{
    public:
        Node()
        {
            m_next = NULL;
            m_prev = NULL;
            m_child = NULL;
        }

        virtual ~Node()
        {
            m_prev = NULL;

            if(m_child != NULL)
            {
                delete m_child;
                m_child = NULL;
            }
```

```
      if(m_next != NULL)
      {
         delete m_next;
         m_next = NULL;
      }
   }


   void AddChild(Node *node)
   {
      if(m_child == NULL)
      {
         m_child = node;
      }
      else
      {
         m_child->AddSibling(node);
      }
   }


   void AddSibling(Node *node)
   {
      Node *ptr = m_next;

      if(m_next == NULL)
      {
         m_next = node;
         node->m_prev = this;
      }
      else
      {
         while(ptr->m_next != NULL)
         {
            ptr = ptr->m_next;
         }

         ptr->m_next = node;
         node->m_prev = ptr;
      }
   }

   virtual void Process()
   {
```

```
            if(m_child != NULL)
               m_child->Process();

            if(m_next != NULL)
               m_next->Process();
         }

      protected:
         Node *m_next;
         Node *m_prev;
         Node *m_child;
   };
```

The second node type is `TransformationNode` and is used to store a transformation. In the Building Blocks Engine, this transformation refers to an orientation and
translation. The `TransformationNode` keeps track of a 3D position in a `Vector3D`
object and an orientation (rotation) in a quaternion. When processing this type of
node, the matrix is calculated from the quaternion and the translation is applied to
it. It is then multiplied to the current matrix on the stack. Upon processing this type
of node, a new matrix is pushed onto the stack. This allows the matrix to be popped
off the stack, thus restoring the previous state of the stack before this node applied
its own information to it. A matrix should only be applied to the children of the
node and not the siblings; children are only affected by their parents, not by their
own siblings. This can be seen in the overloaded `Process()` function of the `Trans-`
`formationMatrix()` class where the order in which the functions are called is done
so in the manner just described. The `TransformationNode` class can be seen listed in
Listing 5.2.

LISTING 5.2   The `TransformationNode` class.

```
class TransformationNode : public Node
{
   public:
      TransformationNode(Vector3D &position, Quaternion &q,
                         RenderInterface *renderer)
      {
         m_renderer = renderer;
         m_position = position;
         m_quaternion = q;
      }
```

```
        virtual ~TransformationNode()
        {
        }

        void Process()
        {
           if(m_renderer != NULL)
           {
              m_renderer->PushMatrix();

              float matrix[16] = { 0 };

              m_quaternion.CreateMatrix(matrix);
              matrix[12] = m_position.x;
              matrix[13] = m_position.y;
              matrix[14] = m_position.z;

              m_renderer->MultiplyToCurrentMatrix(matrix);
           }

           if(m_child != NULL)
              m_child->Process();

           if(m_renderer != NULL)
              m_renderer->PopMatrix();

           if(m_next != NULL)
              m_next->Process();
        }

     protected:
        Vector3D m_position;
        Quaternion m_quaternion;

        RenderInterface *m_renderer;
   };
```

The last node type is the node class GeometryNode and is used for renderable objects. This node references a dynamic model of type DynamicModel. Inside the Process() function of this class, the dynamic model's transformation is applied before the model is drawn. The reason dynamic models have their own transformation is because it is an easy way to apply a dynamic model's physics calculated information in it. If not, the transformation node that parents the GeometryNode would have to be altered for every physics-based object. This also means that the application must have some way to access those specific nodes, or keep pointers to those nodes after being inserted into the scene graph. Dynamic objects in a scene can have data structures that are used to speed physics and collision detection that are separate from the scene graph. Since this information in the Building Blocks Engine is coupled with the dynamic models, it is convenient to get the transformations from those objects, since the node will already have them. Another consideration is that shaders matrix tracking must be applied after the model's transformation in Cg. The GeometryNode is listed in Listing 5.3. A partial look at the DynamicModel class can be seen in Listing 5.4 with all the information relevant to this chapter. The complete DynamicModel class is discussed in Chapter 6, "Physics," in more detail.

LISTING 5.3   The GeometryNode class.

```
class GeometryNode : public Node
{
    public:
        GeometryNode(DynamicModel *model,
                     BB_MODEL_RESOURCE_MANAGER *modelManager,
                     BB_EFFECT_RESOURCE_MANAGER *effectManager,
                     RenderInterface *renderer)
        {
            m_renderer = renderer;
            m_model = model;
            m_modelManager = modelManager;
            m_effectManager = effectManager;
        }

        virtual ~GeometryNode()
        {
            m_renderer = NULL;
            m_model = NULL;
            m_modelManager = NULL;
            m_effectManager = NULL;
        }
```

```
void Process()
{
  if(m_model != NULL && m_modelManager != NULL &&
     m_renderer != NULL)
  {
    ModelResource *modelResPtr = NULL;
    ModelData *mPtr = NULL;
    bbe::EffectResource *effectResPtr = NULL;
    bbe::Effect *effectPtr = NULL;

    modelResPtr = m_modelManager->GetResource(
       m_model->GetModelHandle());

    if(m_effectManager != NULL)
    {
      effectResPtr = m_effectManager->GetResource(
         m_model->GetEffectHandle());
    }

    if(effectResPtr != NULL)
    {
      effectPtr = effectResPtr->GetEffect();
    }

    if(modelResPtr != NULL)
    {
      mPtr = modelResPtr->GetModel();

      if(mPtr != NULL)
      {
        m_renderer->PushMatrix();

        m_renderer->MultiplyToCurrentMatrix(
           m_model->GetTransformation());

        if(effectPtr != NULL)
        {
          effectPtr->ApplyEffect();
        }

        m_renderer->Render(
           BB_RENDER_MODEL_DATA_PARAMS((*mPtr)));
```

```
                m_renderer->PopMatrix();
            }
        }
    }

    Node::Process();
}

protected:
    DynamicModel *m_model;

    BB_MODEL_RESOURCE_MANAGER *m_modelManager;
    BB_EFFECT_RESOURCE_MANAGER *m_effectManager;

    RenderInterface *m_renderer;
};
```

LISTING 5.4   The `DynamicModel` class.

```
class DynamicModel
{
    public:
        DynamicModel()
        {
            for(int i = 0; i < BB_MAX_LOD; i++)
                m_modelHandle[i].Nullify();

            m_effectHandle.Nullify();

            m_isVisible = true;
            m_currentLOD = 0;
        }

        virtual ~DynamicModel()
        {
            for(int i = 0; i < BB_MAX_LOD; i++)
                m_modelHandle[i].Nullify();

            m_effectHandle.Nullify();
        }
```

```
float *GetTransformation()
{
   return m_transformationMatrix.matrix;
}

void SetTransformation(Matrix4x4 m)
{
   m_transformationMatrix = m;
}

Handle<ModelResourceTag> GetModelHandle()
{
   return m_modelHandle[m_currentLOD];
}

Handle<EffectResourceTag> GetEffectHandle()
{
   return m_effectHandle;
}

void SetModelHandle(Handle<ModelResourceTag> &handle)
{
   m_modelHandle[m_currentLOD].Initialize(handle.GetIndex());
}

void SetEffectHandle(Handle<EffectResourceTag> &handle)
{
   m_effectHandle.Initialize(handle.GetIndex());
}

void SetCurrentLOD(int index)
{
   if(index >= 0 && index < BB_MAX_LOD)
      m_currentLOD = index;
}

int GetCurrentLOD()
{
   return m_currentLOD;
}
```

```
      void SetIsVisible(bool val)
      {
         m_isVisible = val;
      }

      bool GetIsVisible()
      {
         return m_isVisible;
      }

   private:
      Handle<ModelResourceTag> m_modelHandle[BB_MAX_LOD];
      Handle<EffectResourceTag> m_effectHandle;
      Matrix4x4 m_transformationMatrix;

      int m_currentLOD;
      bool m_isVisible;
};
```

SCENE GRAPH CREATION

The scene graph for the Building Blocks Engine is a separate class. The scene graph class has functions inside it to add nodes to the hierarchy, delete the hierarchy, and process the nodes in the hierarchy. Many of the scene graph's functionality wraps around the root node's functions. For example, adding a node to the scene graph is done by calling the root node's `AddChild()` function. If the root already has a first child, that child's next pointer is made the second child, and so on. Deleting the scene graph consists of deleting the root node, which will recursively call the destructor on all nodes attached to it. The scene graph class `SceneGraph` can be seen listed in Listing 5.5. An example of using the scene graph and various nodes can also be seen listed in Listing 5.6.

LISTING 5.5   The `SceneGraph` class.

```
class SceneGraph
{
   public:
      SceneGraph()
      {
```

```
                    m_root = NULL;
                }

                virtual ~SceneGraph()
                {
                    Release();
                }

                void Release()
                {
                    if(m_root != NULL)
                    {
                        delete m_root;
                        m_root = NULL;
                    }
                }

                void AddNode(Node *node)
                {
                    if(m_root == NULL)
                        m_root = new Node;

                    m_root->AddChild(node);
                }

                void Process()
                {
                    if(m_root != NULL)
                        m_root->Process();
                }

        private:
            Node *m_root;
        };
```

LISTING 5.6 An example of using the scene graph.

```
        bbe::TransformationNode *group1 =
            new bbe::TransformationNode(bbe::Vector3D(-5, 0, 0),
            bbe::Quaternion(),
            static_cast<bbe::RenderInterface*>(&g_Render));
```

```
bbe::Matrix4x4 boxPos;

boxPos.Translate(0, 0, -5);
model1.SetTransformation(boxPos);

boxPos.Translate(0, 0, 5);
model2.SetTransformation(boxPos);

bbe::GeometryNode *box1Node = new bbe::GeometryNode(
    model1, &g_modelManager, &g_effectManager,
    static_cast<bbe::RenderInterface*>(&g_Render));

bbe::GeometryNode *box2Node = new bbe::GeometryNode(
    model2, &g_modelManager, &g_effectManager,
    static_cast<bbe::RenderInterface*>(&g_Render));

group1->AddChild(box1Node);
group1->AddChild(box2Node);

g_sceneGraph.AddNode(group1);
```

STATE MANAGEMENT WITH SCENE GRAPHS

Many resources are being passed around in a video game. Objects can be made up of more than one texture, more than one shader, and can share many resources. Earlier in this book, we mentioned that it is important to not load the same resource more than once, because the result will be an increase is memory requirements. In this section, we discuss state management; whereas resource management served to improve memory consumption, state management serves to improve performance by managing states.

One state used frequently in a game is a texture state. In a game, many objects share the same texture. In the Building Blocks Engine, these objects can share the same texture memory. The problem is that if one object uses a texture that the next object uses, and if the next object sends that data down the pipeline, it has unnecessarily used time doing so. The thing with all states is that switching them causes some overhead in the system. Textures and shaders are the most expensive states to switch. If a game object is sending the same texture data that is already there, the overhead incurred is unnecessary. If every object in a game is switching states freely, there can be lost opportunities to optimize the process.

State management is the process of grouping objects by their states so that all objects can be rendered that require one state, all objects can be rendered that require another state, and so on. The issue now is what states the objects are sorted by. There is most likely no way to eliminate all state switches in the average game, but the most important ones can be reduced. For example, switching textures and shaders are the most costly states. Grouping objects by shader, and then sub-grouping those by texture will give a boost in performance when compared to switching for all objects. Although it is still possible to have textures in one shader group that are used in another, it would be impossible to handle those together if they use different shaders, because the overhead from one switch is just being replaced by the overhead of another. Thus, in some situations, it might not be possible to eliminate all duplicate switches.

In the Building Blocks Engine, the states of objects are manually handled by grouping objects based on effects using the `EffectNode`. In the scene graph, hierarchy objects can be sorted by shader and then by texture; a feature that can be added to the scene graph system if desired. If you are using a third-party tool to create scenes, an exporter can be created to always sort objects based on their order, so when a game loads the hierarchy, it is already set up to reduce as many state switches as possible based on the sorting choice. Allowing objects to be automatically sorted when they are added to a node can be useful as well.

LEVEL OF DETAIL

Level of detail (LOD) is the process of decreasing an object's polygon count based on its distance from the viewer. In games, as objects move farther from the viewing position, their detail is not as visible to the viewer as if the objects were close. Therefore, it is unnecessary to render objects at max polygon count, since the detail of the object cannot be seen from a certain distance. Level of detail is a technique used to decrease the polygon count of an object so it still looks the same or close to the same as the original object, but with fewer polygons. Fewer polygons can cause a slight increase in performance. Since the majority of the environment's visible objects at any one position are often, especially in outdoor environments, farther from the camera, this increase in performance can add up. Most of the time, the decrease in the model's polygon count goes unnoticed with distance, but in some situations, depending on the difference in shape between the two levels, an artifact can occur where the jump between levels is obvious and the increase can be observed by the viewer. This effect is known as a "detail pop-in." Various algorithms can be performed on a model to decrease its polygon count; those techniques are beyond the scope of this book. A simple way to perform LOD is to use a modeling application to reduce the number of polygons in a model, and to save multiple copies with one for each level of detail.

LOD ON OBJECTS

In the Building Blocks Engine, LOD is handled in the application, not in the scene graph. The DynamicModel class looked at earlier in this chapter has an array of ModelData objects. The size of this array is based on the max levels of detail, which is defined in the header file Defines.h. Each element in the array represents a different LOD of the model. When models are loaded, each LOD is loaded as well. During the update section of a frame in a game, the game can loop through all objects and determine which ones are visible and what LOD that object will have. In the DynamicModel class, a ModelData is returned, as seen in the GeometryNode class. The model returned depends on the LOD that was set.

The LOD is decoupled from everything in the rendering system because that information is more appropriate when the objects are being updated. How these objects are updated is game specific. For example, some games use bounding volume hierarchies (BVHs) solely for the objects in the game world. This BVH would be used not to store model data, but to store generally what objects fall within what node. A transversal through that BVH can be used to update physics and collisions, determine which objects are visible to the viewer, and determine what LOD the objects are. In the DynamicModel class, a flag determines visibility. When the scene graph is rendered, it can look at this flag during geometry nodes and use it to determine if the object should be drawn. That allows the scene graph to maintain the state management and relationships, while allowing the BVH used for the objects to determine visibility and LOD. Another BVH can be used on the static environment, such as a terrain, and can be rendered in conjunction with the scene graph to display an entire scene. In addition, there can be two different BVH hierarchies for the objects; one used for static objects, and one for dynamic objects. Since dynamic objects have special needs, which will be seen later in this chapter, this can be useful. Again, many of these topics are often game specific with no right or wrong answer. A look at the DynamicModel class with the relevant members that deal with LOD can be seen in Listing 5.4.

GEOMETRY SORTING AND CULLING

The key to a fast rendering system is to be able to render only what is visible to the viewer, to display geometry at a resolution (polygon count) that is satisfactory at the distance between the object and the viewer, and to avoid as many unnecessary state switches as possible, among other things. To achieve this, numerous different data structures can be used in video games. The use of a specific implementation is highly game specific, as discussed previously.

When it comes to culling, a frustum can be created around the viewing volume by constructing a list of planes. Objects can be tested within this set of planes for visibility. When an object is tested, a bounding volume around that object is normally used. The fastest bounding volume is a bounding sphere, and is normally used as a quick detection of possible collisions, visibility, and so forth. Normally, a combination of a bounding sphere and some other bounding volume is used, since the bounding sphere test is very fast and can quickly discard most objects in the scene. Since the bounding sphere is a fast but inaccurate test, other types of volume tests can follow; for example, an oriented bounding box.

Culling can also be used for the geometry of the game world. By splitting an environment (e.g., a terrain) into a hierarchy of bounding volumes, a culling algorithm can process it by starting at the root node and testing for visibility. If the root is visible, each of its children is tested. For the children that pass the test, their children are tested, and so on until the entire tree has been processed. This process can eliminate entire branches in the tree, because if a parent is not visible, its children are not visible. This elimination leads to an increase in performance between entire chunks of a game world that has been effectively culled from the rendering process.

A number of different types of data structures can be used to partition a space or a scene in this manner. Each of these types has its strengths and weaknesses, which are highly game specific. Understanding the nature of these different types of partitioning can help developers when deciding on which technique to use in their games. In games, geometry can be partitioned, as seen with terrains, or space itself can be partitioned, which can be used for creating trees of object positions for static and dynamic objects in the game world.

TYPES OF SPACE PARTITIONING

Many different types of partitioning schemes can exist in computer graphics. Some schemes work well with indoor scenes and some with outdoor scenes. All these techniques try to take a complex environment and break it into smaller pieces. These smaller pieces of geometry are easier to manage, and using a tree of these pieces can allow for fast culling of the game world. In the following section, the types of techniques discussed are BSP trees, quad trees, octrees, and portals.

BSP Trees

Binary Space Partitioning (BSP) trees are recursively created trees that use planes to split a convex space. In computers, binary means two, and in a binary tree, a space is split into two halves by a plane. This is done by taking a plane in the scene and determining if something (e.g., polygons, etc.) is on the front side of the plane, back side of the plane, or is clipping the plane. When an object clips a plane (e.g., a triangle clips a plane), it is split into two pieces so that the one piece is on the front side and the second piece is on the backside of the plane. An example of a BSP tree can be seen in Figure 5.3.

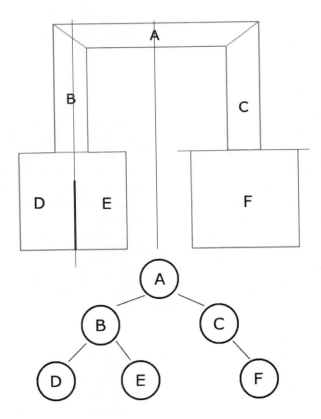

FIGURE 5.3 A BSP tree.

When it comes to rendering, BSP trees can be used to render a scene in front to back order, or vice versa, using the painter's algorithm. This was used in the early days of 3D games when hardware-accelerated Z-buffers did not exist. By drawing a scene from back to front, a game can correctly display a scene from any viewing point in a game. Without depth testing, a game would need to know what order to draw polygons in for them to render correctly. This was the job of a BSP tree when it came to rendering.

BSP trees can be used for other things than rendering, like collision detection. Today, BSP trees are still used in games such as *Half-Life 2*. Traditional BSP trees suffered from overdraw issues, which other techniques, when combined with BSP trees, helped to overcome. One such technique is potential visibility sets, or PVSs. BSP trees can be used with PVSs and the Z-buffer to draw scenes rather fast. BSP trees are well suited for indoor scenes and have been used greatly in first-person shooters and other video game types where the indoor scenes greatly benefited from a BSP tree. The performance of a BSP tree has a number of factors, one of which being whether the tree is balanced. A balanced tree can be processed faster in most situations than an unbalanced tree, and is the type of tree desired in many games.

*k*d Trees

A *k*d tree is a data structure that splits a space into k-dimensions and is a special type of BSP tree. In a BSP tree, arbitrary planes are used to split a space into sections; in *k*d trees, a plane that is perpendicular to a certain axis is used to split the space. As a *k*d tree is being created, it alternates between axes that determine the direction of the splitting plane. In 3D space, the tree would be known as a 3d tree, with 3 replacing the *k*, because it specifies the number of dimensions with *k* being a general term for an unknown number of dimensions. An example of a *k*d tree can be seen in Figure 5.4.

*K*d trees have many different uses, and their performance deals with whether they are balanced. One popular use for a *k*d tree is to use it with photon mapping in ray tracing. Photon mapping is a global illumination technique used to accurately shade an environment in ray tracing. Using a *k*d tree with photon mapping can accelerate the shading process.

Quad Trees

A quad tree is a data structure in which each node is split into four smaller nodes, whereas binary trees split their nodes into two sections. Quad trees are used for splitting up a 2D region into a hierarchy. Quad trees can be used in 3D games because the quad tree splits in two dimensions, meaning that it uses two planes for each node. For example, a plane along the x-axis and a plane along the y-axis at the

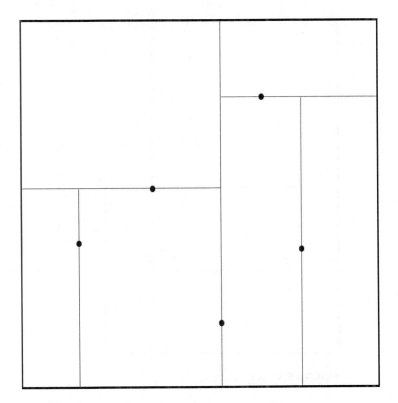

FIGURE 5.4   A *k*d tree.

same point will split a cube into four smaller sections. View frustum culling is used on quad trees to test the bounding box of each node for visibility. An example of a quad tree can be seen in Figure 5.5 where a box is divided into two different levels.

Octrees

An octree is a 3D version of a quad tree where three planes are used to split a node instead of two. With octrees, each node can have eight children; hence, the oct in octree. Octrees, and quad trees, are frequently used for the visibility determination of outdoor scenes such as terrains. They are better suited for outdoor scenes because of the viewing distance those kinds of scenes offer. When it comes to indoor scenes, many walls can easily occlude geometry that otherwise passes the frustum culling test. This causes many polygons to be drawn that should not be; therefore,

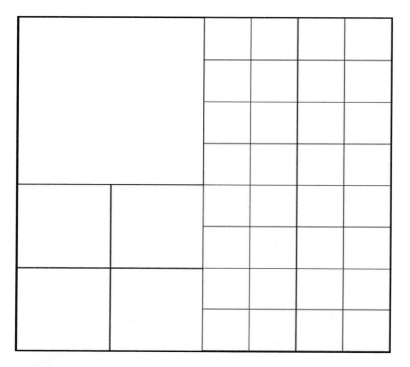

FIGURE 5.5 A quad tree.

there are better options for rendering indoor scenes than to use an octree or a quad tree. An example of an octree can be seen in Figure 5.6.

Portals

Portal rendering is used to render scenes with no overdraws in an efficient manner. In portal rendering, each section of the game world is broken up into sections that are connected by invisible "portals." These portals are planes that mark where two sections meet. Each individual section is known as a sector. When a sector is created, its portals are connected to other sectors. When inside a sector, any sector that is connected to any visible portal that can be seen by the viewer is rendered, and then the sector the viewer is inside is rendered.

Portals are usually created from closed areas such as doors, tunnels, windows, and so forth. Portal rendering is ideally good for indoor scenes, because portals can be clearly defined, whereas with outdoor scenes it is not as easy to define efficient portals or to section off parts of the game world. When rendering a portal, all poly-

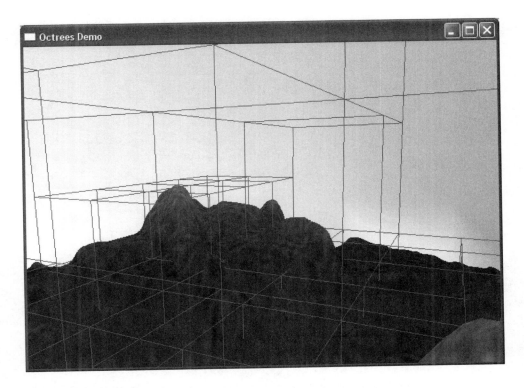

FIGURE 5.6 An octree.

gons that are visible to that portal based on the viewer are clipped to that portal. All clipped polygons are drawn and the rest of the polygons are culled out. An example of portal rendering can be seen in Figure 5.7.

PARTITIONING IN THE BUILDING BLOCKS ENGINE

As an example of defining a bounding volume hierarchy, the Building Blocks Engine creates an octree. This octree is used as an example of how to create a BVH to partition space. The octree takes a bounding box and splits it until some threshold is met. The octree is created by recursively calling the CreateNode() function of the octree node class. This function creates the entire BVH until a level limit condition is met. As mentioned previously, BVH classes are highly game specific. This example is a simple test that allows an empty space to be split up. The class declaration of the OctreeNode class can be seen in Listing 5.7. The CreateNode() function can be

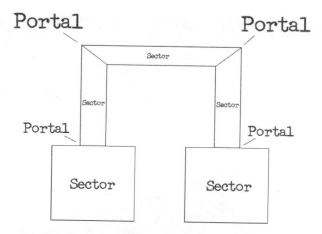

FIGURE 5.7 A portal system.

seen listed in Listing 5.8, and the remaining functions of the class can be seen listed in Listing 5.9. A screen shot of the octree BVH being rendered as wireframe boxes can be seen in Figure 5.8.

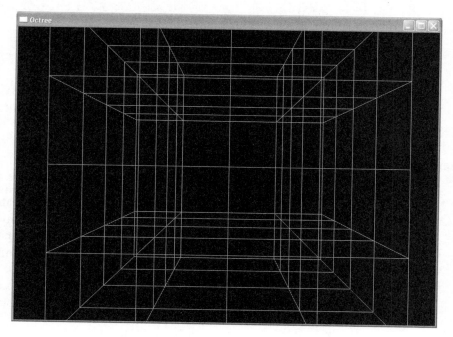

FIGURE 5.8 Wireframe of the octree.

On the companion CD-ROM is a demo application that uses this example octree class as explained in the previous paragraph. The octree is then rendered to the screen so it is visible. The demo application can be found in the BUILDING BLOCKS ENGINE/EXAMPLES/CHAPTER 5 folder and is called OCTREE.

LISTING 5.7   The `OctreeNode` class declaration.

```cpp
class OctreeNode
{
   public:
      OctreeNode();
      virtual ~OctreeNode();

      void CreateNode(Vector3D center, float bbSize,
                      int currentLevel, int maxLevel);

      bool isLeaf() { return m_isLeaf; }
      Vector3D GetCenter() { return m_center; }
      float GetSize() { return m_bbSize; }
      OctreeNode **GetSubNodes() { return m_childNodes; }

   private:
      bool m_isLeaf;
      Vector3D m_center;
      float m_bbSize;

      OctreeNode *m_childNodes[8];
};
```

LISTING 5.8   The `CreateNode()` function.

```cpp
void OctreeNode::CreateNode(Vector3D center, float bbSize,
                            int currentLevel, int maxLevel)
{
   m_bbSize = bbSize;
   m_center = center;

   if(currentLevel >= maxLevel)
   {
      m_isLeaf = true;
```

```
      return;
   }

   float newSize = bbSize / 4;
   m_isLeaf = false;

   Vector3D topFrontLeft (-newSize, newSize,  newSize);
   Vector3D topFrontRight( newSize, newSize,  newSize);
   Vector3D topBackLeft  (-newSize, newSize, -newSize);
   Vector3D topBackRight (newSize, newSize,  -newSize);
   Vector3D bottomFrontLeft (-newSize, -newSize,  newSize);
   Vector3D bottomFrontRight( newSize, -newSize,  newSize);
   Vector3D bottomBackLeft  (-newSize, -newSize, -newSize);
   Vector3D bottomBackRight ( newSize, -newSize, -newSize);

   m_childNodes[TOP_FRONT_LEFT] = new OctreeNode();
   m_childNodes[TOP_FRONT_RIGHT] = new OctreeNode();
   m_childNodes[TOP_BACK_LEFT] = new OctreeNode();
   m_childNodes[TOP_BACK_RIGHT] = new OctreeNode();
   m_childNodes[BOTTOM_FRONT_LEFT] = new OctreeNode();
   m_childNodes[BOTTOM_FRONT_RIGHT] = new OctreeNode();
   m_childNodes[BOTTOM_BACK_LEFT] = new OctreeNode();
   m_childNodes[BOTTOM_BACK_RIGHT] = new OctreeNode();

   currentLevel++;
   m_childNodes[TOP_FRONT_LEFT]->CreateNode((m_center +
      topFrontLeft), bbSize / 2, currentLevel, maxLevel);
   currentLevel—;

   currentLevel++;
   m_childNodes[TOP_FRONT_RIGHT]->CreateNode((m_center +
      topFrontRight), bbSize / 2, currentLevel, maxLevel);
   currentLevel—;

   currentLevel++;
   m_childNodes[TOP_BACK_LEFT]->CreateNode((m_center +
      topBackLeft), bbSize / 2, currentLevel, maxLevel);
   currentLevel—;

   currentLevel++;
   m_childNodes[TOP_BACK_RIGHT]->CreateNode((m_center +
```

```
      topBackRight), bbSize / 2, currentLevel, maxLevel);
   currentLevel—;

   currentLevel++;
   m_childNodes[BOTTOM_FRONT_LEFT]->CreateNode((m_center +
      bottomFrontLeft), bbSize / 2, currentLevel, maxLevel);
   currentLevel—;

   currentLevel++;
   m_childNodes[BOTTOM_FRONT_RIGHT]->CreateNode((m_center +
      bottomFrontRight), bbSize / 2, currentLevel, maxLevel);
   currentLevel—;

   currentLevel++;
   m_childNodes[BOTTOM_BACK_LEFT]->CreateNode((m_center +
      bottomBackLeft), bbSize / 2, currentLevel, maxLevel);
   currentLevel—;

   currentLevel++;
   m_childNodes[BOTTOM_BACK_RIGHT]->CreateNode((m_center +
      bottomBackRight), bbSize / 2, currentLevel, maxLevel);
   currentLevel—;
}
```

LISTING 5.9   The remaining `OctreeNode` functions.

```
OctreeNode::OctreeNode()
{
   m_isLeaf = 0;
   m_bbSize = 0;

   for(int i = 0; i < 8; i++)
      m_childNodes[i] = 0;
}


OctreeNode::~OctreeNode()
{
   for(int i = 0; i < 8; i++)
   {
```

```
            if(m_childNodes[i] != 0)
            {
               delete m_childNodes[i];
               m_childNodes[i] = 0;
            }
        }
     }
```

PORTALS RENDERING IN THE ENGINE

To create a portal rendering system would require, at minimum, the creation of a data structure to represent sectors and one for portals. The sectors can contain the actual geometry and a list of portals, while the portals can contain pointers to two sectors. When a sector it rendered, its vertex list is drawn out. When a portal is processed, the algorithm draws the two sectors that connect to it. To keep an infinite loop from appearing when a sector is drawn repeatedly, a flag can be used for each sector to determine if it was rendered already. The rendering flag can be replaced with a counter that can allow a sector to be drawn a number of times before the recursion is halted. This can be useful for situations in which a sector's portal can connect to itself. This can be done with mirrors, where the portal is the mirror and the connecting sector is to itself, as seen in the *Duke Nukem 3D* game. A portal rendering system can also be used to render worlds in an almost paradoxical way by allowing portals in sectors to connect to themselves or to sectors that are physically nowhere near it. This can be seen in the Xbox 360 game *Prey*, where the character can enter portals in the oddest places that lead to completely different locations in the game world. This can also be seen in that game if the character is looking through an open portal that leads behind it, allowing it to be able to shoot itself in the back. Another example can be seen in Valve's *Portal* game, which, if the dynamic portals are positioned correctly, can allow for the top half of a model to be visible in one portal and the bottom half to be visible in the other portal that can be right next to it. This leads to an object that is leaving one portal to re-enter it over and over again, which was demonstrated in the tech videos released by Valve.

A portal rendering system is created in Chapter 9, "Game Demos," and is made part of a demo called 3D WALKTHROUGH. The demo allows a viewer to navigate a relatively simple game world that is split into sectors that are connected by portals. The demo also has some additional features that are discussed in Chapter 9 in more detail. The demo is simple and straightforward and does not have the paradoxical rendering support as seen in games like *Prey*, but the support can be added and will be added in future versions of the Building Blocks Engine.

EFFECTS

In the Building Blocks Engine, just about everything dealing with rendering is application specific and user defined. For example, when rendering vertices, a custom vertex structure is created, a vertex descriptor is created for that structure, and the information needed to draw a model is passed to the rendering system's Render() function. Effects in the Building Blocks Engine work in the same sense in that they are user defined and often application specific.

Effects are created by creating a class for a specific effect. An effect can be anything from texture mapping, to bump mapping, and so forth. By creating a class for an effect, that effect can have everything it needs to perform its job. This can include shaders, shader parameters, texture handles, and so forth. Everything in an effect is resource managed to allow sharing between objects. Every object in the scene can have its own effect class, or share effect classes if the same shaders, texture, and shader parameters are reused.

In the Building Blocks Engine, all effects derive from the base class Effect. In the scene graph, these effects are applied by the GeometryNode class and are a part of the DynamicModel class. The base class for the Effect class and the classes used for the resource management of an effect can be seen listed in Listing 5.10.

LISTING 5.10   The Effect class.

```
class Effect
{
   public:
      Effect()
      {
      }

      virtual ~Effect()
      {
         Release();
      }

      virtual void ApplyEffect() = 0;

      virtual void Release()
      {
      }
};
```

```
class EffectResourceTag
{

};


class EffectResource
{
   public:
      EffectResource(Effect *effect)
      {
         m_effect = effect;
      }

      virtual ~EffectResource()
      {
         FreeMemory();
      }

      Effect *GetEffect()
      {
         return m_effect;
      }

   private:
      void FreeMemory()
      {
         if(m_effect != NULL)
            delete m_effect;

         m_effect = NULL;
      }

      Effect *m_effect;
};
```

To demonstrate the workings of the Effect class, the Building Blocks Engine has a number of effects already defined in the SOURCE folder on the companion CD-ROM. These effects include texture mapping, multitexturing, a luminance filter, a sepia filter, alpha mapping, reflection mapping, per-vertex lighting, per-pixel lighting, bump mapping, and specular mapping. An example of the texture mapping effect without a shader can be seen in Listing 5.11.

ON THE CD

LISTING 5.11   Texture mapping without a shader.

```
class TextureMapEffect : public Effect
{
    public:
        TextureMapEffect(char *decalFile,
                         std::vector<BB_FILTER_TYPE> *filters,
                         RenderInterface *renderer)
        {
            m_renderer = renderer;

            if(m_renderer != NULL)
            {
                m_renderer->LoadTexFromFile(decalFile, BB_TEX2D_TYPE,
                                            &m_decalTexture);

                m_renderer->ApplyFilters(m_decalTexture, filters);
            }
        }

        virtual ~TextureMapEffect()
        {
        }

        void ApplyEffect()
        {
            if(m_renderer != NULL)
                m_renderer->ApplyTexture(0, m_decalTexture);
        }

    protected:
        BB_TEXTURE m_decalTexture;
        RenderInterface *m_renderer;
};
```

The texture mapping effect has as a member variable a decal texture and a pointer to the rendering system. The constructor of this class takes the texture handle for the object's decal texture. `ApplyEffect()` is called before the object is rendered and the texture is applied to texture unit 0. Because this effect is so simple, so is the class that represents it. To perform multitexture with two decals, a second texture handle can be added to the class. This can be seen listed in Listing 5.12.

LISTING 5.12 Multitexturing without a shader.

```cpp
class MultiTexEffect : public Effect
{
   public:
      MultiTexEffect(char *decalFile1, char *decalFile2,
                     std::vector<BB_FILTER_TYPE> *filters,
                     RenderInterface *renderer)
      {
         m_renderer = renderer;

         if(m_renderer != NULL)
         {
            m_renderer->LoadTexFromFile(decalFile1, BB_TEX2D_TYPE,
                                        &m_decalTexture1);

            m_renderer->ApplyFilters(m_decalTexture1, filters);

            m_renderer->LoadTexFromFile(decalFile2, BB_TEX2D_TYPE,
                                        &m_decalTexture2);

            m_renderer->ApplyFilters(m_decalTexture2, filters);
         }
      }

      virtual ~MultiTexEffect()
      {
      }

      void ApplyEffect()
      {
         if(m_renderer != NULL)
         {
            m_renderer->ApplyTexture(0, m_decalTexture1);
            m_renderer->ApplyTexture(1, m_decalTexture2);
         }
      }

   protected:
      BB_TEXTURE m_decalTexture1, m_decalTexture2;
      RenderInterface *m_renderer;
};
```

Along with nonshader texture mapping, there are also shader versions. The shader versions take a GLSL shader along with the texture handles needed for the effect. The class also has as member variables the necessary GLSL parameters for the model-view projection matrix and the decal image for the texture mapping shader. The shader version of the texture mapping and multitexture classes can be seen in Listing 5.13. A screenshot of the effect in action can be seen in Figure 5.9. On the companion CD-ROM is a demo application in the BUILDING BLOCKS ENGINE/ EXAMPLES/CHAPTER 5 folder called TEXTURE MAPPING that demonstrates how to perform texture mapping with the texture shader effect in a scene graph.

ON THE CD

FIGURE 5.9 Texture mapping in action.

LISTING 5.13 Texture mapping with a shader.

```
class TextureShader : public Effect
{
    public:
```

```
TextureShader(char *vs, char *ps, char *decalFile,
              std::vector<BB_FILTER_TYPE> *filters,
              RenderInterface *renderer)
{
   m_renderer = renderer;

   if(m_renderer != NULL)
   {
      m_renderer->LoadTexFromFile(decalFile, BB_TEX2D_TYPE,
                                  &m_decalTexture);

      m_renderer->ApplyFilters(m_decalTexture, filters);

      m_renderer->CreateShaderFromFile(vs, ps, &m_shader);

      m_renderer->SetupShaderParameter("mvp", m_shader,
                                       &m_mvpParam);

      m_renderer->SetupShaderParameter("decal", m_shader,
                                       &m_decalParam);
   }
}

~TextureShader()
{

}

void ApplyEffect()
{
   if(m_renderer != NULL)
   {
      m_renderer->ApplyShader(m_shader);

      m_renderer->SetShaderParameter1f(m_decalParam, 0);
      m_renderer->ApplyTexture(0, m_decalTexture);
   }
}

void Release()
{
   if(m_renderer != NULL)
```

```
                    m_renderer->DeleteTexture(m_decalTexture);
        }


    protected:
        ShaderHandle m_shader;
        ParameterHandle m_mvpParam;
        ParameterHandle m_decalParam;

        BB_TEXTURE m_decalTexture;

        RenderInterface *m_renderer;
    };
```

LIGHTING

Lighting is a very important effect in modern 3D games, and adds a level of quality that can dramatically increase the detail and renderings of a 3D scene. Lighting usually falls within two main categories—per-vertex lighting and per-pixel lighting—and can be done in real time or pre-processed. The lighting discussed in the next section is done using shaders in real time. More complex and realistic lighting that combine realistic shadows can also be done using pre-processing algorithms. In most games, a combination of real-time and pre-processed lighting is used to increase the rendering quality. It is assumed that you are familiar with lighting in 3D scenes. For more detailed information on lighting, several book resources are listed in Appendix A, "Additional Resources."

Per-Vertex Lighting

Per-vertex lighting is calculated for every vertex of a 3D geometrical shape. Per-vertex lighting is easy to do with and without shaders. To perform the technique without shaders, the lighting contribution can be passed to the rendering system as the vertex color. When using shaders, all that is required is to use a vertex shader, since that is where all the necessary calculations will happen. For per-vertex lighting, the lighting contribution for every vertex can be combined with the total color contribution (i.e., when textures are applied) at that point. See Figure 5.10 for an example of per-vertex lighting in a 3D scene.

The problem with per-vertex lighting is that the quality is dependent on the total number of vertices in a 3D model. To get decent quality in 3D scenes using per-vertex lighting requires games to use a high number of triangles for everything in a scene. This is unacceptable because the more polygons that are processed, the

FIGURE 5.10 Per-vertex lighting.

lower the performance. LOD and other optimizations can help, but for objects that are close, the increased number of polygons that are needed to increase the lighting quality will often be unacceptable. Per-vertex lighting is not recommended, because there are better alternatives that will be looked at later in this section.

ON THE CD

A demo application on the companion CD-ROM called PER-VERTEX LIGHTING can be found in the BUILDING BLOCKS ENGINE/EXMAPLES/ CHAPTER 5 folder and performs the technique on a simple geometrical shape using a GLSL shader, which can be seen in Listing 5.14. The rendering function from the PER-VERTEX LIGHTING demo application can be seen in Listing 5.15. The lighting of a scene is done for every vertex processed. The lighting equation used is a simple diffuse light using the dot product of the light vector and the surface normal that is being shaded (N dot L), and is all done in the vertex shader. The pixel shader in this demo combines the decal texture with the incoming vertex color, which is used to store the vertex total light. The GLSL pixel shader for this demo application can be seen in Listing 5.16.

LISTING 5.14   The vertex shader for per-vertex lighting.

```
varying vec4 color;

uniform vec4 lightPos;
uniform vec4 lightColor;


void main()
{
   gl_Position = gl_ModelViewProjectionMatrix * gl_Vertex;

   vec3 n = gl_NormalMatrix * gl_Normal;

   vec4 lightVec = normalize(gl_Vertex - lightPos);
   float dp = max(dot(n, lightVec.xyz), 0.0);
   color = lightColor * dp;
}
```

LISTING 5.15   The rendering function from the PER-VERTEX LIGHTING demo.

```
void DemoRender()
{
   g_Render.StartRendering(1, 1, 0);

   g_Render.LoadIdentityMatrix();

   g_Render.SetView(0, 3, 5, 0, 0, 0, 0, 1, 0);
   g_Render.RotateMatrix((float)g_xRot, 0, 1, 0);
   g_Render.RotateMatrix((float)g_yRot, 1, 0, 0);

   g_Render.ApplyShader(g_shader);

   g_Render.SetupMatrixTracking(g_mvpParam, BB_MVP_MATRIX,
                                BB_IDENTITY_MATRIX);

   g_Render.SetupMatrixTracking(g_mvInvParam,
                                BB_MODELVIEW_MATRIX,
                                BB_INVERSE_MATRIX);

   g_Render.SetShaderParameter3f(g_lightPos, 0, 5, 8);
   g_Render.SetShaderParameter3f(g_lightCol, 1, 1, 1);
```

```
g_Render.SetShaderTextureParameter(g_decalParam, g_tex);

g_Render.Render(BB_PRIMITIVE_TRI_LIST, &g_desc,
                (char*)g_boxData, g_boxIndices,
                sizeof(g_boxData), g_numBoxIndices,
                sizeof(stVertex));

g_Render.EndRendering();
}
```

LISTING 5.16 The pixel shader for per-vertex lighting.

```
varying vec4 color;


void main()
{
    gl_FragColor = color;
}
```

Per-Pixel Lighting

Per-pixel lighting is the process of calculating the lighting contribution on a per-pixel level than on a per-vertex level. Since there are more pixels than there are vertices, this can instantly lead to a higher quality of lighting when compared to per-vertex lighting. This is because for per-vertex lighting, on a triangle, three colors are interpolated across the surface evenly. When it comes to per-pixel lighting, there is no interpolation; every pixel has its own lighting contribution that affects the final rendered scene. The increase in quality per-pixel lighting offers comes with a decrease in performance. With modern hardware, this is becoming less of an issue and more games are taking advantage of this.

Unlike per-vertex lighting, per-pixel lighting is unaffected by the number of triangles. Instead, per-pixel lighting is affected by the resolution of the rendered scene. With per-pixel lighting, we can move the lighting equation into the pixel shader so that the lighting is evaluated on a per-pixel basis. The per-pixel lighting demo can be seen in Figure 5.11. On the companion CD-ROM in the BUILDING BLOCKS ENGINE/EXAMPLES/CHAPTER 5 folder is a demo application called PER-PIXELLIGHTING. See Listing 5.17 for the shader code for the per-pixel lighting demo application. Note that the per-pixel lighting demo application

ON THE CD

added specular lighting along with the diffuse contribution. The different between the PER-VERTEX LIGHTING and PER-PIXEL LIGHTING demos are the high-level shaders.

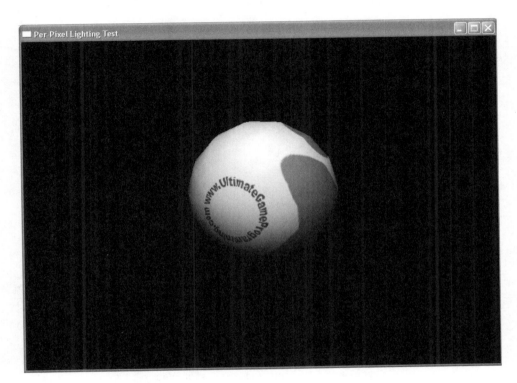

FIGURE 5.11   Per-pixel lighting.

LISTING 5.17   The per-pixel lighting shader.

```
[Vertex Shader]

varying vec2 texCoords;
varying vec3 pos;
varying vec3 normal;
```

```
void main()
{
   gl_Position = gl_ModelViewProjectionMatrix * gl_Vertex;
   pos = gl_Vertex.xyz;
   normal = gl_NormalMatrix * gl_Normal;

   texCoords = gl_MultiTexCoord0.xy;
}


 [Pixel Shader]

varying vec2 texCoords;
varying vec3 pos;
varying vec3 normal;

uniform sampler2D decal;
uniform vec4 lightPos;
uniform vec4 lightColor;
uniform vec4 camPos;
uniform float shininess;


void main()
{
   vec3 lightVec = normalize(lightPos.xyz - pos);
   vec3 n = normalize(normal);

   float d = dot(lightVec.xyz, lightVec.xyz);
   float attenuationFactor = 1.0 / (d * d);

   float dp = dot(n, lightVec);
   vec4 diffuse = vec4(attenuationFactor * lightColor.xyz * dp,1);

   vec3 eyeVec = normalize(camPos.xyz - pos);
   vec3 halfVec = normalize(lightVec.xyz + eyeVec);
   float specularLight = pow(dot(n, halfVec), shininess);
   vec4 specular = vec4(attenuationFactor * lightColor.xyz *
                        specularLight, 1);
```

```
    vec4 col = texture2D(decal, texCoords);

    gl_FragColor = col * (0.3 + diffuse + specular);
}
```

BUMP MAPPING

Bump mapping is a type of per-pixel lighting technique. What separates bump mapping from per-pixel lighting is that traditional bump mapping uses normals in the lighting calculations from a texture known as a bump map, while per-pixel lighting uses vertex, or face, normals. With interpolated vertex normals across a surface, you get a slight change from one point to the next. This change is smooth across the entire surface in traditional per-pixel lighting. By altering the normals of every pixel, you can change the lighting from smooth to bumpy. Using a bump map that has some type of pattern will create lighting on a surface that looks like that pattern; thus causing the illusion of detail. This means that bump mapping is used to add "fake" detail because the slight changes in normals give the appearance that there is more to what is seen than what actually is there. See Figure 5.12 for an example of bump mapping versus traditional per-pixel lighting.

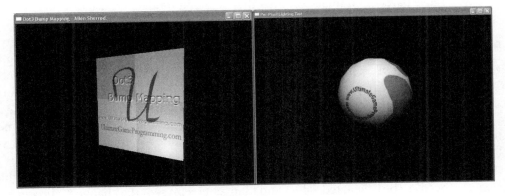

FIGURE 5.12   Bump mapping versus per-pixel lighting.

In bump mapping, the images used store normal values instead of RGB color values. In these images, the RGB color of images actually represents the XYZ direction of a normal. Technically, they are still color images, but since the values in bump maps are not used for colors, they are called bump maps instead of decal textures. There are many tools to create a bump map out of a pattern, or it can be manually calculated. All normals in a bump map must be normalized at some point to achieve the correct results using the technique. Since a bump map is a pattern, we only need to use grayscale color values from images instead of any one component from a source image. That grayscale pixel is normalized with its neighbors (to the right and underneath) using the same formula you would use to normalize a triangle, as discussed in Chapter 4. Do that for all pixels in the image and you have a bump map.

Bump maps look blue because the blue, or Z, component of each pixel is the highest value because the normal is pointing out of the image along the axis.

Object versus Tangent Space Bump Mapping

There are generally two types of bump mapping: object space and texture (tangent) space bump mapping. Object space bump mapping is straightforward and uses the normal from the normal map directly. You must use unique texture coordinates (i.e., no mirroring) when doing object space bump mapping. This is mostly because the normals in the bump map must point in a certain direction, and you can't reuse parts of an image on the other side of a model because technically, the normals should be pointing in a different direction.

Object space bump mapping has other issues that make it a little less attractive than texture space bump mapping. Texture space bump mapping is doing bump mapping in a different space system. By using a TBN matrix (tangent, bi-normal, normal), we can convert a light in object space into texture space and perform the lighting calculations there. This allows us to bypass all the limitations of the object space bump mapping, but requires a bit more setup than before. First, we need to know the tangent (s-tangent), bi-normal (t-tangent), and normal of each vertex. We already know how to get the normal, and the bi-normal is just the cross product between the normal and tangent. The tangent is the only unknown variable that needs to be calculated. The s and t tangents represent the change in direction of the TU and TV texture coordinates.

Bump mapping can use the same code as per-pixel lighting, with the exception of getting the normal from an image and, when dealing with texture-space bump mapping, transforming the light direction vector to texture space (or normal to object space). Listing 5.18 lists the Cg shader used to perform bump mapping in the BUMP MAPPING demo. The BUMP MAPPING demo can be found on the companion CD-ROM in the BUILDING BLOCKS ENGINE/EXAMPLES/CHAPTER 5 folder. There is also a tool on the CD-ROM in the BUILDING BLOCKS ENGINE/

ON THE CD

TOOLS folder called BUMP MAP GENERATOR and it is used to take a grayscale .TGA image (height map) and convert it into a bump map. A detailed explanation of the tool and the tool's source code can be found in Appendix B "Additional Tools."

LISTING 5.18   The texture-space bump mapping shader.

```
[Vertex Shader]

varying vec2 texCoords;
varying vec3 pos;
varying vec3 normal;
varying vec3 sTangent;


void main()
{
   gl_Position = gl_ModelViewProjectionMatrix * gl_Vertex;

   pos = gl_Vertex;
   normal = gl_NormalMatrix * gl_Normal;
   sTangent = gl_Color;
   texCoords = gl_MultiTexCoord0.xy;
}


 [Pixel Shader]

varying vec2 texCoords;
varying vec3 pos;
varying vec3 normal;
varying vec3 sTangent;

uniform sampler2D decal;
uniform sampler2D bump;
uniform vec4 lightPos;
uniform vec4 lightColor;


void main()
{
```

```
        vec3 lightVec = lightPos - pos;
        vec3 n = normalize(normal);

        vec3 binormal = cross(sTangent, n);
        mat3 tbnMatrix = mat3(sTangent, binormal, n);

        lightVec = tbnMatrix * lightVec;
        lightVec = normalize(lightVec);

        n = texture2D(bump, texCoords).xyz;
        n = (n - 0.5) * 2;

        float d = dot(lightVec.xyz, lightVec.xyz);
        float attenuationFactor = 1 / (d * d);

        float dp = max(dot(n, lightVec.xyz), 0);
        vec4 diffuse = vec4(attenuationFactor * lightColor.xyz * dp, 1);

        vec4 col = texture2D(decal, texCoords);

        gl_FragColor = col * (0.3 + diffuse);
    }
```

NORMAL MAPPING

What exactly is normal mapping? Aren't normal mapping and bump mapping the same? As already seen in the previous section, bump mapping is the process of taking a grayscale image that represents a height map and using that information to generate normals. These normals are used in per-pixel lighting to vary the lighting contribution for each pixel to give the illusion of detail on the surface. Normal mapping is similar, but instead of creating normals from a height map, normal mapping uses normals created from a high- and low-resolution polygonal mesh.

Performing bump mapping on a low-resolution model with an image that was generated out of it and a higher resolution model will give the lower resolution geometry the appearance of the high-resolution one. For normal mapping, we create a high-resolution model, a lower resolution model suitable for real-time applications, and a normal map out of the two, and apply that normal map to the low-resolution model in a game to give it the appearance of looking like the high-resolution one.

Normal mapping is a neat little trick that most modern games use in great detail. This can be seen in games like *Gears of War*, *Quake 4*, *Doom 3*, *Halo 3*, and many more using normal mapping to increase the detail and realism in a scene without the high polygon count. Using normal mapping, we can take a scene with millions of polygons and represent it in the same or almost the same detail using several thousand. The purpose of bump mapping as a whole is to add detail to the detail-less. Since bump mapping is an extension to per-pixel lighting, we also get realistic lighting effects when using normal mapping.

There are many ways to create a normal map. We can use a tool like NVIDIA's Melody as seen in Figure 5.13. We could also use ATI's Normal Mapper command-line tool, 3D modeling applications like ZBrush 2 (check out Figure 5.14 for a look at ZBrush 2), 3ds Max, LightWave, Maya, and many more. There are many plug-ins for existing modelers and even built-in support for normal mapping function-

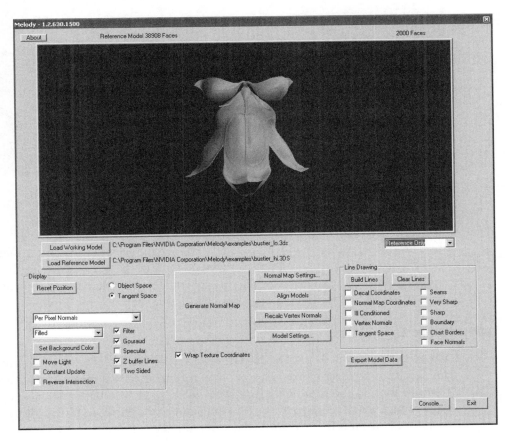

FIGURE 5.13 NVIDIA's Melody in action.

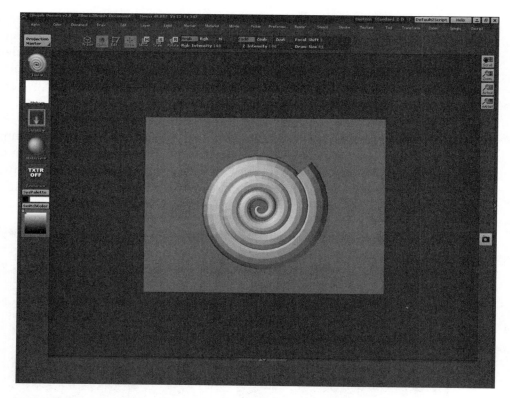

FIGURE 5.14   ZBrush 2 normal mapping.

ality. As long as you have a high polygon reference model and a low polygon model with UV texture coordinates, you can generate one of these images using a normal mapping tool. You can also calculate the normal map manually, but this involves some principles of ray tracing, which is beyond the scope of this book.

LUMINANCE AND SEPIA TONE

The next two effects deal with image filtering. Filtering an image requires running an algorithm across the pixels of a decal texture to alter its appearance. In this section, we look at the luminance and sepia filters. The luminance filter will give a color image an appearance of being black and white. A sepia filter will make an image look like it is being displayed on an old television set.

For the luminance filter, the required vertex inputs are a position and its texture coordinate. The vertex shader passes information to the pixel shader. In the pixel shader, it calculates the new color of the value fetched from the color map by finding the dot product against it, and the luminance coefficient, which is R(0.3), G(0.59), and B(0.11). The result of the dot product is then used as the color of the pixel at that location. Since the value is grayscale, we use the result as the R, G, and B of the final color. See Listing 5.19 for the shader for the luminance filter, and Figure 5.16 for a screenshot of this shader in action.

FIGURE 5.15 Luminance filter screenshot.

LISTING 5.19 The luminance filter in GLSL.

```
[Vertex Shader]

varying vec2 texCoords;

void main()
{
    gl_Position = gl_ModelViewProjectionMatrix * gl_Vertex;
    texCoords = gl_MultiTexCoord0.xy;
```

```
}


 [Pixel Shader]

varying vec2 texCoords;

uniform sampler2D decal;


void main()
{
    vec3 lumConst = vec3(0.30, 0.59, 0.11);

    vec3 color = texture2D(decal, texCoords).xyz;
    float dp = dot(color, lumConst);

    gl_FragColor = vec4(dp, dp, dp, 1);
}
```

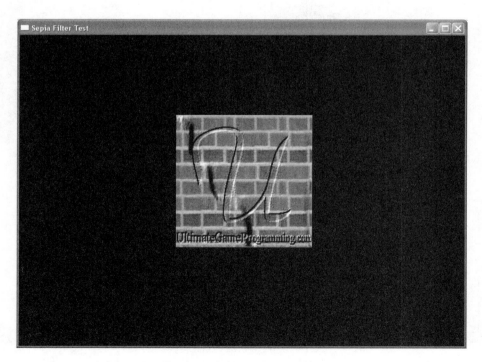

FIGURE 5.16   The sepia effect in action.

The sepia effect builds off the luminance filter to add a new effect, but instead of using the grayscale value as the final color, the shader does a few more operations. For the sepia effect, we have two additional constants: a light value and a dark value. When we get the luminance value of the pixel, we use it as a percentage to interpolate between the light and dark constants. This value can be combined with the color from the decal image to give it the sepia look. See Listing 5.20 for the sepia Cg shader, and Figure 5.17 for a screenshot of the effect in action.

LISTING 5.20   The sepia effect in GLSL.

```
[Vertex Shader]

    varying vec2 texCoords;


    void main()
    {
        gl_Position = gl_ModelViewProjectionMatrix * gl_Vertex;
        texCoords = gl_MultiTexCoord0.xy;
    }


     [Pixel Shader]

    varying vec2 texCoords;

    uniform sampler2D decal;


    void main()
    {
        vec3 lumConst = vec3(0.30, 0.59, 0.11);
        vec4 light = vec4(1.0, 0.9, 0.5, 1.0);
        vec4 dark = vec4(0.2, 0.05, 0.0, 1.0);

        vec4 color = texture2D(decal, texCoords);
        float dp = dot(color.xyz, lumConst);

        vec4 sepia = lerp(dark, light, dp);
        vec3 luminance = lerp(color.xyz, dp, 0.5);
        vec3 final = lerp(luminance, sepia.xyz, 0.5);

        gl_FragColor = vec4(final, 1.0);
    }
```

Both the luminance and sepia effects can be found on the companion CD-ROM in the BUILDING BLOCKS ENGINE/EXAMPLES/CHAPTER 5 folder and are called LUMINANCE and SEPIA, respectively.

SPECULAR MAPPING

When drawing objects with shiny parts that make up the object's body, not all sections are supposed to have specular lighting. The specular contribution is used for shiny surfaces that reflect light sharply in a direction. If a game is modeling an armored medieval solider, it would not want this specular contribution anywhere other than the character's armor and other shiny parts. In the per-pixel lighting demo application mentioned earlier in this chapter, the specular contribution was applied to the entire model. In this section, we look at how to use specular mapping to control which areas of a model have the specular contribution.

The concept is straightforward. An image is used to define which parts of a model's texture allow for specular reflection. This can be done by storing the specular percent, or even a true/false styled value (where an alpha of 0 is false and anything else is considered true), in the alpha channel of the decal image, or by creating a separate texture with the required information. The goal is to have a specular map that can be used to great effect to control the way the specular contribution from the lighting pass affects a model. See this effect in action in Figure 5.17.

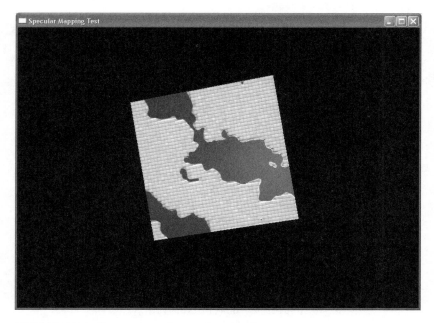

FIGURE 5.17   Screenshot of specular mapping.

There is a demo application on the companion CD-ROM called SPECULAR MAPPING in the BUILDING BLOCKS ENGINE/EXAMPLES/CHAPTER 5 folder. In this demo, we are storing the specular map information in the alpha channel of the decal map, since all we need is the one component and the decal map is not using its alpha channel. Since all we are doing to create this effect is checking the alpha channel and making sure it is not zero before adding the specular value, the shaders are straightforward. See Listing 5.21 for a look at the pixel shader from this demo. There is nothing new or different about the vertex shader, so it is not listed. You can see all

of the demo's code by referring to the CD-ROM. Again, in this demo we are doing per-pixel lighting, but we've added a little conditional statement to keep us from adding the specular contribution to parts of the image the alpha map does not specify.

LISTING 5.21 The SPECULAR MAPPING demo's pixel shader.

```
[Vertex Shader]

varying vec2 texCoords;
varying vec3 pos;
varying vec3 normal;


void main()
{
   gl_Position = gl_ModelViewProjectionMatrix * gl_Vertex;
   pos = gl_Vertex.xyz;
   normal = gl_NormalMatrix * gl_Normal;

   texCoords = gl_MultiTexCoord0.xy;
}


 [Pixel Shader]

varying vec2 texCoords;
varying vec3 pos;
varying vec3 normal;

uniform sampler2D decal;
uniform vec4 lightPos;
uniform vec4 lightColor;
```

```
uniform vec4 camPos;
uniform float shininess;


void main()
{
    vec3 lightVec = normalize(lightPos.xyz - pos);
    vec3 n = normalize(normal);

    float d = dot(lightVec.xyz, lightVec.xyz);
    float attenuationFactor = 1.0 / (d * d);

    float dp = dot(n, lightVec.xyz);
    vec4 diffuse = vec4(attenuationFactor * lightColor.xyz * dp, 1);

    vec3 eyeVec = normalize(camPos.xyz - pos);
    vec3 halfVec = normalize(lightVec.xyz + eyeVec);
    float specularLight = pow(dot(n, halfVec), shininess);
    vec4 specular = vec4(attenuationFactor * lightColor.xyz *
                        specularLight, 1);

    vec4 col = texture2D(decal, texCoords).rgba;

    if(col.a == 0.0)
        specular = vec4(0, 0, 0, 0);

    gl_FragColor = col * (0.3 + diffuse + specular);
}
```

ALPHA MAPPING

Alpha mapping is a simple concept and similar to specular mapping. Normally, when we are doing alpha blending we are blending an entire geometrical surface. This can be done with the alpha component of the vertex color or from a texture image. The interesting thing about a texture image is that we can manipulate the alpha channel so that only parts of an image are transparent. This can lead to many useful things, such as rendering metal fences, chains, blinds, holes, leaves, and much more.

When setting up the alpha blending and its properties, we must take certain steps so we can correctly perform alpha mapping without having to render our primitives from back to front order. Normally, when alpha blending, the current surface being rendered is blended with what is already there. If another surface is drawn that is behind the primitive that came before it, it won't render correctly.

On the companion CD-ROM is a demo application called ALPHA MAPPING in the BUILDING BLOCKS ENGINE/EXAMPLES/CHAPTER 5 folder. The demo application works similar to the specular mapping demo application by specifying the alpha amount for each pixel of a texture image in the alpha channel. Because the demo uses texture mapping with a 32-bit image, the code of interest is not in the shader, which can be seen listed in Listing 5.22, but instead in the rendering function seen in Listing 5.23. A screenshot of the effect can be seen in Figure 5.18.

FIGURE 5.18   ALPHA MAPPING demo screenshot.

LISTING 5.22   The ALPHA MAPPING shader.

```
[Vertex Shader]

varying vec2 texCoords;
```

```
void main()
{
   gl_Position = gl_ModelViewProjectionMatrix * gl_Vertex;
   texCoords = gl_MultiTexCoord0.xy;
}


 [Pixel Shader]

varying vec2 texCoords;

uniform sampler2D decal;


void main()
{
   gl_FragColor = texture2D(decal, texCoords);
}
```

LISTING 5.23 The rendering function of the ALPHA MAPPING demo.

```
void DemoRender()
{
   g_Render.StartRendering(1, 1, 0);
   g_Render.LoadIdentityMatrix();

   g_Render.SetView(0, 3, 5, 0, 0, 0, 0, 1, 0);
   g_Render.RotateMatrix((float)g_xRot, 0, 1, 0);
   g_Render.RotateMatrix((float)g_yRot, 1, 0, 0);

   g_Render.ApplyShader(&g_shader);

   g_Render.SetupMatrixTracking(g_mvpParam, BB_MVP_MATRIX,
                                BB_IDENTITY_MATRIX);

   g_Render.SetShaderTextureParameter(g_decalParam, g_tex);

   g_Render.Enable(BB_ALPHA_TESTING);
   g_Render.SetAlphaFunc(BB_ALPHA_GREATER, 0.5f);
```

```
g_Render.Render(BB_RENDER_MODEL_DATA_PARAMS(g_model));

g_Render.Disable(BB_ALPHA_TESTING);

g_Render.EndRendering();
}
```

CUBE MAPPING

The rendering system of the Building Blocks Engine has support to load 2D and cube map images. Cube map images are six images combined into one. Accessing a cube map requires using three texture coordinates instead of two, because cube maps have a U, V, and R for a texture coordinate. In a shader, a cube map can be represented by the samplerCUBE type, and access to its elements can be done with a call to texCUBE() instead of tex2D(). The texCUBE() function takes a float3 variable for the texture coordinates, while tex2D() takes a float2 variable.

On the companion CD-ROM is a demo application called CUBE MAPPING, which can be found in the BUILDING BLOCKS ENGINE/EXAMPLES/CHAPTER 5 folder. The demo's GLSL shader can be seen in Listing 5.24. Texture mapping with a cube map is the same as with 2D textures, with the exception that three values are specified for each texture coordinate; in the shader, a cube map is specified with samplerCUBE; and the color information from the cube map is accessed by called texCUBE(). The cube map in the demo application was created by a command-line tool called CUBE MAP GENERATOR. The CUBE MAP GENERATOR

tool and its source can be found on the CD-ROM in the BUILDING BLOCKS ENGINE/TOOLS folder. A detailed description of the tool and its source code can be found in Appendix B of this book. The tool takes six .TGA images and creates a cube map. The code used by the rendering system to load a cube map created by this tool can be found on the CD-ROM in the CubeMap.h header file in the

SOURCE folder. For convenience, the rendering function from the CUBE MAPPING demo can be seen in Listing 5.25. A screenshot of the demo can be seen in Figure 5.20.

LISTING 5.24   The CUBE MAPPING shader.

```
[Vertex Shader]

varying vec3 texCoords;
```

```
void main()
{
   gl_Position = gl_ModelViewProjectionMatrix * gl_Vertex;
   texCoords = gl_MultiTexCoord0.xyz;
}


 [Pixel Shader]

varying vec3 texCoords;

uniform samplerCube decal;


void main()
{
   vec4 col = textureCubeLod(decal, texCoords, 1.0);
   gl_FragColor = col;
}
```

LISTING 5.25 The rendering function of the CUBE MAPPING demo.

```
void DemoRender()
{
   g_Render.StartRendering(1, 1, 0);
   g_Render.LoadIdentityMatrix();

   g_Render.SetView(0, 3, 5, 0, 0, 0, 0, 1, 0);
   g_Render.RotateMatrix((float)g_xRot, 0, 1, 0);
   g_Render.RotateMatrix((float)g_yRot, 1, 0, 0);

   g_Render.ApplyShader(g_shader);

   g_Render.SetShaderParameter1i(g_cubeMapParam, 0);
   g_Render.ApplyTexture(0, g_cube);

   g_Render.Render(BB_PRIMITIVE_TRI_LIST, &g_desc,
                   (char*)g_boxData, g_boxIndices,
                    sizeof(g_boxData), g_numBoxIndices,
                    sizeof(stVertex));

       g_Render.EndRendering();
}
```

FIGURE 5.19   A screenshot of the CUBE MAPPING demo.

MODELS AND MESHES

All 3D games need some method to render 3D models. In the Building Blocks Engine, static geometry rendering is supported. In future versions of the Building Blocks Engine, model animation will be included in the framework, but for now, the engine deals with static geometry. Many different file formats exist that can be used to store character models. Most games have their own model format, which is specific to the needs of a game.

In the Building Blocks Engine, there are built-in meshes and OBJ model loading. OBJ models are model files with the extension .OBJ and are a popular format that is exported by many different modeling applications such as 3ds Max, Milkshape3D, and many more. For the built-in meshes, there are header files for the framework that have functions that will fill in ModelData objects with the shape that is desired. The shapes that are built into the framework are squares, boxes, pyramids, spheres, and a single triangle. These shapes were initially created for the test scenes for the Building Blocks Engine and are now part of the framework. When a shape is created, it creates a `ModelData` object and its vertex descriptor. The code used to create the square shape in SquareShape.h can be seen listed in Listing 5.26.

LISTING 5.26 The code used to create a square shape.

```
struct stUnitSquareVertex
{
   float x, y, z;
   float tu1, tv1;
   float nx, ny, nz;
};



#define UNIT_SQUARE_VERTEX_TOTAL 4
#define UNIT_SQUARE_INDEX_TOTAL  6
#define UNIT_SQUARE_STRIDE       sizeof(stUnitSquareVertex)


bool CreateSquareMesh(float size, bbe::ModelData *model)
{
   if(model == NULL)
      return false;

   stUnitSquareVertex UnitSquareData[UNIT_SQUARE_VERTEX_TOTAL] =
   {
       1 * size, -1 * size, 0,  1, 0,  0, 0, 1,
      -1 * size, -1 * size, 0,  0, 0,  0, 0, 1,
      -1 * size,  1 * size, 0,  0, 1,  0, 0, 1,
       1 * size,  1 * size, 0,  1, 1,  0, 0, 1
   };

   unsigned int UnitSquareIndices[UNIT_SQUARE_INDEX_TOTAL] =
   {
      0, 1, 2, 2, 3, 0
   };


   model->Clear();
```

```
model->AddDescriptorElement(BB_ELEMENT_TYPE_VERTEX_3F);
model->AddDescriptorElement(BB_ELEMENT_TYPE_TEX1_2F);
model->AddDescriptorElement(BB_ELEMENT_TYPE_NORMAL_3F);

if(model->SetVertices(BB_PRIMITIVE_TRI_LIST,
    UNIT_SQUARE_VERTEX_TOTAL, UNIT_SQUARE_STRIDE,
    (char*)UnitSquareData) == false)
{
    return false;
}

if(model->SetIndices(UNIT_SQUARE_INDEX_TOTAL,
    UnitSquareIndices) == false)
{
    return false;
}

return true;
}


bool CreateUnitSquareMesh(bbe::ModelData *model)
{
    return CreateSquareMesh(1, model);
}
```

The `CreateSquareMesh()` function in Listing 5.27 creates a flat 2D square along the x- and y-axis, and its indices. The model's vertex descriptor is set, and so is the model's data to the `ModelData` object. The built-in square mesh has its own vertex structure that specifies that a 3D position, texture coordinate set, and a normal is to be set for each point on the mesh. The remaining shapes have similar functions; for example, boxes being created by the `CreateBoxMesh()`, and so forth. A screenshot of an application displaying a square mesh created from the code seen in Listing 5.26 can be seen in Figure 5.20.

OBJ MODEL LOADING

Being able to read in a model from a file is very important. It is also useful to be able to read in a file that can be exported from a modeling application such as 3ds Max. In the Building Blocks Engine, the current version supports loading OBJ models. Users using the framework can load any kind of model they desire. The only step is

FIGURE 5.20 Displaying built-in shapes.

to load the data of the model into a `ModelData` object and set the class's descriptor so the rendering system knows how to render the geometry.

The loading of an OBJ model is similar to that of the square mesh in the general sense. When loading an OBJ model in the Building Blocks Engine, the function `CreateOBJMesh()` is used and is defined in OBJLoader.h. The function calls another function, `LoadOBJ()`, that is also in the same file. `LoadOBJ()` returns a model in a form that cannot be directly set to the ModelData object, so it is converted within the `CreateOBJMesh()` function. The remainder of the function specifies the vertex descriptor and deletes any temporary data. The code used to load an OBJ model, minus `LoadOBJ()`, can be seen in Listing 5.27. A screenshot of the OBJ loader in action can be seen in Figure 5.21. The `LoadOBJ()` function can also be seen in Listing 5.28.

FIGURE 5.21 OBJ loading.

LISTING 5.27 OBJ loading code.

```
struct stOBJMeshVertex
{
    float x, y, z;
    float tu1, tv1;
    float nx, ny, nz;
};

struct stObjModel
{
    float *vertices;
    float *normals;
```

```
        float *texCoords;
        int numFaces;
};


bool CreateOBJMesh(char *fileName, bbe::ModelData *model)
{
    if(model == NULL)
        return false;

    stObjModel *loadedModel = LoadOBJ(fileName);

    if(loadedModel == NULL)
        return false;

    int totalVertices = loadedModel->numFaces * 3;
    stOBJMeshVertex *objMesh = new stOBJMeshVertex[totalVertices];

    if(objMesh == NULL)
        return false;

    int i = 0, v = 0, n = 0, t = 0;

    for(i = 0; i < totalVertices; i++)
    {
        objMesh[i].x = loadedModel->vertices[v++];
        objMesh[i].y = loadedModel->vertices[v++];
        objMesh[i].z = loadedModel->vertices[v++];

        objMesh[i].nx = loadedModel->normals[n++];
        objMesh[i].ny = loadedModel->normals[n++];
        objMesh[i].nz = loadedModel->normals[n++];

        objMesh[i].tu1 = loadedModel->texCoords[t++];
        objMesh[i].tv1 = loadedModel->texCoords[t++];
    }

    model->Clear();

    model->AddDescriptorElement(BB_ELEMENT_TYPE_VERTEX_3F);
    model->AddDescriptorElement(BB_ELEMENT_TYPE_TEX1_2F);
    model->AddDescriptorElement(BB_ELEMENT_TYPE_NORMAL_3F);
```

```
    if(model->SetVertices(BB_PRIMITIVE_TRI_LIST, totalVertices,
        sizeof(stOBJMeshVertex), (char*)objMesh) == false)
    {
        return false;
    }

    model->SetIndices(0, NULL);

    delete[] loadedModel;
    delete[] objMesh;

    return true;
}
```

LISTING 5.28   The `LoadOBJ()` function that is called by `CreateOBJMesh()`.

```
stObjModel *LoadOBJ(char *fileName)
{
    TokenStream tokenStream, tempStream;
    FileInputStream fileInput;
    std::string tempLine, token;
    char *buffer = NULL;
    int fileSize = 0;
    bool validFile = false;

    if(fileInput.OpenFile(fileName, BB_TEXT_FILE) == false)
        return false;

    fileSize = fileInput.GetFileSize();

    if(fileSize <= 0)
        return false;

    buffer = new char[fileSize];

    if(buffer == NULL)
        return false;

    fileInput.Read(buffer, fileSize);
    tokenStream.SetTokenStream(buffer);
```

```
   delete[] buffer;

   // Look for the word Wavefront.
   while(tokenStream.GetNextToken(&token))
   {
      if(strcmp(token.c_str(), "Wavefront") == 0)
      {
         validFile = true;
         break;
      }
   }

   if(validFile == false)
      return NULL;

   tokenStream.ResetStream();

   int totalVertices = 0, totalNormals = 0,
      totalTexC = 0, totalFaces = 0;

   while(tokenStream.MoveToNextLine(&tempLine))
   {
      tempStream.SetTokenStream((char*)tempLine.c_str());
      tokenStream.GetNextToken(NULL);

      if(!tempStream.GetNextToken(&token))
         continue;

      if(strcmp(token.c_str(), "v") == 0) totalVertices++;
      else if(strcmp(token.c_str(), "vn") == 0) totalNormals++;
      else if(strcmp(token.c_str(), "vt") == 0) totalTexC++;
      else if(strcmp(token.c_str(), "f") == 0) totalFaces++;

      token[0] = '\0';
   }

   float *verts = new float[totalVertices * 3];
   float *norms = new float[totalNormals * 3];
   float *texC = new float[totalTexC * 2];
   int *faces = new int[totalFaces * 9];
   int vIndex = 0, nIndex = 0, tIndex = 0, fIndex = 0, index = 0;
```

```
tokenStream.ResetStream();

while(tokenStream.MoveToNextLine(&tempLine))
{
    tempStream.SetTokenStream((char*)tempLine.c_str());
    tokenStream.GetNextToken(NULL);

    if(!tempStream.GetNextToken(&token))
        continue;

    if(strcmp(token.c_str(), "v") == 0)
    {
        tempStream.GetNextToken(&token);
        verts[vIndex] = (float)atof(token.c_str());
        vIndex++;

        tempStream.GetNextToken(&token);
        verts[vIndex] = (float)atof(token.c_str());
        vIndex++;

        tempStream.GetNextToken(&token);
        verts[vIndex] = (float)atof(token.c_str());
        vIndex++;
    }
    else if(strcmp(token.c_str(), "vn") == 0)
    {
        tempStream.GetNextToken(&token);
        norms[nIndex] = (float)atof(token.c_str());
        nIndex++;

        tempStream.GetNextToken(&token);
        norms[nIndex] = (float)atof(token.c_str());
        nIndex++;

        tempStream.GetNextToken(&token);
        norms[nIndex] = (float)atof(token.c_str());
        nIndex++;
    }
    else if(strcmp(token.c_str(), "vt") == 0)
    {
        tempStream.GetNextToken(&token);
```

```
            texC[tIndex] = (float)atof(token.c_str());
            tIndex++;

            tempStream.GetNextToken(&token);
            texC[tIndex] = (float)atof(token.c_str());
            tIndex++;
         }
      else if(strcmp(token.c_str(), "f") == 0)
      {
         for(int i = 0; i < 3; i++)
         {
            tempStream.GetNextToken(&token);
            int len = strlen(token.c_str());

            for(int s = 0; s < len + 1; s++)
            {
               char buff[64];

               if(token[s] != '/' && s < len)
               {
                  buff[index] = token[s];
                  index++;
               }
               else
               {
                  buff[index] = '\0';
                  faces[fIndex] = (int)atoi(buff);
                  fIndex++;
                  index = 0;
               }
            }
         }
      }
   }

   token[0] = '\0';
}

stObjModel *model = new stObjModel;

if(!model)
   return NULL;
```

```
memset(model, 0, sizeof(stObjModel));

model->numFaces = totalFaces;

vIndex = 0, nIndex = 0, tIndex = 0, fIndex = 0, index = 0;

model->vertices = new float[totalFaces * 3 * 3];

if(totalNormals)
    model->normals = new float[totalFaces * 3 * 3];

if(totalTexC)
    model->texCoords = new float[totalFaces * 3 * 2];

for(int f = 0; f < totalFaces * 9; f+=3)
{
    model->vertices[vIndex + 0] =
        verts[(faces[f + 0] - 1) * 3 + 0];

    model->vertices[vIndex + 1] =
        verts[(faces[f + 0] - 1) * 3 + 1];

    model->vertices[vIndex + 2] =
        verts[(faces[f + 0] - 1) * 3 + 2];

    vIndex += 3;

    if(model->texCoords)
    {
        model->texCoords[tIndex + 0] =
            texC[(faces[f + 1] - 1) * 2 + 0];

        model->texCoords[tIndex + 1] =
            texC[(faces[f + 1] - 1) * 2 + 1];

        tIndex += 2;
    }

    if(model->normals)
    {
        model->normals[nIndex + 0] =
            norms[(faces[f + 2] - 1) * 3 + 0];
```

```
        model->normals[nIndex + 1] =
            norms[(faces[f + 2] - 1) * 3 + 1];

        model->normals[nIndex + 2] =
            norms[(faces[f + 2] - 1) * 3 + 2];

        nIndex += 3;
      }
    }

    delete[] verts;
    delete[] norms;
    delete[] texC;
    delete[] faces;

    return model;
}
```

SUMMARY

Rendering in games is a very large area of study in game development. When it comes to data structures, there are many different scene management techniques to explore, each with its own strengths and weaknesses. The environment and other factors will determine what technique(s) is right for most scenes. Regardless of what technique is used, games need to find a way to manage the scene data effectively, or else run the risk of horrible performance. In this chapter, we discussed various ways to do this with level of detail, space partitioning, and state management.

The rendering system of the Building Blocks Engine is not complete compared to what will be added to future versions of the framework. At the end of this book is a discussion on various methods that can be used to improve and add to the rendering system. Because the point of the Building Blocks Engine is to give users a starting point, many more topics and techniques will need to be researched and implemented.

The next chapter deals with physics in the Building Blocks Engine. Physics is becoming a huge topic in game development and something all 3D game engines can benefit from.

CHAPTER EXERCISES

1. Add a point light source that uses per-pixel lighting as an effect. Use distance attenuation with the per-pixel lighting effect discussed earlier in this chapter.
2. Create an application that uses level of detail as an object is farther from the camera. For the lowest level, use a billboard to represent the object instead of a 3D mesh.
3. Add code to the scene graph that allows it to sort nodes based on their type (geometry, transformation, etc.). Sort the geometry nodes in that subgroup based on the shader it uses. Add to the rendering system code to allow the same textures and shaders to not be applied if they are already there. This can be done by keeping pointers to the currently applied resources in the rendering system and checking the addresses of it and an object that is about to be applied to see if they match.

Part

III

Physics, AI, and Scripting

6 Physics

In This Chapter

- Overview
- Point Masses
- Rigid Bodies
- Soft Bodies
- Collision Detection and Response
- Improvements
- Physics Demos

In recent years, physics in games have become a very important topic for game developers to tackle. Physics allow for more realistic behaviors in a gaming environment. Physics deal with the motions of objects in a virtual scene, and their interactions with their environments. In games, this interaction comes in the form of collision detection and response with the physical geometry of both the game world and the various objects that populate that world. Realistic and accurate physics in a video game are becoming a selling point much like advanced artificial intelligence and realistic graphics. With an increase in physics comes an increase of immersion in a gaming world that will become increasingly realistic as hardware becomes more and more powerful. Moreover, with physics comes an increase in various effects like particle systems.

The purpose of this chapter is to generally discuss the types of physics that exist primarily in game development and how they are incorporated into a game engine framework. As an example of using physics in a game engine, the Building Blocks Engine implements a physics system to work on point masses and cloth implemented using soft bodies. Although not a complete physics system it does pave the way for some expansion and improvements, and is far along enough to create some pretty cool simulations. This chapter assumes that readers have some experience with game math (e.g., vectors) and a general idea of physics. Appendix A, "Additional Resources," lists various resources that deal with physics and physics in game development.

Overview

Computer processing is becoming more advanced every year. Because of this increase in computing power, game developers are able to use a system's resources in different ways. In the past, graphics were at the forefront of game development, but now that graphics are so realistic, it seems that the game development scene is using additional resources to increase the level of realism in other parts of a game. Today, physics are becoming a real focus by game developers because they can add the following to a game:

- New game play elements that were not possible or probable before physics were used in games
- Increased level of realism in the various parts of an environment (e.g., gravity, water resistance, friction with touching surfaces, etc.)
- Improved collision detection and response to that collision with all objects in an environment
- Rag doll physics for character models or any game objects that are made up of a hierarchy

■ Realistic movements and rotations that are physically accurate and natural looking

Physics can be used as the basis of a game itself as seen with Valve's upcoming game *Portal* that is shipping with the second *Half-Life 2* expansion pack called *Episode 2*. With an increase in computing power comes an increase in realism. Today, computers are shipping with duo-core or more processors. There are even physics processors like Ageia's *Physx* dedicated physics hardware and next-generation GPU graphics cards being used as general-purpose processors for physics instead of rendering scenes. An example of this is using SLI and multiple NVIDIA graphics cards, with one or more for graphics physics. Physics software development kits such as Havok's *Havok FX* also can be used with GPUs to create physics simulations on a graphics card using Shader Model 3.0. As mentioned earlier, this chapter looks at game physics briefly. It is important to have an understanding of game physics for the following reasons:

■ When using a third-party physics system, it is important to have an idea of the physics concepts to understand what it going on in code.
■ When implementing physics in a game, it is important to have an understanding of the concept to create such a system.
■ An understanding of physics is needed to be able to build upon an already existing system created by another party.

NEWTON PHYSICS

Sir Isaac Newton came up with philosophies on mechanics in the late 1600s. His theories held true for the day-to-day interaction of objects that existed in the real world. Although his philosophies fall apart when trying to describe the universe, as Einstein showed centuries later with his findings, Newton's philosophies are good to use in video games and simulations because they are often fast to process and easy to understand. Newton's laws of motion are world famous, and include:

■ A body will remain at rest or continue to move in a straight line at a constant velocity unless it is acted upon by an external force.
■ The acceleration of a body is proportional to the resultant force acting on the body (acceleration), and is in the same direction as the resultant force.
■ For every action, there is an equal and opposite reaction.

Newton's laws of motion generally say that objects do not naturally come to a stop; forces must bring an object to a stop. Whether this force is friction between two surfaces colliding against one another or some kind of drag in a fluid (including air), an object will eventually be brought to a stop. If no force is acting on an object, there is no stopping or moving the object.

In Newton physics, objects need forces to act upon them to be manipulated in some way. In dynamics, the equation $F = ma$ says that a resultant force equals the mass of an object times its acceleration. This means that a force can be calculated if an application knows the mass of an object and the accelerations acting on the mass. The equation can be written as $a = F/m$ to say that the acceleration equals force divided by mass, or force times the inverse of mass. In games, the forces acting on a body are often known, and what is needed is to calculate the acceleration. Acceleration represents the rate of change in an object's velocity. With the change in velocity (acceleration), one can update the velocity of an object, which is then used to update the position of an object. In games, the variables that are known tend to be the current position of an object, its current velocity, and the object's mass and other physical properties. By applying all outside forces on an object, the change in velocity can be calculated and its position updated. What makes these properties useful in games is that they can easily be represented using vectors. Using the math library discussed in Chapter 4, "Rendering Systems," the Building Blocks Engine already has everything it needs to start performing physics.

In games, real-time calculations are often used. To apply real-time calculations to physics equations, a time delta is used and is multiplied by the various equations. A time delta is the rate of change in time. By using the following equation, a game can calculate the position of any object at any time:

$$x \mathrel{+}= (v + a * t) * t \tag{6.1}$$

where x is the position, v is the velocity, a is the linear acceleration (change in velocity) being applied to the center of gravity, and t is the time delta. The more mass an object has, the more resistant it is to forces. Using Equation 6.1, as long as the mass of an object is known and its current velocity, a position can be updated with respect to time once the total acceleration has been calculated. To get an object's acceleration, a game can add up all the forces acting on an object and multiply that by the inverse of its mass. To calculate the speed of an object, one can get the magnitude of the velocity vector. Each of these items, except the time, can be represented in more than one dimension (e.g., created and used by vectors). In the natural world, various different forces exist outside individual objects acting on one another, including:

- Gravitational force
- Electromagnetic
- Weak nuclear
- Strong nuclear

By taking these four types of forces into consideration, just about every physical problem in the natural world can be handled based on general observations. In games, the main natural force is gravity, and is the most well known.

Kinematics is the study of the motion of bodies and the forces acting on those bodies. In kinematics, three types of bodies are dealt with: point masses, soft bodies, and rigid bodies. Rigid bodies' shapes do not change, and deal with an object's linear and angular motion (orientation). If they do change, it is assumed the change is negligible. With point masses, angular motion is not taken into consideration, and linear motion is the only property calculated. This is because point masses are considered infinitely small objects with a negligible orientation. Soft bodies are objects that have a position and orientation and can change shape (e.g., cloth). Earlier in this chapter, the equation to update an object's linear motion was examined. For point masses, this is enough. More discussion on point masses and rigid bodies appears later on in this chapter. In games, point masses are used mostly for particle systems, whereas rigid bodies are used for objects with volumes such as characters and other dynamic game objects. When trying to simulate the real world, games will need to update an object's position and orientation (rotation). This will be discussed later in this chapter.

GAME PHYSICS

You can either create a physics system or use an already existing system created by a third-party such as Ageia, Havok, and so forth. Using a third-party tool is highly recommended in most situations for the following reasons:

- Third-party tools are heavily tested and oftentimes used in multiple games so they are proven.
- Third-party tools are maintained and updated.
- Some third-party tools are optimized.
- Much time and resources can be saved by not creating a system from the ground up.
- It is not necessary to create a custom system with the level of sophistication of existing tools.

Although creating a physics system is not necessary in most cases, it can be a very educational experience, and necessary if a custom tool is the only option based on certain requirements or restrictions. Regardless, learning about how physics systems work is important in understanding how third-party tools work on a high level. The same can be argued about creating a custom game engine from the ground up.

BUILDING BLOCKS PHYSICS SYSTEM

The purpose of the Building Blocks Engine is to create a framework that can be built upon and learned from by hobby and student game developers. The physics system in the Building Blocks Engine is not a complete solution with all of the bells and whistles of modern physics systems seen in professional games, but it is enough to start working with dynamics in virtual worlds. The Building Blocks Engine will have the following features:

- Support for point masses
- Support for point mass collision detection
- Support for springs that will be used with cloth simulation

ON THE CD

The framework will have classes to represent point masses, springs, and a class dedicated to solving collisions. The physics system will make use of every class created in the math library discussed in Chapter 4. The physics system for the Building Blocks Engine can be found on the companion CD-ROM in the SOURCE folder.

POINT MASSES

A point mass in physics is an object whose dimensions are extremely small when compared to the object being observed at a distance that is relevant to the problem. Because of the size of the point mass at the distance it is being observed, most of its information can be neglected because it has little or no impact. Point masses are often created as a single point in space that is assumed small, but its size and orientation are not considered. Point masses are a simplification of objects.

In games, point masses are ideally used for particle systems in the virtual world. A particle in a game is an object whose only properties related to physics are its position and velocity. Because of this, point masses are perfect for particle systems. In particle systems, the textured particles often have no rotation and are camera-aligned 2D quads. Point masses can collide with other point masses, but doesn't often occur in real-time simulations. This is because point masses are often used for particles, and if thousands of particles are being emitted from one emitter, the number of collision queries and responses can affect performance. This is especially true if several emitters exist in a game level. In the early days of gaming, particle systems and effects were simple and often used animated sprites. Today, using physics with these systems allows them to behave more realistically and dynamically to the changes in the environment, and not look repetitive like a pre-created animated sprite texture.

Games can use point masses to simulate quite a few different effects in games, ranging from the simple to the more complex. For point masses, these effects include but are not limited to:

- Smoke
- Fire
- Rain
- Snow
- Sparks
- Debris
- Blood splats
- Cloth (using springs and point masses)
- Moving water
- Additional soft bodies using springs and point masses

POINT MASS DESIGN

ON THE CD

For the Building Blocks Engine, a point mass is implemented in the `PointMass` class on the companion CD-ROM in the BUILDINGBLOCKSENGINE/SOURCE folder in the files PointMass.h and PointMass.cpp. With point masses, the following properties are important when trying to represent them in a general way:

- Mass
- Position
- Velocity
- Total forces acting on the object

For specific effects using point masses with particle systems, other properties can be used to describe an object. These properties are often members of a particle class and not the point mass itself, since the point mass is only a mathematical representation of an object's position and movement in the virtual world. For particles and particle systems, the following properties can be considered depending on the type of effect a game is trying to achieve:

- Color and color delta
- Energy and energy delta
- Opacity and opacity delta
- Texture(s)

When discussing the implementation, the PointMass class will take into account all the items that were said to make up point masses in game physics. Because some of the properties used in point masses are the same as some of those used in rigid bodies, the class derives from a base class, which can later be used for creating the rigid body system. This base class is called PhysicsObject and can be seen listed in Listing 6.1.

LISTING 6.1 The PhysicsObject class.

```
class PhysicsObject
{
   public:
      PhysicsObject();
      virtual ~PhysicsObject();

      virtual void Update(float dt) = 0;

      virtual float GetDragArea() = 0;
      virtual float GetDragCoefficient() = 0;
      virtual float GetLiftCoefficient() = 0;

      virtual float GetVolumeUnderHeight(float height) = 0;

      virtual void SetMass(float m)
      {
         m_mass = m;
         m_massInv = 1 / m;
      }

      virtual float GetMass() { return m_mass; }

      virtual float GetVolume() { return m_volume; }

      virtual void SetLift(float lVal, Vector3D lVec)
      {
         m_lift = lVal;
         m_liftVector = lVec;
      }
```

```
        virtual float GetLift() { return m_lift; }
        virtual Vector3D GetLiftVec() { return m_liftVector; }

        virtual float GetSpeed() { return m_speed; }

        virtual Vector3D GetOldPosition() { return m_oldPosition; }

        virtual void SetPosition(Vector3D pos) { m_position = pos; }
        virtual Vector3D GetPosition() { return m_position; }

        virtual void SetForce(Vector3D f) { m_force = f; }
        virtual Vector3D GetForce() { return m_force; }
        virtual void AddForce(Vector3D f) { m_force += f; }

        virtual void SetVelocity(Vector3D v) { m_velocity = v; }
        virtual Vector3D GetVelocity() { return m_velocity; }
        virtual void AddVelocity(Vector3D v) { m_velocity += v; }

        virtual Vector3D GetAcceleration() { return m_acceleration; }

        virtual Matrix4x4 GetTransformation() = 0;

    protected:
        float m_mass;
        float m_massInv;
        float m_volume;
        float m_lift;
        float m_speed;

        Vector3D m_oldPosition;
        Vector3D m_position;

        Vector3D m_force;
        Vector3D m_velocity;
        Vector3D m_acceleration;

        Vector3D m_liftVector;
};
```

The `PhysicsObject` class seen in Listing 6.1 has member variables for the mass, inverse of mass, volume, lift, speed, position, total force, velocity, acceleration, and lift direction of an object. For the mass, that property is a must for physics calculations. The inverse of mass is used because many calculations need to divide by mass. By using the inverse, the calculations can perform a multiplication instead of a division. This is done because multiplication is faster processing-wise than division on the CPU.

The volume of an object is used for simulations with water and buoyancy. The lift property is used for objects that can fly when given enough speed. The speed is the magnitude of the object's velocity, and can be used to tell the game how fast an object is going.

The old and current position variables are used to move the object, with the old position keeping track of the last known position of the object. The force is the total forces acting on the body, which are summed before being applied to the physics object. The velocity is the direction of the object's movement, and the acceleration is the change in that object's velocity. As different forces act on a body, the acceleration changes. This change in acceleration thus changes the velocity, which in turn changes the position of the object.

In the following sections, we discuss the implementation to the point mass system in more detail. That discussion is followed by another on collision detection and response. An example of point masses used for a particle system can be seen in Figure 6.1.

FIGURE 6.1 Point masses used for a snow particle system.

POINT MASS IMPLEMENTATION

The point mass class, `PointMass`, implements all virtual functions of the base class. For the functions that are not affected by point masses, a default value is returned, like 0. For example, lift deals with objects that have the capability to fly like the wings of an airplane using lift. Point masses do not use this in their calculations, so a value of 0 is returned for the lift coefficient. The same can be said with the drag area and drag coefficient. The `PointMass` class can be seen listed in Listing 6.2.

LISTING 6.2   The `PointMass` class.

```
class PointMass : public PhysicsObject
{
    public:
        PointMass()
        {
        }

        virtual ~PointMass()
        {
        }


        virtual void Update(float dt);


        virtual float GetDragArea()
        {
            return 0;
        }

        virtual float GetDragCoefficient()
        {
            return 0.05f;
        }

        virtual float GetLiftCoefficient()
        {
            return 0;
        }
```

```
virtual float GetVolumeUnderHeight(float height)
{
    if(m_position.y >= height)
        return 0;

    return 1;
}


virtual Matrix4x4 GetTransformation();
};
```

The Update() function takes a time delta and is used to update the point mass object. The next four functions deal with the drag, lift, and the percentage the object is under a specified height. The drag is used for objects that collide with other objects, causing friction (e.g., a box being pushed along the ground). The lift, as mentioned earlier, deals with objects that can fly. The GetVolumeUnderHeight() function simply returns 0 if the point mass is above a height, and 1 if it is below. This is used for trying to determine how much of an object is submerged in water for buoyancy. Since point masses have no volume, they are either totally under or totally above a height in the PointMass class. Rigid bodies are handled differently and need more calculations to handle buoyancy.

The only two functions implemented for point masses that do not return default values to satisfy the base class' virtual functions are Update() and Get Transformation(). The GetTransformation() function returns a 4x4 matrix that describes the transformation of the point mass. Since point masses only deal with position, the matrix returned is a translated matrix based on the current position of the point mass. The second function, Update(), updates all of the point mass relevant member variables based on the time delta that is passed into the function dt. The function starts by recording the last position and calculating the acceleration, which is $F = m/a$ or $F = (1/m)a$. With the change in velocity (acceleration), the time delta can be applied to it and the linear velocity can then be updated to reflect its new information. With the new velocity, the new position can be calculated with respect to time and the speed can be calculated by getting the magnitude of the velocity. Once an update has occurred on a physics object, the total forces acting on the body must be reset. Every frame, the total forces acting on a body are determined and calculated, so once those forces are applied, it is reset for the next frame. The bodies of the Update() and GetTransformation() functions can be seen listed in Listing 6.3.

LISTING 6.3   The two PointMass functions.

```
void PointMass::Update(float dt)
{
   m_oldPosition = m_position;

   // The a = F * (1 / m) is the same as a = F / m.
   m_acceleration = m_force * m_massInv;

   m_velocity += m_acceleration * dt;
   m_position += m_velocity * dt;

   m_speed = m_velocity.Magnitude();

   m_force = Vector3D(0, 0, 0);
}


Matrix4x4 PointMass::GetTransformation()
{
   Matrix4x4 matrix;
   matrix.Translate(m_position);

   return matrix;
}
```

RIGID BODIES

In game physics, a point mass is considered an object with a position but no volume, or the volume is negligible. Rigid bodies are objects with a finite volume, position, and orientation. Rigid bodies are rigid, meaning their shape is not deformable and they represent a solid body. In other words, the shape of a rigid body stays the same regardless of the forces acting on the body. For example, if enough pressure is applied to a steel pipe, it will eventually start to bend. In games, if that pipe is represented by a rigid body, its shape shouldn't change no matter what forces are being applied to the object. Soft bodies can be used for objects that can change shape and are often a combination of point masses and springs where a spring connects two point masses together. An example of a soft body is cloth used in cloth animation physics. Rigid bodies deal with topics such as:

- Inertia
- Angular momentum
- Angular velocity
- Volume
- Contact points of a collision
- Impulses

Rigid bodies are bounding volumes that generally represent an object. Rigid bodies can be boxes, spheres, or any other shape that can be used as a volume. Oriented bounding boxes are often used as rigid boxes. What shape is used will depend on the implementation of the various calculations. A hierarchy of different rigid bodies can be used to represent a complex object and allow for realistic-looking simulations when compared to using one bounding volume for the entire object.

This version of the Building Blocks Engine does not have initial support for rigid bodies, but future versions will look at adding the support in the physics system. Hardware is becoming fast enough to process rigid bodies more quickly, which allows many dynamic objects to be on the screen at once and is something that can be looked at for the future. An example of rigid bodies can be seen in Figure 6.2.

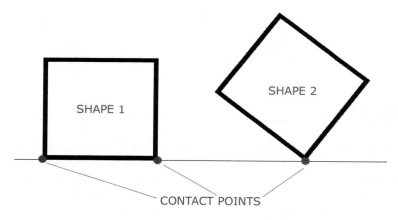

FIGURE 6.2   Rigid bodies.

SOFT BODIES

Rigid bodies in games can be used to create realistic approximations in a gaming environment. The catch with using rigid bodies is that the objects are assumed not deformable (change their shape). Soft bodies are used to solve this limitation by allowing various forces on an object to bend and deform the object. Steps can be taken to allow objects to break under enough force as a special effect. At this time, the most heavily used soft bodies are cloth and hair. Cloth simulations have many uses in games, as seen in the *Splinter Cell* series from UbiSoft. Cloth simulations can be used for flags, capes, drapes, and so fourth.

Soft bodies work by using springs and point masses. A spring is an object that connects two point masses. This spring has a tension amount that affects how the object's point masses can stretch and bend in relation to one another. A spring's capability to stretch can be seen in Equation 6.2, where:

- x is the distance the spring is elongated by
- k is the spring constant
- F is the resulting force exerted by the spring

$$F = -kx \qquad\qquad (6.2)$$

Later in this chapter, we look at creating a simple cloth animation system using springs and the point mass system from the previous section. An example of a soft body can be seen in Figure 6.3.

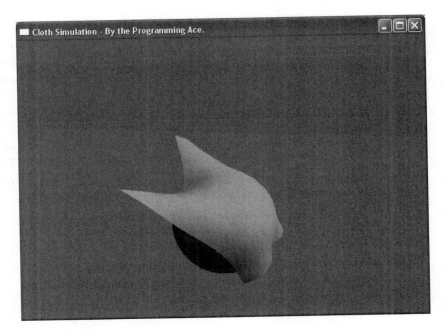

FIGURE 6.3   A soft body.

COLLISION DETECTION AND RESPONSE

Up until now, this chapter has been about the representation of physics controlled objects using point masses, soft bodies, and rigid bodies. These objects are able to have forces applied to them such as gravity in very realistic manners that move and orient (rigid and soft bodies) the objects. In game physics, an equally important area involves collision detection and response between objects. The code up to this point can have physics performed on objects, but they have no way to interact with one another (e.g., one box colliding into another and responding). In this section, we discuss the Building Blocks Engine's physics response.

COLLISION RESPONSE

Collision response is handled in the Building Blocks Engine through a separate class called `CollisionResponse`. This class is used to take two objects and test them for collision. If collision is found, the objects respond to that collision; otherwise, the collision check functions return false. In this class, there are functions to perform sphere-to-sphere, sphere-to-frustum, and sphere-to-plane collision detection. The sphere collision test uses point masses that are acting as spheres. Even though a point mass does not have a volume in its calculations, if collision is to happen between them, some kind of volume needs to be assumed because infinitely small objects cannot collide in code. Although point mass volumes don't affect their own calculations, a volume can be used to determine how big an object is so there is a way to know what area to test upon collision. Additional functions that can be added to this class are point masses acting as boxes, ellipsoids, and so forth.

A polytope is a convex polyhedron and is the base class used to create the oriented bounding box. Any convex shade can be created as a polytope, but the Building Blocks Engine has only one implementation of it with the OBB class. A convex shape is a shape where each face of the shape can see each other face without being blocked by any other faces. An example of this can be seen in Figure 6.4. The rigid body system that will be implemented in future versions of the Building Blocks Engine uses the oriented bounding box class to create a rigid box.

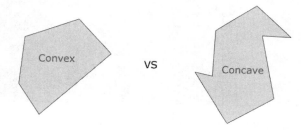

FIGURE 6.4   Convex versus a concave shape.

The public functions of the CollisionResponse class are all that is needed to check for and respond to collision between objects in the framework. If the function returns true, collision has occurred and has been handled; otherwise, it returns false. To check for any collisions in the class, all that is needed are the two objects being tested. The CollisionResponse class can be seen listed in Listing 6.4.

LISTING 6.4   The CollisionResponse class.

```
class CollisionResponse
{
    public:
        CollisionResponse();
        virtual ~CollisionResponse();

        // Point Mass Collision as Spheres.
        bool ResponseToCollision(PointMass *p1, float radius1,
                                 PointMass *p2, float radius2,
                                 float e);

        bool ResponseToCollision(PointMass *p1, float radius1,
                                 Frustum &frustum, float e);

        bool ResponseToCollision(PointMass *p1, float radius1,
                                 Plane &plane, float e);
};
```

SPHERE-TO-SPHERE COLLISIONS

In the following sections, point mass collision detection and response functions are examined. Point masses are simpler than rigid bodies, and their code is much shorter. To test for collision between two spheres, the first ResponseToCollision() function is used and takes as parameters the first point mass, its radius, the second point mass, its radius, and a value used to slightly offset the calculations, which can be used to apply a little cushion between the objects so they are not touching when collision is detected.

Inside the sphere-to-sphere collision, check that the BoundingSphere class' collision detection functions are used since that code already exists in the class. If this test passes, both objects' velocities and positions are altered so they no longer collide. How fast and from what direction each sphere hits will determine the direction they are reflected. The code for the sphere-to-sphere collision detection and response can be seen listed in Listing 6.5.

LISTING 6.5 Sphere-to-sphere collisions.

```
bool CollisionResponse::ResponseToCollision(PointMass *p1,
   float radius1, PointMass *p2, float radius2, float e)
{
   if(p1 == 0 || p2 == 0)
      return false;

   Vector3D pos1 = p1->GetPosition();
   Vector3D pos2 = p2->GetPosition();
   Vector3D vel1 = p1->GetVelocity();
   Vector3D vel2 = p2->GetVelocity();

   float mass1 = p1->GetMass();
   float mass2 = p2->GetMass();

   BoundingSphere s1, s2;

   s1.m_center = pos1;
   s1.m_radius = (double)radius1;

   s2.m_center = pos2;
   s2.m_radius = (double)radius2;


   if(s2.CollisionCheck(s1) == true)
   {
      Vector3D massDir = pos2 - pos1;
      float massDirLength = massDir.Magnitude();
      float massTotal = mass1 + mass2;
      float radiusTotal = radius1 + radius2;

      massDir.Normalize();

      if(massDirLength < radiusTotal)
      {
         p2->SetPosition(pos1 + massDir * (radiusTotal + e));
      }

      float v1 = massDir.Dot3(vel1);
      float v2 = massDir.Dot3(vel2);
      float vp1 = ((mass1 - (e * mass2)) * v1 + (1 + e) *
                  mass2 * v2) / massTotal;
```

```
      float vp2 = ((mass2 - (e * mass1)) * v2 + (1 + e) *
                    mass1 * v1) / massTotal;

      p1->SetVelocity(vel2 + (massDir * (vp2 - v2)));
      p2->SetVelocity(vel1 + (massDir * (vp1 - v1)));

      return true;
   }

   return false;
}
```

PLANE COLLISIONS

Planes are used a lot in game development for collision detection. In the Collision Response class, planes are handled by every type of object that can collide with them. For the sphere-to-plane test, all that is needed are the point mass, its radius, and a plane. The plane class already has code to test for sphere-to-plane collisions, so that function is used for the collision detection part. If collision has occurred, the sphere is reflected based on the plane's normal and its incoming velocity. In the Collision Response class, it is assumed the planes in a scene are static and can't be moved, so only the sphere or other object will need to be updated. To test a frustum for collision against a sphere, this sphere-to-plane function can be used against all planes that make up the frustum. A frustum can be an enclosed area such as a box, and can be used to keep an object inside an area, which is used a lot in games. The sphere-to-plane collision detection and response function can be seen in Listing 6.6.

LISTING 6.6 Sphere-to-plane collisions.

```
bool CollisionResponse::ResponseToCollision(PointMass *p1,
   float radius1, Plane &plane, float e)
{
   if(p1 == 0)
      return false;

   if(plane.Intersect(p1->GetPosition(), radius1) == false)
      return false;

   p1->SetVelocity(plane.Reflect(p1->GetVelocity(), e));

   return true;
}
```

PHYSICS SPACE

Forces can be applied to objects from various areas of a game world. Objects can be fully submerged in fluids, partially submerged, or not at all. Objects can have drag and lift and be affected by gravity. Regardless of what forces are acting on an object, that object will need some way to calculate the various total forces that are acting on it to make a simulation believable.

In the Building Blocks Engine, forces that can be exerted on an object from the environment are represented by the class PhysicsSpace. A PhsyicsSpace object can be created to represent the air, a body of water, conditions in outer space, conditions on other planets, and so forth. In the majority of the demo applications discussed later in this chapter, a PhysicsSpace object is used to exert gravity onto objects in the scene.

The PhysicsSpace class has a gravitational force, flag for determining if it is air (not water), density of the space, and surface height if it is water as member variables. For methods, the class is made up of mostly accessor functions and a function called InfluenceObject(). InfluenceObject() is used to take a physics object (e.g., point mass, rigid body, and so forth) and apply its environmental influences on it. The function allows a percentage to be passed in as a way to control how much influence the space has on an object. This is used in situations in which an object is partially inside more than one space. For example, a box can be floating in water, causing it to be partially submerged and only requiring a percent of the water's influence and the normal atmosphere outside the water. The PhysicsSpace class can be seen listed in Listing 6.7.

LISTING 6.7 The PhysicsSpace class declaration.

```
class PhysicsSpace
{
   public:
      PhysicsSpace();
      virtual ~PhysicsSpace();

      void InfluenceObject(PhysicsObject *obj,
                           scalar influencePct);

      void SetDensity(float density)
      {
         m_density = density;
      }
```

```
float GetDensity()
{
   return m_density;
}

void SetSurfaceHeight(float height)
{
   m_surfaceHeight = height;
}

float GetSurfaceHeight()
{
   return m_surfaceHeight;
}

void SetGravity(PhysicsVec g)
{
   m_gravity = g;
}

Vector3D GetGravity()
{
   return m_gravity;
}

void SetIsAirAtmosphere(bool val)
{
   m_isAir = val;
}

bool isAirAtmosphere()
{
   return m_isAir;
}


private:
   PhysicsVec CalDrag(Vector3D dir, float V,
                      float A, float CW);

   PhysicsVec CalLift(Vector3D dir, Vector3D liftNormal,
                      float V, float A, float CL);
```

```
      PhysicsVec CalBuoyancy(float volume);


   protected:
      float m_density;
      float m_surfaceHeight;

      Vector3D m_gravity;

      bool m_isAir;
   };
```

The main function in the `PhysicsSpace` class is `InfluenceObject()`, and tallies all forces in the environment. It adds up the total gravity, drag, and lift forces. Once added, these forces are passed to the `PhysicsObject`'s `AddForce()` function. If a space is represented by water, buoyancy can be calculated, which is done in the function by calling the private method `CalBuoyancy()`. If the object in question has any speed to it, the drag forces in the space are applied to the object. If there is any lift for the object, that too is added to the total forces. In game physics, many forces can act on an object. Once all of these forces are added up, the `PhsyicsObject`'s `Update()` function can be called to update the object's dynamics. The `InfluenceObject()` function can be seen in Listing 6.8.

LISTING 6.8   The `InfluenceObject()` function.

```
   void PhysicsSpace::InfluenceObject(PhysicsObject *obj,
                                      float influencePct)
   {
      if(obj == 0)
         return;

      Vector3D velocity, totalForces(0, 0, 0);
      float speed = obj->GetSpeed();

      if(speed != 0.0f)
         velocity = obj->GetVelocity() / speed;

      // Apply any buoyancy.
      if(m_isAir != true)
      {
         totalForces += CalBuoyancy(obj->GetVolume());
      }
```

```
// Apply any gravity.
totalForces += m_gravity;

// Apply any drag.
if(speed != 0.0f )
{
    totalForces += CalDrag(velocity, speed,
                           obj->GetDragArea(),
                           obj->GetDragCoefficient());
}

// Apply any lift.
if(obj->GetLift() > 0.0f)
{
    totalForces += CalLift(velocity, obj->GetLiftVec(),
                           speed, obj->GetLift(),
                           obj->GetLiftCoefficient());
}

// Update object's total.
obj->AddForce(totalForces * influencePct);
}
```

The remaining functions outside of the accessor functions are the private methods `CalDrag()`, `CalLift()`, and `CalBuoyancy()`. `CalDrag()` calculates the drag in the space and takes as parameters the object's velocity, speed, drag area, and drag coefficient. Once calculated, a vector is returned representing the drag force for that object. `CalLift()` calculates the lift force for an object and takes as parameters the object's velocity, lift direction, speed, lift area, and lift coefficient. `CalBuoyancy()` calculates the buoyancy by taking the gravity that exists in the environment and applying the space's density and volume to it. The force is also inverted (* –1), because buoyancy causes objects to rise in water, while gravity pulls objects toward the center of the earth. The remaining function of the `PhysicsSpace` class can be seen in Listing 6.9.

LISTING 6.9 The private functions of the `PhysicsSpace` class.

```
Vector3D PhysicsSpace::CalDrag(Vector3D dir, float V,
                               float A, float CW)
{
    Vector3D drag;
```

```
        if(V != 0)
        {
            float d = (float)0.5 * m_density * (V * V) * A * CW;
            drag = (dir * -1) * d;
        }

        return drag;
    }


    Vector3D PhysicsSpace::CalLift(Vector3D dir, Vector3D liftNormal,
                                   float V, float A, float CL)
    {
        Vector3D drag, lift;

        if(V != 0)
        {
            Vector3D cross;

            drag = dir * -1;

            cross = drag.CrossProduct(liftNormal);
            lift = cross.CrossProduct(drag);
            lift.Normalize();

            float l = (V * V) * ((scalar)0.5 * m_density) * A * CL;
            lift = lift * l;
        }

        return lift;
    }


    Vector3D PhysicsSpace::CalBuoyancy(float volume)
    {
        if(m_isAir ==  true)
            return Vector3D ();

        return m_gravity * (m_density * volume * -1);
    }
```

IMPROVEMENTS

The physics system for the Building Blocks Engine has a small bit of functionality when compared to the other systems of the framework, and much more can be added to it and many improvements can be applied. Physics in games must be as fast as possible, so code optimizations are a must for any modern physics system and math library. A few optimizations and additions that can be applied to the code include:

- Scene management for environments and other objects
- Rigid body support
- Rag doll physics
- Vehicle physics
- SSE math optimizations
- Performing physics on a dedicated piece of hardware
- General soft bodies
- Possibly GPU physics
- Multithreading for physics that is done on the CPU

Scene management was discussed in Chapter 5, "Rendering Scenes and Scene Graphs" and the benefits various scene and space partitioning techniques gave the rendering system can also be given to the physics system. By using a bounding volume hierarchy, collision against an environment can be processed very quickly. Moreover, using BVH with static and dynamic objects can allow for quick collision detection and response because the BVH would allow only the objects that are close to the object in question to be tested. This can cause a huge leap in performance depending on the number of objects in the scene. Since rigid and soft body collisions are complex and expensive, this is a definite performance boost. In addition, by using SSE math optimizations, a boost in the math library can occur, which in turn boosts the performance of the physics system since it uses the math library to a greater extent than any other system in the framework.

Rag doll animation is one of the benefits of having physics in a game. Rag doll can allow for all kinds of realistic behaviors by objects being thrown around by forces in the game world. Rag doll animation requires models that are built out of hierarchies like animated characters that use skeleton systems (bone animation) in their calculations.

Vehicle physics are important to allow for realistic vehicle physics in a scene depending on the type of game being made. In a racing game, vehicle physics can greatly enhance the gameplay experience by offering a realistic simulation of the real world.

In games, soft bodies are starting to see more use than in the past. The most common soft body is a piece of cloth like the ones seen in the *Splitter Cell* games by UbiSoft. When it comes to soft bodies, any object that can change its shape can be a soft body, unlike rigid bodies whose shape must stay constant throughout the entire application simulation. A general set of classes to represent soft bodies can be added to the framework.

Although processors are fast, they are still finite in the amount of power they have. With all the different systems working in a game—artificial intelligence, networking, game logic, and so forth—physics must use whatever resources it can to perform its task. This translates into a limited number of objects that can be processed in real time at an acceptable rate. One way to improve this would be to use a dedicated piece of hardware whose sole purpose is to calculate physics much like a graphics card has traditionally been used solely to calculate a rendered scene. One popular piece of hardware that can be used for physics is the Physx card by Ageia. Another alternative is to use programmable GPUs to calculate physics. This was already demonstrated by both NVIDIA and ATI and is more than possible with Shader Model 3.0 hardware. Since physics is floating-point math, GPUs are able to do the calculations if programmed to do so. The challenge is getting the information to and from the GPU, but with the next generation of graphics cards, there is little to worry about physics in games. The only recommendation is to use multiple GPUs with at least one for physics and one for rendering to keep performance up; however, with the cost of some newer GPUs, not everyone will be able to afford it.

Physics Demos

The remainder of this chapter focuses on a few different physics demos that were created using the code discussed in this chapter. Each of the demos in this section is simple and is used to test that the code works and to illustrate physics in a graphical application. As a bonus, the final demo of this chapter will implement cloth simulation where an object controlled by the user can interact with the cloth dynamically in real time. The demos that are going to be covered can be found on the companion CD-ROM in the BUILDING BLOCKS ENGINE/EXAMPLES/ CHAPTER 6 folder and include:

ON THE CD

- Constant velocity
- Gravity
- Sphere-to-sphere collisions
- Sphere-to-plane collisions
- Cloth simulation

CONSTANT VELOCITY DEMO

The constant velocity application demonstrates how to apply a velocity on an object that does not change throughout the execution of the application. The demo application itself has a box that moves from the left side of the screen to the right. Once the box passes the right side of the screen, the object is repositioned to its start so the simulation can loop. Earlier in this chapter, we looked at the equation

$$F = ma \tag{6.3}$$

where force equals mass multiplied by acceleration. Acceleration is the change (delta) in velocity. If the velocity is constant, the equation used to update a position can be expressed as

$$P = P + V * t \tag{6.4}$$

where the new position equals the old position plus the velocity (which is constant) multiplied by a time delta. Because the point mass class calculates the acceleration and so forth, this equation can be used instead of using the Update() function of the class. Since this is a simple demo, it will use the function regardless, although a faster and simpler version can be used since the velocity is constant and does not change throughout the remainder of the application.

The demo application's main source file (main.cpp) has in its global section a DynamicModel object that is used to store the displayable mesh to the screen, a point mass for the object, time values used for supporting time-based updates, resource managers (which are optional for such a simple application), a scene graph (which again is optional and not necessary), rotation values for allowing the mouse to rotate the scene, and the rendering system and quit flag. The global section of the CONSTANT VELOCITY demo can be seen in Listing 6.10.

LISTING 6.10 The global section of the CONSTANT VELOCITY demo.

```
// Models to be displayed.
bbe::DynamicModel g_object;


// Object's Physics information.
bbe::PointMass g_objMass;
```

```
// Time values for real time simulation.
float g_lastTime = 0, g_currentTime = 0;


// Resource managers.
BB_MODEL_RESOURCE_MANAGER g_modelManager;
BB_EFFECT_RESOURCE_MANAGER g_effectManager;


// Scene graph.
bbe::SceneGraph g_sceneGraph;


// Scene rotations.
int g_xRot = 0, g_oldXRot = 0;
int g_yRot = 0, g_oldYRot = 0;


// Rendering System.
bbe::OpenGLRenderer g_Render;


// Flag used to quit.
bool g_quitDemo = false;
```

The first two functions of the demo's source file are `DemoResize()` and `DemoInitialize()`, with `DemoResize()` being the same function we've seen for every demo in the book. The initialize function starts by setting up the rendering system and resizing the window. Once successful, the function sets the default rendering states used throughout the demo application. Next, the model that is displayed to the screen is created, its texture mapping effect created, and both are added to their respective resource managers. Once that operation is successful, the function sets up the scene graph and returns true. The `DemoResize()` and `DemoInitialize()` functions can be seen in Listing 6.11.

LISTING 6.11 The `DemoResize()` and `DemoInitialize()` functions from the CONSTANT VELOCITY demo.

```
void DemoResize(int width, int height)
{
    g_Render.SetViewPort(0, 0, width, height);
    g_Render.ResizeWindow(45.0f, 0.1f, 1000, width, height);
}
```

```cpp
bool DemoInitialize(bbe::RenderParams &params)
{
    bool result = false;

    params.m_colorBits = 24;
    params.m_depthBits = 16;
    params.m_stencilBits = 8;
    params.m_fullscreen = WINDOW_FULLSCREEN;
    params.m_height = WINDOW_HEIGHT;
    params.m_width = WINDOW_WIDTH;
    params.m_maxCacheBytes = 2000;
    params.m_maxCacheIndices = 2000;

    if(g_Render.Initialize(&params) != BB_SUCCESS)
        return false;

    DemoResize(WINDOW_WIDTH, WINDOW_HEIGHT);

    g_Render.SetClearColor(0, 0, 0, 255);
    g_Render.Enable(BB_DEPTH_TESTING);
    g_Render.Enable(BB_SMOOTH_SHADING);
    g_Render.Enable(BB_TEXTURE_2D);

    bbe::ModelData *objectMesh = new bbe::ModelData();

    if(objectMesh == NULL)
        return false;

    result = bbe::CreateCubeMesh(5, objectMesh);

    if(result == false)
        return false;


    std::vector<BB_FILTER_TYPE> filters;
    filters.push_back(BB_MIN_LINEAR_FILTER);
    filters.push_back(BB_MAG_LINEAR_FILTER);

    bbe::Effect *effect = NULL;

    effect = new bbe::TextureShader("resources/passThrough.cg",
        "resources/decal.tga", &filters,
        static_cast<bbe::RenderInterface*>(&g_Render));
```

```
        if(effect == NULL)
           return false;


        g_modelManager.Create(new bbe::ModelResource(objectMesh),
           "CUBE MODEL", g_object.GetModelHandlePtr());

        g_effectManager.Create(new bbe::EffectResource(effect),
           "TEXTURE MAPPING", g_object.GetEffectHandlePtr());


        bbe::GeometryNode *objectNode = NULL;

        objectNode = new bbe::GeometryNode(&g_object,
           &g_modelManager, &g_effectManager,
           static_cast<bbe::RenderInterface*>(&g_Render));

        g_sceneGraph.AddNode(objectNode);


        g_objMass.SetPosition(bbe::Vector3D(-120, 0, 0));
        g_objMass.SetVelocity(bbe::Vector3D(15, 0, 0));
        g_objMass.SetMass(1);

        g_lastTime = bbe::GetTimeSeconds();

        return true;
     }
```

The last functions from the CONSTANT VELOCITY demo include `DemoUpdate()`, `DemoRender()`, and `DemoShutdown()`. `DemoShutdown()` destroys the rendering system and releases all memory from the scene graph and resource managers, and `DemoRender()` renders the scene graph. `DemoUpdate()` starts by gathering input from the keyboard and mouse. Once done with the input, the function moves on to updating the physics used in the demo. This is done by finding the time delta, calling the point mass' `Update()` function, and updating the `DynamicModel`'s position using the newly calculated position. The remaining functions from the CONSTANT VELOCITY demo can be seen in Listing 6.12. A screenshot of the CONSTANT VELOCITY demo application can be seen in Figure 6.5.

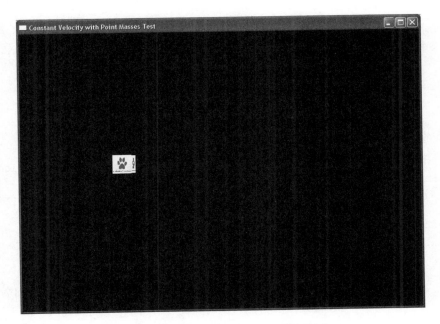

FIGURE 6.5   A screenshot of the CONSTANT VELOCITY demo.

LISTING 6.12   The remaining function from the CONSTANT VELOCITY demo.

```
void DemoUpdate()
{
    int mouseX = 0, mouseY = 0;

    bbe::GetMousePosition(&mouseX, &mouseY);


    if(bbe::isButtonDown(BB_BUTTON_ESCAPE))
    {
        g_quitDemo = true;
    }

    if(bbe::isButtonDown(BB_BUTTON_MOUSE_LEFT))
    {
        g_xRot -= (mouseX - g_oldXRot);
        g_yRot -= (mouseY - g_oldYRot);
    }
```

```
        g_oldXRot = mouseX;
        g_oldYRot = mouseY;


        g_currentTime = bbe::GetTimeSeconds();
        float dt = g_currentTime - g_lastTime;


        g_objMass.Update(dt);
        g_object.SetTransformation(g_objMass.GetTransformation());


        bbe::Vector3D pos = g_objMass.GetPosition();

        // Move back to the start.
        // This allows for the simulation to "loop".
        if(pos.x > 120)
            g_objMass.SetPosition(bbe::Vector3D(-120, 0, 0));


        g_lastTime = bbe::GetTimeSeconds();
    }


void DemoRender()
{
    g_Render.StartRendering(1, 1, 0);
    g_Render.LoadIdentityMatrix();

    g_Render.SetView(0, 0, 200, 0, 0, 0, 0, 1, 0);
    g_Render.RotateMatrix((float)g_xRot, 0, 1, 0);
    g_Render.RotateMatrix((float)g_yRot, 1, 0, 0);

    g_sceneGraph.Process();

    g_Render.EndRendering();
}


void DemoShutdown()
{
    g_Render.Shutdown();
```

```
        g_effectManager.Release(g_object.GetEffectHandle());
        g_modelManager.Release(g_object.GetModelHandle());

        g_sceneGraph.Release();
    }
```

GRAVITY DEMO

The next demo application demonstrates performing gravity in a physics environment. Gravity is a force that can be applied to all objects in a scene. In a gaming application, gravity can be a 3D vector that points in the direction of the force. In most applications, this direction will point in the down direction. Many different forces can act on an object, such as friction, lift, buoyancy, and so forth.

The global section of the GRAVITY demo application can be seen in Listing 6.13. In this demo application is a box that starts from the top of the screen and starts to fall when gravity starts to take over. For extra measure, there is another shape in the scene that represents the floor. There will be code in the update section to make sure the box does not go past this to give the impression of the box colliding with the ground. The code also uses the PhysicsSpace class to apply the influence of gravity in the environment to the object. The remaining variables in the global section include the resource managers, time values, scene graph, rotation values, rendering system, and quit flag.

LISTING 6.13   The global section of the GRAVITY demo.

```
// Models to be displayed.
bbe::DynamicModel g_object, g_ground;

// Object's Physics informaiton.
bbe::PointMass g_objMass;

// Physical space in which the object lives.
bbe::PhysicsSpace g_3dSpace;

// Time values for real time simulation.
float g_lastTime = 0, g_currentTime = 0;

// Resource managers.
BB_MODEL_RESOURCE_MANAGER g_modelManager(32);
BB_EFFECT_RESOURCE_MANAGER g_effectManager(32);
```

```
// Scene graph.
bbe::SceneGraph g_sceneGraph;

// Scene rotations.
int g_xRot = 0, g_oldXRot = 0;
int g_yRot = 0, g_oldYRot = 0;

// Rendering System.
bbe::OpenGLRenderer g_Render;

// Flag used to quit.
bool g_quitDemo = false;
```

The first two functions in the GRAVITY demo application are DemoResize()
and DemoInitialize(). The initialization function starts by initializing the rendering system. It then creates a box that will have the physics applied to it, and creates
a square mesh for the ground, both using the built-in shapes code looked at in
Chapter 5. After that operation, the function continues as it did for the CON-
STANT VELOCITY demo application until the physics information is initialized.
Here, gravity is added to the PhysicsSpace object so it can be applied later in the
simulation. Since the ground doesn't move, the box is the only object affected by
physics. The DemoResize() and DemoInitialize() functions can be seen in Listing
6.14.

LISTING 6.14   The DemoResize() and DemoInitialize() functions.

```
void DemoResize(int width, int height)
{
   g_Render.SetViewPort(0, 0, width, height);
   g_Render.ResizeWindow(45.0f, 0.1f, 1000, width, height);
}


bool DemoInitialize(bbe::RenderParams &params)
{
   bool result = false;

   params.m_colorBits = 24;
   params.m_depthBits = 16;
   params.m_stencilBits = 8;
   params.m_fullscreen = WINDOW_FULLSCREEN;
   params.m_height = WINDOW_HEIGHT;
```

```
params.m_width = WINDOW_WIDTH;
params.m_maxCacheBytes = 2000;
params.m_maxCacheIndices = 2000;

if(g_Render.Initialize(&params) != BB_SUCCESS)
    return false;

DemoResize(WINDOW_WIDTH, WINDOW_HEIGHT);

g_Render.SetClearColor(0, 0, 0, 255);
g_Render.Enable(BB_DEPTH_TESTING);
g_Render.Enable(BB_SMOOTH_SHADING);
g_Render.Enable(BB_TEXTURE_2D);


// Create meshes.
bbe::ModelData *objectMesh = new bbe::ModelData();

if(objectMesh == NULL)
    return false;

result = bbe::CreateCubeMesh(5, objectMesh);

if(result == false)
    return false;

bbe::ModelData *groundMesh = new bbe::ModelData();

if(groundMesh == NULL)
    return false;

result = bbe::CreateXZPlaneMesh(50, groundMesh);

if(result == false)
    return false;


// Load textures and effects.
std::vector<BB_FILTER_TYPE> filters;
filters.push_back(BB_MIN_LINEAR_FILTER);
filters.push_back(BB_MAG_LINEAR_FILTER);

bbe::Effect *effect = NULL;
```

```
effect = new bbe::TextureShader("resources/passThrough.cg",
    "resources/decal.tga", &filters,
    static_cast<bbe::RenderInterface*>(&g_Render));

if(effect == NULL)
    return false;


// Resource manage objects.
g_modelManager.Create(new bbe::ModelResource(objectMesh),
    "CUBE MODEL", g_object.GetModelHandlePtr());

g_modelManager.Create(new bbe::ModelResource(groundMesh),
    "GROUND MODEL", g_ground.GetModelHandlePtr());

g_effectManager.Create(new bbe::EffectResource(effect),
    "TEXTURE MAPPING", g_object.GetEffectHandlePtr());

// Copy handle to the same resource for the ground.
int index = -1;
index = g_effectManager.GetRegisteredIndex("TEXTURE MAPPING");
g_ground.GetEffectHandlePtr()->Initialize(index);


// Scene graph.
bbe::GeometryNode *objectNode = NULL, *groundNode = NULL;

objectNode = new bbe::GeometryNode(&g_object,
    &g_modelManager, &g_effectManager,
    static_cast<bbe::RenderInterface*>(&g_Render));

if(objectNode == NULL)
    return false;

groundNode = new bbe::GeometryNode(&g_ground,
    &g_modelManager, &g_effectManager,
    static_cast<bbe::RenderInterface*>(&g_Render));

if(groundNode == NULL)
    return false;


g_sceneGraph.AddNode(objectNode);
g_sceneGraph.AddNode(groundNode);
```

```
// Physics initialize.
g_objMass.SetPosition(bbe::Vector3D(0, 50, 0));
g_objMass.SetMass(1);

// Apply gravity going down almost 10 units.
g_3dSpace.SetGravity(bbe::Vector3D(0.0f, -9.81f, 0.0f));

g_lastTime = bbe::GetTimeSeconds();

return true;
}
```

The last functions of the GRAVITY demo application are `DemoShutdown()`, `DemoRender()`, and `DemoUpdate()`, where the first two mentioned are the same as they were in the CONSTANT VELOCITY demo application. The `DemoUpdate()` gets the input before moving on to the physics again. Here, the position of the object is obtained and a test is executed to see if the box hasn't passed a certain height (hit the floor). If not, the `PhysicsSpace` object's influence is applied to the object; otherwise, nothing is applied. The object's position is updated and the function returns. The remaining functions of the GRAVITY demo application can be seen in Listing 6.15. A screenshot of the GRAVITY demo can be seen in Figure 6.6.

FIGURE 6.6 A screenshot of the GRAVITY demo.

LISTING 6.15 The remaining functions of the GRAVITY demo application.

```
void DemoUpdate()
{
    int mouseX = 0, mouseY = 0;

    bbe::GetMousePosition(&mouseX, &mouseY);

    if(bbe::isButtonDown(BB_BUTTON_ESCAPE))
        g_quitDemo = true;

    if(bbe::isButtonDown(BB_BUTTON_MOUSE_LEFT))
    {
        g_xRot -= (mouseX - g_oldXRot);
        g_yRot -= (mouseY - g_oldYRot);
    }

    g_oldXRot = mouseX;
    g_oldYRot = mouseY;


    g_currentTime = bbe::GetTimeSeconds();
    float dt = g_currentTime - g_lastTime;

    bbe::Vector3D pos = g_objMass.GetPosition();

    // Fake collision against the ground.
    if(pos.y > 5.3f)
        g_3dSpace.InfluenceObject(&g_objMass, 1);
    else
        g_objMass.SetVelocity(bbe::PhysicsVec(0, 0, 0));

    g_objMass.Update(dt);
    g_object.SetTransformation(g_objMass.GetTransformation());

    g_lastTime = bbe::GetTimeSeconds();
}


void DemoRender()
{
    g_Render.StartRendering(1, 1, 0);
    g_Render.LoadIdentityMatrix();
```

```
    g_Render.SetView(0, 50, 200, 0, 0, 0, 0, 1, 0);
    g_Render.RotateMatrix((float)g_xRot, 0, 1, 0);
    g_Render.RotateMatrix((float)g_yRot, 1, 0, 0);

    g_sceneGraph.Process();

    g_Render.EndRendering();
}


void DemoShutdown()
{
    g_Render.Shutdown();

    g_effectManager.Release(g_object.GetEffectHandle());
    g_modelManager.Release(g_object.GetModelHandle());

    g_effectManager.Release(g_ground.GetEffectHandle());
    g_modelManager.Release(g_ground.GetModelHandle());

    g_sceneGraph.Release();
}
```

SPHERE-TO-SPHERE COLLISION DEMO

The SPHERE-TO-SPHERE COLLISION demo detects collision between two spheres. Each sphere starts at a different corner of the screen with velocities heading toward one another. When they collide, they respond and change directions. Once both objects are out of view, their positions and velocities are reset so the simulation can loop. This demo does not use the PhysicsSpace class as the GRAVITY demo did, so the collision response can be observed better. When the two objects collide near the middle of the screen, they are reflected in opposite directions based on their velocities and moment of impact.

The global section of the SPHERE-TO-SPHERE COLLISION demo has two dynamic objects that will be modeled as spheres in this demo application. Beneath that are two physics point masses, one for each object, and the remaining objects are for the time, resource managers, rotational values, rendering system, and quit flag. The global section of the SPHERE-TO-SPHERE COLLISION demo can be seen in Listing 6.16.

LISTING 6.16 The global section of the SPHERE-TO-SPHERE COLLISION demo.

```
// Models to be displayed.
bbe::DynamicModel g_object1, g_object2;


// Object's Physics informaiton.
bbe::PointMass g_obj1Mass, g_obj2Mass;


// Time values for real time simulation.
float g_lastTime = 0, g_currentTime = 0;


// Resource managers.
BB_MODEL_RESOURCE_MANAGER g_modelManager(32);
BB_EFFECT_RESOURCE_MANAGER g_effectManager(32);


// Scene graph.
bbe::SceneGraph g_sceneGraph;


// Scene rotations.
int g_xRot = 0, g_oldXRot = 0;
int g_yRot = 0, g_oldYRot = 0;


// Rendering System.
bbe::OpenGLRenderer g_Render;


// Flag used to quit.
bool g_quitDemo = false;


void DemoResize(int width, int height)
{
    g_Render.SetViewPort(0, 0, width, height);
    g_Render.ResizeWindow(45.0f, 0.1f, 1000, width, height);
}
```

The next code of interest is the DemoInitialize() function. This demo creates the rendering system and default states before creating the two sphere objects that will be displayed to the screen. These objects are added to the resource manager (which is more a test of the resource manager and is not necessary), and the texture mapping effects are loaded for each object. The remainder of the function sets up the scene graph and initializes the point masses for both objects that will appear in the scene. The DemoInitialize() function of the SPHERE-TO-SPHERE COLLISION demo can be seen in Listing 6.17.

LISTING 6.17   The DemoInitialize() function.

```
bool DemoInitialize(bbe::RenderParams &params)
{
    bool result = false;

    params.m_colorBits = 24;
    params.m_depthBits = 16;
    params.m_stencilBits = 8;
    params.m_fullscreen = WINDOW_FULLSCREEN;
    params.m_height = WINDOW_HEIGHT;
    params.m_width = WINDOW_WIDTH;
    params.m_maxCacheBytes = 2000;
    params.m_maxCacheIndices = 2000;

    if(g_Render.Initialize(&params) != BB_SUCCESS)
        return false;

    DemoResize(WINDOW_WIDTH, WINDOW_HEIGHT);


    g_Render.SetClearColor(0, 0, 0, 255);
    g_Render.Enable(BB_DEPTH_TESTING);
    g_Render.Enable(BB_SMOOTH_SHADING);
    g_Render.Enable(BB_TEXTURE_2D);


    // Create models.
    bbe::ModelData *object1Mesh = new bbe::ModelData();
    bbe::ModelData *object2Mesh = new bbe::ModelData();

    if(bbe::CreateSphereMesh(5, 15, 15, object1Mesh) == false)
        return false;
```

```
if(bbe::CreateSphereMesh(5, 15, 15, object2Mesh) == false)
   return false;

// Resource manage.
g_modelManager.Create(new bbe::ModelResource(object1Mesh),
   "sphere 1", g_object1.GetModelHandlePtr());

g_modelManager.Create(new bbe::ModelResource(object2Mesh),
   "sphere 2", g_object2.GetModelHandlePtr());


// Load textures and effects.
std::vector<BB_FILTER_TYPE> filters;
filters.push_back(BB_MIN_LINEAR_FILTER);
filters.push_back(BB_MAG_LINEAR_FILTER);


bbe::Effect *effect1 = NULL;
effect1 = new bbe::TextureShader("resources/passThrough.cg",
   "resources/decal.tga", &filters,
   static_cast<bbe::RenderInterface*>(&g_Render));

if(effect1 == NULL)
   return false;

bbe::Effect *effect2 = NULL
effect2 = new bbe::TextureShader("resources/passThrough.cg",
   "resources/decal2.tga", &filters,
   static_cast<bbe::RenderInterface*>(&g_Render));

if(effect2 == NULL)
   return false;

// Resource manage.
g_effectManager.Create(new bbe::EffectResource(effect1),
   "effect 1", g_object1.GetEffectHandlePtr());

g_effectManager.Create(new bbe::EffectResource(effect2),
   "effect 2", g_object2.GetEffectHandlePtr());


// Scene graph.
bbe::GeometryNode *obj1Node = NULL, *obj2Node = NULL;
```

```
obj1Node = new bbe::GeometryNode(&g_object1, &g_modelManager,
    &g_effectManager,
    static_cast<bbe::RenderInterface*>(&g_Render));

if(obj1Node == NULL)
    return false;

obj2Node = new bbe::GeometryNode(&g_object2, &g_modelManager,
    &g_effectManager,
    static_cast<bbe::RenderInterface*>(&g_Render));

if(obj2Node == NULL)
    return false;

g_sceneGraph.AddNode(object1Node);
g_sceneGraph.AddNode(object2Node);


// Physics init.
g_object1PointMass.SetPosition(bbe::Vector3D(-120, 50, 0));
g_object1PointMass.SetVelocity(bbe::Vector3D(15, -15, 0));
g_object1PointMass.SetMass(1);

g_object2PointMass.SetPosition(bbe::Vector3D(-120, -50, 0));
g_object2PointMass.SetVelocity(bbe::Vector3D(15, 15, 0));
g_object2PointMass.SetMass(1);


g_lastTime = bbe::GetTimeSeconds();

return true;
}
```

The remaining function of interest is DemoUpdate(). In this function, the objects are first updated. If the position of the objects moves past a certain height, the objects are reset so the application can loop. After the objects have been updated, a CollisionSolver object tests if the two objects collide with one another. If so, the appropriate response is taken; otherwise, the objects are left alone. The collision response occurs on both objects that are passed into the object, so the function only needs to be called once to ensure that both objects no longer touch and are fully updated. The remaining functions from the SPHERE-TO-SPHERE COLLISION demo application can be seen in Listing 6.18. A screenshot of the SPHERE-TO-SPHERE COLLISION demo can be seen in Figure 6.7.

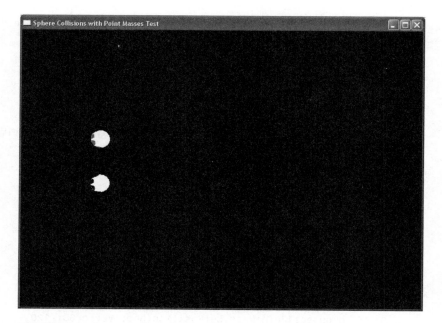

FIGURE 6.7 A screenshot of the SPHERE-TO-SPHERE COLLISION demo.

LISTING 6.18 The remaining functions from the SPHERE-TO-SPHERE COLLISION demo.

```
void DemoUpdate()
{
   int mouseX = 0, mouseY = 0;

   bbe::GetMousePosition(&mouseX, &mouseY);

   if(bbe::isButtonDown(BB_BUTTON_ESCAPE))
      g_quitDemo = true;

   if(bbe::isButtonDown(BB_BUTTON_MOUSE_LEFT))
   {
      g_xRot -= (mouseX - g_oldXRot);
      g_yRot -= (mouseY - g_oldYRot);
   }

   g_oldXRot = mouseX;
   g_oldYRot = mouseY;
```

```
// Time update.
g_currentTime = bbe::GetTimeSeconds();
float dt = g_currentTime - g_lastTime;


// Update obj 1.
g_obj1Mass.Update(dt);
g_object1.SetTransformation(g_obj1Mass.GetTransformation());

bbe::Vector3D pos = g_obj1Mass.GetPosition();

// Reset position once past screen.
if(pos.y > 100)
{
    g_obj1Mass.SetPosition(bbe::Vector3D(-120, 50, 0));
    g_obj1Mass.SetVelocity(bbe::Vector3D(15, -15, 0));
}


// Update obj 2.
g_obj2Mass.Update(dt);
g_object2.SetTransformation(g_obj2Mass.GetTransformation());

pos = g_obj2Mass.GetPosition();

// Reset position once past screen.
if(pos.y < -100)
{
    g_obj2Mass.SetPosition(bbe::Vector3D(-120, -50, 0));
    g_obj2Mass.SetVelocity(bbe::Vector3D(15, 15, 0));
}


// Test for collision and respond.
bbe::CollisionResponse collisionSolver;

collisionSolver.ResponseToCollision(&g_obj1Mass, 5,
    &g_obj2Mass, 5, 0.01f);


g_lastTime = bbe::GetTimeSeconds();
}
```

```
void DemoRender()
{
    g_Render.StartRendering(1, 1, 0);
    g_Render.LoadIdentityMatrix();

    g_Render.SetView(0, 0, 200, 0, 0, 0, 0, 1, 0);
    g_Render.RotateMatrix((float)g_xRot, 0, 1, 0);
    g_Render.RotateMatrix((float)g_yRot, 1, 0, 0);

    g_sceneGraph.Process();

    g_Render.EndRendering();
}


void DemoShutdown()
{
    g_Render.Shutdown();

    g_effectManager.Release(g_object1.GetEffectHandle());
    g_modelManager.Release(g_object1.GetModelHandle());

    g_effectManager.Release(g_object2.GetEffectHandle());
    g_modelManager.Release(g_object2.GetModelHandle());

    g_sceneGraph.Release();
}
```

Sphere and Plane Collisions Demo

The next demo is the SPHERE AND PLANE COLLISION application. This demo application builds off the SPHERE-TO-SPHERE COLLISION demo and adds a room where each wall is a plane the objects can collide off. In this demo are three objects, one for the room and the other two as spheres. The room does not have any physics attributes, so only point masses are used for the spheres. A list of planes is stored for the entire room so collision detection can be performed on the plane list. The remainder of the global section is the same as it was for the SPHERE-TO-SPHERE COLLISION demo application. The global section from the SPHERE AND PLANE COLLISION can be seen in Listing 6.19.

LISTING 6.19   The global section of the SPHERE AND PLANE COLLISION demo.

```cpp
// Models to be displayed.
bbe::DynamicModel g_object1, g_object2, g_room;


// Object's Physics informaiton.
bbe::PointMass g_obj1Mass, g_obj2Mass;


// Room bounds.
std::vector<bbe::Plane> g_roomPlanes;


// Time values for real time simulation.
float g_lastTime = 0, g_currentTime = 0;


// Resource managers.
BB_MODEL_RESOURCE_MANAGER g_modelManager(32);
BB_EFFECT_RESOURCE_MANAGER g_effectManager(32);


// Scene graph.
bbe::SceneGraph g_sceneGraph;


// Scene rotations.
int g_xRot = 0, g_oldXRot = 0;
int g_yRot = 0, g_oldYRot = 0;


// Rendering System.
bbe::OpenGLRenderer g_Render;


// Flag used to quit.
bool g_quitDemo = false;


void DemoResize(int width, int height)
{
    g_Render.SetViewPort(0, 0, width, height);
    g_Render.ResizeWindow(45.0f, 0.1f, 1000, width, height);
}
```

The initializing function starts the same way it did for the last demo. After creating the two sphere meshes, it creates the room. CreateCubeMesh() takes as parameters the size of the cube, the object that will store the cube's data, and a list to store the planes that make up the cube. The last parameter is optional, and for this demo is used to automatically create the planes when the mesh is being built. So far, the cube creation function is the only one that can take an array of planes and add one plane for every surface of a mesh. The remainder of the function is the same as it was for the SPHERE-TO-SPHERE COLLISION demo application. The DemoInitialize() function can be seen in Listing 6.20.

LISTING 6.20   The DemoInitialize() function of the SPHERE AND PLANE COLLISION demo.

```
bool DemoInitialize(bbe::RenderParams &params)
{
    params.m_colorBits = 24;
    params.m_depthBits = 16;
    params.m_stencilBits = 8;
    params.m_fullscreen = WINDOW_FULLSCREEN;
    params.m_height = WINDOW_HEIGHT;
    params.m_width = WINDOW_WIDTH;
    params.m_maxCacheBytes = 2000;
    params.m_maxCacheIndices = 2000;

    if(g_Render.Initialize(&params) != BB_SUCCESS)
        return false;

    DemoResize(WINDOW_WIDTH, WINDOW_HEIGHT);

    g_Render.SetClearColor(0, 0, 0, 255);
    g_Render.Enable(BB_DEPTH_TESTING);
    g_Render.Enable(BB_SMOOTH_SHADING);
    g_Render.Enable(BB_TEXTURE_2D);
    g_Render.Enable(BB_BACK_CCW_CULLING);


    // Create models.
    bbe::ModelData *object1Mesh = new bbe::ModelData();
    bbe::ModelData *object2Mesh = new bbe::ModelData();
    bbe::ModelData *roomMesh = new bbe::ModelData();

    if(bbe::CreateSphereMesh(5, 15, 15, object1Mesh) == false)
        return false;
```

```
if(bbe::CreateSphereMesh(5, 15, 15, object2Mesh) == false)
    return false;

if(bbe::CreateCubeMesh(50, roomMesh, &g_roomPlanes) == false)
    return false;

// Resource manage.
g_modelManager.Create(new bbe::ModelResource(object1Mesh),
    "OBJECT 1", g_object1.GetModelHandlePtr());

g_modelManager.Create(new bbe::ModelResource(object2Mesh),
    "OBJECT 2", g_object2.GetModelHandlePtr());

g_modelManager.Create(new bbe::ModelResource(roomMesh),
    "ROOM", g_room.GetModelHandlePtr());


// Load textures and effects.
std::vector<BB_FILTER_TYPE> filters;
filters.push_back(BB_MIN_LINEAR_FILTER);
filters.push_back(BB_MAG_LINEAR_FILTER);


bbe::Effect *effect1 = NULL;
effect1 = new bbe::TextureShader("resources/passThrough.cg",
    "resources/decal.tga", &filters,
    static_cast<bbe::RenderInterface*>(&g_Render));

if(effect1 == NULL)
    return false;

bbe::Effect *effect2 = NULL;
effect2 = new bbe::TextureShader("resources/passThrough.cg",
    "resources/decal2.tga", &filters,
    static_cast<bbe::RenderInterface*>(&g_Render));

if(effect2 == NULL)
    return false;

// Resource manage.
g_effectManager.Create(new bbe::EffectResource(effect1),
    "effect 1", g_object1.GetEffectHandlePtr());
```

```
        g_effectManager.Create(new bbe::EffectResource(effect2),
            "effect 2", g_object2.GetEffectHandlePtr());

        // Copy handle to the same resource for the room.
        int index = -1;
        index = g_effectManager.GetRegisteredIndex("effect 2");
        g_room.GetEffectHandlePtr()->Initialize(index);


        // Scene graph.
        bbe::GeometryNode *object1Node = NULL, *object2Node = NULL,
                        *roomNode = NULL;

        object1Node = new bbe::GeometryNode(&g_object1,
            &g_modelManager, &g_effectManager,
            static_cast<bbe::RenderInterface*>(&g_Render));

        object2Node = new bbe::GeometryNode(&g_object2,
            &g_modelManager, &g_effectManager,
            static_cast<bbe::RenderInterface*>(&g_Render));

        roomNode = new bbe::GeometryNode(&g_room,
            &g_modelManager, &g_effectManager,
            static_cast<bbe::RenderInterface*>(&g_Render));

        g_sceneGraph.AddNode(object1Node);
        g_sceneGraph.AddNode(object2Node);
        g_sceneGraph.AddNode(roomNode);


        // Physics init.
        g_obj1Mass.SetPosition(bbe::Vector3D(-40, 30, 0));
        g_obj1Mass.SetVelocity(bbe::Vector3D(15, -25, 0));
        g_obj1Mass.SetMass(1);

        g_obj2Mass.SetPosition(bbe::Vector3D(-40, -30, 0));
        g_obj2Mass.SetVelocity(bbe::Vector3D(15, 25, 0));
        g_obj2Mass.SetMass(1);

        g_lastTime = bbe::GetTimeSeconds();

        return true;
    }
```

The update function of the SPHERE TO PLANE COLLISION demo updates each object at a time. It then follows up by solving any collisions that occur between the two objects. Once the object-to-object collision is taken care of from the previous demo, the SPHERE TO PLANE COLLISION demo application loops through the planes of the room and tests those for collision against each object. Any collisions that occur are responded to just like any other object. Normally, planes are static, and in the case of a set of planes making up a room, they have no need to move. When the collision response is handled between objects like a sphere and a plane, only the sphere is moved if collision occurs. `DemoUpdate()` and the demo's remaining function can be seen in Listing 6.21. A screenshot of the SPHERE TO PLANE COLLISION demo can be seen in Figure 6.8.

FIGURE 6.8 A screenshot of the SPHERE TO PLANE COLLISION demo.

LISTING 6.21 The remaining functions of the SPHERE TO PLANE COLLISION demo.

```
void DemoUpdate()
{
    int mouseX = 0, mouseY = 0;

    bbe::GetMousePosition(&mouseX, &mouseY);
```

```
if(bbe::isButtonDown(BB_BUTTON_ESCAPE))
   g_quitDemo = true;

if(bbe::isButtonDown(BB_BUTTON_MOUSE_LEFT))
{
   g_xRot -= (mouseX - g_oldXRot);
   g_yRot -= (mouseY - g_oldYRot);
}

g_oldXRot = mouseX;
g_oldYRot = mouseY;



// Update time.
g_currentTime = bbe::GetTimeSeconds();
float dt = g_currentTime - g_lastTime;


// Update object 1.
g_obj1Mass.Update(dt);
g_object1.SetTransformation(g_obj1Mass.GetTransformation());

// Update object 2;
g_obj2Mass.Update(dt);
g_object2.SetTransformation(g_obj2Mass.GetTransformation());


// Respond to any collisions between the balls.
bbe::CollisionResponse collisionSolver;

collisionSolver.ResponseToCollision(&g_obj1Mass, 5,
   &g_obj2Mass, 5, 0.001f);

// Respond to any collisions against the room.
for(int i = 0; i < (int)g_roomPlanes.size(); i++)
{
   collisionSolver.ResponseToCollision(&g_obj1Mass, 5,
      g_roomPlanes[i], 5.5f);

   collisionSolver.ResponseToCollision(&g_obj2Mass, 5,
      g_roomPlanes[i], 5.5f);
}
```

```
        g_lastTime = bbe::GetTimeSeconds();
}


void DemoRender()
{
    g_Render.StartRendering(1, 1, 0);
    g_Render.LoadIdentityMatrix();

    g_Render.SetView(0, 0, 200, 0, 0, 0, 0, 1, 0);
    g_Render.RotateMatrix((float)g_xRot, 0, 1, 0);
    g_Render.RotateMatrix((float)g_yRot, 1, 0, 0);

    g_sceneGraph.Process();

    g_Render.EndRendering();
}


void DemoShutdown()
{
    g_Render.Shutdown();

    g_effectManager.Release(g_object1.GetEffectHandle());
    g_modelManager.Release(g_object1.GetModelHandle());

    g_effectManager.Release(g_object2.GetEffectHandle());
    g_modelManager.Release(g_object2.GetModelHandle());

    g_effectManager.Release(g_room.GetEffectHandle());
    g_modelManager.Release(g_room.GetModelHandle());

    g_sceneGraph.Release();
}
```

CLOTH SIMULATION

The last physics-based demo application for this chapter is cloth simulation. The cloth simulation performed here is straightforward and builds off the point mass class seen earlier in this chapter, along with springs. A spring is an object that connects two point masses. The springs have a tension amount that allows the two point masses to be pulled away from one another until the tension threshold is reached. At that point, the spring starts to pull the masses back toward one another. Springs keep the point masses connected and are similar to real springs.

The CLOTH SIMULATION demo application can be found on the companion CD-ROM in the BUILDING BLOCKS ENGINE/EXAMPLES/CHAPTER 6 folder. In the demo application, a class is derived from the PointMass class called Spring-Mass. This class adds extended functionality to the point mass class, which includes a flag that can be used to lock a point mass in place and a normal for lighting. The point masses for the cloth simulation are used as vertices for the cloth geometry. This grid of point masses is drawn using triangle lists. The SpringMass class can be seen listed in Listing 6.22.

LISTING 6.22 The SpringMass class derived from the PointMass class with extended functionality.

```
class SpringMass : public PointMass
{
   public:
      SpringMass()
      {
         m_fixed = false;
      }

      Vector3D GetNormal()
      {
         return m_normal;
      }

      Vector3D *GetNormalPtr()
      {
         return &m_normal;
      }

      void SetNormal(Vector3D &n)
      {
         m_normal = n;
      }

      void NormalizeNormal()
      {
         m_normal.Normalize();
      }
```

```
        bool isFixed()
        {
            return m_fixed;
        }

        void SetIsFixed(bool val)
        {
            m_fixed = val;
        }


    private:
        Vector3D m_normal;
        bool m_fixed;
};
```

The next class is the `Spring` class, which represents a physics spring. This class has pointers to two point masses, a tension amount, a spring constant, and a length for the distance between the two point masses. The class also has two functions; the first used to set the member variables of the class, and the second used to update the point masses that the spring connects with the spring force. To calculate the spring force, the spring vector is first obtained. This is used to calculate the spring's tension, which is the spring's constant times the magnitude minus the spring's length, divided by the length. The spring vector and tension are used to add a force to both point masses, with the second point mass receiving the inverse of the force. Calling the `Update()` function of the spring class will add the spring's force to both point masses to which it is connected. The `Spring` class can be seen listed in Listing 6.23.

LISTING 6.23   The `Spring` class.

```
    class Spring
    {
        public:
            Spring()
            {
                m_ball1 = 0;
                m_ball2 = 0;
                m_tension = 0;
                m_constant = 0;
                m_length = 0;
            }
```

```
        virtual ~Spring()
        {

        }

        void SetSpring(float t, float c, float l,
                       SpringMass *m1, SpringMass *m2)
        {
           m_tension = t;
           m_constant = c;
           m_length = l;

           m_ball1 = m1;
           m_ball2 = m2;
        }

        void Update()
        {
           if(m_ball1 == 0 || m_ball2 == 0)
              return;

           Vector3D springVec = m_ball2->GetPosition() -
                                m_ball1->GetPosition();

           m_tension = m_constant * (springVec.Magnitude() -
                       m_length) / m_length;

           springVec.Normalize();

           m_ball1->AddForce(springVec * m_tension);
           m_ball2->AddForce((springVec * m_tension) * -1);
        }


   private:
      SpringMass *m_ball1;
      SpringMass *m_ball2;

      float m_tension;
      float m_constant;
      float m_length;
};
```

The cloth simulation is done using a class called Cloth. This class has a list of point masses, a list of springs, a constant used for the springs, a damper used to offset the velocity, and a list of renderable vertices. The majority of the member functions in the Cloth class are accessor functions, with the exception of Initialize(), RecalculateMesh(), and Shutdown(). Shutdown()is used to release all memory the class allocates during the creation of the cloth. RecalculateMesh()is used to update the list of renderable vertices and normals every time the cloth is updated by the physics system. Initialize()is used to create the cloth, and takes as parameters the size of the cloth, the mass to set for each point mass, the spring constant to use, the length of each spring, and a damper. The cloth is technically a square whose polygon count is determined by the size (grid size) that is passed into the initializing function. By treating each vertex of this square as a point mass, physics can be applied to the body. Using collision detection on the individual point masses allows the object to act as a cloth. The Cloth class can be seen in Listing 6.24. The body for the Initialize() class can be seen in Listing 6.25.

LISTING 6.24   The Cloth class.

```
struct stClothVertex
{
    bbe::Vector3D pos, normal;
};


class Cloth
{
    public:
        Cloth()
        {
            m_balls = 0;
            m_constant = 0;
            m_totalBalls = 0;
            m_dampFactor = 0;
            m_totalSprings = 0;
            m_springs = 0;
            m_vertices = 0;
            m_totalVertices = 0;

            m_descriptor.AddElement(BB_ELEMENT_TYPE_VERTEX_3F);
            m_descriptor.AddElement(BB_ELEMENT_TYPE_NORMAL_3F);
        }
```

```
~Cloth()
{

}

bool Initialize(int gridSize, float mass, float springConst,
                float springLen, float damp);

void RecalculateMesh();
void Shutdown();

void UpdateSprings()
{
   for(int j = 0; j < m_totalSprings; ++j)
   {
      m_springs[j].Update();
   }
}

stClothVertex *GetVertices()
{
   return m_vertices;
}

int GetVertexSizeInBytes()
{
   return GetVertexStride() * m_totalVertices;
}

int GetVertexStride()
{
   return sizeof(stClothVertex);
}

bbe::VertexDescriptor GetDescriptor()
{
   return m_descriptor;
}

int GetGridSize()
{
   return m_gridSize;
}
```

```cpp
        bbe::SpringMass *GetMasses()
        {
           return m_balls;
        }

        int GetTotalMasses()
        {
           return m_totalBalls;
        }

        bbe::Spring *GetSprings()
        {
           return m_springs;
        }

        int GetTotalSprings()
        {
           return m_totalSprings;
        }

    private:
        int m_gridSize;

        stClothVertex *m_vertices;
        int m_totalVertices;

        bbe::VertexDescriptor m_descriptor;

        bbe::SpringMass *m_balls;
        int m_totalBalls;

        bbe::Spring *m_springs;
        int m_totalSprings;

        float m_constant;
        float m_dampFactor;
};
```

LISTING 6.25   The body of the `Initialize()` function.

```cpp
bool Cloth::Initialize(int gridSize, float mass,
                       float springConst, float springLen,
                       float damp)
```

```
{
   int springIndex = 0;

   m_constant = springConst;
   m_dampFactor = damp;
   m_gridSize = gridSize;

   m_totalBalls = m_gridSize * m_gridSize;

   m_totalSprings = (m_gridSize - 1) * m_gridSize * 2;
   m_totalSprings += (m_gridSize - 1) * (m_gridSize - 1) * 2;
   m_totalSprings += (m_gridSize - 2) * m_gridSize * 2;

   m_balls = new bbe::SpringMass[m_totalBalls];
   m_springs = new bbe::Spring[m_totalSprings];

   if(m_balls == 0 || m_springs == 0)
      return false;

   // Set the mass for all balls.
   for(int i = 0; i < m_totalBalls; i++)
   {
       m_balls[i].SetMass(mass);
       m_balls[i].SetVelocityDamper(m_dampFactor);
   }

   // Calculate the m_springs not on the right edge.
   for(i = 0; i < m_gridSize; i++)
   {
      for(int j = 0; j < m_gridSize - 1; j++)
      {
         m_springs[springIndex++].SetSpring(0, m_constant,
            springLen, &m_balls[i * m_gridSize + j],
               &m_balls[i * m_gridSize + j + 1]);
      }
   }

   // Calculate the m_springs not on the bottom edge.
   for(i = 0; i < m_gridSize - 1; i++)
   {
      for(int j = 0; j < m_gridSize; j++)
      {
         m_springs[springIndex++].SetSpring(0, m_constant,
            springLen, &m_balls[i * m_gridSize + j],
```

```
          &m_balls[(i + 1) * m_gridSize + j]);
   }
}

// Calculate the m_springs not on the right or bottom edge.
for(i = 0; i < m_gridSize - 1; i++)
{
   for(int j = 0; j < m_gridSize - 1; j++)
   {
      m_springs[springIndex++].SetSpring(0, m_constant,
         springLen * 1.5f, &m_balls[i * m_gridSize + j],
         &m_balls[(i + 1) * m_gridSize + j + 1]);
   }
}

// Calculate the m_springs from one below and left but not
// on the right or bottom edge.
for(i = 0; i < m_gridSize - 1; i++)
{
   for(int j = 1; j < m_gridSize; j++)
   {
      m_springs[springIndex++].SetSpring(0, m_constant,
         springLen * 1.5f, &m_balls[i * m_gridSize + j],
         &m_balls[(i + 1) * m_gridSize + j - 1]);
   }
}

// Calculate the m_springs not on or next to the right edge.
for(i = 0; i < m_gridSize; i++)
{
   for(int j = 0; j < m_gridSize - 2; j++)
   {
      m_springs[springIndex++].SetSpring(0, m_constant,
         springLen * 2.0f, &m_balls[i * m_gridSize + j],
         &m_balls[i * m_gridSize + j + 2]);
   }
}

// Calculate the m_springs not on or next to the bottom edge.
for(i = 0; i < m_gridSize - 2; i++)
{
   for(int j = 0; j < m_gridSize; j++)
   {
      m_springs[springIndex++].SetSpring(0, m_constant,
```

```
            springLen * 2.0f, &m_balls[i * m_gridSize + j],
            &m_balls[(i + 2) * m_gridSize + j]);
      }
   }

   m_totalVertices = (m_gridSize - 2) * (m_gridSize - 2) * 6;
   m_vertices = new stClothVertex[m_totalVertices];

   return true;
}
```

The next function is RecalculateMesh(), which is used to calculate the normals of the cloth's mesh and the vertices. This data is the information that is rendered to the scene. This function should be called after the physics update the cloth, which should be at most one per frame. The body for the RecalculateMesh() can be seen in Listing 6.26 along with the Shutdown() function of the Cloth class.

LISTING 6.26   The RecalculateMesh() function.

```
void Cloth::RecalculateMesh()
{
   bbe::Vector3D *p0 = 0, *p1 = 0, *p2 = 0,
                 *p3 = 0, *p4 = 0, *p5 = 0;

   bbe::Vector3D *n0 = 0, *n1 = 0, *n2 = 0,
                 *n3 = 0, *n4 = 0, *n5 = 0;
   int index = 0;

   // Reset normals.
   for(int i = 0; i < m_totalBalls; i++)
      m_balls[i].SetNormal(bbe::Vector3D(0, 0, 0));

   // Recalculate all normals for the cloth mesh.
   for(i = 0; i < m_gridSize - 1; ++i)
   {
      for(int j = 0; j < m_gridSize - 1; ++j)
      {
         p0 = &m_balls[i * m_gridSize + j].GetPosition();
         p1 = &m_balls[i * m_gridSize+j + 1].GetPosition();
         p2 = &m_balls[(i + 1) * m_gridSize + j].GetPosition();

         p3 = &m_balls[(i + 1) * m_gridSize + j].GetPosition();
         p4 = &m_balls[i * m_gridSize + j + 1].GetPosition();
         p5 = &m_balls[(i + 1) * m_gridSize + j + 1].GetPosition();
```

```
        n0 = m_balls[i * m_gridSize + j].GetNormalPtr();
        n1 = m_balls[i * m_gridSize+j + 1].GetNormalPtr();
        n2 = m_balls[(i + 1) * m_gridSize + j].GetNormalPtr();

        n3 = m_balls[(i + 1) * m_gridSize + j].GetNormalPtr();
        n4 = m_balls[i * m_gridSize + j + 1].GetNormalPtr();
        n5 = m_balls[(i + 1) * m_gridSize + j + 1].GetNormalPtr();

        bbe::Vector3D tempN1, tempN2;
        tempN1.Normalize(*p0, *p1, *p2);
        tempN2.Normalize(*p3, *p4, *p5);

        *n0 += tempN1; *n1 += tempN1; *n2 += tempN1;
        *n3 += tempN2; *n4 += tempN2; *n5 += tempN2;
    }
}

for(i = 0; i < m_totalBalls; i++)
{
    m_balls[i].NormalizeNormal();
}

// Update mesh.
for(int y = 0; y < m_gridSize - 2; y++)
{
    for(int x = 0; x < m_gridSize - 2; x++)
    {
        // V1.
        m_vertices[index].pos =
            m_balls[y * m_gridSize + x].GetPosition();

        m_vertices[index++].normal =
            m_balls[y * m_gridSize + x].GetNormal();

        // V2.
        m_vertices[index].pos =
            m_balls[y * m_gridSize + x + 1].GetPosition();

        m_vertices[index++].normal =
            m_balls[y * m_gridSize + x + 1].GetNormal();

        // V3.
        m_vertices[index].pos =
            m_balls[(y + 1) * m_gridSize + x].GetPosition();
```

```
            m_vertices[index++].normal =
               m_balls[(y + 1) * m_gridSize + x].GetNormal();

            // V4.
            m_vertices[index].pos =
               m_balls[(y + 1) * m_gridSize + x].GetPosition();

            m_vertices[index++].normal =
               m_balls[(y + 1) * m_gridSize + x].GetNormal();

            // V5.
            m_vertices[index].pos =
               m_balls[y * m_gridSize + x + 1].GetPosition();

            m_vertices[index++].normal =
               m_balls[y * m_gridSize + x + 1].GetNormal();

            // V6.
            m_vertices[index].pos =
               m_balls[(y + 1) * m_gridSize + x + 1].GetPosition();

            m_vertices[index++].normal =
               m_balls[(y + 1) * m_gridSize + x + 1].GetNormal();
         }
      }
   }


void Cloth::Shutdown()
{
   if(m_balls != 0)
   {
      delete[] m_balls;
      m_balls = 0;
   }

   if(m_springs != 0)
   {
      delete[] m_springs;
```

```
        m_springs = 0;
    }

    if(m_vertices != 0)
    {
        delete[] m_vertices;
        m_vertices = 0;
    }
}
```

The last file in the demo application is the main.cpp source file. The demo application displays two objects: the cloth, and a sphere that can be moved throughout the scene that can interact with the cloth. The global section of the main.cpp source file has a ModelData object used for rendering the sphere, the sphere's position, the sphere's radius, the cloth, the PhysicsSpace object used for applying gravity, shader information, the rendering system, and values used for rotating the scene. The demo application allows the sphere to be moved using the keyboard's up and down arrow keys. The cloth itself will hang suspended in the air with two of its corners locked into place, while the rest is free to fall around the environment. The global section of the main.cpp source file can be seen listed in Listing 6.27.

LISTING 6.27   The global section of the Cloth demo.

```
// Models to be displayed.
bbe::ModelData g_object;

// Main sphere object's position and radius.
// The sphere is user controlled.
float g_spherePos[3] = { 0, -2, 0 };
float g_sphereRadius = 3.0f;

// Dynamic cloth.
Cloth g_cloth;

// Shader ID.
bbe::ShaderHandle g_shader;
```

```
// Shader parameters.
bbe::ParameterHandle g_lightPos;
bbe::ParameterHandle g_lightCol;

// Physical space in which the object lives.
bbe::PhysicsSpace g_3dSpace;

// Time values for real time simulation.
float g_lastTime = 0, g_currentTime = 0;

// Scene rotations.
int g_xRot = 0, g_oldXRot = 0;
int g_yRot = 0, g_oldYRot = 0;

// Rendering System.
bbe::OpenGLRenderer g_Render;

// Flag used to quit.
bool g_quitDemo = false;
```

The next function is DemoInitialize(), which starts by setting up the rendering system. It then creates the sphere mesh and the shader the demo uses for lighting. Next, the cloth is created by calling the Cloth class' Initialize() function, and the cloth's default position is specified. This position is set above the sphere so the cloth can fall on it when the application begins. The remainder of the function sets the physics information before exiting. The DemoInitialize() function can be seen in Listing 6.28.

LISTING 6.28   The DemoInitialize() function.

```
bool DemoInitialize(bbe::RenderParams &params)
{
   bool result = false;

   params.m_colorBits = 24;
   params.m_depthBits = 16;
   params.m_stencilBits = 8;
   params.m_fullscreen = WINDOW_FULLSCREEN;
   params.m_height = WINDOW_HEIGHT;
   params.m_width = WINDOW_WIDTH;
```

```
params.m_maxCacheBytes = 2000;
params.m_maxCacheIndices = 2000;

if(g_Render.Initialize(&params) != BB_SUCCESS)
    return false;

DemoResize(WINDOW_WIDTH, WINDOW_HEIGHT);

g_Render.SetClearColor(0, 0, 0, 255);
g_Render.Enable(BB_DEPTH_TESTING);
g_Render.Enable(BB_SMOOTH_SHADING);


// Create meshes.
result = bbe::CreateSphereMesh(g_sphereRadius, 15, 15,
                                &g_object);

if(result == false)
    return false;


// Load shader.
result = g_Render.CreateShaderFromFile("resources/vs.glsl",
                                        "resources/ps.glsl",
                                        &g_shader);

if(result == false)
    return false;

g_Render.SetupShaderParameter("lightPos", g_shader,
                                &g_lightPos);

g_Render.SetupShaderParameter("lightColor", g_shader,
                                &g_lightCol);


// Create the cloth.
int gridSize = 10;

if(!g_cloth.Initialize(gridSize, 0.01f, 15.0f, 1.0f, 0.85f))
    return false;
```

```
// Set the cloth grid to a default location.
int index = 0;
bbe::Vector3D pos;
bbe::SpringMass *ptr = g_cloth.GetMasses();

// Create flat grid.
for(int i = 0; i < gridSize; ++i)
{
    for(int j = 0; j < gridSize; ++j)
    {
        index = i * gridSize + j;

        pos.x = (float)j - (gridSize - 1) / 2;
        pos.y = 5.0f;
        pos.z = (float)i - (gridSize - 1) / 2;

        ptr[index].SetIsFixed(false);
        ptr[index].SetPosition(pos);
    }
}

// Fix location for two of the corners.
ptr[0].SetIsFixed(true);
ptr[gridSize - 1].SetIsFixed(true);


// Physics initialize.
g_3dSpace.SetIsAirAtmosphere(true);
g_3dSpace.SetGravity(bbe::Vector3D(0.0f, -0.98f, 0.0f));

g_lastTime = bbe::GetTimeSeconds();

return true;
}
```

The next function is DemoUpdate(), which starts by detecting and responding to
the various inputs the application cares about. After the input is handled, the function performs the physics updates on the scene. For the physics update, all the
springs have their Update() functions called, which adds the spring forces to all point
masses that make up the cloth. The function moves on to apply the total forces from
the physics space (mainly gravity) on all the point masses in the cloth. By adding
gravity, the cloth can fall from its default position until it collides with the sphere, or
until the cloth backends fall as far as the springs will allow them.

Once the new positions of the cloth have been calculated, the next step would be to perform collision detection against the scene. In the demo application, this consists of performing collision detection against the main sphere object in the scene. If there is collision, the collision response code will reposition the cloth so it lies on top of the sphere but does not penetrate its geometry. With the new and final updated positions for a frame, the mesh can be recalculated and the updating is done. The `DemoUpdate()` function can be seen in Listing 6.29. The rendering and shutdown functions from the `Cloth` demo application can be seen in Listing 6.30. A screenshot of the `Cloth` demo application can be seen in Figure 6.9.

LISTING 6.29   The `DemoUpdate()` function.

```
void DemoUpdate()
{
    int mouseX = 0, mouseY = 0;

    bbe::GetMousePosition(&mouseX, &mouseY);

    if(bbe::isButtonDown(BB_BUTTON_ESCAPE))
        g_quitDemo = true;

    if(bbe::isButtonDown(BB_BUTTON_ARROW_UP))
        g_spherePos[2] -= 0.05f;

    if(bbe::isButtonDown(BB_BUTTON_ARROW_DOWN))
        g_spherePos[2] += 0.05f;

    if(bbe::isButtonDown(BB_BUTTON_MOUSE_LEFT))
    {
        g_xRot -= (mouseX - g_oldXRot);
        g_yRot -= (mouseY - g_oldYRot);
    }

    g_oldXRot = mouseX;
    g_oldYRot = mouseY;


    // Update physics.
    bbe::CollisionResponse collisionSolver;
    bbe::PointMass sphere;
    sphere.SetMass(1);
```

```
// Update time.
g_currentTime = bbe::GetTimeSeconds();
float dt = g_currentTime - g_lastTime;

// Update all spring forces.
g_cloth.UpdateSprings();

// Update all point masses of the soft body.
bbe::SpringMass *ptr = g_cloth.GetMasses();

for(int i = 0; i < g_cloth.GetTotalMasses(); ++i)
{
 // Allow for some points not to move.
   if(ptr[i].isFixed())
   {
      ptr[i].SetVelocity(bbe::Vector3D());
   }
   else
   {
      // Apply gravity.
      g_3dSpace.InfluenceObject(&ptr[i], 1);

      // Update all forces that are on the point mass.
      ptr[i].Update(dt * 0.8f);
   }
}

// Apply collisions with the cloth and the main sphere.
for(i = 0; i < g_cloth.GetTotalMasses(); ++i)
{
   collisionSolver.ResponseToCollision(&sphere, g_sphereRadius,
      &ptr[i], 0.1f, 0.06f);

   // Keep sphere un-moveable.
   sphere.SetPosition(bbe::Vector3D(g_spherePos[0],
                      g_spherePos[1], g_spherePos[2]));

   sphere.SetVelocity(bbe::Vector3D(0, 0, 0));
}

// Update mesh and normals.
g_cloth.RecalculateMesh();
```

```
        g_lastTime = bbe::GetTimeSeconds();
    }
```

LISTING 6.30   The `DemoRender()` and `DemoShutdown()` functions.

```
void DemoRender()
{
    g_Render.StartRendering(1, 1, 0);
    g_Render.LoadIdentityMatrix();

    g_Render.SetView(0, 5, 30, 0, 0, 0, 0, 1, 0);
    g_Render.RotateMatrix((float)g_xRot, 0, 1, 0);
    g_Render.RotateMatrix((float)g_yRot, 1, 0, 0);

    g_Render.ApplyShader(g_shader);

    g_Render.SetShaderParameter4f(g_lightPos, 0, 10, 10, 0);
    g_Render.SetShaderParameter4f(g_lightCol, 0.8f, 0.8f, 0.8f, 0);


    // Render cloth.
    g_Render.Render(BB_PRIMITIVE_TRI_LIST, &g_cloth.GetDescriptor(),
                    (char*)g_cloth.GetVertices(), NULL,
                    g_cloth.GetVertexSizeInBytes(), 0,
                    g_cloth.GetVertexStride());


    // Render sphere object.
    g_Render.PushMatrix();

        g_Render.TranslateMatrix(g_spherePos[0],
                                 g_spherePos[1],
                                 g_spherePos[2]);

        g_Render.Render(BB_RENDER_MODEL_DATA_PARAMS(g_object));

    g_Render.PopMatrix();

    g_Render.EndRendering();
}
```

```
void DemoShutdown()
{
   g_Render.Shutdown();
   g_cloth.Shutdown();
}
```

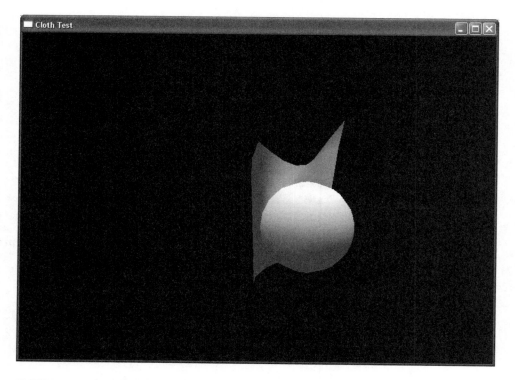

FIGURE 6.9   A screenshot of the CLOTH SIMULATION demo.

SUMMARY

Physics is a huge and complex field of study. In games, physics are becoming increasingly important as hardware becomes more powerful. In the Building Blocks Engine, there is code to work with point masses and simple cloth. In games, the detection of collisions and their response are needed to create realistic simulations. If additional or more detailed information on physics is required, check out Appendix A for book resources that can be a great help when learning about the different game physics. Much information and detail go into modern physics systems, and the implementation of such a system is not trivial.

The next chapters look at artificial intelligence and scripting in video games. Artificial intelligence is used to create realistic behaviors in games by nonhuman characters and players. Scripting is a part of application development that allows the logic of an application to be controlled outside the program. Scripting has many uses in games, which will be examined briefly.

CHAPTER EXERCISES

1. Extend the cloth demo application to work with boxes and spheres.
2. Use the Point Mass class to create a simple particle system. The system can have textured squares falling from random positions in a 3D scene moving along random velocities. After a certain amount of time (e.g., 10 seconds), the particles can have their positions and velocities reset.

7 Artificial Intelligence

In This Chapter

- Overview
- Path Finding
- Finite State Machines
- Scripting AI
- Additional AI Techniques

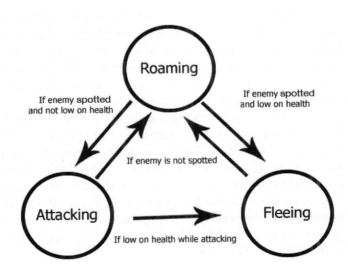

Artificial intelligence (AI) has been around in games since the beginning of gaming itself in one form or another. When playing a video game against a computer opponent, one must be challenged to some degree to achieve some difficultly in completing the game. As games become more complex, so does their realism. One part of this increase in realism comes from AI just as importantly as any other area of game development. Like physics a few years ago, AI is one aspect that can make a game stand out from the rest of the games on the market, which can increase a game's popularity and sales. AI is no trivial topic in game development and a field of study unto itself. In games, there is the major challenge of trying to model realistic behavior in real time with limited resources available to the gaming application.

There are many different algorithms and techniques for creating artificial behavior in a virtual simulation such as a video game. Not all games require the same complexity as other games in various game genres. For example, a side-scrolling game's AI would not be as complex as that of a tactical squad-based first-person shooting game. In this chapter, we discuss AI in general game development by looking at a few different topics that can be seen in various games. The key to a good AI in a game requires a balance between performance and realism through simulated intelligence. Not all AI has to have actual intelligence.

OVERVIEW

In this chapter, we discuss a few different topics in AI, including chasing and evading, finite state machines (FSMs), neural networks, path finding, patterns, fuzzy logic, flocking behaviors, probability, and scripting artificial intelligence. In Chapter 9, "Game Demos," a demo implement 5 simple levels of AI. This chapter will serve as an overview of some of the topics and techniques that can be found in games dealing with artificial intelligence.

One of the most important areas of AI deals with path finding. Path finding is the ability for an AI game object to go from point A to point B, while looking like it has some kind of intelligence. A character running in circles or looking as if it is having some kind of mental breakdown when trying to navigate a simple path will cause the appearance in intelligence in the game to be nonexistent. Artificial intelligence does not have to be complex to look complex in most situations. It is about controlling the perception of the game world in the eyes of the players who are engaging in the game title. The following section starts the discussion dealing with path finding in AI in games.

PATH FINDING

Path finding is important in any type of video game. It doesn't matter how intelligent the characters in the game application are if they can't navigate the environment they are in. Path finding opens many doors in video games by allowing nonplayable characters to navigate just about any environment presented. In games there can be characters chasing other characters, groups of objects moving together as a group, the ability for characters to go through the game on their own without any human interference, and so forth. For example, in *Halo® 2*, the path finding is good to the point where gamers can get in a vehicle's passenger seat and allow the game AI solider to drive to the next destination in the game world. Another example of this can be seen in *Saint's Row* for the Xbox 360. The nonplayable characters need to navigate an area, as seen with a fast-moving vehicle in the aforementioned games, and must realistically avoid any obstacles such as debris, other vehicles, buildings, other characters, and so forth.

In this chapter, we discuss chasing and evading, A* path finding, and patterns (animation paths) seen in video games. In AI there is no one perfect technique because each topic has its own strengths and weaknesses that depend on the gaming environment that makes up the game's virtual world, the resources available to the game, and the nature of the game itself. When it comes to learning about AI as a hobby, we recommend researching many different topics before settling on one because some techniques might be more efficient in certain situations.

CHASING AND EVADING

Chasing and evading is a classic type of behavior seen in games throughout history—a nonplayer character is either going after something (chasing) or moving away from something (evading). Maybe there is a situation in which an enemy missile is locked onto a game character and is taking on the chasing behavior. Or maybe an enemy is dangerously low on health and must run away from a game character to survive. Regardless of the situation and game, chasing and evading is a useful technique in games that can get away with doing it in an acceptable manner (i.e., realistic enough for the simulation). Chasing and evading have been around for quite some time in one form or another in 2D games. Chasing and evading is a classic type of AI and can have its uses.

When it comes down to it, an object will have to decide whether it will want to chase or evade another object. Based on the decision, the next step would be to execute the action in a way that is appropriate for the game. Deciding whether a game character will want to chase or evade can be complex depending on the game. The game would need to set up conditions and rules that allow the AI to examine a situation and make a decision based on the information at hand. This can be done with FSMs, neural networks, and other techniques, which are discussed later in this chapter. Once the decision is made, the game has to virtually move the object in a direction, and must worry about obstacles that might lie somewhere within the object's path. Unless an object can move through the geometry in the environment, obstacle avoidance would definitely need to be done and handled—which can complicate things depending on the environments.

Chasing and evading is done by coming to a decision and making an action take place based on the results of that decision. If a game character is physically chasing another object, it must be moved from its current location toward the object it is chasing (its destination). If a game character is evading another object, it needs to move in a direction in opposition to the direction of the object that is doing the chasing. This movement can be random, if possible based on the game environment and game rules, or it will need to do some extra determination work to choose the best option. Listing 7.1 lists an example for a simple conditional statement that can be used in a chasing decision, and Listing 7.2 for evading. Figure 7.1 illustrates a visual example of a chasing and evading algorithm.

LISTING 7.1 Simple chasing between objects A and B.

```
if(objectA.x > objectB.x)
{
    objectA.x—;
}
else if(objectA.x < objectB.x)
{
    objectA.x++;
}

if(objectA.y > objectB.y)
{
    objectA.y—;
}
else if(objectA.y < objectB.y)
{
    objectA.y++;
}
```

LISTING 7.2   Simple evading between objects A and B.

```
if(objectA.x > objectB.x)
{
    objectA.x++;
}
else if(objectA.x < objectB.x)
{
    objectA.x—;
}

if(objectA.y > objectB.y)
{
    objectA.y++;
}
else if(objectA.y < objectB.y)
{
    objectA.y—;
}
```

Example of Chasing

Example of Evading

FIGURE 7.1   Example of chasing and evading.

A* PATH FINDING

The A* (A-Star) path finding algorithm is used in video games to great extent and is probably one of the most popular methods. A* path finding works by finding the best route from a start position to a destination using a node-based approach. A game world is broken up by nodes or tiles. When the A* algorithm is executed, a path is determined from the start to the end based on a scoring system. The algorithm is efficient but does take a bit of CPU cycles to execute. Figure 7.2 illustrates an example of an environment split up by nodes where the node centers are the filled circles.

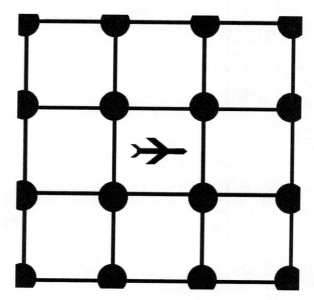

FIGURE 7.2 A game world for A* path finding.

The A* algorithm is not an easy one to grasp for most beginners to artificial intelligence. The number of nodes, node positions, and having to define them is not an easy task. For a search area, which is an area in which the AI can look for a destination, programmers must be sure to avoid obstacles and find the best route, assuming one exists. Even though A* is not as simple as the chase and evading algorithm seen earlier, it will give a game a very realistic path-finding capability for the game characters and is very efficient. Programmers implementing the A* path finding algorithm must be careful because the performance of the algorithm can be affected negatively. Having a ton of objects in the game world and/or too many nodes can have an unacceptable effect on performance.

PATTERNS

Patterns in video games can give characters the appearance of intelligence without the actual intelligence. Many gamers have seen them before with examples such as patrolling enemy guards, nonplayable characters in a village, and so forth. Any object that moves along a pre-defined path or paths is operating along a pattern. Taking the patrolling guard as an example, this could include a guard walking down the hall, stopping at a door, peeking in the door, and then continuing along its route. Although it might sound complicated, it really isn't anything more than a scripted event designed to look as if the character is behaving in a realistic manner. To recreate such an animation, one would need a walking animation to play while the object is moving along a path, and an animation of a guard performing a peeking animation for when it gets to the door. In such an example, there is no real intelligence going on, but just pre-defined behavior being executed in real time.

In the book *Ultimate Game Programming with DirectX* there was a chapter that created and worked with pre-defined animation paths for moving objects from one point to another. This included straight lines, curves, and circular paths. In the book, readers where able to put them together to create an animation route that could be used to create the sequence of animations for the patrolling guard example in the previous paragraph. Patterns can be used with AI to create a life-like simulation. For example, while executing a pattern, if the guard spotted the main character it could break away from the pre-defined pattern and start operating on its AI code to determine the actions that need to take place. Patterns have always been a huge part of games and are definitely worth looking at, especially when combined with AI.

FINITE STATE MACHINES

FSMs in AI are a set of code used to control the states of an object. In the case of video games, they can be used to control the AI of a nonplayer character, among other things. An FSM defines a set of conditions that are used to change an object from one state to another. FSMs are easy to implement and easy to debug so they've gained a lot of use in video game AI. If a programmer can plan on paper all the states he needs to have for a behavior and what conditions must occur to cause state transitions, he can code an FSM. Often, the hardest part of making an FSM is deciding all of the states and conditions, and making sure everything flows logically. FSMs are an old concept that has been used since the early days of game development, are very useful, and something worth learning about in general.

THE BASICS OF FSM

To begin making an FSM, a programmer will have to create a model of the object's behavior he wants to capture. For example, consider a simple game that has enemy characters roaming an environment randomly. If the enemy sees the character, they can start to chase/attack that character. However, if the enemy has low health, they might be programmed to run and hide from the main character. From this simple description, one can deduce that there are three states: one for roaming, one for attacking, and one for fleeing. To transition from the roaming state to the attacking state, the enemy must be able to see the main character. To transition from the roaming state to the fleeing state, the enemy has to be able to see the main character and has to have low health. For the state machine to transition from the attacking or the fleeing state back to roaming state, the enemy would have to lose view of the main character. In a situation in which the game does not allow the enemies to regain health, there would be no way to go from fleeing to attacking because the enemy would be in danger unless there was some other action or state that could intervene.

In the basic example game mentioned in the previous paragraph, there were three states and five conditions. By following the information about the object's behavior, it can be said that the main character is able to be spotted by an enemy, attacked by an enemy, or have an enemy run from it. If the enemy does not see the main character, it could simply walk around the environment randomly patrolling the area. Figure 7.3 illustrates the AI diagram model for the FSM just described.

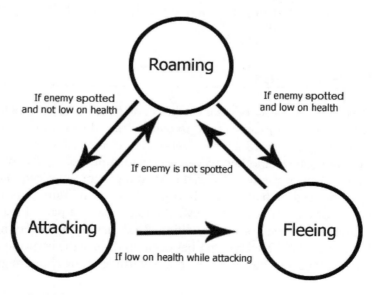

FIGURE 7.3 A simple finite state machine.

AN FSM EXAMPLE

Once a programmer has the behavior planned, the next step would be to code the FSM. Luckily for most situations, this can boil down to having a structure to hold an enemy's AI state and a set of if statements, or switch conditional statements, to test and control the transitions from one state to the other. A look at pseudocode that implements the behavior described can be seen in Listing 7.3 where the FSM is implemented as a switch statement.

LISTING 7.3   Pseudocode for the FSM.

```
#define ROAMING_STATE     1
#define ATTACKING_STATE  2
#define FLEEING_STATE     3

#define LOW_HEALTH       20


struct AI_State
{
   int health = 100;
   int aiState = ROAMING_STATE;
};


// During Game Update for an Enemy


AI_State enemy;


switch(enemy.aiState)
{
   case ROAMING_STATE:

      if(CanSeePlayer() == TRUE)
      {
         if(enemy.health <= LOW_HEALTH)
            enemy.aiState = FLEEING_STATE;
         else
            enemy.aiState = ATTACKING_STATE;
      }
```

```
            break;

        case ATTACKING_STATE:

            if(CanSeePlayer() == false)
            {
                enemy.aiState = ROAMING_STATE;
            }
            else
            {
                if(enemy.health <= LOW_HEALTH)
                    enemy.aiState = FLEEING_STATE;
            }

        break;

        case FLEEING_STATE:

            if(CanSeePlayer() == false)
            {
                enemy.aiState = ROAMING_STATE;
            }

        break;
    };
```

In Listing 7.3 is a pseudocode implementation of an FSM using the states and conditions that were described and modeled in Figure 7.3. It took a switch statement and a set of if/else statements to test and control the execution of the FSM. Finite state machines can be complex and large when trying to model complex behavior. As seen in Listing 7.3, they can also be small when trying to model simple behavior.

SCRIPTING AI

Scripting in games has the added capability to allow developers and users of a game to modify or add behaviors to a game by editing a file(s) instead of having to modify and rebuild the game's source code. Artificial intelligence has had a great use for scripting in the past and has allowed many games to allow users to create bots, which are computer-controlled AI characters, among other things using their own custom defined behavior. There are a few different types of scripting out there, as no one type is the same as another. Depending on the type of AI a developer has in a game and the type of control he wishes to allow outside of the game's source code will depend on which one is right for that game. There are also many existing scripting libraries and languages like Game Monkey Script, Java Script, C#, LUA, Python, and many more. Each has its own strengths, weaknesses, and performance. It is not always necessary to create a custom scripting language, compiler, and so forth from the ground up when there are so many already out there. The needs of the developer and how the existing scripting systems stack up can make a difference in the final decision.

SCRIPTING TECHNIQUES

When it comes to scripting, one can take an approach of using command scripts, scripts to set properties (property scripts), and compiled scripts. A command script is a script with a list of commands in it. When a command is read in and parsed, the machine does whatever it was instructed to do by the command. Command scripts are generally interpreted and executed on-the-fly by reading a command from the file and doing a string comparison to determine what action needs to take place. Listing 7.4 lists an example of a command script file. In the fictional example in Listing 7.4, there are commands for printing a string to a screen, clearing a screen, and exiting a script.

LISTING 7.4 A command script.

```
Print "Hello World"
Print "Goodbye World"

Clear

Print "Hello Again World"

Exit
```

A property script defines properties. A property in a script has a name, similar to a variable name, and a value. A programmer can use property scripts to set tweakable values in an AI system to alter the behavior of game objects. A simple property script could specify a different property and its value on each line of the file. When the property script loads in the file, it reads each line one by one and parses the name of the property and its value. Normally, property names are at the beginning of the line and the value comes after a space (or series of spaces) after the name. Listing 7.5 lists an example of a property script.

LISTING 7.5   A property script.

```
Width 800
Height 600
Fullscreen true
Title "Some String"
```

Compiled scripts are similar to Java, C, C++, and so forth because they are transformed by a program known as a compiler into a form that can be easily processed by a computer. The system in an application that processes a compiled script is called the virtual machine. A virtual machine will execute a script and mimic the behavior of a computer's CPU to some degree. Compiled scripts and their virtual machines are the hardest of the three types of scripting talked about so far to implement, but can be a great asset to have depending on the type of AI developers will be implementing in their games. When it comes to compiled scripts, developers might want to look at using a pre-existing scripting system instead of creating their own from the ground up. If time is an issue during development, acquiring a scripting system might be a necessity rather than a personal preference.

ADDITIONAL AI TECHNIQUES

Many more topics go into the realm of AI. In this chapter, we briefly talk about fuzzy logic, neural networks, and flocking in games. Additional resources on AI can be found in Appendix A, "Additional Resources." Artificial intelligence is a very important and unavoidable topic in game development. As the game community grows and games become more complex, so do the AI requirements the gaming community expects and demands of its products.

FUZZY LOGIC

Fuzzy logic was created at the University of California Berkeley in 1965 by a professor named Lotfi Zadeh. Fuzzy logic is a technique used to present problems to a computer in a manner in which humans naturally solve them. The way people and machines operate and process information is very different from one another. Humans beings can make decisions without knowing all the facts (if any) and by generalizing facts. Computers, on the other hand, often have access to precise measurements and information that humans don't need and don't often care for when they make their decisions.

Fuzzy logic enables developers to solve problems using linguistic terms with a computer. In fuzzy logic, everything is a matter of degree. Something can be true (1), false (0), and fall within the gray area between the two extremes. This provides a varying degree of truth when dealing with values between true and false.

In games, fuzzy logic can be used by computer-controlled characters to do things like threat assessments, classification (i.e., character ranks), state control like turning on streetlights when it gets dark outside, and things of that nature. The great thing about fuzzy logic is that it allows developers to solve problems like humans instead of like a machine. The opposite can be said when learning to program for the first time. Many coders had to learn to solve problems like a computer rather than how they naturally would handle them. Fuzzy logic is the type of technique that can look at a situation in a general sense and make a believable decision without hard measurements and facts. One of the main characteristics of fuzzy logic is its capability to look at a situation generally and base a decision on its assessment.

Neural Networks

Artificial neural networks, or just neural networks, are a type of AI technique that aims to simulate the human brain. In the human brain are billions of neurons that are connected to thousands of other neurons. This complex network works by sending information from one neuron to another via the axon and dendrites. In computer simulations of neural networks, systems do not have billions of neurons firing off information all over the place; instead, they might have a few dozen or so. This makes computer neural networks a much simpler type of network than the human brain. Regardless of this simplification, developers can still use it to create some pretty believable and interesting simulations.

One thing about an artificial neural network is that it has the capability to learn. What this means is that while the AI is engaged in a simulation it is learning and getting "smarter." This allows for many possibilities that can be used in games. For example, this can be used in a fighting game in which the computer AI learns a gamer's fighting style, and moves and adapts to better defend against it. The process of adapting to a situation can make a computer-controlled simulation more lifelike. Although not fully explored in modern games, it is only a matter of time when hardware power will increase to give enough additional resources for game AI to use neural networks to a higher degree than what they are now. The ability to learn and adapt will become a huge selling point for games, because the challenge such gameplay can offer can be unlike anything seen before.

Neural networks are not easy to test or debug, mainly because the system can learn and change its behavior in a somewhat unpredictable manner. If the behavior cannot be predicted, it is much harder to debug. Something like an FSM would be easier to test, but the power of a neural network might be more appealing based on the type of game a developer is creating. Neural networks might not even be necessary in a game because of its complexity, and other techniques might prove more efficient in many situations.

FLOCKING

Often in games, a gamer will see a bunch of units that are moving as a group throughout the game world. These groups can include flocks of birds, a crowd of people, a school of fish, a pack of wolves, a squadron of fighter planes, and so forth. With these types of units, it is more realistic for groups of units to move together rather than individually. For example, if an enemy were being attacked by a pack of wolves, it would look more realistic to have the wolves attacking together than one at a time randomly and individually.

In AI there is a technique known as a flocking algorithm. By flocking, a developer can add group behavior to multiple units in a game to give them the impression of working together. This effect is more powerful in aiding to immerse a player into a gaming world even when used for subtle effects like flocking birds around village scenery. In classic flocking, three simple rules must be followed in the simulation:

Cohesion: Have each unit steer toward the average position of its neighbors.

Alignment: Have each unit steer in a direction that aligns itself to the average heading of its neighbors.

Separation: Have each unit steer to avoid hitting one another.

By following these three rules, a developer can apply a flocking behavior to nonplayer character objects in their game scenes. The type of game a developer is making will determine whether it is important to invest time learning how to use flocking in an AI world. If a developer combines flocking to a physics-based environment, they can control the steering by applying forces to the rigid bodies of the 3D objects. This technique is definitely worth looking into if there is any need to have group behavior in a game with nonplayer units. Figure 7.4 illustrates an example of a flocking behavior.

FIGURE 7.4   Flocking.

SUMMARY

Artificial intelligence is one of those areas that will rapidly grow in the game industry as more powerful hardware is released to the market. The AI in a game is dependent on the type of game being played. Although this chapter briefly talked about various topics dealing with AI in games, this was just the beginning of a very large and complex field of study. Appendix A has a list of resources to aid in learning more about artificial intelligence.

In the next chapter, we discuss game scripting and the various types of scripting systems that can be used in game development. Chapter 9, "Game Demos," focuses on the creation of various demos that are built from the Building Blocks Engine. In Chapter 9, a finite state machine will be created and used for controlling the AI and the game execution. Artificial intelligence is a huge topic and very important in game development.

8 Scripting

In This Chapter

- Overview
- Parsing Tokens
- Property Scripting
- Command Scripting
- GameMonkey Script

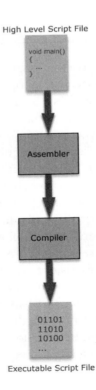

High Level Script File

```
void main()
{
    ...
}
```

Assembler

Compiler

```
01101
11010
10100
...
```

Executable Script File

Scripting in applications has long been a feature many games take advantage of to great use. Games are complex pieces of software that often have many smaller yet complex subsystems that work together to create an end product. Many parts of a game can be defined outside the application itself, and sometimes this code can be modified by the end users. There is no hard rule of thumb for a script. If it can manipulate the logic of an application outside the program itself, it can be considered a script. Scripting systems can be simple text parsers or complex systems capable of executing an instruction stream of compiled code within them. Scripting systems that execute compiled code are often the most complex, but can be the most powerful.

This chapter is about scripting in game applications. The scripting systems used by the Building Blocks Engine will be examined throughout the text. Scripting can be a complex task, especially when talking about virtual machines and compiled scripts. Appendix A, "Additional Resources," has several resources on scripting in general and in video games that can be useful to those trying to create their own scripting system in their games and applications. In this chapter, we look at a few different types of text parsing scripting systems, and creating and using compiled scripts using a tool called GameMonkey Script.

OVERVIEW

Scripting in applications allows application logic to be defined outside the application itself in a file. This file is called a script file, and is often a text file created by a standard text editor. Other times, it is a binary file that was created from another application called a compiler. Scripts are files that traditionally favor rapid development over execution efficiency. The syntax most scripting files contain is often instructions with less restrictions and strictness than full-blown programming languages like C++.

Scripts are written using a scripting language. A scripting language is often a programming language that borrows from other well-known languages and simplifies them for rapid development. This can translate into various things, such as the ability to use variables and functions in a typeless manner, or not having to group code into functions, to name a few. A scripting language can have any syntax. In games, these syntaxes are often modeled after high-level programming language to make them easier to work with by experienced programmers than the average gamer with no development experience.

Scripting systems come in two main types: interpreted and compiled. Each type of script has different strengths and weaknesses, and its own varying levels of difficulty to implement. In the following section, both types of scripting systems are examined. The Building Blocks Engine will have examples of each type later in the chapter. The simple interpreted scripting systems of the engine will be created and implemented from scratch.

INTERPRETED SCRIPTS

An interpreted script is opened, read in piece by piece, and executed on the fly. An interpreted script is often defined in an ASCII text file. When a script is interpreted, string comparisons and parsing are taking place internally. Code that reads interpreted scripts is called an interpreter. If there is an error somewhere in the script file, the interpreter will report that error when it tries to execute the code. Normally, interpreted scripts are not checked for errors and are executed until one such error arises or the script finishes.

An example of an interpreted script is HTML, and an interpreter is a Web browser. When HTML files are being read for display, they are parsed, and the browser displays whatever it is told to. If an error occurs, in most HTML files the problem is noticeable from the visual output when compared to what was desired. In parts of a Web file that contains non-HTML code, like JavaScript, when errors are encountered they are often reported by some kind of error indicator. With Internet Explorer on Windows operating systems, this error is usually a yellow warning sign icon in the lower section of the browser window.

Interpreted scripts are the easiest to implement because all that is needed is code to read a text file, compare strings, and code in the application for handling any commands or instructions it reads. An example of an interpreted script can be seen listed in Listing 8.1, which has three commands: display, clear, and end. Each of these commands is self-explanatory and demonstrate the nature of some scripting syntaxes.

LISTING 8.1 An example of a simple interpreted script.

```
display "Hello World"
display "Nice to meet you!"

clear

display "Goodbye World..."
display "...Nice knowing you!"

display "This is an example of an interpreted scrip!"

clear
```

```
display "Ultimate Game Engine Design and Architecture"
display "Chapter 8: Scripting"

clear

display "Interpreted Scripting "
display "is read on the fly in most cases "
display "until the end of the file or "
display "until an error is encountered."

end
```

COMPILED SCRIPTS

Compiled scripts are more complicated than interpreted scripts. Compiled scripts are often run through a compiler much like traditional programming languages. The compiler transforms the scripts into a form that can be processed quickly by an application. Inside the application sits a system called a virtual machine, whose job is to execute the instruction stream of a compiled script. An instruction stream is made up of opcodes and operands that define the logic of the script code. The main differences between compiled scripts and interpreted include but are not limited to:

- Interpreted scripts are often ASCII text files, whereas compiled scripts are often binary files.
- Compiled scripts require some kind of compiler to transform human-readable code into instructions for the machine.
- Compiled scripts run inside a virtual machine, whereas interpreted scripts are parsed on the fly.
- Compiled scripting systems are much harder to implement than interpreted scripts.
- Compiled scripts are checked for errors during the compilation process, not during the execution.
- The compiled scripts (after compilation) are much more complex files than their high-level counterpart.
- Interpreted scripts are not assumed correct in their syntax, whereas compiled scripts are because the compiler should have caught any errors.

A virtual machine is code that executes an instruction stream that was read in from a script into the application. For speed reasons, this instruction stream is often assumed valid, and that validation is often left to the compiler to handle and enforce. Because the instruction stream of a compiled script can be processed faster than the text parsing and string comparisons of an interpreted script, they are often far faster performance wise in many senses.

One main feature of compiled scripting systems is host binding. When a virtual machine binds itself to host functions, those functions can be called from inside the script itself as if the function existed in the script. The functions of an application can also call script functions as if the host application has those functions defined. This feature is what makes compiled scripts so powerful, especially in games. In addition, other topics like memory management and multithreading are both extremely complex and extremely useful. An example of a compiled script can be seen in Figure 8.1

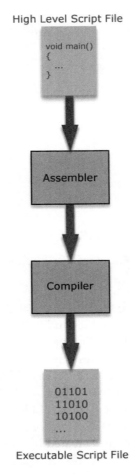

FIGURE 8.1 A compiled script.

PARSING TOKENS

Parsing tokens makes interpreting and compiling happen in code. A token is any group of text that is separated by a delimiter. A delimiter can be anything such as a white space, a new-line, a semicolon, and so fourth. Parsing tokens is done by breaking a file into a token stream. A tool that breaks a file into tokens is called a lexer. An example of a file being broken into a token stream can be seen in Figure 8.2. By breaking up a file into tokens, each token can be processed individually.

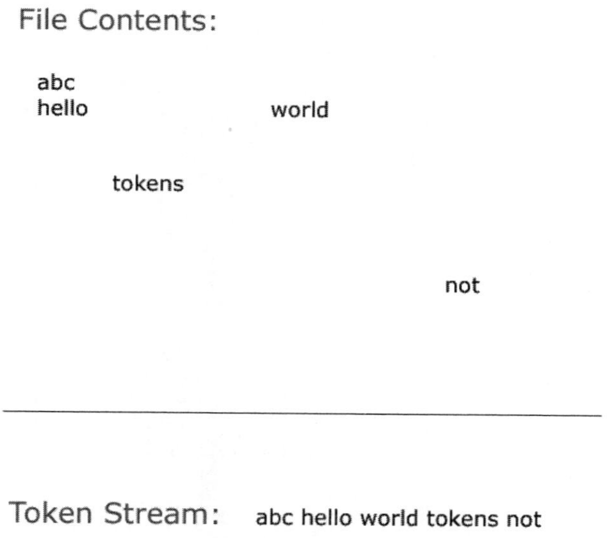

File Contents:

abc
hello   world

        tokens

                                not

Token Stream: abc hello world tokens not

FIGURE 8.2 Breaking a file into tokens.

Being able to break a file into tokens has many uses in computer applications. In Chapter 5, "Rendering Scenes and Scene Graphs," the upcoming token parsing class for the Building Blocks Engine was used to parse an .OBJ model file and extract its contents so the meshes can be viewed by the rendering system. A simple lexer for the Building Blocks Engine was coded as an example, but in the real world, there are other options. These options include using FLEX for lexing, and BISON for parsing tokens created by FLEX. FLEX is a free program that takes expressions and can turn a file into tokens. The free program BISON is used to read grammar description files like the ones created by FLEX and creates a C program out of it. This generated C code is the code for a parser for a user-defined grammar or language. The code can be compiled and executed.

FLEX and BISON are not covered in this book. For the Building Blocks Engine, a class called TokenStream is used to break a file up into tokens. The implementation for the TokenStream class will be discussed in the next section. When creating a compiler it is recommended that tools such as FLEX and BISON (or LEX and YACC) are researched.

IMPLEMENTING A TOKEN PARSER

The class to parse tokens in the Building Blocks Engine is simple. It takes a file's data and can get the next token from the file with every call to the function GetNextToken(). The functions of the class include ResetStream(), GetNextToken(), SetTokenStream(), and MoveToNextLine(). MoveToNextLine()is used to move to the position after the next new-line character in the file, and takes as a parameter an std::string object that will store the skipped line. ResetStream()will move to the start of the data (file), and SetTokenStream() will set the data to be parsed to the class. This can be the character data of anything, but will mostly be used with files. The member variables of the class are two indexes that are used internally to keep track of its current position in the data and the data itself. The class declaration of the TokenStream class can be seen in Listing 8.2. The code for the TokenStream class can be found on the companion CD-ROM in the BUILDING BLOCKS ENGINE/ SOURCE folder in the files TokenStream.h and TokenStream.cpp.

ON THE CD

LISTING 8.2   The TokenStream class.

```cpp
class TokenStream
{
   public:
      TokenStream();
      ~TokenStream();

      void ResetStream();

      void SetTokenStream(char *data);
      bool GetNextToken(std::string *buffer);
      bool GetNextToken(std::string *token, std::string *buffer);

      bool MoveToNextLine(std::string *buffer);

   private:
      int m_startIndex, m_endIndex;
      std::string m_data;
};
```

When opening TokenStream.cpp on the CD-ROM, the first file is called isValidIdentifier() and is used to test if the character being passed in is a letter, number, or symbol and not a character such as a new-line, end-of-file, white space, and so forth. This function is used during the parsing to extract text from the data and uses invalid characters as delimiters. The isValidIdentifier() can be seen in Listing 8.3. Listing 8.4 lists the class' constructor, destructor, SetTokenStream(), and ResetStream() function bodies.

LISTING 8.3   The function isValidIdentifier().

```cpp
bool isValidIdentifier(char c)
{
   // Ascii from ! to ~.
   if((int)c > 32 && (int)c < 127)
      return true;

   return false;
}
```

LISTING 8.4   The constructor, destructor, SetTokenStream() and ResetStream() of TokenStream.

```cpp
TokenStream::TokenStream()
{
   ResetStream();
}


TokenStream::~TokenStream()
{
}


void TokenStream::ResetStream()
{
   m_startIndex = m_endIndex = 0;
}


void TokenStream::SetTokenStream(char *data)
{
   ResetStream();
   m_data = data;
}
```

The next two functions are the `GetNextToken()` functions. The second function calls the first and takes as a parameter a token to look for and an address to store the first token after the search token. The `GetNextToken()` takes a brute force approach to moving through the character data until it gets to a delimiter. Once it finds a delimiter, all the text that was read since the beginning of the function is returned through the function's address string parameter. The function does look for strings, which it will keep grouped together whenever it comes to a pair of quotes. The two `GetNext` functions can be seen in Listing 8.5.

LISTING 8.5 The `GetNextToken()` functions.

```cpp
bool TokenStream::GetNextToken(std::string *buffer)
{
   bool inString = false;
   m_startIndex = m_endIndex;
   int length = m_data.length();

   while(m_startIndex < length &&
         isValidIdentifier(m_data[m_startIndex]) == false)
   {
      m_startIndex++;
   }

   m_endIndex = m_startIndex + 1;

   if(m_data[m_startIndex] == '"')
      inString = !inString;

   if(m_startIndex < length)
   {
      while(m_endIndex < length &&
            (isValidIdentifier(m_data[m_endIndex]) ||
            inString == true))
      {
         if(m_data[m_endIndex] == '"')
            inString = !inString;

         m_endIndex++;
      }

      if(buffer != NULL)
      {
```

```
              int size = (m_endIndex - m_startIndex);
              int index = m_startIndex;

              buffer->reserve(size + 1);
              buffer->clear();

              for(int i = 0; i < size; i++)
              {
                 buffer->push_back(m_data[index++]);
              }
           }

           return true;
       }

       return false;
   }


   bool TokenStream::GetNextToken(std::string *token,
                                  std::string *buffer)
   {
       std::string tok;

       if(token == NULL)
          return false;

       while(GetNextToken(&tok))
       {
          if(stricmp(tok.c_str(), token->c_str()) == 0)
             return GetNextToken(buffer);
       }

       return false;
   }
```

The final function in the class is MoveToNextLine(). Much like GetNextToken(), this function moves through the data in a brute force manner looking for a newline character or until there is no more data. Once it finds it, the function takes all the data read in so far and returns it to the std::string address parameter if it is not NULL. The final function of the TokenStream class, MoveToNextLine(), can be seen in Listing 8.6.

LISTING 8.6   The last function of the `TokenStream` class.

```cpp
bool TokenStream::MoveToNextLine(std::string *buffer)
{
    int length = m_data.length();

    if(m_startIndex < length && m_endIndex < length)
    {
        m_startIndex = m_endIndex;

        while(m_endIndex < length &&
              (m_data[m_endIndex] != '\n' &&
               m_data[m_endIndex] != '\r' &&
               m_data[m_endIndex] != '\0'))
        {
            m_endIndex++;
        }

        if(m_endIndex - m_startIndex >= length)
            return false;

        if(buffer != NULL)
        {
            int size = (m_endIndex - m_startIndex);
            int index = m_startIndex;

            buffer->reserve(size + 1);
            buffer->clear();

            for(int i = 0; i < size; i++)
            {
                buffer->push_back(m_data[index++]);
            }
        }
    }
    else
    {
        return false;
    }

    return true;
}
```

PROPERTY SCRIPTING

The Building Blocks Engine has a property scripting system. A property script is a script that has properties and values defined in it. A property can be thought of as a variable and a value. Property scripts are good for cases in which a list of values can be stored in a file for an application to quickly parse and use. Property scripts are often plain text files with a property on each line. The types of properties are dependent on the system being implemented. For example, properties can be integers, floats, strings, or anything else that can be coded and represented in a file. An example of a property script can be seen in Listing 8.7.

LISTING 8.7   A property script.

```
Fullscreen   True
Width        800
Height       600
Name         "Some Window Name"
```

PROPERTY SCRIPT IMPLEMENTATION

The property scripting system is implemented in the Building Blocks Engine using the TokenStream class discussed earlier in this chapter. The property script is parsed by getting a token, which is the property, and then getting the following token after it, which is the value. This pair is then added to a list and the parsing continues until the end of the file. Once a file has been parsed, the property script will then have an entire list of properties and their values as strings. A property script is highly specific on the application, so if an application needs a certain property it will know what type that property should be in and will be able to convert the value string to the data type it expects.

For the Building Blocks Engine, there are two main objects. The first is a structure called Property, which is used to hold a name/value pair. The second is a class called PropertyScript, which is used to parse a file and to fill in a list of Property objects. Both of these can be seen in Listing 8.8. The property script code can be found on the companion CD-ROM in the Property.h and Property.cpp files in the BUILDING BLOCKS ENGINE/SOURCE folder.

ON THE CD

LISTING 8.8   The Property structure and PropertyScript class.

```
struct Property
{
    std::string m_propertyName;
```

```
        std::string m_value;
};


class PropertyScript
{
    public:
        PropertyScript() {}
        virtual ~PropertyScript() {}

        bool Load(char *fileName);
        bool GetPropertyValue(std::string property,
                                std::string *val);

    private:
        std::vector<Property> m_list;
};
```

There are two functions in the `PropertyScript` class other than the class' constructor and destructor functions, called `Load()` and `GetPropertyValue()`. The `Load()` function uses the `FileInputStream` and `TokenStream` classes, with the `FileInputStream` object being used to load in an entire file's data and the `TokenStream` object taking that loaded data. Once the entire file is loaded, a loop is executed to parse all tokens from the script. The `Load()` function can be seen in Listing 8.9.

The last function, `GetPropertyValue()`, takes as parameters a property to search for and the address to a string object where the value will be saved once it is found. For the search, a linear walkthrough is performed and string comparisons are made to look for the correct property. Once that property is found, its value is set to the point pointer and the function returns true. If the property was not found, the function returns false. The `GetPropertyValue()` function's body can be seen listed in Listing 8.10.

LISTING 8.9   The `Load()` function.

```
bool PropertyScript::Load(char *fileName)
{
    TokenStream tokenStream;
    FileInputStream fileInput;
    Property prop;
    int fileSize = 0;
    char *buffer = NULL;
    bool result = true;
```

```
      if(fileInput.OpenFile(fileName, BB_TEXT_FILE) == false)
         return false;

      fileSize = fileInput.GetFileSize();

      if(fileSize <= 0)
         return false;

      buffer = new char[fileSize];

      if(buffer == NULL)
         return false;

      fileInput.Read(buffer, fileSize);
      tokenStream.SetTokenStream(buffer);

      delete[] buffer;

      while(result == true)
      {
         result = tokenStream.GetNextToken(&prop.m_propertyName);

         if(result == true)
            result = tokenStream.GetNextToken(&prop.m_value);

         m_list.push_back(prop);
      }

      return true;
   }
```

LISTING 8.10   The GetPropertyValue() function.

```
   bool PropertyScript::GetPropertyValue(std::string property,
                                         std::string *val)
   {
      if(val == NULL)
         return false;

      for(int i = 0; i < (int)m_list.size(); i++)
      {
         if(m_list[i].m_propertyName == property)
         {
```

```
        *val = m_list[i].m_value;
        return true;
      }
    }

    return false;
  }
```

COMMAND SCRIPTING

In command scripting, a text file is parsed and interpreted on the fly. With command scripting, there are commands that are read from a file. When an application reads a command, it does what it says. The command that is read will depend on the number of parameters, if any, that go with the command. This is highly dependant on the application. A Basic-like language can be created using the TokenStream class and command scripting.

Because of the nature of command scripting, there is no command script system in the Building Blocks Engine because it is so dependant on the application. Since command scripting is easy to do with the TokenStream class, a demo application on the companion CD-ROM in the BUILDING BLOCKS ENGINE/ EXAMPLES/CHAPTER 8 folder exists and is called COMMAND SCRIPTING. The sample command script from the demo can be seen in Listing 8.11 and has three different commands: Print, which will print a line of text; PrintLine, which will do the same as Print but will also attach a new-line at the end of the string; and DisplayDemoInfo, which the application will respond to by simply printing the name of the application to the screen along with a few other small pieces of text.

ON THE CD

LISTING 8.11 The COMMAND SCRIPTING demo's script.

```
Print "Hello World"
PrintLine ""

PrintLine "Good bye world!!!"
PrintLine "Hello world again!"

Print "Command Scripting"
PrintLine ""

DisplayDemoInfo
```

In the demo application's main source file, three functions are called when one of the commands is parsed. Each of these functions is named directly after the command. All commands except for `DisplayDemoInfo` will take a string as a parameter and display it to the screen. `Print` will print out a string as long as it is not an empty pair of quotes. In the example script file, this was used to simply print out a newline without any text. The three functions used to execute each command are listed in Listing 8.12.

LISTING 8.12   The functions called for each command.

```
void Print(string &str)
{
   if(str != "\"\"")
      cout << str;
}


void PrintLine(string &str)
{
   Print(str);
   cout << endl;
}


void DisplayDemoInfo()
{
   cout << "Command Scripting Demo!" << endl;
   cout << "Ultimate Game Engine Design & Architecture" << endl;
   cout << "Chapter 8" << endl << endl;
}
```

The `main()` function for the demo application loads an entire file into memory and sets it to a `TokenStream` object. Once set, the function `GetNextToken()` is called in a loop until the end of the file. When each command is read, it is compared to the commands the application is aware of. Which command is read will determine the next step taken. If either of the `Print` commands is read, `GetNextToken()` is called again to get the string that is to be displayed to the screen. Because `Display-DemoInfo` has no values, `GetNextToken()` is not called. The `main()` function of the COMMAND SCRIPTING demo application can be seen listed in Listing 8.13.

LISTING 8.13 The `main()` function for the COMMAND SCRIPTING demo.

```
int main(int args, char **argc)
{
    bbe::TokenStream tokenStream;
    bbe::FileInputStream fileInput;
    string command, value;
    int fileSize = 0;
    char *buffer = NULL;

    if(fileInput.OpenFile("commands.txt", BB_TEXT_FILE) == false)
    {
        cout << "Error reading commands.txt!" << endl << endl;
        return 0;
    }

    fileSize = fileInput.GetFileSize();

    if(fileSize <= 0)
    {
        cout << "Error reading commands.txt!" << endl << endl;
        return 0;
    }

    buffer = new char[fileSize];

    fileInput.Read(buffer, fileSize);
    tokenStream.SetTokenStream(buffer);

    delete[] buffer;

    while(tokenStream.GetNextToken(&command))
    {
        if(command == "Print")
        {
            tokenStream.GetNextToken(&value);
            Print(value);
        }
        else if(command == "PrintLine")
        {
            tokenStream.GetNextToken(&value);
            PrintLine(value);
        }
        else if(command == "DisplayDemoInfo")
```

```
        {
            DisplayDemoInfo();
        }
    }

    cout << endl << endl;

    return 1;
}
```

GAMEMONKEY SCRIPT

GameMonkey Script is a cross-platform scripting system that can be used in applications (targeted toward games). GameMonkey Script takes high-level script files and compiles them to a native format. This format is executed by the GameMonkey virtual machine that is running inside an application. GameMonkey can be downloaded from the GameMonkey website and installed with ease. The scripting system has been known to work on consoles, Windows, Mac, Linux, and just about any system on which C++ code can be compiled. The scripts for GameMonkey are similar to LUA, with an example being listed in Listing 8.14. For a more detailed introduction to GameMonkey, see the resources in Appendix A. Because the syntax of GameMonkey scripts is so similar to C, it will be assumed that anyone reading this book can easily read a GameMonkey script. An example of declaring variables and using conditional statements can be seen in Listing 8.15, while an example of defining and calling functions can be seen in Listing 8.16.

LISTING 8.14   A GameMonkey script.

```
a = 10;
b = 5;

if(a == 10)
{
    print("a == 10");
}

if(b < 5)
{
    print("b < 5");
}
```

```
else if(b > 5)
{
   print("b > 5");
}
else
{
   print("b == 5");
}
```

LISTING 8.15   Calling functions.

```
addFunction = function(a, b)
{
   return a + b;
};


result = addFunction(10, 5);

print(result);
```

To use GM in an application, a virtual machine object must be created of the type gmMachine. A GM virtual machine can execute script commands using the ExecuteString() function. This function can be used to execute a single line or an entire file by simply passing a null-terminating string to it. An example of this can be seen in Listing 8.15. To define a gmMachine object, the inclusion of the header file gmThread.h is necessary. This header file is a part of the GameMonkey Script SDK download you can get from their site. An example script that will be referenced for the rest of this section can be seen in Listing 8.16, where the global keyword is used to mark a function as being accessible outside the script.

LISTING 8.16   Executing a string.

```
#include<gmThread.h>

using namespace std;


int main(int args, char argc[])
{
   gmMachine gvm;
```

```
    // Test executing hard coded simple scripts.
    gvm.ExecuteString("print(\"Script Test!\");");
    gvm.ExecuteString("print(\"\");");

    return 1;
}
```

LISTING 8.17   Test script used throughout the rest of this section.

```
global AddTest = function(lVal, rVal)
{
    return lVal + rVal;
};


global Display = function()
{
    retVal = HostMultiply(5, 2);

    print("Display() called the host function HostMultiply()");
    print("HostMultiply(5, 2) returned:", retVal);
};
```

The function ExecuteString() is used to execute any script in the system. This function takes several parameters, but the most important three for the purposes of this book are the script data, a thread index, and a flag for whether execution of the script should start right away or wait. If false is sent as the flag, the function Execute() will have to be called to manually execute a script. The Execute() function takes a single parameter, is the script's thread index.

If there is an error compiling the script, an error log can be obtained by creating a gmLog object and calling GetLog() from the virtual machine. This will allow the application to loop through and extract all the errors that occurred during the compilation. An example of executing a script stored in a std::string object, checking for errors, and executing threads can be seen in Listing 8.18.

LISTING 8.18   Executing threads and error checking.

```
if(gvm.ExecuteString(str.c_str(), 0, false) != 0)
{
    gmLog &errorLog = gvm.GetLog();
    bool flag = true;
    const char *errorString = NULL;
```

```
    errorString = errorLog.GetEntry(flag);

    while(errorString)
    {
       cout << "Error: " << errorString << endl;
       errorString = errorLog.GetEntry(flag);
    }
}

// Execute script.
gvm.Execute(0);
```

Functions inside the script can be called from the application. Parameters can also be passed to script-defined functions. This is done by creating a gmCall object and calling its BeginGlobalFunction() function. Any function inside the script that was specified with the global keyword can be called. The BeginGlobalFunction() function takes as parameters the virtual machine and the function name that will be called. Parameters can be sent to the function by calling AddParam*(), where the * is Int for an integer parameter, Float is for floats, and so on. When the gmCall's End() function is called, the script function is executed within the virtual machine. If the function returned a value, the function GetReturned*() can be called to retrieve it and to use it in the application. An example of calling a function defined in a script can be seen in Listing 8.19.

LISTING 8.19 Calling a script function and sending it parameters.

```
gmCall scriptCall;
int retVal = 0;


if(scriptCall.BeginGlobalFunction(&gvm, "AddTest"))
{
   scriptCall.AddParamInt(50);
   scriptCall.AddParamInt(22);
   scriptCall.End();

   if(scriptCall.GetReturnedInt(retVal))
   {
      cout << "Script function Add() returned: " <<
      retVal << endl;
   }
```

```
        else
        {
           cout << "Add() return NOT INTEGER!" << endl;
        }
     }
     else
     {
        cout << "Script function Add() NOT FOUND!" << endl;
     }
```

Similar to how script functions can be called in the application, application functions can be called within the script. The first step is to register the host application's function with the virtual machine. This is done by sending a gmFunctionEntry object to the RegisterLibrary() function of the virtual machine. Once registered, any function inside the script can call it. Listing 8.20 shows an example of this. In the example, a script function is called that calls the host application function as an example. Listing 8.17 lists the example script the example in Listing 8.20 is using as a test for this feature. The function that was registered so that it can be called from within a script can be seen in Listing 8.21. In Listing 8.21, a return value is pushed onto the script thread so the script can have access to that data.

LISTING 8.20   Registering a host function and calling a script function that uses it.

```
static gmFunctionEntry hostLibraries[] =
{
   {"HostMultiply", gmHostMultiply},
};

gvm.RegisterLibrary(hostLibraries, sizeof(hostLibraries) /
                    sizeof(hostLibraries[0]));


if(scriptCall.BeginGlobalFunction(&gvm, "Display"))
{
   scriptCall.End();
}
else
{
   cout << "Script function Display() NOT FOUND!" << endl;
}
```

LISTING 8.21   Host application function called from within the script.

```
int GM_CDECL gmHostMultiply(gmThread *a_thread)
{
    GM_CHECK_NUM_PARAMS(2);
    GM_CHECK_INT_PARAM(lVal, 0);
    GM_CHECK_INT_PARAM(rVal, 1);

    int retVal = lVal * rVal;

    a_thread->PushInt(retVal);

    return GM_OK;
}
```

The demo applications in the next chapter will use GameMonkey Script for the game demos that will be created. For this chapter, a demo application that does everything mentioned in this section in one application can be found on the companion CD-ROM. The demo application is called GAME MONKEY and can be found in the BUILDING BLOCKS ENGINE/EXAMPLES/CHAPTER 8 folder. The property scripting and lexing classes can also be found on the CD-ROM in the BUILDING BLOCKS ENGINE/SOURCE folder.

ON THE CD

SUMMARY

Scripting in applications can be simple, as seen with the property and command scripting in this chapter, or more complicated by using compiled scripts. Using a third-party scripting tool made the feature of compiled scripts easier to work with because all the hard work of creating such a system from the ground up has already been done. A few different resources in Appendix A can be used for those looking to create their own compiled scripting system and virtual machine.

In the next chapter, a few simple games there were made using the Building Blocks Engine for this book will be examined. The scripting systems discussed in this chapter will be used in the implementation of those demos, and the other information throughout this entire book.

CHAPTER EXERCISES

1. Add support to load already compiled scripts into the system.
2. Add user-defined structure support to the GameMonkey Script class.
3. Add garbage collection support for user-defined structure binds to the GameMonkey Script class.

Part IV

Demos

9 Game Demos

In This Chapter

- Overview
- Black Jack Game Demos
- 3D Walkthrough Demo

The Building Blocks Engine has come quite a way for a simple game engine. The framework can render organized 3D objects with shaders, perform input detection through the keyboards, mice, and Xbox 360 controllers, play sound clips, perform simple physics, and perform scripting using interpreted scripts through a property scripting system or through compiled scripts through the use of GameMonkey Script. At this time, there are eight different major systems spanning over 100 files and thousands of lines of code. Regardless of the amount of work that was already done on the framework, much more will need to be done before it can be used to create a moderate game that can be seen on the market today.

In this chapter, a few simple game demos are discussed that were created for this book as a way to test the various different systems working together as one in applications. Each of these game demos uses similar code and functions, so they will be described in a general sense. Other topics are discussed, such as features that can be added to improve the demos.

OVERVIEW

The simple game demos created for this book include a simple 3D walkthrough and a black jack game. The black jack game will be a card game with simple black jack rules that will support player versus the CPU, and the 3D walkthrough game will create a simple portal system and first-person controls/view. The full code for each of these demos can be found on the companion CD-ROM in the BUILDING BLOCKS ENGINE/EXAMPLES/CHAPTER 9 folder.

ON THE CD

Each of these games is discussed in the following section in more detail. The demos are simple enough to where no real game design was performed in the planning and implementation of them. Game design is the process of describing everything dealing with a game, and everything can be planned in a game design. A game design is normally a document, called a design document, which describes a game in detail. Game design documents include but are not limited to:

- Game rules
- Game play
- Game mechanics
- Characters
- Locations
- Backgrounds
- Theme
- Reference materials
- Presentation
- Content

Using game design documents can allow for a smoother and more direction-controlled game development experience than immediately starting to write a game once a concept has been thought of. Game design is a topic unto itself, and several great resources on the subject can help aspiring game developers get into the game development process. Each of these resources can be found in Appendix A, "Additional Resources." Game design is very important for professional game development and is recommended to all designing a game to look into.

THE BUILDING BLOCKS ENGINE

The Building Blocks Engine is a game engine created for and throughout the writing of this book. As the framework stands now, it can create small demos, like the ones featured on *UltimateGameProgramming.com*, or simple games. To take the engine to the next level, many additional tools and utilities will have to be designed and implemented. Each of these additions varies in difficulty level, and many are game- and genre-specific topics. The core system of the Building Blocks Engine currently uses STL data structures, has a resource manager, an archive filesystem, and timing and file input/output utilities. A few improvements can be made to the already existing core system, including:

- Improved archive format and loader
- A GUI application for archive system that allows for manipulation of the archive files in a natural way
- A memory management system
- An improved resource manager depending on the implementation of the memory management system

The second and third major subsystems of the Building Blocks Engine include the game math library and the input detection system. The game math library has quite a number of different structures that are used commonly in game development. Many of the functions in each of these objects were implemented based on what was needed for the various demos of this book at the time of writing. Each game math object could have had much more code and is lightweight. The improvement that can be made to the math library was mentioned earlier in the book with the use of SSE math instructions. SIMD types of math instructions like SSE can drastically improve the performance of mathematical operations in an application. For games that are majority math, this optimization is very important.

The input system of the Building Blocks Engine is currently the simplest system in the entire framework because it is made up of two small functions and a class to allow for the input detection of Xbox 360 controller input on Windows operating systems. The main feature that can be added to this system is the support of game pads, joysticks, and so forth across all operating systems to allow for non-keyboard and mouse interaction outside of using Xbox 360 controllers on Windows.

The next two major subsystems are the sound and the networking systems. The sound system is the third smallest system after the scripting and input systems of the framework. The sound system has major improvements that were mentioned in Chapter 3, "Input, Sound, and Networking," including:

- Streaming audio for OpenAL and XACT
- Compressed audio
- Support for 5.1 sound
- 3D sound support for XACT

The networking system wrapped around sockets using a class called Socket, which was in turn used as a member variable array in a class called Network. The improvements to the networking system can include but are not limited to:

- Encryption for transmitting data
- Fast compression for data
- Varying packet sizes
- An incoming message queue that is processed based on the time allocated to the networking system

The last three major subsystems of the Building Blocks Engine include the scripting, physics, and rendering systems. The scripting system uses GameMonkey Script for compiled scripts, a property scripting class, and a class to break up data into a token stream. The property system can be improved by allowing the application to choose the delimiters and improving the search of the property list. The TokenStream class can also be improved a number of ways, one being in its design. The class uses a brute force method of extracting data. There might be a better way to go about getting tokens. In addition, a token list can be gathered and stored for each line. This would make the MoveToNextLine() function much simpler and clearer in its implementation.

The physics system has support for representing point masses and bodies using springs, and collision detection and response between various different objects. The physics system is heavily based on the math library, so any optimizations to the math library will affect the physics system. Additions to the physics system can include but are not limited to:

- Rigid bodies
- Rag doll
- Vehicle and plane physics
- Bounding volume hierarchies for speeding up collision checks
- Various internal optimizations for the different classes of the physics system
- Stacking for multiple rigid bodies that can stack on one another
- Physics hierarchies for allowing objects to be controlled and represented by multiple different dynamic rigid bodies instead of just one

The last major subsystem, the rendering system, uses OpenGL to render geometry. The system has support for shaders, textures, and off-screen rendering using OpenGL frame buffer objects. When rendering geometry, the OpenGL class uses vertex buffer objects, which offer a fast way to use AGP memory, if available, to send data to the hardware. This is what Direct3D uses in its vertex buffers when rendering to the screen. A few additions and improvements to the rendering system include:

- Create state classes and use those to switch states instead of the large conditional statements used in the class' various functions
- Support for depth and stencil destination targets with the frame buffer objects, which can be used for various shadowing techniques, and so forth
- Multiple pass approach when rendering geometry that is larger than the max size of the vertex buffer object
- Decouple the dependency on Cg shaders in a such a way that the system can be used to create GLSL shaders if desired
- Support for rendering bitmap fonts by using textures and 2D quads
- Support for loading and using additional file formats for textures such as DDS, JPG, BMP, etc.
- Support for compressed textures such as 3Dc, DXTn, etc.
- Anti-aliasing techniques
- Motion blur and other post-processing techniques for cinematic quality rendering in real time
- Support for Direct3D 10 on Windows Vista

The engine has a long way to go, but has already covered a lot of ground. Additional improvements can be made to the framework that do not necessarily fit in any one subsection. Many of these additions and improvements can depend on if they are needed by a certain game or games that will be created by the Building

Blocks Engine or by future versions of the framework. These additions and improvements include but are not limited to:

- Animated character models and game objects (not handled in a rendering system but is rendered once calculated)
- Animation paths for cut-scenes and moving objects in a scene
- Improved cameras using springs and dampers, zoom in/out capability, etc.
- XML for game resources such as materials
- A level editor
- A GUI editor and GUI system
- Tools for calculating global illumination
- Realistic water rendering
- Realistic sky rendering
- Realistic vegetation and tree rendering
- Exporters for all the major file formats for game models, environments, and texture images

Although the Building Blocks Engine has a ton of code and files, it is lightweight when compared to what it will be once these items are implemented into the framework. Professional modern game engines are extremely complex systems that require the talents of many different engineers to create. The reason why the Building Blocks Engine was kept relatively simple was the sheer complexity involved in game engine design and development in general.

It was mentioned repeatedly throughout this book that Appendix A has various resources that can help in the educational process of game and engine development. These resources cover all areas of a game and are highly recommended. Game engine design and development is a process that evolves with the changing times, technology, and social atmospheres. The expectations and the requirements set by gamers will always challenge game developers to push the envelope of what was done in games and other simulations.

The following sections of this chapter take a brief look at the various games created for this chapter. The next chapter marks the end of this book and the start of game engine development.

GAME DEMOS

The various aspects of the demos that are important to this chapter will be briefly discussed. In this section, the thought processes and how the demos work and are coded are discussed. In other words, this is not a tutorial on how to create these games, but an explanation on the code in general. These demos can be found on the companion CD-ROM in the BUILDING BLOCKS ENGINE/EXAMPLES/ CHAPTER 9 folder. The black jack game is located in the BLACK JACK folder, and the 3D walk through demo is located in the WALKTHROUGH folder.

THE BLACK JACK GAME

The black jack game was created with simple rules. The player can either hit or stay when it is his turn. The game itself works in a straightforward manner and uses a finite state machine, as described in Chapter 7, "Artificial Intelligence," to handle the transitions from one game state to another, and the artificial intelligence. The game was created to allow the player to play against the CPU. The CPU itself is simple in that it will hit if it has a total card count of 16 or less, or will stay unless the player has a higher card total. The goal of black jack is to get as close to 21 without going over and without being less than the opponent. At the end of each round, the cards are revealed to show what both players had and to show who won or if there was a tie. The cards are dealt using random numbers. When a card is dealt, the game checks to make sure that card is not already out, or it will keep generating random numbers until a unique one can be given out. There are 52 cards in the average deck. Because this black jack game will be simple with simple rules, all aces are considered 11, instead of 11 or 1.

The game is broken into states. When the game is first started, it is in the initialize state. Once the game finishes the initialization process, it automatically switches to the menu state. When at the menu state, the game displays the main menu of the game and waits for the player to start or quit the game. The "to start a game message" is displayed to tell the player what button to click to begin the game. For the black jack game and all other games, this will be a symbol of the Xbox 360 start button or an image representing the space bar for those without the controller.

The states that can be transitioned to from the menu state are game start and game quit. If the Escape key or the back button on the Xbox 360 controller is pressed, the game quits by shutting down, cleaning up, and exiting, which happens when the quit state is set. If a game is started, the menu screen is no longer displayed and the game board appears. From here, there is an indicator to press Escape to quit to the main menu or to press a button to deal. As the dealing starts, the game state transitions from the game start state to the game deal state upon the button press. From here, the game goes through the process of giving the player and the CPU random but unique cards.

After the deal state, the game alternates between the player move state and the CPU move state until both players choose stay or if they go over 21. When all moves are done, the game compares totals and the player that is both under or equal to 21 and is higher than the second player wins. If it is a tie, a tie message is displayed; otherwise, the player that won is displayed. During any of the three status screens (tie, player win, CPU win), the game displays a message to press Escape to back out to the menu (or Back on the Xbox 360 controller), or press any button to play again. If the player backs out, the menu state is set; otherwise, the gameplay start state is set. The transitioning of the states continues in this manner until the user ends the game. Figure 9.1 displays the finite state machine (FSM) used for the game AI, and Figure 9.2 displays the finite state machine used for the game's execution states.

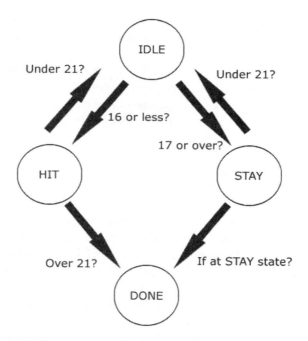

FIGURE 9.1 The FSM for the game AI.

The game itself is implemented in a class called BlackJackGame. This class has member functions to resize the project matrix if the window is resized, initialize the game, update the game, render the game, shut down the game, and process the main menu and the game level, among several other private functions that are used internally by the game itself. Each of the games discussed in this chapter will follow the

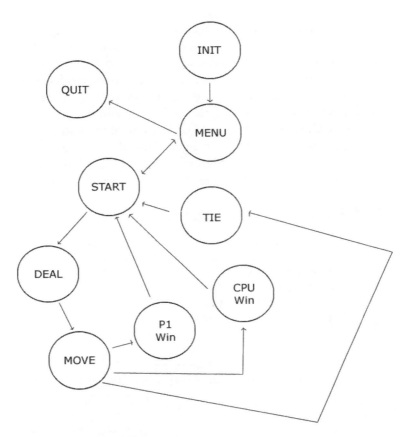

FIGURE 9.2   The FSM for the game execution.

same format. The function to initialize the game, GameInitialize(), will load all the textures, models, and so forth the game needs. The GameUpdate() function executes game logic, input detection, and state switches. The actual code the GameUpdate() executes depends on the game state. The same goes for the rendering function GameRender(). If the game is at the menu state, ProcessMainMenu() is called. If the game is at the gameplay state, the ProcessGameLevel() function is called. Each of these functions will display and handle whatever is needed for the state it represents. The Shutdown() function is used to delete all used memory in the game. The other private functions of the class include DrawCards(), which is used to display the playing cards both players have; DealCards(), which deals the first two cards to the players;

GiveCard(), which is used when a player "hits"; IsCardOut(), which is used to test if a card was already dealt; ProcessAI(), which controls the CPU artificial intelligence; and PlayerHit(), which is called when the human player chooses to "hit."

The member variables of the class include the rendering system, a model for a card that can be used by all cards since they are the same shape, a texture for each card that can be drawn from the deck, the main menu background geometry and texture, GUI elements to display during one of the status screens (player win, CPU win, etc.), the current state of the game, the players' hands (the cards they have during the game), flags if the player chooses to "stay," and a flag to test if the game should quit. The BlackJackGame class can be seen in Listing 9.1.

LISTING 9.1   The BlackJackGame class.

```
// General Defines.
#define WINDOW_NAME        "Black Jack"
#define WINDOW_CLASS       "UPGCLASS"
#define WINDOW_WIDTH       800
#define WINDOW_HEIGHT      600
#define WINDOW_FULLSCREEN  0


// Finite state machine's states.
enum BLACK_JACK_GAME_STATE { BJ_GAME_INITIALIZING,
                             BJ_GAME_MENU,
                             BJ_GAME_PLAY_START,
                             BJ_GAME_PLAY_DEALING,
                             BJ_GAME_PLAY_PLAYER_MOVE,
                             BJ_GAME_PLAY_CPU_MOVE,
                             BJ_GAME_PLAY_PLAYER_WIN,
                             BJ_GAME_PLAY_CPU_WIN,
                             BJ_GAME_PLAY_PLAYER_CPU_TIE,
                             BJ_GAME_QUIT };


// Background IDs.
enum BLACK_JACK_GUI { BJ_GUI_MENU = 0, BJ_GUI_START,
                      BJ_GUI_P1_MOVE, BJ_GUI_CPU_MOVE,
                      BJ_GUI_P1_WIN, BJ_GUI_CPU_WIN,
                      BJ_GUI_P1_CPU_TIE, BJ_TOTAL_GUI };
```

```cpp
// Used for testing if a keyboard button is up.
enum BLACK_JACK_KEYS { BJ_ENTER_KEY = 0, BJ_ESC_KEY,
                       BJ_H_KEY, BJ_S_KEY,
                       BJ_TOTAL_KEYS };


// Info dealing with the deck.
#define BJ_TOTAL_SUITS        4
#define BJ_TOTAL_SUIT_CARDS   13
#define BJ_TOTAL_CARDS        BJ_TOTAL_SUITS * BJ_TOTAL_SUIT_CARDS


// Structure for an individual card.
struct Card
{
   bbe::BB_TEXTURE m_decal;
   int m_suite;
   int m_face;
};


// Game class.
class BlackJackGame
{
   public:
      BlackJackGame();
      virtual ~BlackJackGame();

      void Resize(int width, int height);

      virtual bool GameInitialize(bbe::RenderParams &params);
      virtual void GameUpdate();
      void GameRender();
      virtual void GameShutdown();

      virtual int EnterGameLoop() = 0;

   protected:
      void ProcessMainMenu();
      void ProcessGameLevel();
      void DrawCards();
      void DealCards();
```

```
        int GiveCard();
        bool IsCardOut(int suite, int face);
        void ProcessAI();
        void PlayerHit();

    protected:
        // Rendering system.
        bbe::OpenGLRenderer m_render;

        // One model data, 52 cards in a deck, and
        // a decal for the back of a card.
        bbe::ModelData m_cardGeometry;
        Card m_cards[BJ_TOTAL_CARDS];
        bbe::BB_TEXTURE m_cardBack;

        // Background geometry.
        bbe::ModelData m_background;

        // GUI (P1 Win, CPU Win, tie, etc).
        bbe::ModelData m_guiElement;
        bbe::BB_TEXTURE m_guiTextures[BJ_TOTAL_GUI];

        // Cards for each player and score totals.
        std::vector<int> m_playerCards;
        std::vector<int> m_cpuCards;
        int m_playerTotal, m_cpuTotal;

        // Flag if the player stays or is over 21.
        bool m_cpuStay;
        bool m_playerStay;

        // States for game's finite state machine.
        BLACK_JACK_GAME_STATE m_currentGameState;

        // For keyboard input (button up detection).
        bool m_buttonKeys[BJ_TOTAL_KEYS];

        // Flag to quit application.
        bool m_quitDemo;
};
```

The BlackJackGame class is a base class that OS specific classes can derive from. Using Windows as an example, the Win32 version is called BlackJackGameWin32. The class has Win32 specific member variables inside it. An overloaded GameInitialize() function is also specified in the derived class, so that the Win32 window can be created and the Win32 objects for the RenderParams object can be passed to the base class, which passes it to the rendering system. Also overloaded in that class are GameUpdate(), GameShutdown(), and EnterGameLoop(). The BlackJackGameWin32 class can be seen in Listing 9.2. The Win32 GameInitialize() function can be seen in Listing 9.3, and the EnterGameLoop() and GameShutdown() functions of the Win32 class are listed in Listing 9.4. The EnterGameLoop() function is defined in the base class as a pure virtual function, so derived classes can implement their own game loops (application loops).

LISTING 9.2   The BlackJackGameWin32 class.

```
class BlackJackGameWin32 : public BlackJackGame
{
   public:
      BlackJackGameWin32(HINSTANCE hInst) : BlackJackGame()
      {
         m_hInst = hInst;
      }

      virtual ~BlackJackGameWin32()
      {
      }

      bool GameInitialize();
      void GameUpdate();
      int EnterGameLoop();
      void GameShutdown();

   private:
      HWND m_hwnd;
      HINSTANCE m_hInst;

      bbe::X360Controller m_360Pads[4];
};
```

LISTING 9.3 The GameInitialize() function for Win32 (partial).

```cpp
bool BlackJackGameWin32::GameInitialize()
{
   DEVMODE dmScreenSettings;
   bbe::RenderParams params;

   if(!WINDOW_FULLSCREEN)
   {
      m_hwnd = CreateWindowEx(0, WINDOW_CLASS, WINDOW_NAME,
         WS_OVERLAPPEDWINDOW | WS_VISIBLE | WS_SYSMENU |
         WS_CLIPCHILDREN | WS_CLIPSIBLINGS, 100, 100,
         WINDOW_WIDTH, WINDOW_HEIGHT, 0, 0, m_hInst, NULL);
   }
   else
   {
      ... SET dmScreenSettings ...

      m_hwnd = CreateWindowEx(0, WINDOW_CLASS, WINDOW_NAME,
         WS_POPUP | WS_VISIBLE, 0, 0, WINDOW_WIDTH, WINDOW_HEIGHT,
         0, 0, m_hInst, NULL);

      SetForegroundWindow(m_hwnd);
   }

   if(!m_hwnd)
      return false;

   ShowWindow(m_hwnd, SW_SHOW);
   UpdateWindow(m_hwnd);

   // Setup X360 controller and render params.
   params.m_handle.m_hwnd = m_hwnd;
   params.m_handle.m_hInstance = m_hInst;

   if(m_360Pads[0].Initialize(0) == BB_FAIL)
      return false;

   return BlackJackGame::GameInitialize(params);
}
```

LISTING 9.4 The `GameShutdown()` and `EnterGameLoop()` functions in Win32.

```
int BlackJackGameWin32::EnterGameLoop()
{
   MSG msg;

   while(!m_quitDemo)
   {
      if(PeekMessage(&msg, 0, 0, 0, PM_REMOVE))
      {
         if(msg.message == WM_QUIT)
            break;

         TranslateMessage(&msg);
         DispatchMessage(&msg);
      }
      else
      {
         GameUpdate();
         GameRender();
      }
   }

   GameShutdown();

   return (int)msg.wParam;
}


void BlackJackGameWin32::GameShutdown()
{
   BlackJackGame::GameShutdown();

   if(WINDOW_FULLSCREEN)
      ChangeDisplaySettings(NULL, 0);

   UnregisterClass(WINDOW_CLASS, m_hInst);
}
```

The main function of all operating systems is different, so a main function for each demo on each system is specified. For Win32, this is `WinMain()`, and it handles the Win32 stuff before allowing the black jack game to take over. The code for the main function is straightforward and can be seen listed in Listing 9.5. A screenshot of the black jack game can be seen in Figure 9.3 on page 479.

LISTING 9.5 The `WinMain()` function.

```
BlackJackGameWin32 *g_blackJackGame = NULL;


int WINAPI WinMain(HINSTANCE hInstance, HINSTANCE prev,
                   LPSTR cmd, int show)
{
   int result = 0;

   g_blackJackGame = new BlackJackGameWin32(hInstance);

   if(g_blackJackGame == NULL)
   {
      MessageBox(NULL, "Error creating g_blackJackGame!",
                 "Error", MB_OK);
      return 0;
   }

   WNDCLASSEX windowClass;
   memset(&windowClass, 0, sizeof(WNDCLASSEX));
   windowClass.cbSize = sizeof(WNDCLASSEX);
   windowClass.style = CS_HREDRAW | CS_VREDRAW;
   windowClass.lpfnWndProc = WndProc;
   windowClass.hInstance = hInstance;
   windowClass.hIcon = LoadIcon(NULL, IDI_APPLICATION);
   windowClass.hCursor = LoadCursor(NULL, IDC_ARROW);
   windowClass.lpszClassName = WINDOW_CLASS;
   windowClass.hIconSm = LoadIcon(NULL, IDI_APPLICATION);

   if(!RegisterClassEx(&windowClass))
      return 0;

   if(g_blackJackGame->GameInitialize() == false)
   {
      MessageBox(NULL, "Error in initialize!", "Error", MB_OK);
   }
   else
```

```
    {
        result = g_blackJackGame->EnterGameLoop();
    }

    g_blackJackGame->GameShutdown();
    delete g_blackJackGame;
    g_blackJackGame = NULL;

    return result;
}
```

The GameUpdate() function in the Win32 class is used to call the base class' GameUpdate() function and to test for Xbox 360 controller input. Since Xbox 360 controllers can be used on Microsoft systems using XINPUT, this is handled in the Win32 class. During the black jack game, only limited amounts of input can be handled. The first set of input deals with the menu state when the player is given the option to quit the application by pressing the Back button on the controller, or to start the game by pressing the Start button. From there, the same options are given to the player when the game starts and the deal is about to take place, with the exception that the quit action quits to the main menu instead of the application. From there, during the game the player can hit with the "A" button or stay with the "B" button. When a game is over and the victory conditions are displayed (e.g., win, lose, and so forth), the player can either press Start again to start a new game, or Back to quit to the menu. With keyboard input, the same options are given in the base class GameUpdate() function with the escape, enter, "H," and "S" keys. The Win32 overloaded GameUpdate() function can be seen in Listing 9.6.

LISTING 9.6 The Win32's derived GameUpdate() function.

```
void BlackJackGameWin32::GameUpdate()
{
    // Win32 specific input using Xbox 360 controllers.
    if(m_360Pads[0].Update() == BB_SUCCESS)
    {
        switch(m_currentGameState)
        {
            case BJ_GAME_MENU:
                if(m_360Pads[0].isButtonUp(BB_BUTTON_BACK))
                    m_quitDemo = true;
```

```
                        if(m_360Pads[0].isButtonUp(BB_BUTTON_START))
                            m_currentGameState = BJ_GAME_PLAY_START;
                        break;

                    case BJ_GAME_PLAY_START:
                    case BJ_GAME_PLAY_PLAYER_WIN:
                    case BJ_GAME_PLAY_CPU_WIN:
                    case BJ_GAME_PLAY_PLAYER_CPU_TIE:
                        if(m_360Pads[0].isButtonUp(BB_BUTTON_BACK))
                            m_currentGameState = BJ_GAME_MENU;

                        if(m_360Pads[0].isButtonUp(BB_BUTTON_START))
                            m_currentGameState = BJ_GAME_PLAY_DEALING;
                        break;

                    case BJ_GAME_PLAY_PLAYER_MOVE:
                        if(m_playerStay == false)
                        {
                            if(m_360Pads[0].isButtonUp(BB_BUTTON_A))
                            {
                                PlayerHit();
                                m_currentGameState = BJ_GAME_PLAY_CPU_MOVE;
                            }
                            else if(m_360Pads[0].isButtonUp(BB_BUTTON_B))
                            {
                                m_playerStay = true;
                                m_currentGameState = BJ_GAME_PLAY_CPU_MOVE;
                            }
                        }
                        break;

                    default:
                        break;
                }
            }

        BlackJackGame::GameUpdate();
    }
```

The first three functions of the game's class are the constructor, destructor, and
Resize(). The constructor sets all variables to default values, while the destructor
calls GameShutdown() to release all memory the application has consumed through-

out its execution. The Resize() function is used to set the projection matrix whenever the window is resized. Because this game is not a 3D game, orthogonal projection is used. The BlackJackGame class constructor, destructor, and Resize() functions can be seen in Listing 9.7.

LISTING 9.7   The constructor, destructor, and Resize() functions.

```
BlackJackGame::BlackJackGame()
{
    m_currentGameState = BJ_GAME_INITIALIZING;
    m_quitDemo = false;
    m_playerStay = false;
    m_cpuStay = false;

    for(int i = 0; i < BJ_TOTAL_KEYS; i++)
        m_buttonKeys[i] = false;
}


BlackJackGame::~BlackJackGame()
{
    GameShutdown();
}


void BlackJackGame::Resize(int width, int height)
{
    m_render.SetViewPort(0, 0, width, height);

    m_render.ResizeWindowOrtho(-width, width, -height,
                                 height, 0, 1);
}
```

The next function is GameInitialize() and is a one-time call function. This means that the function was meant to be called once at the startup of the application. All memory allocated by this function is freed by the GameShutdown() function. The function starts like many Initialize() functions seen throughout all of the demos of this book by setting up the rendering parameters, initializing the rendering system, setting the project by resizing the window, and setting up the default rendering states. The function then moves on to create the geometry that will make up the background, which will be used by the main menu and the game. Every game state has it own image that is displayed as the background. A few improvements can be made here that are looked at at the end of this section. Once all of the background images are loaded, the function loads all the cards and initializes them, updates the game's state to move to the menu, and calls srand() to seed the random number generator for the dealing of the cards. A card is represented by a structure called Card. This structure contains a texture for an individual card, the face value of the card, and the suite value of the card. The suite can be clubs, spades, diamonds, or hearts, which are represented by integers 0 through 3. A face value can be 1 through 10 for number cards, 11 for an ace, and 10 for face cards (i.e., kings, queens, and jacks). The GameInitialize() function can be seen in Listing 9.8.

LISTING 9.8   The GameInitialize() function.

```
bool BlackJackGame::GameInitialize(bbe::RenderParams &params)
{
   params.m_colorBits = 24;
   params.m_depthBits = 16;
   params.m_stencilBits = 8;
   params.m_fullscreen = false;
   params.m_height = WINDOW_HEIGHT;
   params.m_width = WINDOW_WIDTH;
   params.m_maxCacheBytes = 2000;
   params.m_maxCacheIndices = 2000;

   if(m_render.Initialize(&params) != BB_SUCCESS)
      return false;


   Resize(WINDOW_WIDTH, WINDOW_HEIGHT);

   m_render.SetClearColor(0, 0, 0, 255);
   m_render.Enable(BB_DEPTH_TESTING);
   m_render.Enable(BB_SMOOTH_SHADING);
   m_render.Enable(BB_TEXTURE_2D);


   std::vector<BB_FILTER_TYPE> filters;
   filters.push_back(BB_MIN_LINEAR_FILTER);
   filters.push_back(BB_MAG_LINEAR_FILTER);
   filters.push_back(BB_MIP_LINEAR_FILTER);
```

```
// Create background full-screen square.
if(bbe::CreateSquareMesh(WINDOW_WIDTH, WINDOW_HEIGHT,
   &m_background) == false)
{
   return false;
}

// Background images.
std::string resourceStr[BJ_TOTAL_GUI] =
{
   "resources/menu.tga",
   "resources/GamePlayStart.tga",
   "resources/GamePlayP1Move.tga",
   "resources/GamePlayCPUMove.tga",
   "resources/GamePlayP1Win.tga",
   "resources/GamePlayCPUWin.tga",
   "resources/GamePlayP1CPUTie.tga"
};

// Load all background images.
for(int i = 0; i < BJ_TOTAL_GUI; i++)
{
   if(m_render.LoadTexFromFile(const_cast<char*>(
      resourceStr[i].c_str()),
      BB_TEX2D_TYPE, &m_guiTextures[i]) == false)
      {
         return false;
      }

      m_render.ApplyFilters(m_guiTextures[i], &filters);
}


int tempIndex = 0;
char file[64] = { 0 };

// Create card geometry.
if(bbe::CreateSquareMesh(128, 128, &m_cardGeometry) == false)
   return false;

// Load image for the back of a card.
if(m_render.LoadTexFromFile("resources/Cards/CardBack.tga",
```

```
         BB_TEX2D_TYPE, &m_cardBack) == false)
   {
      return false;
   }

   m_render.ApplyFilters(m_cardBack, &filters);


   // Load all card images.
   for(int f = 0; f < BJ_TOTAL_SUIT_CARDS; f++)
   {
      for(int s = 0; s < BJ_TOTAL_SUITS; s++)
      {
         tempIndex = s * BJ_TOTAL_SUITS + f;
         sprintf(file, "resources/Cards/Card%d%d.tga", s, f);

         m_cards[tempIndex].m_suite = s;
         m_cards[tempIndex].m_face = f;

         if(m_render.LoadTexFromFile(file,
            BB_TEX2D_TYPE,
            &m_cards[tempIndex].m_decal) == false)
         {
            return false;
         }
      }
   }


   // Ready to move to menu.
   m_currentGameState = BJ_GAME_MENU;


   // Used for random number generators.
   srand((unsigned)time(0));

   return true;
}
```

The BlackJackGame GameUpdate() function is responsible for detecting and handling keyboard input, game logic, and testing for victory conditions. The state of
the game drives this function. During the menu state, all input dealing with that is

detected and handled. The same goes for the gameplay itself. The game logic is a set of code that handles the dealing of the cards during the dealing state, handles the player's move, and processes the artificial intelligence for the CPU. The victory conditions are determined once both players have made all the moves they can. This can be determined by either player choosing to "stay" when satisfied with the cards he has or if he went over 21. The GameUpdate() function can be seen in Listing 9.9.

LISTING 9.9   The BlackJackGame GameUpdate().

```
void BlackJackGame::GameUpdate()
{
    // Used for testing if a button is up rather than down.
    if(bbe::isButtonDown(BB_BUTTON_ESCAPE))
        m_buttonKeys[BJ_ESC_KEY] = true;
    else if(bbe::isButtonDown(BB_BUTTON_ENTER))
        m_buttonKeys[BJ_ENTER_KEY] = true;
    else if(bbe::isButtonDown(BB_BUTTON_H))
        m_buttonKeys[BJ_H_KEY] = true;
    else if(bbe::isButtonDown(BB_BUTTON_S))
        m_buttonKeys[BJ_S_KEY] = true;


    // Input.
    switch(m_currentGameState)
    {
        case BJ_GAME_MENU:
            if(bbe::isButtonUp(BB_BUTTON_ESCAPE,
                m_buttonKeys[BJ_ESC_KEY]))
            {
                m_buttonKeys[BJ_ESC_KEY] = false;
                m_quitDemo = true;
            }

            if(bbe::isButtonUp(BB_BUTTON_ENTER,
                m_buttonKeys[BB_BUTTON_ENTER]))
            {
                m_buttonKeys[BJ_ENTER_KEY] = false;
                m_currentGameState = BJ_GAME_PLAY_START;
            }
            break;
```

```
case BJ_GAME_PLAY_START:
case BJ_GAME_PLAY_PLAYER_WIN:
case BJ_GAME_PLAY_CPU_WIN:
case BJ_GAME_PLAY_PLAYER_CPU_TIE:
   if(bbe::isButtonUp(BB_BUTTON_ESCAPE,
      m_buttonKeys[BJ_ESC_KEY]))
   {
      m_buttonKeys[BJ_ESC_KEY] = false;
      m_currentGameState = BJ_GAME_MENU;
   }

   if(bbe::isButtonUp.isButtonUp(BB_BUTTON_ENTER,
      m_buttonKeys[BB_BUTTON_ENTER]))
   {
      m_currentGameState = BJ_GAME_PLAY_DEALING;
   }
   break;


case BJ_GAME_PLAY_PLAYER_MOVE:
   if(m_playerStay == false)
   {
      if(bbe::isButtonUp(BB_BUTTON_H,
         m_buttonKeys[BJ_H_KEY]))
      {
         m_buttonKeys[BJ_H_KEY] = false;

         PlayerHit();
         m_currentGameState = BJ_GAME_PLAY_CPU_MOVE;
      }
      else if(bbe::isButtonUp(BB_BUTTON_S,
            m_buttonKeys[BJ_S_KEY]))
      {
         m_buttonKeys[BJ_S_KEY] = false;

         m_playerStay = true;
         m_currentGameState = BJ_GAME_PLAY_CPU_MOVE;
      }
   }
   break;
```

```
        default:
            break;
    }


// Game logic.
switch(m_currentGameState)
{
    case BJ_GAME_PLAY_DEALING:
        m_playerStay = false;
        m_cpuStay = false;

        DealCards();
        m_currentGameState = BJ_GAME_PLAY_PLAYER_MOVE;
        break;

    case BJ_GAME_PLAY_PLAYER_MOVE:
        if(m_playerTotal > 21)
        {
            m_playerStay = true;
            m_currentGameState = BJ_GAME_PLAY_CPU_MOVE;
        }
        break;

        case BJ_GAME_PLAY_CPU_MOVE:
        if(m_cpuStay != true)
            ProcessAI();


        if(m_playerStay != true)
            m_currentGameState = BJ_GAME_PLAY_PLAYER_MOVE;
        break;

        default:
            break;
    }


// Victory conditions.
if(m_cpuStay == true && m_playerStay == true)
{
    // Any over 21?
    if(m_cpuTotal <= 21 && m_playerTotal > 21)
```

```
                      m_currentGameState = BJ_GAME_PLAY_CPU_WIN;
                  else if(m_playerTotal <= 21 && m_cpuTotal > 21)
                      m_currentGameState = BJ_GAME_PLAY_PLAYER_WIN;
                  else
                  {
                      // Any tie...
                      if(m_playerTotal > 21 && m_cpuTotal > 21)
                         m_currentGameState = BJ_GAME_PLAY_PLAYER_CPU_TIE;
                      else if(m_playerTotal == m_cpuTotal)
                         m_currentGameState = BJ_GAME_PLAY_PLAYER_CPU_TIE;
                      else
                      {
                         // Cpu over player else player over Cpu.
                         if(m_cpuTotal > m_playerTotal)
                            m_currentGameState = BJ_GAME_PLAY_CPU_WIN;
                         else
                            m_currentGameState = BJ_GAME_PLAY_PLAYER_WIN;
                      }
                  }

                  m_cpuStay = m_playerStay = false;
               }
           }
```

The next four functions are GameRender(), GameShutdown(), ProcessMainMenu(), and ProcessGameLevel(). GameShutdown()deletes everything at the end of a game. ProcessMainMenu()will draw the main menu during that game state. GameRender() will call either ProcessMainManu() or ProcessGameLevel() depending on the game state. ProcessGameLevel(), will draw the game backgrounds and the players' cards. These functions can be seen in Listing 9.10.

LISTING 9.10   The GameRender(), GameShutdown(), ProcessMainMenu(), and ProcessGameLevel() functions.

```
      void BlackJackGame::GameRender()
      {
         m_render.StartRendering(1, 1, 0);
         m_render.LoadIdentityMatrix();


         switch(m_currentGameState)
         {
```

```
          case BJ_GAME_MENU:
              ProcessMainMenu();
              break;


          default:
              ProcessGameLevel();
              break;
      }


    m_render.EndRendering();
}


void BlackJackGame::GameShutdown()
{
    m_render.Shutdown();
}


void BlackJackGame::ProcessMainMenu()
{
    m_render.SetView(0, 0, 1, 0, 0, 0, 0, 1, 0);

    m_render.TranslateMatrix(0, 0, 0.1f);
    m_render.ApplyTexture(0, m_guiTextures[BJ_GUI_MENU]);
    m_render.Render(BB_RENDER_MODEL_DATA_PARAMS(m_background));
}


void BlackJackGame::ProcessGameLevel()
{
    m_render.SetView(0, 0, 1, 0, 0, 0, 0, 1, 0);


    // Draw background.
    switch(m_currentGameState)
    {
      case BJ_GAME_PLAY_START:
          m_render.ApplyTexture(0, m_guiTextures[BJ_GUI_START]);
          break;
```

```
      case BJ_GAME_PLAY_PLAYER_MOVE:
         m_render.ApplyTexture(0, m_guiTextures[BJ_GUI_P1_MOVE]);
         break;


      case BJ_GAME_PLAY_CPU_MOVE:
         m_render.ApplyTexture(0, m_guiTextures[BJ_GUI_CPU_MOVE]);
         break;


      case BJ_GAME_PLAY_PLAYER_WIN:
         m_render.ApplyTexture(0, m_guiTextures[BJ_GUI_P1_WIN]);
         break;


      case BJ_GAME_PLAY_CPU_WIN:
         m_render.ApplyTexture(0, m_guiTextures[BJ_GUI_CPU_WIN]);
         break;


      case BJ_GAME_PLAY_PLAYER_CPU_TIE:
        m_render.ApplyTexture(0, m_guiTextures[BJ_GUI_P1_CPU_TIE]);
         break;


      default:
         break;
   }


   m_render.TranslateMatrix(0, 0, 0.1f);
   m_render.Render(BB_RENDER_MODEL_DATA_PARAMS(m_background));


   // Draw cards.
   switch(m_currentGameState)
   {
      case BJ_GAME_PLAY_PLAYER_MOVE:
      case BJ_GAME_PLAY_CPU_MOVE:
      case BJ_GAME_PLAY_PLAYER_WIN:
      case BJ_GAME_PLAY_CPU_WIN:
      case BJ_GAME_PLAY_PLAYER_CPU_TIE:
```

```
        DrawCards();
        break;


    default:
        break;
    }
}
```

DrawCards() is used to render the players' cards. This function works by displaying all the player's cards at the bottom of the screen and all the CPU cards at the top of the screen. The player can only see the CPU's cards at the end of the game, so while the game is executing, a texture of the back of the cards is displayed. Each card is drawn on top of the other, slightly to the right of the last. A player can only have a finite total number of cards without going over 21. The size of the cards and the screen allows for plenty of room for all cards to be drawn. The DrawCards() function can be seen in Listing 9.11.

LISTING 9.11   The DrawCards() function.

```
void BlackJackGame::DrawCards()
{
    float z = 0;
    float x = 200;
    int index = 0;


    for(int i = 0; i < (int)m_playerCards.size(); i++)
    {
        m_render.PushMatrix();

            m_render.TranslateMatrix((float)(i * 40) - x,
                                     -300,
                                     0.2f + z);

            index = m_playerCards[i];
            m_render.ApplyTexture(0, m_cards[index].m_decal);

            m_render.Render(BB_RENDER_MODEL_DATA_PARAMS(
                            m_cardGeometry));
```

```
      m_render.PopMatrix();

   z += 0.01f;
}


z = 0;


for(i = 0; i < (int)m_cpuCards.size(); i++)
{
   m_render.PushMatrix();

      m_render.TranslateMatrix((float)(i * 40) - x,
                               300,
                               0.2f + z);


      // Only draw CPU cards at the end.
      if(m_currentGameState >= BJ_GAME_PLAY_PLAYER_WIN &&
         m_currentGameState <= BJ_GAME_PLAY_PLAYER_CPU_TIE)
      {
         index = m_cpuCards[i];
         m_render.ApplyTexture(0, m_cards[index].m_decal);
      }
      else
      {
         m_render.ApplyTexture(0, m_cardBack);
      }


      m_render.Render(BB_RENDER_MODEL_DATA_PARAMS(
                   m_cardGeometry));

   m_render.PopMatrix();

   z += 0.01f;
}
}
```

The next function is DealCards() and is called at the start of every game. This function is responsible for clearing the players' hands and giving each two initial cards. In black jack, two cards are dealt at the start of each game, and this function does just that. To get a new card, the function GiveCard() is called, which takes that new card and inserts it into the player's hand. The player's total is also incremented to reflect the newly added card. The index for the cards ranges from 0 to 14, where 0 is a 2 and 14 is a king. An 11 is an ace, and anything above that (jack, queen, king) is a face card with a value 10. When updating the player's total, two can be added to all values under 11 to offset the range to map the card it represents. When all cards have been handed out, the function returns to the caller. The DealCards() function can be seen listed in Listing 9.12.

LISTING 9.12   The DealCards() function.

```
void BlackJackGame::DealCards()
{
    int cardIndex = -1;

    m_playerCards.clear();
    m_cpuCards.clear();

    m_playerTotal = m_cpuTotal = 0;
    m_cpuStay = m_playerStay = false;

    // Get first two player cards.
    cardIndex = GiveCard();
    m_playerCards.push_back(cardIndex);
    m_playerTotal += (m_cards[cardIndex].m_face + 2) > 11 ? 10 :
                        m_cards[cardIndex].m_face + 2;

    assert(m_cards[cardIndex].m_face >= 0);


    cardIndex = GiveCard();
    m_playerCards.push_back(cardIndex);
    m_playerTotal += (m_cards[cardIndex].m_face + 2) > 11 ? 10 :
                        m_cards[cardIndex].m_face + 2;

    assert(m_cards[cardIndex].m_face >= 0);
```

```
// Get first two CPU cards.
cardIndex = GiveCard();
m_cpuCards.push_back(cardIndex);
m_cpuTotal += (m_cards[cardIndex].m_face + 2) > 11 ? 10 :
                    m_cards[cardIndex].m_face + 2;

assert(m_cards[cardIndex].m_face >= 0);


cardIndex = GiveCard();
m_cpuCards.push_back(cardIndex);
m_cpuTotal += (m_cards[cardIndex].m_face + 2) > 11 ? 10 :
                    m_cards[cardIndex].m_face + 2;

assert(m_cards[cardIndex].m_face >= 0);
}
```

The next two functions are GiveCard() and IsCardOut(). GiveCard() randomly generations a suite ID and a face number. Once it has these two values, it checks to make sure the card is not already in someone's hand. Since the total number of possible cards a player can have is small, this search is done linearly. The function returns the index to the card in the m_cards array (which is of type Card). Both the GiveCard() and IsCardOut() functions can be seen listed in Listing 9.13.

LISTING 9.13 The GiveCard() and IsCardOut() functions.

```
int BlackJackGame::GiveCard()
{
   int suite = 0;
   int face = 0;


   do
   {
      suite = rand() % 4;
      face = rand() % 14;
   }
   while(IsCardOut(suite, face) == true ||
         suite < 0 || face < 0 || suite > 3 ||
         face > 13);
```

```
      return suite * BJ_TOTAL_SUITS + face;
}


bool BlackJackGame::IsCardOut(int suite, int face)
{
   int card = suite * BJ_TOTAL_SUITS + face;


   for(int i = 0; i < (int)m_cpuCards.size(); i++)
   {
      if(m_cpuCards[i] == card)
         return true;
   }


   for(i = 0; i < (int)m_playerCards.size(); i++)
   {
      if(m_playerCards[i] == card)
         return true;
   }

   return false;
}
```

The remaining functions are ProcessAI() and the PlayerHit(). ProcessAI() checks if the CPU's total is under 16 or is greater than the player's. If so, it will choose to stay; otherwise, it will hit. Knowing what the player has can allow the game to be a bit more challenging. If the CPU knows it will lose, it will hit in an attempt to change the outcome. If the CPU goes over 21, it will automatically have to stay (which has dual uses for both staying and "bust"). The PlayerHit() function works in a similar fashion to ProcessAI(), with PlayerHit()giving the player a new card upon request. If the player goes over 21, the function will force the player to stay (bust). Both functions can be seen in Listing 9.14.

LISTING 9.14   The ProcessAI() and PlayerHit() functions.

```
   void BlackJackGame::ProcessAI()
   {
      if(m_cpuTotal > 16 && m_cpuTotal >= m_playerTotal ||
```

```
      m_cpuTotal > 21)
   {
      m_cpuStay = true;
      return;
   }

   int cardIndex = -1;

   // If the CPU does not stay, it hits.
   cardIndex = GiveCard();
   m_cpuCards.push_back(cardIndex);
   m_cpuTotal += (m_cards[cardIndex].m_face + 2) > 11 ? 10 :
                   m_cards[cardIndex].m_face + 2;

   assert(m_cards[cardIndex].m_face >= 0);
}


void BlackJackGame::PlayerHit()
{
   if(m_playerTotal > 21)
   {
      m_playerStay = true;
      return;
   }

   int cardIndex = -1;

   // Allow the hit.
   cardIndex = GiveCard();
   m_playerCards.push_back(cardIndex);
   m_playerTotal += (m_cards[cardIndex].m_face + 2) > 11 ? 10 :
                      m_cards[cardIndex].m_face + 2;

   assert(m_cards[cardIndex].m_face >= 0);
}
```

The black jack game is simple with simple black jack rules. When a game is first executed, the main menu appears. When a user decides to start a game of black jack, the cards are dealt and the players alternate turns until one is the victor. On

Windows, the user has the option of using an Xbox 360 game controller. Screenshots of the black jack game can be seen in Figures 9.3 and 9.4.

When looking at the simple black jack game, a number of small improvements could have a huge effect on the overall game, including:

- Adding a font system to use for in-game text instead of loading multiple large images with the text on them as a stand-in.
- All graphics can use some polish.
- Adding a graphical user interface to the game can be helpful. For example, having virtual buttons for "hit" and "stay" can be a nice alternative to hitting specific keyboard keys.
- Multiple human players are easy to add and could be a nice touch.
- Placing all resources in an archive file might be nice to make it hard for gamers to access the game's assets.
- Allowing an ace to be a 1 or 11 would make the game more like traditional black jack.
- The addition of splitting and double downs is also a part of black jack that can be added.
- The scripting system can be used for the artificial intelligence.

FIGURE 9.3   A screenshot of the black jack game's main menu.

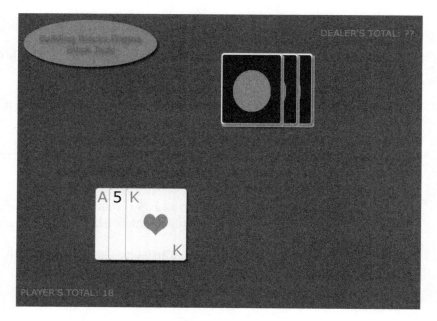

FIGURE 9.4   A screenshot of the black jack game.

THE 3D WALKTHROUGH DEMO

The next demo is a simple first-person walkthrough that creates a simple portal rendering system as discussed in Chapter 5, "Rendering Scenes and Scene Graphs." Although not a game, the demo is a 3D application that brings together a number of the different topics discussed throughout this book. Creating a 3D game takes a lot of work and would require a lengthy book to describe getting started in 3D game programming. In this chapter, the demo focuses on moving around a 3D environment using a simple portal system that was discussed earlier in the book. The various elements used in this demo application include:

■ Xbox 360 controllers
■ OpenAL audio
■ 3D environments
■ Collisions between the camera and the environment
■ A simple portal rendering system

A portal rendering system is a system in which a game world is split up into areas known as sectors. These sectors store all the geometry, objects, and materials needed for that area. Inside each sector are a number of portals. A portal is a connection from one sector to another. This connection can be a window, door, or some other space where an opening can go either directly from one area to another or can connect indirectly. Portals can be used to connect areas that are not physically close or touching one another, which can lead to some interesting effects.

The algorithm of a portal rendering system works at a basic level by first rendering the area the viewer is in. Once drawn, all portals in that area are checked for visibility. If a portal is visible, the area that connects to that portal is rendered. This process continues recursively until all visible areas have been drawn to the screen. Because of the advancements of modern hardware, it is not necessary to clip polygons to portals before rendering an area. This is because the process of clipping polygons to a portal will be slower than allowing the hardware to handle the culling and Z tests.

A bounding sphere can surround the small area that defines a portal. This can allow the Frustum class to quickly reject any portals that are not visible. This was first discussed in Chapter 4 "Rendering Systems," and the Frustum class can be seen listed in Listing 9.15.

LISTING 9.15   The Frustum class.

```
class Frustum
{
   public:
      Frustum();


      void CalculateFrustum(float *viewProj,
                       BB_COORDINATE_TYPE type);



      void AddPlane(Plane &pl);
      bool GetPlane(int index, Plane *out);
      int GetTotalPlanes() { return (int)m_frustum.size(); }


      bool isPointVisible(float x, float y, float z);

      bool isSphereVisible(float x, float y,
                       float z, float radius);
```

```
        bool isCubeVisible(float x, float y, float z, float size);
        bool isBoxVisible(Vector3D min, Vector3D max);
        bool isOBBVisible(OBB &obb);


    private:
        std::vector<Plane> m_frustum;
};
```

The 3D camera used to navigate around the 3D environment is the camera system that was created in Chapter 4. In most 3D first-person games, the movements of the camera are handled by the arrow keys and the "W," "S," "A," and "D" keys (which often can be changed). The Camera class can be seen listed in Listing 9.16.

LISTING 9.16   The Camera class.

```
class Camera
{
    public:
        Camera();

        Camera(Vector3D &pos, Vector3D &lookAt,
                Vector3D &up, Vector3D &right);


        void MoveCamera(Vector3D &direction, float speed);
        void StrafeCam(float speed);

        void RotateCamera(float angle, Vector3D &axis);
        void RotateCamera(float deltaX, float deltaY);


        void SetPosition(Vector3D &pos) { m_pos = pos; }
        void SetLookDirection(Vector3D &at) { m_lookAt = at; }
        void SetUpDirection(Vector3D &up) { m_up = up; }
        void SetRightDirection(Vector3D &right) { m_right = right; }

        Vector3D GetPosition() { return m_pos; }
        Vector3D GetLookDirection() { return m_lookAt; }
        Vector3D GetUpDirection() { return m_up; }
        Vector3D GetRightDirection() { return m_right; }
```

```
        private:
            Vector3D m_pos, m_lookAt, m_up, m_right;
    };
```

The only code in the 3D demo not seen in this book so far deals with the sectors and the portals. The application is coded in the same way the black jack game was earlier in this chapter, minus the game-specific functions and variables. The remaining code for the demo uses code that was seen in previous chapters. The WALKTHROUGH 3D demo application can be found on the companion CD-ROM in the BUILDING BLOCKS ENGINE/EXAMPLES/CHAPTER 9 folder. The game's class declaration can be seen in Listing 9.17. Because the demo application is not a game, it has less code overall than the black jack game.

ON THE CD

LISTING 9.17   The demo's class declaration.

```
// Finite state machine's states.
enum WALKTHROUGH_GAME_STATE { WT_GAME_INITIALIZING,
                              WT_GAME_MENU,
                              WT_GAME_PLAY,
                              WT_GAME_QUIT };


// Demo class.
class WalkThrough3D
{
    public:
        WalkThrough3D();
        virtual ~WalkThrough3D();


        void Resize(int width, int height);


        virtual bool GameInitialize(bbe::RenderParams &params);
        virtual void GameUpdate();

        void GameRender();

        virtual void GameShutdown();
        virtual int EnterGameLoop() = 0;
```

```
protected:
    void ProcessMainMenu();
    void ProcessGameLevel();


protected:
    // Rendering system.
    bbe::OpenGLRenderer m_render;


    // List of sectors.
    std::vector<Sector*> m_areas;


    // Sound system.
    bbe::OpenALSystem m_soundSystem;


    // Global sound source.
    bbe::OpenALSoundSource m_globalSource;


    // Menu.
    bbe::ModelData m_menu;
    bbe::BB_TEXTURE m_menuTexture;
    bbe::OpenALSoundBuffer m_menuSound;


    // States for game's finite state machine.
    WALKTHROUGH_GAME_STATE m_currentGameState;


    // Flag to quit application.
    bool m_quitDemo;
};
```

The demo only has states for the application's initialization, menu, quit, and play (walkthrough). The demo only exits when the player backs out of the demo to the main menu, and then out of the application. When the demo renders the scene, it renders the sector the viewer is in first, and then all sectors that are visible from the visible portals in that sector. A portal in the simple demo application is a class with pointers to two areas (sectors). The class also has a piece of geometry that can represent the portal. This geometry is not drawn to the screen and is used for testing for visibility. The Portal class can be seen listed in Listing 9.18.

The last class in the demo application is the Sector class, which has the renderable geometry for the area and a list of portals. The demo application's Process-GameLevel() function renders the sectors to the screen. The Sector class declaration can be seen in Listing 9.19.

LISTING 9.18   Partial look at the Portal class implementation.

```
class Portal
{
    public:
        Portal();
        virtual ~Portal();


        void SetArea1(Sector *area)
        {
            m_area1 = area;
        }


        void SetArea2(Sector *area)
        {
            m_area2 = area;
        }


        Sector *GetArea1()
        {
            return m_area1;
        }


        Sector *GetArea2()
        {
            return m_area2;
        }
```

```
            BB_MODEL GetGeometry()
            {
               return m_geometry;
            }


      private:
         Sector *m_area1;
         Sector *m_area2;

         BB_MODEL m_geometry;
};
```

LISTING 9.19 Partial look at the `Sector` implementation.

```
class Sector
{
   public:
      Sector();
      virtual ~Sector();


      void SetGeometry(BB_MODEL geometry)
      {
         m_geometry = geometry;
      }


      BB_MODEL GetGeometry()
      {
         return m_geometry;
      }


      void SetTexture(bbe::BB_TEXTURE tex)
      {
         m_decal = tex;
      }


      bbe::BB_TEXTURE GetTexture()
      {
```

```
            return m_decal;
        }


        void SetIsRendered(bool val)
        {
            m_rendered = val;
        }


        bool GetIsRendered()
        {
            return m_rendered;
        }


        void SetPortal(Portal &p)
        {
            m_portals.push_back(p);
        }


        std::vector<Portal> *GetPortals()
        {
            return &m_portals;
        }


    private:
        bool m_rendered;

        BB_MODEL m_geometry;
        bbe::BB_TEXTURE m_decal;

        std::vector<Portal> m_portals;
};
```

ON THE CD

The entire source for the 3D demo can be found on the companion CD-ROM under the BUILDING BLOCKS ENGINE/EXAMPLES/CHAPTER 9/ WALKTHROUGH folder, and a screenshot of the application in action can be seen in Figure 9.5. The entire environment was hard coded as a simple area with a few polygons inside the GameInitialize() function. Possible features that can be added to the demo using code developed in this book include:

- Programmable shaders for advanced effects such as bump mapping and other per-pixel lighting techniques
- Particle systems for special effects
- Scripting for defining what level to load
- Text support to the rendering system so text information can be displayed to the screen such as the average frames per second and so forth

FIGURE 9.5   The walkthrough demo.

SUMMARY

Game engine design and game programming are two different fields that come together to create a video game product. The number of professionals required can include game engineers, artists, sound engineers, game programmers, level designers, game designers, and much more, each with varying levels within each field of expertise.

In this chapter, two relatively simple games were created to demonstrate the various subsystems of the Building Blocks Engine's framework working together to reach a common goal. Although not impressive on their own, they are a huge milestone for those learning to create and design their own game engines. The information in this book can be used by those using third-party engines much like the description in Chapter 6 of learning physics to understand third-party tools better if the need to create such a system was not considered.

The next chapter, "Conclusions," marks the end of this book. The development of the Building Blocks Engine and games that use it does not stop with this chapter and will continue at *UltimateGameProgramming.com*. Many of the improvements and additions discussed in this chapter will be implemented, and in future versions of the framework to allow the engine to be more useful for making 3D games.

CHAPTER EXERCISES

1. Add for the ability to make bets to the blackjack game.
2. Add more rooms to the 3D Walkthrough demo that are connected by portals.
3. Add multiple meshes for each sector to store static geometry for the areas.

Part V

Game Over

10 Conclusions

In This Chapter

- Additions and Improvements
- Additional Scripting Capabilities
- Final Thoughts

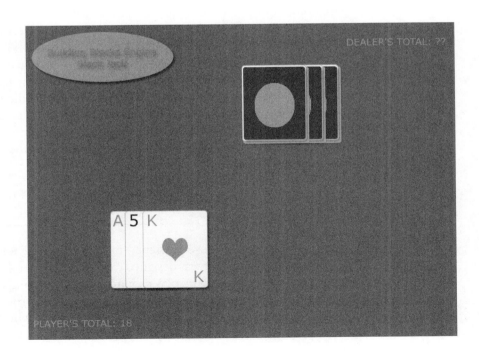

This chapter marks the completion of the early version of the Building Blocks Engine and this book on game engine design and architecture. The Building Blocks Engine is a simple game engine that can be expanded upon or used as is to build gaming applications and demos on the PC. Many features and tools can and will be added to the engine that will make the framework much more efficient and effective to use in game development. Because the engine is relatively small, the need for additional development is evident as seen in the simple types of games it is able to make as is. Modern games are becoming content-driven, which requires a number of tools for the different engineers working on a game project, who include technical artists, technical level designers, and game scripting programmers to name a few different technical fields. To create a gaming project with the Building Blocks Engine a number of tools and code will have to be developed and added to the framework.

The purpose of this chapter is to look at what was done in the book, what can be done, and what will be done in the future with the Building Blocks Engine. Many topics can be used when designing and implementing a game engine framework, some of which will be discussed in this chapter.

Game development is an always-expanding process, and the engineering challenges that come with new hardware will increase with the times. Game development and game programming trends will change and evolve through the years to match the emergence of new technologies. Examples of emerging trends can be seen with electronically distributed content, which is being made more popular on current generation gaming consoles like the Xbox 360 with the Xbox Live Marketplace. Another example of trends in game programming can be seen in multithreaded applications that make use of multicore architectures and episodic content that makes use of high-speed Internet connectivity as seen with Valve's Steam service. Game development is always evolving with the changing times and social atmospheres. Also, in-game advertisements are being used to help offset the cost required to create next-generation gaming titles.

ADDITIONS AND IMPROVEMENTS

The Building Blocks Engine was never designed to be a complete solution for all game development needs. Instead, it was designed to be a tool used by hobbyists and student programmers to learn from and play around with. The engine was designed to be easy to read and digest for those looking to get into engine programming for the first time. Because of this, a lot can go into future versions of the Building Blocks Engine framework, including but not limited to:

- Additional data structures used in game development
- Memory management
- Support for additional input devices
- Streaming audio
- Streaming data
- Enhanced features for the networking system
- Data compression
- Data encryption
- Improved custom physics system
- Graphical additions and enhancements
- An animations system
- Environment editing tools
- Exporters for common file formats such as 3ds Max™'s .3DS file format, for example
- Additional core tools
- Improved rendering system and scene graph
- Improved resource manager
- Optimized math library (e.g., SSE instructions)
- Additional scripting capabilities
- And much more

ADDITIONAL DATA STRUCTURES

In Chapter 2, "Engine Core," we discussed a few STL data structures that were used by the Building Blocks Engine and by the various game demos created in Chapter 10, "Conclusions." Using C++ STL data structures has great benefits in computer programming in general because of how efficient and effective the data structures are. When it comes to games, additional data structures exist in game development that STL alone does not cover, including but not limited to:

- Binary space partitioning trees
- K-D trees
- Sphere trees
- Quad-trees
- Portals
- Bounding volume hierarchies
- Graphs

Many of the data structures will be implemented in future releases of the Building Blocks Engine, and a number of them deal with scene rendering. Research and experimentation is required when deciding to use a data structure that is used for speed-critical processes like scene management, fast physics calculations with collision detection, and so forth before one is chosen. Different algorithms and data structures will have different performance results on an environment. This result can often be dependent on the overall design of the environment, the polygon count, number of static and dynamic items, the physics calculations, and so forth. If one technique is not enough, different techniques can be combined to create hybrid data structures that make use of the best of each.

MEMORY MANAGEMENT

Memory management was first discussed in Chapter 2. Memory management in computer science is a complex and challenging topic that is still being researched by computer scientists all over the field. By using a memory management system, an application can use a system's resources in the best possible way by improving performance, decreasing leaks and critical errors like dangling pointers, and a number of other beneficial features that are valued in application development. When extending upon the Building Blocks Engine or creating another game engine, it is important that memory management is addressed, researched, and if needed, implemented into the game engine's framework. The version of the Building Blocks Engine in this book did not include a plan on a memory management system, but future versions of the framework or future engines that are created will implement such a system, and an improved resource management system for game files and data. Regardless if a game is being developed on the PC or on a home gaming console, it is important that memory management is taken into consideration because the benefits are huge.

SUPPORT FOR ADDITIONAL INPUT DEVICES

The input system for the Building Blocks Engine did a decent job with the task it was given. It allowed the ability to get standard keyboard and mouse device states, and to use Xbox 360 controllers on the Windows XP and higher operating systems on the PC. One improvement would be to add game controller support (i.e., normal game pads, steering wheels, joysticks) for all operating systems so users can use non-Xbox 360 controllers as a game controller in gaming applications. Another feature that can be added is support for extended keyboard and mouse functionality that goes beyond what the standard devices can do. Today, many devices on the market have additional features that are not standard, including but are not limited to:

- Force feedback
- Additional buttons
- LCD screens
- Shortcut keys

The input system in this version of the Building Blocks Engine uses functions instead of classes outside the Xbox 360 controller class. Another change that can be made is to create classes for each input device. This will also allow the classes to be extended upon when new features are required by a project. Because the input detection requirements are simple, the current version of the engine uses two simple functions for keyboards and mice instead of two classes for each.

STREAMING AUDIO

Chapter 3, "Input, Sound, and Networking," discussed the creation of a sound system that can play audio files by using either OpenAL or XACT. These audio systems worked by loading a sound clip into memory and then playing that sound when it was requested by the application. For small sound files, this works well, but when trying to work with larger audio files, there are some issues. The first issue is that it needs to be loaded in completely, which can take up a lot of memory. The second issue is the time it takes to process a large sound file for playback in the sound system. One solution to working with large audio files is to incorporate a streaming feature into the audio system. For XACT, this can be done using streaming wave banks, and for OpenAL, this can be done using .OGG sound files, which can be compared to the popular .MP3 audio files used greatly today.

Streaming data can allow applications to play large audio files without the memory footprint, and can play the sound as soon as possible without waiting for the entire data to be loaded in and prepped. Future versions of the Building Blocks Engine will have the capability to stream audio files in applications. Some uses for being able to load large files into an application include music files, ambient sounds, and audio for cut-scenes, to name a few. Each of these items can be very important in large, complex 3D video games. Although the Building Blocks Engine can play sound effects and small sound files, that still might not be enough for all types of gaming applications. In addition, by using compressed sound files, developers can save on storage space and the amount of memory that needs to be streamed from a source. Streaming sound can also be very important for games that load content dynamically. Such types of games can be seen with open-world-style games like *Grand Theft Auto*.

STREAMING DATA

Streaming sound files for game audio is very beneficial to video games. Other aspects of a video game title can also be streamed from a source into the application dynamically. Streaming materials and environment data as needed also requires less memory, as seen in games like *Legacy of Kain Soul Reaver*, *Grand Theft Auto 3* through *San Andreas*, *Need for Speed Most Wanted*, and *Saint's Row*, to name a few.

Being able to stream an environment quickly from a disk into the game can allow developers to create much more massive worlds. This is definitely a very good feature to have in open-world-style games where players can roam wherever they want at any time. It is also a good feature to have on systems with a limited amount of resources available to the application. Systems have a finite amount of resources. On consoles, the hardware is fixed and traditionally has been lower than high-end PCs. Streaming can have many benefits that can help to side step limitations in hardware to a degree.

The implementation of a streaming system can become very complex. Everything from textures, to shaders, to materials, to geometry data, to sound might need to be quickly loaded and made game-ready at an instant. The archive filesystem of the Building Blocks Engine was designed and coded in a way that the file stream to the archive can be kept open as files are loaded from the hard drive into memory, thereby saving some CPU overhead. To stream data from a source, the data would have to be as game ready as possible to make the process fast. For example, it might not be performance friendly to have to decrypt every file that needs to be loaded into a game that needs to stream its data. Although there is much more to streaming than what was seen with the archive filesystem, it can be a good start in the right direction.

ENHANCED FEATURES FOR THE NETWORKING SYSTEM

The networking system for the Building Blocks Engine used wrapper classes for sockets. The system was straightforward and comprised of three classes: `Packet`, `Socket`, and `Network`. The `Packet` class was used to send a packet of character information to a destination. The `Socket` class wrapped the socket's API and represented a single connection. The `Network` class was created to store a list of connected sockets, a main application socket, and wrapped around the `Socket` class.

A number of topics and features can be added to the networking system to improve it. A queue can be used to hold all incoming networking messages in a list, possibly a priority queue, and can be processed one at a time for a specified amount of time during each frame. Another possible addition is the feature of compressed data. Data compression can reduce the amount of bandwidth that is used to transmit data. If the data can be decompressed and used by the game quickly, compression is definitely a topic worth looking into. This is especially true for games that make use of heavy networking traffic in online games.

Security

Online security is very important when it comes to transmitting data from one computer to another. For the Internet, browsers can send information securely from one computer to a server using very strong encryption. This can be seen in many Web sites such as Amazon.com, ebay.com, and many more that process credit card orders virtually. When it comes to games, security is becoming increasingly important.

Besides personal information, other data will need to be protected in a video game. Users can use things such as packet replay or other such techniques to cheat in a game. By manipulating data that is transmitted online, some gamers can give themselves unfair advantages that can affect the overall online experience for those gamers who are not looking to cheat. Keeping cheaters from playing their games using various hacks and exploits is a never-ending battle. Although it might not be necessary or probable to make a game 100-percent cheatproof, it is important to make it as difficult as possible for malicious users to modify and alter the game in a way that is negative to the overall experience or a threat to the network.

Load Balancing

Load balancing is the distribution of traffic across a network so no one server is overwhelmed by the activity that is taking place. In a network, when one server starts to become overwhelmed by activity, another server with more capacity will step in and start to take some of the load.

What makes load balancing important? In games, especially game servers that are always up and running with a tremendous amount of users, there are often situations in which the number of requests and information being sent and received from a server is unknown. When a server starts to get overwhelmed, developers use load balancing to help with the traffic load. In games, especially games for which users are paying membership fees, developers need a way to ensure that their server can stay up and efficient at all times. If the server crashes, they need another to take its place. If the server is overwhelmed, developers will need that pressure relieved— and load balancing is a way to do so.

IMPROVED CUSTOM PHYSICS

Physics are becoming very popular in this generation of game development and will continue to grow. A strong physics system can allow developers to create interesting effects in their gaming applications that are realistic and can add to the overall game experience. In the Building Blocks Engine, a physics system was started, but many things can be added to it to make it more effective. For starters, rag doll physics with skeleton meshed objects can add a great deal of realism to any scene. Another addition is vehicle and airplane physics in the physics system. Many different types of games use vehicles to some extent, and it could be helpful to have a good physics system to handle those objects realistically—which can go a long way to immersing a player into the gaming experience. Some additional features that can be added to the Building Blocks Engine include:

- Rag doll
- Vehicle physics
- Rigid bodies
- Improved springs
- Improved cloth simulation
- Additional soft bodies
- Optimizations to the Math library
- Optimizations to the Physics library
- Optimizations using scene partitioning

The system can also benefit from optimizations; for example, using various data structures to speed up the physics calculations by splitting the game world into various hierarchies. This was explored a little in Chapter 5, "Rendering Scenes and Scene Graphs," when an octree was used to demonstrate splitting a space into sections. This same idea can apply to application to collision detection in a physics system to speed the number of tests that are done on the dynamic objects in the scene. By having items in separate nodes, the test for collision can be greatly increased because the number of tests for each object is limited to only objects in their nodes. Using bounding spheres within those nodes can be used to quickly reject geometry that does not touch within each node.

GRAPHICS ADDITIONS AND ENHANCEMENTS

When it comes to graphics, many techniques out there are used to increase the realism of a scene. Graphical techniques tend to be either pre-processed or real-time effects. For pre-processed techniques, developers have things like ambient occlusion, radiosity, spherical harmonics, and many more. When it comes to real-time effects, the list goes on and includes topics like deferred shading, dynamic cube mapping, displacement mapping, hardware skinning, per-pixel lighting techniques, and much more. Not all graphical techniques have to rely on powerful hardware to be realized as with many pre-computed (pre-processed) graphics solutions. This also makes processing pre-processed data much faster when the game is running than trying to simulate them in real time with the hardware. The amount of processing power a technique needs will determine if a technique can be done in real time or if the only option is to do it with pre-processed data.

There are also techniques that can increase the quality of the rendered scene. Things like multisampling, which performs anti-aliasing on a rendered scene, can help reduce artifacts that can decrease the overall look of a scene. The level of quality developers are going for will depend on how much of a performance hit can be incurred with multisampling. When it comes to enhancing the Building Blocks Engine, the list is almost limitless. One addition that would prove very useful is to create tools for calculating pre-processed data such as radiosity-based light maps for diffuse and soft shadows.

AN ANIMATIONS SYSTEM

This book does not cover complex models and animations, but anyone creating a modern 3D game will encounter them. When it comes to models, developers have the option of creating their own model file format or using an existing format. By creating a custom format, developers have total control over the format and how it is structured. By using an existing file format, developers have to adhere to the structure the author of the format intended it to have, assuming they want the format to be compatible with applications that can read it.

When specifying custom file formats, developers will often have to write different model exporters for the various tools they use. These tools can include Maya, 3ds Max, LightWave, ZBrush, TrueSpace, and many more. Writing exporters with one of these tools is not always easy, but is often the obstacle that arises when trying to get modeled and animated creations from a modeling application to a custom file format.

Animations are key to any video game. In modern video games, the most used types of animation systems are skeleton, or bone, animations. These are very realistic in terms of the animations they reference and their capability to be physically manipulated (using physics) in a 3D virtual world. Skeleton animation fixes the problems developers once had with geometry key-framed animations and are generally easy to use. When adding an animation system in a game engine for dynamic character models, it is recommended that developers look into skeleton animation. Taking animation data from a motion capture system is also done heavily in the game development industry and is used to create ultra realistic animations in games.

Other types of animations, such as moving platforms and objects that follow pre-defined paths, are also typical in modern games and can be of great value to look into. The book *Ultimate Game Programming with DirectX* looked at creating and working with various animation paths that were able to take an object and move it around a 3D space along a path that was specified in code. Many games have seen guards patrolling an area, and with animation paths, developers can make that possible in their games.

ENVIRONMENT EDITING TOOLS

3D gaming worlds are complex pieces of geometry comprised of many different things. As games become more complex, so do the scenes that make up the various levels and environments. The creation of complex environments requires game developers to use various tools that aid in the construction of the gaming world. Modern game worlds can have, for example, the following types of objects in a scene:

- Light sources
- Particle systems
- Textured geometry
- Static objects
- Dynamic objects
- Triggers

Some of the biggest named game engines have their own editors for game environments. These editors are often tools that work with the various features of the game engine to allow for rapid creation of game worlds. The creation of such a tool is no trivial task. The Building Blocks Engine could use an editor to create levels either by use of a custom environment editor or by creating an exporter to an already existing tool such as 3ds Max.

EXPORTERS

Exporters have many uses in game development, and allow tools to save out content to a specific format. Developers can write exporters for the tools they use to a format their games can understand. This allows developers to use third-party tools that are easily purchased or downloaded for use. All commonly used tools (e.g., 3ds Max) have exporters to common formats. As the Building Blocks Engine grows, various exporters will be created for many different popular tools so content can be created and dropped into the environments running from the engine framework. In addition, exporters for environment editors that are available can be created so that the Building Blocks Engine has a way to create entire gaming worlds. If a third-party tool is used, it will limit what can be done, but will save time versus the creation of custom tools.

ADDITIONAL CORE TOOLS

The core system for the Building Blocks Engine was first discussed in detail in Chapter 2. A few core tools were created for the Building Blocks Engine, but much more can be added to improve that area of the framework. The core of the framework is an important section of a game engine, and the tools and their efficiency are very important. Some tools that can be added to the core include:

- Application profilers
- Improved archive filesystem
- Multithreading

Application Profilers

A profiler is a tool that is used to gain valuable performance and statistical information about an application as it is running. Using a profiler in game development can allow developers to find bottlenecks in their system, some of which might be difficult to find without such a tool. One popular profiler is NVIDIA's NVPerfHUD. The use of a good profiler can give developers the information needed to make minor to major increases in performance.

Improved Archive Filesystem

The archive filesystem for the Building Blocks Engine was a simple system that allowed the packing of many different files into one. The archive system allowed the extraction of individual files such as textures, shaders, and so forth to take place using a constantly opened file stream. Because of the simplicity of the archive filesystem for the engine framework, the following are a few improvements that can be made to the system in the future:

- The ability to append files to the archive file
- Compression
- Encryption
- The ability to create new folders, if necessary, when extracting files to the hard drive from the archive
- A GUI application used to work with archive files

Multithreading

The game industry is starting to see a new trend emerge that uses and takes advantage of multicore processors by using multithreading. Duo-core, quad-core, and higher are replacing the single-core processors and are becoming standard. With multicore processors, more than one processor is being used on a chip. Taking advantage of this feature will allow developers to get the most out of a piece of hardware by maximizing performance. The design and implementation of multithreaded applications are more complex than non-multithreaded applications, but the potential gain is worth considering.

The number of tools that can be added to the core of the Building Blocks Engine is enormous. A few additional tools mentioned previously include:

- Memory management
- Journaling services
- Log filesystem
- Streaming data

IMPROVED RENDERING SYSTEM AND SCENE GRAPH

The rendering system for the Building Blocks Engine consisted of an OpenGL wrapper rendering class, classes for Cg-related objects, and a simple scene graph. Many things can be added to the rendering system to make it more useful. Besides additional rendering effects, many optimizations can be made to the framework. Possible additions include:

- SIMD optimizations to the math library
- Additional nodes for the scene graph, such as nodes to handle dynamic models or even a octree (or other) data structure used for dynamic and static models
- The ability to allow the scene graph to automatically sort objects for state management
- Additional graphical effects
- Generalize the shader system so it can be replaced more easily
- DirectX 10 support
- An animation system for dynamic models
- Tools for creating pre-processed data such as light-maps, etc.

Graphical User Interface

Another addition to the rendering system is a graphical user interface (GUI), which is displayed on the screen and comprised of a number of components. These components are used to interact with the interface, which in turn can interact with the application. In games, most GUIs are used as heads-up displays and menu screens. Components that can appear on the GUI include:

- Text labels
- Text areas
- Buttons
- Check boxes
- Picture controls
- List boxes
- Sliders
- Drop-down boxes
- Radio buttons
- Progress bars

IMPROVED RESOURCE MANAGER

The resource management system for the Building Blocks Engine was lightweight. It allowed for the insertion of resources into a template class. A number of improvements can be added to the resource management system. One would be to alter the way the resource manager blocks duplicate data from the manager. The current process checks if a resource name exists twice when inserting new items in the list. The first check is done outside the resource manager to test if a new resource should be allocated, and the second occurs inside the resource manager. One solution would be to assume that any resources being added by the Create() function do not already exist, or to change the structure of the system so the only check needs to occur inside the resource manager.

Another addition would be to allow for dynamic loading of resources from the manager when items are needed. This feature would take the system one step closer to being a streaming system for content to be dynamically loaded.

OPTIMIZED MATH LIBRARY

The math library was not designed with speed in mind. The main goal of improving the math library is to optimize it. One optimization that can be added is the support of SIMD instructions. SIMD (Single Instruction Multiple Data) instruction sets can be used to speed up mathematical operations on the CPU. Because the math library uses so many mathematical operations many times every frame, this improvement can have drastic effects. When adding support for such instructions, the original non-SIMD math instructions can be used as a fallback if SIMD support is not detected, allow users with hardware support for these instructions performance benefits.

ADDITIONAL SCRIPTING CAPABILITIES

The scripting code used by the Building Blocks Engine framework was done with the help of GameMonkey Script and custom-made code for parsing tokens and property scripting. GameMonkey Scripts allowed applications to make use of compiled scripts. These scripts were able to control the host application in a way other types of scripting could not, or at least as effectively or efficiently. The parsing tokens class was used to break up a file into a stream of individual tokens that were separated by a delimiter. This tool was used as a foundation for building the property scripting system for the engine's framework. Tools such as FLEX and BISON could be used instead of manually writing parsers and lexers, and is recommended.

Another type of scripting capability that can be added to the engine's framework that might be helpful is an XML parsing system. XML is similar to HTML; XML is used to describe data, while HTML is used to describe data visually. The *Project Offset* engine framework uses XML for describing materials and other various things that can allow for a smoother development process. Future versions of the Building Blocks Engine will implement an XML system into the framework.

FINAL THOUGHTS

This book started with an idea: to create a game engine that students and hobby programmers can build off to create their own frameworks, or at least be able to learn from so they can start their own engines from scratch. Throughout this book, the purpose was to try to take readers through the thought process used when developing the Building Blocks Engine. It is hoped that readers will leave this book with a sense of understanding of what it takes to put together a game engine, even if that engine is simple in terms of code, complexity, and design.

This book introduced many topics that were put into practice with a 3D game engine that spanned many different areas of game development. Everything from data structures to input, networking, sound, graphics, and more was covered to the extent that it can be built upon without being overwhelming. Many more topics and information were not included in the engine's framework, many of which were discussed in this chapter. A lot of work goes into the development of a game engine, and it often takes the talents of many individuals. Hopefully, after reading this book, you have a new appreciation for all the hard work professionals do on engines that are far more complex and far bigger.

The Building Blocks Engine will continue to grow at *UltimateGameProgramming.com* with bug fixes, new and improved code, new tools, and many demo applications. Although there is a higher demand for game programmers and other professionals, it is still important to have an understanding of what goes into a game engine. Game engines are big business in themselves, so there will always be a need for engineers with the knowledge and skills to create and maintain them. This is especially true as technology changes and trends, both social and technological, evolve.

Appendix

A   Additional Resources

Included here is a list of recommended books and Web sites you can explore for more advanced information dealing with game programming, physics, artificial intelligence, game design, art, modeling, and so forth. Additional resources that might be of some use beyond those listed here can be found at *UltimateGame Programming.com*.

RECOMMENDED BOOKS

The books in this section can be of some use to those looking to expand their knowledge of the different areas of game development. Reading these books is optional, but recommended for those looking for more detailed knowledge about many of the topics discussed in this book and beyond.

Data Structures and Algorithms for Game Developers deals with data structures and algorithms used in general programming and game development. It is geared toward game developers and covers many useful topics such as arrays, link lists, scene management techniques, and more. A data structure is defined as a way data is stored in memory. The most basic data structure is the array, and something everyone who has worked with C++ is familiar with. Games are driven by data structures, and a book on this topic is essential to those learning how to create games.

Ultimate Game Programming with DirectX deals with learning DirectX using C++ for beginner hobby and student programmers. In it, a simple first-person shooter game is created. The majority of the book's content focuses on learning DirectX and the various tools that make up Microsoft's suite.

Memory Management: Algorithms and Implementation in C++ discusses the ins and outs of writing a memory management system in C++. This book includes information dealing with performance, garbage collection, and so forth. In Chapter

2, "Core," memory management is briefly touched upon as an introduction. This book can be useful for those looking to go deeper into the subject and to implement their own system.

The *Cg Tutorial* teaches readers how to use NVIDIA's high-level graphics programming language for multiple platforms (OpenGL, Direct3D, PlayStation® 2, etc.). NVIDIA's Cg was one of the first high-level programming languages available to developers, and this book is a great resource for getting into advanced graphics. It is easy to read and definitely worth checking out, even if you are using other high-level languages for your graphics programming needs other than Cg.

The *Game Programming Gems* series is a long-running series of books written by game developers *for* game developers. These books are targeted to an advanced audience and are not suited for beginners, but are valuable for anyone looking to get into game development. This series will be a valuable resource for many years to come.

The *ShaderX* series, similar to the *Game Programming Gems* series, is comprised of books written by professionals for an advanced audience. This series mostly deals with graphics programming, and can be a great asset when trying to learn new and advanced graphical techniques.

Ultimate Game Design: Building Game Worlds deals with game design, an important topic of which all serious game developers should have some knowledge.

AI for Game Developers is an artificial intelligence book aimed at the game development community. This inexpensive and lightweight book is a great resource for anyone who wants to get into AI programming in video games.

Physics for Game Developers is another lightweight book aimed at game developers. It deals with physics mathematics and programming and is a great resource for getting into the topic. Physics is not an easy subject, and a book aimed at game developers is very useful.

Game Scripting Mastery deals with scripting in video games. In this book, the author takes readers from the basics to advanced topics dealing with creating a scripting language from scratch. The book shows how to implement an assembler, virtual machine, high-level compiler, and custom high and low programming languages.

Head First Design Patterns is an easy-to-read, fun, and excellent book on the subject of design patterns. Design patterns are very important in professional software development, and something everyone can find some value in.

RECOMMENDED WEBSITES

The websites in this section can be of some use to those looking to expand their knowledge of the different areas of game development. For additional websites and web articles, visit *UltimateGameProgramming.com* for more detailed information.

Ultimate Game Programming (*www.UltimateGameProgramming.com*) is a general game programming site that focuses on areas such as graphics with OpenGL, Direct3D, ray tracing, input, sound, and much more. Anyone can access the site's community for game development help, news, and other information.

OpenGL (*www.OpenGL.org*) is the rendering system used in this book for the graphics aspects of the Building Blocks Engine. The OpenGL website has a plethora of information on the API and can be a valuable resource for anyone using it for graphics. The website also has a community (forums) that can be used to gain additional information on the various aspects of OpenGL.

Pixologic (*www.Pixologic.com*) is the maker of ZBrush2®, a 3D modeling and texturing tool that is gaining popularity. ZBrush2 is easy to use and can be a great experience for anyone looking to get into modeling and texturing. At this time, Pixologic is offering a free trial version of the application on its website.

The Microsoft Developer Network, or MSDN (*http://MSDN.Microsoft.com*), is a great place to visit if you need documentation on a well-known API, language, and so forth. Here, you can get DirectX documentation, OpenGL, C/C++, Visual Basic, and much more.

The NVIDIA Developer Network (*http://developer.nvidia.com/page/home.html*) is a place you can go to get articles and open source demo applications that deal with the latest and greatest in graphics programming. You can also download the NVIDIA SDK, which is full of demos, tools, and other resources.

The ATI's Developer Network (*www.ati.com/developer*) page is similar to the NVIDIA page in that it provides information, demo source code, and articles that deal with graphics programming on ATI-based hardware.

The 3DLabs Developer Network page (*http://developer.3dlabs.comThe 3DLabs*) has a ton of information on GLSL, graphics programming, and other information that deals with 3DLabs-based hardware.

Adobe®'s Photoshop® CS (*www.adobe.com/products/photoshop/main.html*) is a great product to use for creating textures and other such images and art.

Appendix

B Additional Tools

I n this appendix, we look at three different simple tools that were coded and used for a few examples in this book, including a Bump Map Creator, Archive Creator, and Cube Map Generator. Each of these tools can be found on the companion CD-ROM under the BUILDING BLOCKS ENGINE/TOOLS folder complete with source code.

ON THE CD

BUMP MAP CREATOR

The Bump Map Creator tool takes a height map in the form of a grayscale TGA image and converts it into a bump map. This bump map is saved so it can be loaded by an application and used for the bump mapping effect. The tool works by using the same TGA loading code that was used by the OpenGL rendering system to load the source image. For each pixel, the tool uses the current pixel, the one to the right of it, and the pixel underneath it to create a normal that will replace the current pixel's color. This normal is calculated by using the triangle normalizing code in the Vector3D class seen in Chapter 2, "Engine Core."

The tool uses arguments that are passed into the application for the source file and the destination filenames, allowing different images to be created with the same tool without having to recompile the source code. The first half of the tool's main.cpp source file is in Listing B.1, where the code makes sure two arguments are defined—one for the source image and one for the destination—and loads the source image's data. An optional third augment can be specified that stores the scale for the bump map. The scale is used to increase the depth detail of the bump map to make it stronger.

513

LISTING B.1   The first half of the Bump Map Creator's main.cpp file.

```cpp
#include<iostream>
#include<TGA.h>
#include<Vector3D.h>

using namespace std;


int main(int args, char *arg[])
{
   cout << "Normal Map Creator 1.0" << endl;
   cout << "Created by Allen Sherrod aka The Programming Ace" <<
          endl;
   cout << "www.UltimateGameProgramming.com" << endl;
   cout << "Supported file formats: TGA" << endl << endl;


   if(args < 2)
   {
      cout << "No arguments defined." << endl;
      return 0;
   }


   int scale = 1;
   scale = (arg[3] != NULL) ? atoi(arg[3]) : 1;
   scale = (!scale || scale == 0L) ? 1 : scale;


   if(arg[1] == NULL || arg[2] == NULL)
   {
      cout << "No source or destination file defined." << endl;
      return 0;
   }


   int srcWidth = 0, srcHeight = 0, srcComp = 0, component = 3;
   unsigned char *src = NULL, *ptr = NULL;

   src = LoadTGA(arg[1], srcWidth, srcHeight, srcComp);
   ptr = src;
```

```
if(src == NULL)
{
    cout << "Error loading image." << endl;
    return 0;
}
```

The second half of the main function in the main.cpp file loops through all pixels and calculates the normal values. Once the bump map is created, it is saved to a file using a new function, WriteTGA(), that is added to the TGA code. The WriteTGA() function is just like its loading counterpart, except it uses fwrite() instead of fread(). The second half of the main function is in Listing B.2, and the WriteTGA() function can be seen in Listing B.3. An example of using the tool from the command line can be seen in Listing B.4, where the source and destination files and scale are specified. The example in Listing B.4 assumes that the source image is in the same folder as the application, and the bump map will be saved in the same location.

LISTING B.2   The second half of the Bump Map Creator's main.cpp file.

```
bbe::Vector3D e1, e2, normal;

// Convert each pixel to a normal vector.
for(int y = 0; y < srcHeight; y++)
{
    for(int x = 0; x < srcWidth; x++)
    {
        int width  = (x == srcWidth - 1) ? 0  : srcWidth;
        int offset = (x == srcWidth - 1) ? 0  : component;
        int height = (y == srcHeight - 1) ? 0 : width *
                    offset;


        // Get triangle of pixels (Red since greyscale).
        float height1 = ((float)ptr[0] / 255) * scale;
        float height2 = ((float)ptr[0 + offset] / 255) * scale;
        float height3 = ((float)ptr[0 + height] / 255) * scale;

        bbe::Vector3D p1((float)x, (float)y, height1);
        bbe::Vector3D p2((float)x + 1, (float)y, height2);
        bbe::Vector3D p3((float)x, (float)y + 1, height3);
```

```
                     // Normalize the triangle of pixels.
                     e1 = p2 - p1;
                     e2 = p3 - p1;
                     e1.Normalize();
                     e2.Normalize();


                     normal = e1.CrossProduct(e2);
                     normal.Normalize();



                     // Save in 0 to 255 range.
                     ptr[0] = (unsigned char)(127.0f * normal.x + 128.0f);
                     ptr[1] = (unsigned char)(127.0f * normal.y + 128.0f);
                     ptr[2] = (unsigned char)(127.0f * normal.z + 128.0f);

                     // Move to the start of the next pixel.
                     ptr += component;
                }
           }


           // Save image.
           if(!WriteTGA(arg[2], srcWidth, srcHeight, component, src))
           {
              cout << "Error saving normal image." << endl;
              return 0;
           }


           delete[] src;


           cout << "Normal map creation successful." << endl;

           return 0;
```

LISTING B.3   The WriteTGA() function.

```
           bool WriteTGA(char *file, int width, int height, int comp,
                        unsigned char *outImage)
           {
              FILE *pFile = 0;
              unsigned char tgaHeader[12] = {0, 0, 2, 0, 0, 0,
                                              0, 0, 0, 0, 0, 0};
```

```cpp
unsigned char header[6];
unsigned char bits = 0;
unsigned char tempColors = 0;


// Open file for output.
pFile = fopen(file, "wb");

// Check if the file opened or not.
if(pFile == NULL)
   return false;


// Set the color mode, and the bit depth.
bits = comp * 8;

// Save the width and height.
header[0] = width % 256;
header[1] = width / 256;
header[2] = height % 256;
header[3] = height / 256;
header[4] = bits;
header[5] = 0;


// Write the headers to the top of the file.
fwrite(tgaHeader, sizeof(tgaHeader), 1, pFile);
fwrite(header, sizeof(header), 1, pFile);

// Now switch image from RGB to BGR.
for(int i = 0; i < width * height * comp; i += comp)
{
   tempColors = outImage[i];
   outImage[i] = outImage[i + 2];
   outImage[i + 2] = tempColors;
}


// Finally write the image.
fwrite(outImage, width * height * comp, 1, pFile);
```

```
      // close the file.
      fclose(pFile);
      return true;
}
```

LISTING B.4 Calling the application from the command line.

```
NormalMapCreator.exe height.tga normal.tga 20
```

ARCHIVE CREATOR

The Archive Creator works similar to the Bump Map Creator in that it takes arguments from the command line. The tool's arguments are the total number of files being added to the archive, the archive's name that will be created, and a list of files to pack into the archive. The tool uses the archive code created in Chapter 2 and requires little work to create an archive. Because all the work is done by the archive code, this tool's source code is much shorter than the Bump Map Creator. The entire main.cpp source file for the Archive Creator can be seen in Listing B.5. The tool can take any number of files as long as the first argument specifies the total, and the second argument is the name of the archive file.

LISTING B.5 The Archive Creator application.

```
#include<iostream>
#include<Archive.h>

using namespace std;


int main(int args, char **arg)
{
   cout << "Archive Creator." << endl;
   cout << "Created by Allen Sherrod." << endl;
   cout << "Ultimate Game Engine Design and Architecture." <<
            endl << endl;


   // Total files, archive name, and at least 1 file.
   if(args < 3)
   {
      cout << "Not enough arguments defined." << endl;
```

```cpp
      return 0;
}

// Arg 1 is total files, 2 is archive file,
// 3+ are all file names to go into archive.

if(arg[1] == NULL)
{
   cout << "No total files defined." << endl;
   return 0;
}


int totalFiles = atoi(arg[1]);

for(int i = 2; i < totalFiles; i++)
{
   if(arg[i] == NULL)
   {
      cout << "Argument " << i << " is NULL!" << endl;
      return 0;
   }
}

bbe::ArchiveFileHeader *headers =
   new bbe::ArchiveFileHeader[totalFiles];

bbe::Archive archiveFile;

for(i = 0; i < totalFiles; i++)
{
   headers[i].SetFileName(arg[i + 3]);
}


if(archiveFile.WriteArchiveFile(arg[2], headers, totalFiles))
{
   cout << "Archive " << "NAME" << " created!\n";
}
else
{
   cout << "Archive " << "NAME" << " NOT created!\n";
}
```

```
        archiveFile.CloseArchive();

        delete[] headers;

        return 1;
    }
```

CUBE MAP GENERATOR

The Cube Map Generator takes six TGA files and creates a cube map the Building
Blocks Engine can read. The cube map's file format specifies the width, height, and
color components of each face of the cube map followed by all the TGA images that
make up the cube map. The tool uses command-line arguments just as the previous two tools. It requires six images to be specified for each face of the cube map,
and a destination file. The only restriction is that all faces of the cube map must
have the same width, height, and components. The code for the Cube Map Generator can be seen in Listing B.6.

LISTING B.6 The Cube Map Generator application.

```
        #include<iostream>
        #include<Tga.h>

        using namespace std;


        int main(int args, char **arg)
        {
            cout << "Cube Map Generator." << endl;
            cout << "Created by Allen Sherrod." << endl;
            cout << "Ultimate Game Engine Design and Architecture." <<
                    endl << endl;

            bool result = true;

            if(args < 7)
            {
                cout << "Not enough arguments defined." << endl;
                return 0;
            }
```

```cpp
if(arg[1] == NULL || arg[2] == NULL || arg[3] == NULL ||
   arg[4] == NULL || arg[5] == NULL || arg[6] == NULL ||
   arg[7] == NULL)
{
   cout << "Error with one or more arguments!" << endl;
   return 0;
}

unsigned char *img1 = NULL, *img2 = NULL, *img3 = NULL,
              *img4 = NULL, *img5 = NULL, *img6 = NULL;

int w1 = 0, w2 = 0, w3 = 0, w4 = 0, w5 = 0, w6 = 0;
int h1 = 0, h2 = 0, h3 = 0, h4 = 0, h5 = 0, h6 = 0;
int c1 = 0, c2 = 0, c3 = 0, c4 = 0, c5 = 0, c6 = 0;

img1 = LoadTGA(arg[1], w1, h1, c1);
img2 = LoadTGA(arg[2], w2, h2, c2);
img3 = LoadTGA(arg[3], w3, h3, c3);
img4 = LoadTGA(arg[4], w4, h4, c4);
img5 = LoadTGA(arg[5], w5, h5, c5);
img6 = LoadTGA(arg[6], w6, h6, c6);

if(img1 == NULL || img2 == NULL || img3 == NULL ||
   img4 == NULL || img5 == NULL || img6 == NULL)
{
     cout << "One or more images not found." << endl;
     return 0;
}

if(w2 != w1 || w3 != w1 || w4 != w1 || w5 != w1 || w6 != w1)
{
   cout << "Different width resolutions." << endl;
   result = false;
}

if(h2 != h1 || h3 != h1 || h4 != h1 || h5 != h1 || h6 != h1)
{
   cout << "Different height resolutions." << endl;
   result = false;
}
```

```
if(c2 != c1 || c3 != c1 || c4 != c1 || c5 != c1 || c6 != c1)
{
   cout << "Different components." << endl;
   result = false;
}

if(c1 != 3 && c1 != 4)
{
   cout << "Not 24 or 32 bits in components." << endl;
   result = false;
}

FILE *fp = fopen(arg[7], "wb");

if(fp == NULL)
   result = false;

cout << "Images loaded." << endl;

if(result != false)
{
   int c = c1 * 8;

   fwrite(&w1, 1, sizeof(int), fp);
   fwrite(&h1, 1, sizeof(int), fp);
   fwrite(&c, 1, sizeof(int), fp);

   fwrite(img1, 1, w1 * h1 * c1, fp);
   fwrite(img2, 1, w1 * h1 * c1, fp);
   fwrite(img3, 1, w1 * h1 * c1, fp);
   fwrite(img4, 1, w1 * h1 * c1, fp);
   fwrite(img5, 1, w1 * h1 * c1, fp);
   fwrite(img6, 1, w1 * h1 * c1, fp);
}
else
{
   cout << "ERROR" << endl;
}

fclose(fp);

cout << "Cube Map Created." << endl;
```

```
        if(img1) delete[] img1;
        if(img2) delete[] img2;
        if(img3) delete[] img3;
        if(img4) delete[] img4;
        if(img5) delete[] img5;
        if(img6) delete[] img6;

        return 1;
}
```

Appendix

C About the CD-ROM

The companion CD-ROM for *Ultimate Game Engine Design and Architecture* contains all of the project files for your use as you work through the book.

FOLDERS

The files on this disc are organized into folders as follows:

Figures: All of the figures from the book, organized in folders by chapter.

Building Blocks Engine: The book's project source code and chapter examples.

Building Blocks Engine/Diagrams: Visual diagrams used for the book's project.

Building Blocks Engine/Examples: All book examples organized by chapter.

Building Blocks Engine/Lib: Win32 libraries for the book's game engine project.

Building Blocks Engine/Linux Libraries: Linux libraries for the book's game engine project.

Building Blocks Engine/Framework: Mac OSX Carbon frameworks for the book's game engine project.

Building Blocks Engine/Projects: Workspace projects used for compiling the book's engine code for all operating systems.

Building Blocks Engine/Source: The book's engine's entire source code.

Building Blocks Engine/Tools: Various tools that were created for use with the book's game engine.

GENERAL SYSTEM REQUIREMENTS

The system requirements for this CD-ROM are:

- Windows 2000/XP Operating System or better
- Mac OS X
- Linux (Ubuntu distribution was used for this book)
- Pentium 1 GHz
- 256 MB RAM
- 400 MB Hard Drive Space
- CD-ROM Drive
- OpenGL Compatible 3D Graphics Accelerator
- Shader Model 2.0 Compatible Graphics Card

Index